DAVID JACQUES LOUIS 1748-1825
LES SABINES ARRETANT LE COMBAT ENTRE
LES ROMAINS ET LES SABINS.

KNOPF GUIDES

This is a Borzoi Book
published by Alfred A. Knopf

Completely revised and
updated in 2006

Copyright © 1995 Alfred A. Knopf, New York.
All rights reserved under International and
Pan-American Copyright Conventions.
Published in the United States by Alfred
A. Knopf, a division of Random House, Inc.,
New York, and simultaneously in Canada by
Random House of Canada Limited, Toronto.
Distributed by Random House, Inc., New York.

Knopf, Borzoi Books, and the colophon are
registered trademarks of Random House, Inc

www.aaknopf.com

ISBN 0-375-71036-1

Originally published in France by Nouveaux-
Loisirs, a subsidiary of Editions Gallimard,
Paris, 1994. Copyright © 1994 by Editions
Nouveaux-Loisirs / Réunion des Musées
Nationaux

Series editors
Shelley Wanger and Clémence Jacquinet

Translated by
Susan Mackervoy, Anthony Roberts and
Simon Dalgleish

Translation for the updated edition
Clive Unger-Hamilton

Edited and typeset by
Book Creation Services, London

Printed and bound in France by
Kapp Lahure Jombart (Evreux),
Diguet Deny

ILLUSTRATIONS
Pierre-Marie Valat, Philippe Biard, Jean-Michel
Kacédan, Dominique Duplantier, Laure Massin
Nature: Anne Bodin, Frédéric Bony,
Jean Chevallier, François Desbordes, Claire
Felloni, Gilbert Houbre, Jean-Michel Kacédan,
Catherine Lachaud, Pascal Robin, John
Wilkinson.

PHOTOGRAPHY
Patrick Léger, Patrick Horvais;
Michel Chassat for the Louvre Museum
COMPUTER MAPS
Maps of the museum
Conception by the Louvre Museum; graphic
design B. Pell; artistic input Ph. Apeloig
Endpaper maps
Edigraphie

RÉUNION DES MUSÉES NATIONAUX
EDITORIAL AND COMMERCIAL SERVICES
Jean-Jacques Lugbull, Béatrice Foulon

TEXTS
The texts for this guide were written by the
editorial department of Guides Gallimard, with
the exception of the following sections:
Nature (pages 15 to 24): Pierre-Jean
Trombetta and Guilhem Lesaffre
History (pages 25 to 48), itinerary in
The Louvre and its history (pages 121 to
132) and **The Louvre as seen by painters**
(pages 87 to 96): Geneviève Bresc
Arts and traditions and **Behind the scenes**
(pages 49 to 70): Marc Plocki and Françoise
Mardrus
The Louvre through visitors's eyes
(pages 97 to 112): Jean Galard; texts taken
from Les Visiteurs du Louvre, RMN, 1993, in
collaboration with Anne-Laure Charrier
Itineraries around the Louvre quarter
(pages 273 to 312): Vincent Bouvet
**Itineraries for practical information
section**: Violaine Bouvet-Lanselle

Guides Gallimard and the Réunion des Musées
Nationaux would like to thank all those who
contributed to this guide.

*Although every care has been taken in the
editing and publishing of this book, especially
during reprints, certain information may be
contradicted by more recent research, leading
to changes in attribution and dates. In
addition, some works may be placed back into
storage, lent out for exhibitions, withdrawn for
restoration or moved to other display rooms
for museographical purposes.*

THE
LOUVRE

KNOPF GUIDES

CONTENTS

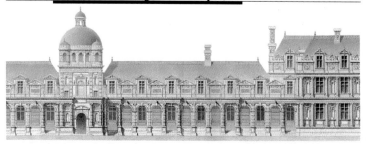

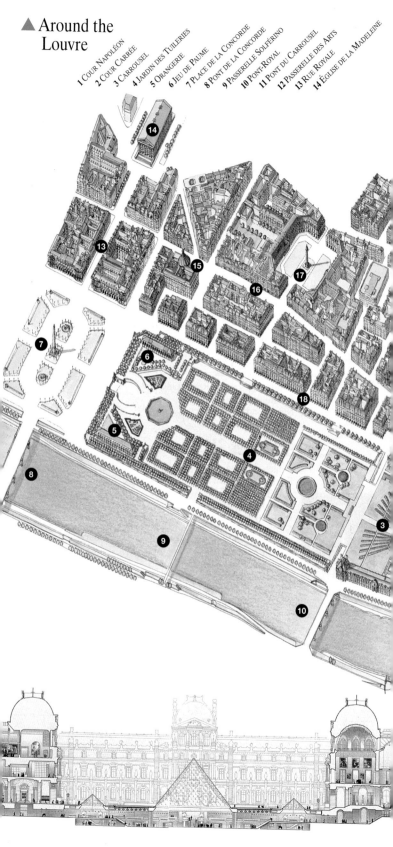

▲ Around the Louvre

1 Cour Napoléon
2 Cour Carrée
3 Carrousel
4 Jardin des Tuileries
5 Orangerie
6 Jeu de Paume
7 Place de la Concorde
8 Pont de la Concorde
9 Passerelle Solférino
10 Pont-Royal
11 Pont du Carrousel
12 Passerelle des Arts
13 Rue Royale
14 Église de la Madeleine

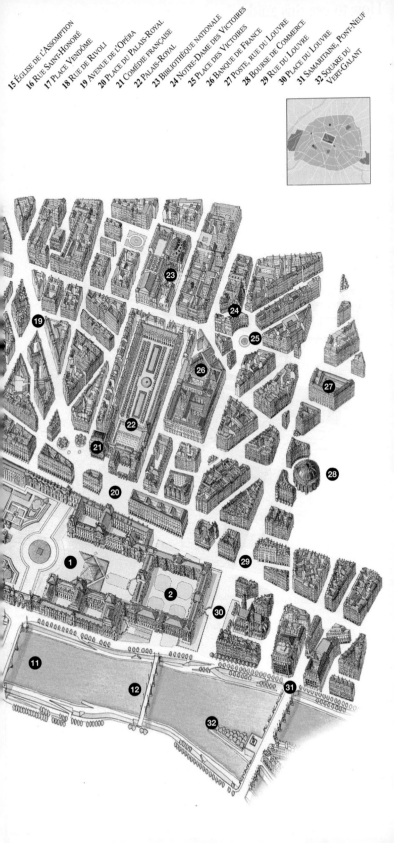

How to use this guide

The symbols at the top of each page refer to the different parts of the guide.

■
●
▲ Nature
◆ Keys to understanding
Itineraries
Practical information

The itinerary map at the start of each section shows the numbered rooms referred to and the main stairways.

Each section is marked in a different color; the color-code chart is given on pages 114–15, and page 317.

The color-coding used here is the same as that used in the museum itself.

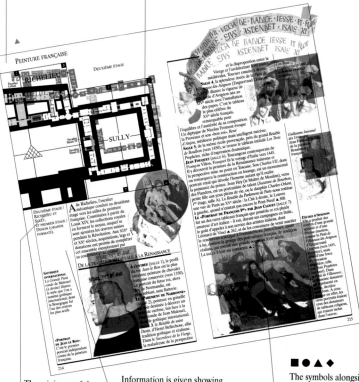

The mini map of the museum shows the location of a particular section and its position in relation to the Pyramide.

Information is given showing the relevant section (SULLY, DENON or RICHELIEU) and floor(s) for the different works.

■ ● ▲ ◆

The symbols alongside a title or within the text itself provide cross-references to a theme or place dealt with elsewhere in the guide

---

NOTE:

The Louvre consists of four levels which have been

referred to throughout this guide as follows:

Entresol = Entresol (i.e. mezzanine)
Rez-de-chaussée = Ground floor
Premier étage = First floor
Deuxième étage = Second floor

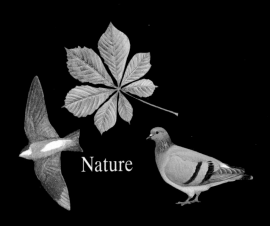

Nature

The site

19th- and 20th-century embankments
Medieval and modern embankments
Alluvial silt
Ancient alluvial deposits
Coarse limestone

Escarpment

Remains of a 14th-century house, demolished when city walls were built during the reign of Charles V

In this area of Paris, the bedrock of coarse limestone and alluvial gravel is overlaid with fertile silt deposits. As a result, it has been continuously occupied from prehistoric times onward. Below the area now covered by the Louvre and the Tuileries the traces of human occupation can be found in layers extending from the Neolithic age to modern times. From the layers came the sparse evidence of our earliest ancestors' brief presence, the remains of large medieval private houses, the city walls of Paris and the tilers' workshops after which the 16th-century palace was named. All these pages in the great book of the capital's history were uncovered during work on the Grand Louvre.

TOPOGRAPHY OF THE SITE
The site of the Louvre is a continuation, at the far western tip, of the hill of St-Germain-l'Auxerrois. To the south is an alluvial bank over 110 feet high which dominates the surrounding landscape. To the north, protected by this bank, is a plain which slopes down gently toward the Rue St-Honoré.

ORNAMENTAL NAIL-CLEANER
This nail- and ear-cleaner made of bone in the shape of a unicorn, dates from the 14th century.

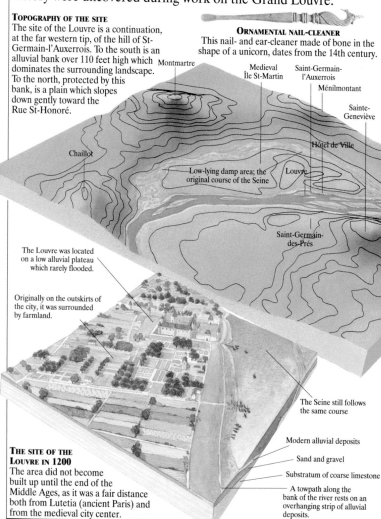

Montmartre

Medieval Île St-Martin

Saint-Germain-l'Auxerrois

Ménilmontant

Sainte-Geneviève

Chaillot

Hôtel de Ville

Low-lying damp area; the original course of the Seine

Louvre

Saint-Germain-des-Prés

The Louvre was located on a low alluvial plateau which rarely flooded.

Originally on the outskirts of the city, it was surrounded by farmland.

The Seine still follows the same course

Modern alluvial deposits

Sand and gravel

Substratum of coarse limestone

A towpath along the bank of the river rests on an overhanging strip of alluvial deposits.

THE SITE OF THE LOUVRE IN 1200
The area did not become built up until the end of the Middle Ages, as it was a fair distance both from Lutetia (ancient Paris) and from the medieval city center.

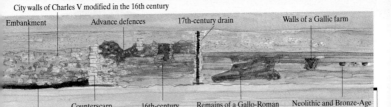

City walls of Charles V modified in the 16th century

Embankment   Advance defences   17th-century drain   Walls of a Gallic farm

Salt deposit   Counterscarp   16th-century tilers' furnace   Remains of a Gallo-Roman quarry (silt works)   Neolithic and Bronze-Age ditches and silo

CROSS-SECTION OF THE COUR DU CARROUSEL
Excavations brought a large number of objects to light, as well as the remains of buildings.

NEOLITHIC REMAINS
Neolithic and protohistoric pots.

Bastille

Butte-aux-Cailles

Seine

Bièvre

14TH-CENTURY JUGS
These vessels were made to hold liquids, particularly wine. The vase on the right has a remarkable tortoiseshell decoration.

GLASS
The shape and the white-colored decoration of this stemmed glass are typical of the 14th century.

19TH-CENTURY PIPE BOWLS
One of five hundred pipe bowls discovered, this one depicts a soldier in the colonial army.

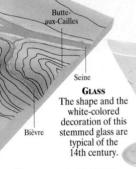

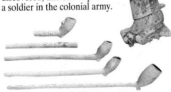

17TH- AND 18TH-CENTURY CLAY PIPES
More than 60 manufacturers and 50 different styles have been identified. Pipe bowls became larger as the price of tobacco fell.

SMALL GALLIC NECROPOLIS
The tombs dating from the end of the 1st century AD were partially destroyed by a Gallo-Roman quarry.

LEAD-SMELTERS' WORKSHOP
This 14th-century workshop was devoted to lead smelting; below are the refining furnaces, above is the forge.

16TH-CENTURY POTTERY
Everyday objects: dishes, bowls, small bottles and jugs.

TILERS AT THE TUILERIES
Around a dozen ovens have been discovered on this site, indicating that a large number of tilers' workshops were located here from the end of the 13th century to the 16th century. In the vault on the lefthand side a worker kept the fire burning. The heat was carried through two channels (*alandiers*) baking the tiles laid out in the heating chamber on the right.

Materials of the Louvre

The Louvre features a remarkable range of building materials, from the limestone of the building's main body, the brickwork contributed by the Industrial Revolution, to 20th-century concrete. Marble completes the picture; the Louvre offers an infinite variety of marbles, from the very whitest reserved for sculpture, to the most richly colored which decorate floors, walls and plinths. I.M. Pei's Louvre also holds its own, owing its combination of brilliance and sobriety to the use of Burgundian stone.

PARIS LIMESTONE
The stones used to build the medieval Louvre ▲ 122 came from quarries in the Paris basin; many bear marks made by the workers.

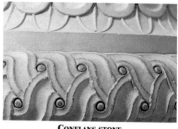

CONFLANS STONE
Percier and Fontaine used very fine limestone in the Salle des Cariatides ▲ 125, enabling the sculptor to produce this delicate ornamentation.

VERMICULATED STONE
The Île-de-France stone in the Cour du Sphinx ▲ 126 was worked in the 17th century. The quality of the stone itself is overshadowed by the random carved motif.

IMPERIAL MARBLE
Napoleon I's architects looked to antiquity and Italy for inspiration. They used the finest white Carrara marble which contrasts with the more veined French marble.

IMPERIAL BRICKWORK
Napoleon III's stables ▲ 132, which today provide a perfect setting for Italian sculpture, are constructed of vaulted brickwork with limestone supports.

MOLDED CONCRETE
Pei used two types of concrete: for the Hall Napoléon he used a fine white one; in the medieval Louvre he used a rough gray concrete imprinted with wooden planks.

This engraving shows the enormous stones used to build the pediment of the Colonnade in 1672.

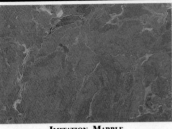

IMITATION MARBLE
Since 1935 the walls of Anne of Austria's apartments have been covered with stucco work which looks just like marble, providing a good backdrop for Roman sculptures ▲ *178*.

GRAY MARBLE
A gray marble with the traces of brown, red and white typical of Belgian quarries, can be seen in the Greek sculpture rooms of the Louvre ▲ *166*.

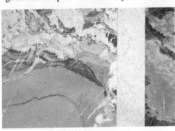

GEOMETRIC PATTERNS
Marbles lend themselves to the creation of ornamental floors like that in the Galerie Michel-Ange ▲ *195*, which uses a variety of French marbles including some from Corsica.

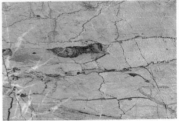

PLINTHS
In the 19th century a variety of colored marbles was used to make the plinths, including the serancolin marble shown here, as well as cracked and sea-green marbles.

GRAFFITI
Graffiti from 1862 can be seen on this close-up of the wall in the Rotonde d'Apollon ▲ *126*. The delicate yellow marble is threaded with fine blue and gray veins.

EXPLOSION OF COLOR
The marble used to decorate the Musée Charles X ▲ *128* at the beginning of the 19th century is one of the most spectacular and colorful in the Louvre.

CHASSAGNE STONE
The stone of Chassagne (Burgundy), seen here with rose tints, goes perfectly with the marble sculptures of the Cour Marly ▲ *188*, one of Louis XIV's favorite haunts.

BURGUNDY STONE
The newly opened Richelieu wing is faced in a very close-grained white stone which has been highly polished to produce a pleasing satin-smooth surface.

Thanks to progress in water treatment processes, the water of the Seine is now less polluted than it has been for many years. The present cloudy appearance of the water is due simply to suspended mineral particles. As a result of this significant improvement in water quality, aquatic plants have been reintroduced and over twenty species of fish have returned, even in the stretch of the river which runs through the city center. There is also the winter parade of seagulls with their circling flight, giving the city an unexpected seaside atmosphere.

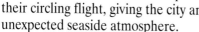

Male

Female   Herring gull   Yellow-backed gull

GRAY WAGTAIL
The wagtail scurries along the quays, pecking away as it runs.

HERRING AND LESSER BLACK-BACKED GULLS
The herring gull can be seen throughout the year but is more common in winter. The black-backed gull is a seasonal visitor and can be spotted mainly in summer and autumn. Both species adapt well to town life.

KINGFISHER
A migrant bird that is generally seen in Paris in autumn and in spring.

MALE MALLARD
These ducks are quite tame but cautious, especially during the nesting season. Variations of plumage are common.

COOT
Only in winter can a few coots be seen on the river, driven there from frozen ponds near the capital.

The Seine

Two centuries ago the Seine was used as a trading route, a washing-place and a watering-place for animals; it also had high levels of organic pollution.

DACE
This fish can tolerate poor-quality water better than other species.

GUDGEON
Gudgeon are very gregarious fish, swimming along the river bed in shoals.

ON THE RIVERBANKS
The riverside ▲ 306 supports plants well-suited to the conditions, both above and below water-level. Plants which thrive in damp conditions grow in the tiniest crevices.

The pretty spikes of purple loosestrife can be seen from May to August.

Mosses and algae flourish close to outflows.

Young, hardy wall rocket manages to survive in cracks.

PIKE
This powerful, well-armed predator feeds on other fish, crayfish or ducklings.

BREAM
With their flat, curved bodies adult bream stay in deep water during the day.

ROACH
Shoals of roach thread through the underwater vegetation.

Curled pondweed

The introduced aquatic vegetation attracts the fish.

Water milfoil

The Tuileries

ENGLISH OAK
An English (or pedunculate) oak, the
only example of its species in the Tuileries,
was planted to mark the bicentenary
of the French Revolution.

Through the changing seasons of
the year, the Tuileries gardens is inhabited by an astonishing
range of wildlife, often hidden from view. Insects, fish and birds
make up a complete animal population that flourishes in the
trees, among the flowers, on stones and in the water. Migrant
birds from distant lands can be found in the trees and sky above
the Tuileries. The plant kingdom is represented not only by trees
of various species but also by a range of wild plants which grow
up at random, and often fall victim to the gardeners' efforts.

Spring plumage   Winter plumage

STARLING
This bird walks across
the lawns of the
Tuileries in small
groups looking for
insect larvae.

TREECREEPER
This small climbing
bird with its bark-
colored plumage
often goes unnoticed
by visitors.

**LESSER SPOTTED
WOODPECKER**
Scarcely bigger than a
sparrow, this
woodpecker is seen
mainly in winter.

DUNNOCK
The dunnock with its
delicate slate-gray
coloring creeps under
the bushes, hidden
from view.

Lime leaf

Maple leaf

Horse chestnut leaf

The Tuileries ▲ *278* has a dense covering of nearly 3,000 trees belonging to around thirty species. Horse chestnuts and limes predominate, but maples, elms, and ornamental trees are also found in the gardens.

MAGPIE
From the end of the winter the magpie builds its nest of twigs high up in a chestnut or plane tree.

JAY
Despite its raucous screeching cries the jay is difficult to spot among the foliage.

WOODPIGEON
This pigeon can be identified by the white patch on its neck and its white wing patches.

Female

Male

CARP
Shoals of carp flourish in the two large ornamental lakes of the Tuileries; they are so successful that some must be removed from time to time to prevent overcrowding.

BLACKBIRD
One of the most common birds of the Tuileries. The male is identified by its ebony plumage, which contrasts with the brown and speckled tones of his mate.

Animals of the Louvre

KESTREL
It is not unusual to see a kestrel wheeling above the palace before settling on a chimney or a roof.

Old buildings provide many opportunities for nearby animals and birds. Crevices in walls, carved motifs, cornices and roof trussings offer homes to those species which have adapted to man-made sites. The Louvre has its own habitual residents. Birds are the most common of these, but some unexpected mammals, like bats, have also settled here. All seem unperturbed by the noise and movement of the constant flow of tourists.

BLACK REDSTART
In the summer this pretty little bird can be seen hunting around for insects on the roofs.

HOUSE MARTIN
On its return from Africa the house martin seeks out its nest made of mud hanging under a cornice.

HOUSE SPARROW
The smallest of cavities can provide a home for this opportunist little sparrow.

PIPISTRELLE BAT
In the evening a few of these small bats can be seen flying around the museum buildings.

SWIFT
From the end of April to August, swifts streak through the sky before plunging into their nesting holes.

History

| 1000 | 1050 | **1066**
Battle of
Hastings | **1099**
1st Crusade and
capture of Jerusalem | 1100 | 1150 | **1180–1223**
Reign of
Philippe Auguste | **1226–70**
Reign of
Louis IX | 1 |
| | | | | | | 1200 | 1250 | |

1187
Construction of
St Thomas' church
at the Louvre   **1214**
Bouvines

The Pietà of St-Germain-des-Prés, painted around 1500, features a rare depiction of the medieval Louvre. Here we see the fortress façade overlooking the Seine, viewed from the left bank.

The beginning to Charles V

BEGINNINGS

Excavations have revealed traces of protohistoric habitation to the west of the Île de la Cité on the north bank of the Seine. A bank of clay has preserved the remains from the effect of floods ● *16*.

In the Gallo-Roman period this area on the outskirts of Lutetia was farmland. Ditches, various types of boundary and clay quarries have been discovered here. Today's Rue St-Honoré follows the course of the road which connected this district with the town to the east.

THE MEDIEVAL LOUVRE

Under the reign of Philippe Auguste, Paris became the capital of France. Faced with the town's rapid growth and the increasing military resources required to defend it, the king ordered his citizens to build a town wall. In 1190 when the king left for the Crusades, the decision was taken to enclose the town with a strong rampart. On the river side it was to have a royal fortress which would function as an outpost of the palace in the city with the aim of countering potential invaders from the Seine; the Louvre was born. It was a flatland chateau with a circular keep placed at the center of a solid quadrangle of walls defended by towers. In 1214 in the Bouvines Philippe Auguste's army overcame a coalition of German, Flemish and English troops to defend the kingdom. The Louvre gradually lost its strategic function as a military bulwark and prison. The western suburbs of the city were growing, and Étienne Marcel, the merchants' provost and leader of the town council, set up a new system of defense after the Paris Rebellion of 1358, surrounding the first wall with a second defensive structure larger than the first. Charles V ordered the completion of the new barrier which was reinforced by a wide moat. The Louvre then became a richly decorated royal residence which housed the king's magnificent library of manuscripts (1360–4). After Charles V's death the English conquerors installed the young Henry V in the Louvre and the Regent Bedford acquired the royal library.

As the French fought to regain the kingdom, violent battles took place around Charles V's city walls. Joan of Arc was wounded at the Porte St-Honoré.

26

| 1348 Great Plague | 1453 Fall of Byzantium | 1517 Beginning of the Reformation | 1572 St Bartholomew's Day Massacre | 1598 Edict of Nantes |

| 350 | 1400 | 1450 | 1500 | 1550 | 1600 | 1650 |

| 1358 Paris Rebellion | 1380 Death of Charles V | 1528 Destruction of the Louvre's Great Tower | 1546 Pierre Lescot converts the Old Louvre. | 1594 Henri IV enters Paris |

From the Renaissance to the Fronde

THE RENAISSANCE PALACE

The kings of the 15th century neglected Paris and the Louvre in favor of other residences, notably the chateaux of the Loire. François I thought Philippe Auguste's tower too austere and had it demolished in 1528; in 1540 he organized festivities in honor of Charles V. In 1546, he commissioned his architect Pierre Lescot to replace one section of the old medieval rampart with a new wing. Henri II (1547–59) completed this project, as well as beginning a second

wing at right angles to the first and added the sturdy Royal Pavilion overlooking the Seine, intended for the king's own apartments. Jean Goujon added sculptural details to the exterior. After

Henri II's death his widow Catherine de' Medici had the Tuileries Palace built overlooking an Italian-style garden. At the same time Charles IX undertook further building work to connect the Royal Pavilion with the Seine by a small gallery, itself joined by a long passage to the Tuileries Palace along the river, completed in 1566. A new fortified city wall was constructed even further to the west, surrounding the Tuileries Gardens and the St-Honoré quarter.

THE GREAT BUILDERS

Two kings were the force behind the conversion of the Louvre; François I (opposite) and Henri IV (below, on the medallion). Henri IV was the first to plan a palace-complex, joining the two existing buildings (the Louvre and the Tuileries) into a whole. He housed his artists and his works of art here, and had mulberry trees planted to provide silk.

HENRI IV'S GRAND PLAN

Henri IV's ceremonial entry into Paris in 1594 after the civil war, confirmed Paris as France's political and cultural center. He made the Louvre into a "royal city", creating a hall

to house his classical treasures and installing his artists in the Grande Galerie built alongside the Seine by his architects Androuet du Cerceau and Métezeau. He

planned to create a vast complex of courts between the Louvre and the Tuileries, but did not have the time to carry out his projects. He was stabbed by Ravaillac in 1610 and died at the Louvre, leaving power in the hands of the regency. Louis XIII took up where his father had left off. The painter Nicolas Poussin came back from Rome to decorate the interior of the Grande Galerie, while the architect Mercier was commissioned to make the Cour Carrée four times larger, and to build the Pavillon de l'Horloge along with its adjoining wing. This scheme was

Fresco in the Galerie des Cerfs in Fontainebleau illustrating Henri IV's Grand Plan

supported by the powerful Cardinal Richelieu who lived in the residence bearing his name between 1627 and 1633. After this Richelieu built the Palais-Cardinal,

which became the Palais-Royal after it was bequeathed to the king in 1642. Anne of Austria later lived here with the young Louis XIV during the Regency. They fled to St-Germain during the turmoils of the Fronde in 1650 and again in 1651.

1661–1715	1685		1715–74
Reign of Louis XIV	Revocation of the		Reign of Louis XV
	Edict of Nantes		

1650　　　**1660**　　　**1670**　　　**1680**　　　**1690**　　　**1700**　　　**1710**　　　**1720**

1656–8	**1665**	**1660–99**	**1699**	**1711**
Romanelli's	Bernini's	The Academies move to the	The first Salon	Watteau's *Embarkation*
decorations	project	Louvre	at the Louvre	*for the Island of Cythera*
at the Louvre				

From Louis XIV to the Revolution

THE LOUVRE UNDER LOUIS XIV

Once peace had been restored, the king moved into the Louvre, where large-scale improvements were being carried out. The queen mother's apartments were sumptuously decorated; Romanelli's frescos and Anguier's stuccos can still be seen today ▲ *126*, while a theater, the Salle des Machines, was built in the Tuileries. Under the personal reign of Louis XIV (above right), the last remnants of the medieval building were destroyed, while improvements and additions continued. The architect Le Vau rebuilt the terrace of the Petite Galerie (now the Galerie d'Apollon), which was destroyed by fire in 1661, and completed the enlargement of the Cour Carrée. In 1665 the architect Bernini, chosen by competition, was invited to Paris where he made plans for an oriental façade. However this very ambitious project never saw the light of day. It was superseded by a plan devised by a group of architects headed by Claude Perrault, who built the Colonnade (below). The great and powerful of the kingdom inhabited the area around the Louvre: Mazarin lived in the Hôtel Tubeuf, renamed Palais Mazarin; the former queen of England, the king's aunt lived in the Palais-Royal; her daughter Henriette, who married Philippe, Louis XIV's brother and later Duc d'Orléans, established the Bourbon-d'Orléans branch of the family in this palace. As for Louis XIV, he bought the Palais Brion, an outbuilding of the Palais-Royal, as a home for his first official mistress, Louise de la Vallière, and used the Hôtel du Petit Bourbon, next to St-Germain-l'Auxerrois, as a theater and a furniture store. Louis XIV's choice of Versailles as his official residence marked the end of royal residency in Paris.

THE ARTISTS' AND PHILOSOPHERS' QUARTER

This quarter lived under the shadow of the court. Residences such as the Hôtels de Longueville and de Rambouillet, where the "Précieuses" met (destroyed in 1850), as well as more modest houses, were the last homes of famous figures such as Corneille, who died in 1684, Mignard (Rue de Richelieu) in 1695, Rigaud (Rue Louis-le-Grand) in 1743, La Fontaine and indeed Molière, who paced up and down these streets the day before his final performance. The king gave his favorite artists the use of studios in the entresol of the Louvre gallery, the Tuileries Palace and the pavilions in the gardens. After his death, authors, actors and creative artists of all kinds moved out to the surrounding district. Academies were established at the Louvre, bringing with them their books and collections. The Academy of Painting and Sculpture set up its annual exhibition there (the Salon). The Louvre quarter became a hotbed of intellectual and artistic activity taking over from the Marais district opposite the Faubourg St-Germain. Philosophers frequented the salons of Mme Geoffrin in Rue St-Honoré, and of Helvetius in Rue Ste-Anne.

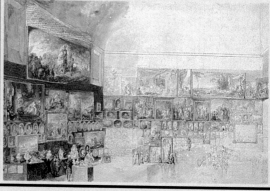

| 1730 | 1740 | 1751–80 Compilation of the *Encyclopédie* | 1760 | 1774–92 Reign of Louis XVI | 1770 | July 14, 1789 Storming of the Bastille | 1780 | August 10, 1792 Fall of the monarchy | 1790 | 1800 |

1763
Port Royal
destroyed
by fire

1768–90
Plans for a museum
at the Louvre

August 10, 1793
National museum
opened at the Louvre

THE LOUVRE MUSEUM

The Louvre remained incomplete and abandoned, left to artists and courtiers. It became a subject of public debate in the age of Enlightenment, prompting demands for the palace to be completed and the royal collections to be opened to the public (these were soon exhibited in the Palais du Luxembourg). Gradually the plans for a Louvre museum took shape with the support of the Royal Directors of Buildings. The last of these, Angiviller, purchased paintings, commissioned statues of eminent figures and had pictures restored. The Revolution realized this plan and the museum, displaying mainly paintings by the old masters, was opened in the Grande Galerie on August 10, 1793, the anniversary of the monarchy's collapse. Works of art seized during military conquests were added to the collection and magnificent classical treasures were displayed in the former queen mother's apartments.

COMTE D'ANGIVILLER (1730–1809)

He was appointed Royal Director of Buildings in 1774, and was a member of both the Academy of Science and the Royal Academy of Painting and Sculpture. His major ambition was to open to the public a royal museum at the Louvre. In the portrait opposite he is shown proudly holding the plan of the Grande Galerie which was to house Louis XVI's museum.

THE TUILERIES, PALACE OF STATE

Louis XVI returned to the Tuileries in 1789 but was driven out again by the riot of August 10, 1792 (below). The Convention held session here before First Consul Bonaparte (right) made it his ceremonial palace. When he became Napoleon I, Emperor of France, he revived Henri IV's grand plan to combine the Louvre and the Tuileries. "Big is beautiful" he used to say and was delighted by the plan for an imperial city devised by his architects Percier and Fontaine. Yet the buildings completed by the fall of the Empire are few in number: part of the north wing (below) bordering the new Rue de Rivoli, a "Saint-Napoléon" chapel and the Arc

de Triomphe, which was built as a gateway to the Tuileries Gardens on the Carrousel in 1806.

	1830	1848	1870	1871
	July	Revolution	End of the	Paris
	Revolution		Second Empire	Commune
1800	1820 1840	1860	1880	1900
1803	1826	1827	1849–53	July 25, 1852	May 23, 1871	1882
The Louvre:	Champollion	Naval	Restoration of	Visconti and	Fire at the	Ruins of the
Musée	at the Egyptian	museum	the Louvre, by	Lefuel begin work	Tuileries and	Tuileries
Napoléon	museum	established	Félix Duban.	on New Louvre.	Palais-Royal	demolished

From the Restoration to the Grand Louvre

PALACE OF STATE AND GOVERNMENT

The Tuileries Palace was the residence of the head of state in Paris until 1870. The Louvre functioned partly as an administrative annexe. State openings of parliament took place in the Henri II wing until Napoleon III built a special chamber in his "New Louvre" (which now houses the museum ▲ *131*). Charles X (below, presenting awards to artists at the Salon of 1827) installed the Conseil d'État (Council of State) in the ceremonial rooms of the Cour Carrée; it was moved to its current home at the Palais-Royal in 1871. The Ministry of Finance was located on the site of today's Hôtel Continental, Rue de Rivoli, before moving to the Rivoli wing of the Louvre from 1872 to 1989. The Ministry of Foreign Affairs was located in Rue des Capucines from 1820 until the Hôtel du Quai d'Orsay was built in 1853. The Ministry of Justice is located on the Place Vendôme. During the revolutionary era

An assembly held during the Restoration in the State Room of the Henri II wing (today room 32, first floor, Sully wing).

attacks and popular uprisings inevitably affected the government institutions. In 1820 the Duc de Berry was killed at the Opéra, then in the Square Louvois ▲ *298* (right). Ten years later, Charles X was overthrown in the July Revolution; the rebels attacked the Louvre, gained entry and vented their fury on pictures of the king. In the disturbances of February 1848 the

Tuileries were attacked and pillaged and the Palais-Royal was burned down.

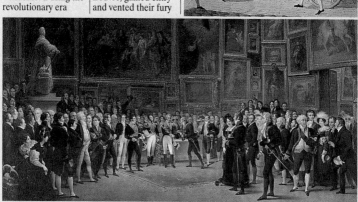

1914–18		1939–45	1958		1989	
World War One		World War Two	Beginning of the		Fall of the	
			Fifth Republic		Berlin wall	

| 1900 | 1920 | 1940 | 1960 | | 1990 | 2006 |

	1930	1953	1981	1989	1998
	Naval museum	Georges Braque is asked	Plan for	The Pyramide	Work is
	moved to the	to produce a ceiling for	"Grand	is opened	completed
	Palais de Chaillot	the Royal Antechamber	Louvre"		

A HUGE DOUBLE PALACE: THE LOUVRE AND THE TUILERIES

The restored monarchy had been content to add only a few bays to the north wing of the Tuileries. Only with the Second Republic (1848–51) did major construction work begin again. Victor Hugo called upon the government of 1848 to make the Louvre a "Mecca for intellectuals", and the revolutionary government decided by decree to complete the palace, which became one of France's largest building sites at a time when national building programs were leading the struggle against unemployment. Louis-Napoleon, the Prince-President, undertook to finance the project. When he became Emperor he decided to make it a showcase of his power. Baron Haussmann ordered the demolition of the run-down district between the Louvre and the Tuileries and built the Avenue de l'Opéra as a major axis connecting the new palace with the opera house; this project was carried out by Charles Garnier. Architects Visconti and then Lefuel built the "New Louvre", finally completing the old palace. (The architect Visconti is shown presenting his project to Napoleon III and the Empress Eugénie, right). The new buildings around the "Cour Napoléon" which were opened in 1857, glorified the regime with a prominent place given to decorative images of the Emperor and imperial allegories. In 1861, things took off again when architect Lefuel came up with the idea of an "imperial city". He destroyed one third of the Louvre gallery and the Pavillon Flore to make way for his new buildings; the large *guichets* (passages) and the Flore wing are the result of his scheme. When war broke out and the empire fell in 1870, the palace was a trapeze-shaped quadrangle at the center of the district. The Louvre and Tuileries complex was at its height, incorporating the redesigned Jardin des Tuileries. The 1871 fire reduced the Tuileries and part of the Palais-Royal to ashes.

THE "GRAND LOUVRE"

The Pyramide and alterations to the open spaces around the museum are the visible part of the "Grand Louvre" project which covers all the underground area beneath the Cour Napoléon and the Cour du Carrousel, as illustrated in the cut-away diagram (right). In the foreground, from left to right, are the Louvre amphitheater and school, the car park and the rooms of the Carrousel area. Behind this is the Carrousel shopping area, lit by an inverted pyramid.

THE MUSEUM TAKES OVER

The museum gradually took over the sites occupied by government bodies. The Union Centrale des Arts Décoratifs moved into the Marsan wing after it was rebuilt. The Louvre acquired the Flore wing in 1964. The departure of the Ministry of Finance in 1989 finally gave the Louvre control of the Richelieu wing. Some sections have been transferred to other buildings – America, Asia, ethnography, and most recently the second half of the 19th-century collection were moved to the Musée d'Orsay in 1986.

Nonetheless the size of the Louvre's collections required a major reconstruction project; the "Grand Louvre" scheme was devised by President Mitterrand in 1981 to meet these needs. Archeological excavations formed the first stage of the project, followed by the construction of an entrance hall crowned by I.M. Pei's glass pyramid, opened in 1989, and the opening of the Richelieu wing and Carrousel du Louvre in 1993. The Sully and Denon wings were completed in 1997 and 1998.

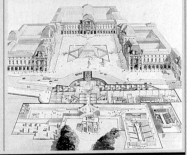

▲ 1200: Philippe Auguste's château.　　▼ 1380: Charles V's moat.

▲ 1572: The Valois palace and Tuileries.　　▼ 1610: Henri IV's Grand Plan.

▲ 1643 Louis XIII has the Cour Carrée made four times larger.

The Louvre is eight hundred years old: in 1200 it was a fortress, today it is the largest museum in the world. Kings and emperors, as well as presidents of the Republic, have all played a part in creating this immense architectural puzzle, a veritable encyclopedia of France's history, and a mirror of changing architectural fashions. This evolution is illustrated by ten models, here photographed from above, which are displayed in the rooms that the museum has set aside to display its history (the Hall Napoléon).

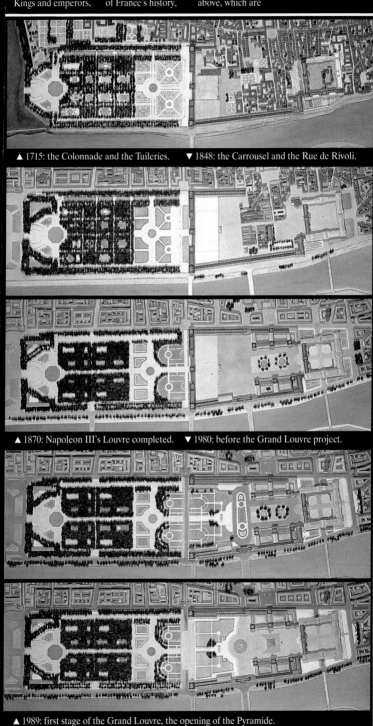

▲ 1715: the Colonnade and the Tuileries.   ▼ 1848: the Carrousel and the Rue de Rivoli.

▲ 1870: Napoleon III's Louvre completed.   ▼ 1980: before the Grand Louvre project.

▲ 1989: first stage of the Grand Louvre, the opening of the Pyramide.

● The medieval suburb

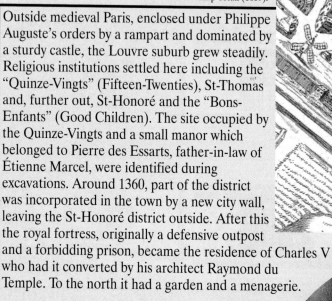

Outside medieval Paris, enclosed under Philippe Auguste's orders by a rampart and dominated by a sturdy castle, the Louvre suburb grew steadily. Religious institutions settled here including the "Quinze-Vingts" (Fifteen-Twenties), St-Thomas and, further out, St-Honoré and the "Bons-Enfants" (Good Children). The site occupied by the Quinze-Vingts and a small manor which belonged to Pierre des Essarts, father-in-law of Étienne Marcel, were identified during excavations. Around 1360, part of the district was incorporated in the town by a new city wall, leaving the St-Honoré district outside. After this the royal fortress, originally a defensive outpost and a forbidding prison, became the residence of Charles V who had it converted by his architect Raymond du Temple. To the north it had a garden and a menagerie.

FRESCO FRAGMENT
Fragments of secular frescos were discovered during excavations. Originally they decorated the walls of a small medieval manor (left, a fragment of painted plaster).

THE LOUVRE CHATEAU
It can be seen in the background of the *Retable of the Paris Parlement* (above, ▲ 215). The figures of King Charles V (left) and of the queen (▲ 184) became part of the royal collection in the 17th century after the last medieval buildings were destroyed. They may originally have decorated the palace gateway.

Excavations have revealed the size of the fortifications. Above, the wide moat of Charles V's city wall.

THE SCHOLAR KING

This picture of Charles V in his library (below) reminds us that he was a collector of rare manuscripts, which he kept in his ornately decorated library tower at the Louvre. In 1373 librarian Gilles Malet listed 973 works.

THE QUINZE-VINGTS

This hospice was founded in 1254 by Saint Louis for three hundred blind people (15 times 20), on the site of the current Richelieu wing. It was transferred to Rue de Charenton in 1780.

● The Louvre under the Valois

The Valois stayed frequently at the Louvre. Intrigues, balls and marriages took place in the residence which Henri II had modernized to suit contemporary taste. It was here, on August 24, 1572, the day after the King of Navarre married the king's sister, that the St Bartholomew's Day Massacre took place, announced by the bells of St-Germain-l'Auxerrois. During the turmoil of the Wars of Religion, the Louvre was a base for a weak regime until Henri III abandoned it after the "day of the barricades" (1588), and was also witness to the excesses of the Paris League.

THE LOUVRE: SCENE OF THE ST BARTHOLOMEW'S DAY MASSACRE
The terrible massacre of Protestants ordered by Charles IX took place under the windows of the chateau and even within its walls. Blood spattered the bedchamber of the young Marguerite de Valois, who had just married Henri de Navarre, the future Henri IV, himself a Protestant. The massacre took place after the assassination of Admiral de Coligny, who is commemorated by a 19th-century statue behind the Oratoire church ▲ 305.

THE TUILERIES
Catherine de' Medici had the garden designed by Bernard de Carnessequi, a Florentine landscape gardener, between 1563 and 1578. It was here in 1573 that a reception was held for the Polish ambassadors who had come to offer the crown to the future Henri III (opposite, right). In the background are avenues covered with bowers and vines bordering squares of lawn which offer a variety of attractions including a grotto ● 75, an echo and a maze.

THE TILER'S KILN

In the Tuileries gardens stood the grotto which ceramicist Bernard Palissy (1510–89 ▲ 205) decorated with lizards, snakes and rockeries. The famous researcher left behind a number of trial pieces which were discovered in a tiler's kiln during excavations in the Carrousel gardens ▲ 277.

"HIDEOUT" OF THE VALOIS

The pictures of the St Bartholomew's Day Massacre (left) may be unrealistic, but they evoke vividly the atmosphere of this large-scale carnage. Romantic versions of history were to present the Louvre as the Valois' hideout during these events. In the 19th century the window of the Petite Galerie (on the Seine side) was designated "Charles IX's Balcony": the king was supposed to have shot at Protestants with his crossbow from here. The legend is untrue since this part of the palace was completed under Henri IV.

THE PARIS LEAGUE

The Louvre was occupied by the Paris League after Henri III's departure (1588). It was here that the "torture of the Sixteen" took place, so-called after the sixteen men hanged in the great hall for having ordered the execution of President Brisson.

The Revolution

The Tuileries palace was Louis XVI's home after he was brought back from Versailles; after the fall of the monarchy it became a national palace, headquarters of the Convention and then of the Senate until the Bonapartist coup on November 9, 1799. The Revolution unfolded around this center of government, from the Prince of Lambesc's charge on July 14, 1789 to Bonaparte's cannons on the steps of St-Roch. Here too was the center of political debate: the Palais-Royal with its orators, the Club des Feuillants, the Assembly in the Salle du Manège and the "Fête de l'Être Suprême" (Festival of the Supreme Being).

THE FALL OF THE MONARCHY
On the morning of August 10, 1792, the King and his family fled to the Assembly in the Salle du Manège at the Tuileries. The monarchy was abolished and the royal family was taken to the Temple. Parisians, along with citizens of Marseilles who had come to the capital to overthrow the monarchy, attacked the Tuileries palace which was poorly defended by lightly armed Swiss guards. The rebels fired cannons before entering the hallway and the apartments inside, slaughtering the Swiss guards. These victims of the Revolution are commemorated by a grandiose pyramid in the garden.

THE PLACE DE LA CONCORDE
The guillotine was set up on the former Place Louis XV, renamed Place de la Révolution, in 1792. The emblems of royal power were also burned here (right). In its final decree, in 1795, the Convention renamed the square Place de la Concorde, to wipe out these tragic memories (1795) ▲ 280.

38

THE SALLE DU MANÈGE
The Republic was proclaimed on September 21, 1792 ▲ *288* in the former riding school of the Tuileries, built by Robert de Cotte (1720).

FESTIVAL OF THE SUPREME BEING
Designated by Robespierre to counter atheism by exalting Nature and the human soul, this festival took place on June 8, 1794.
An optimistic vision of humanity was expressed in a grandiose national liturgy; the procession with the "Incorruptible" at its head passed before a circular platform set up in front of the palace.

THE CONVENTION
The former Salle des Machines in the Tuileries Palace ● *78* became the Salle de l'Assemblée and was redecorated by the Convention. It was here, on the last day of the Revolution, (May 20, 1795), that the head of deputy Ferraud was presented by the rebellious people to the President of the Convention, who admitted defeat.

●Napoleon's treasures

The Musée Central des Arts opened at the Louvre on August 10, 1793. It was renamed Musée Napoléon in honor of Bonaparte in 1803. In addition to collections of paintings seized from the King, the churches and the émigrés, the Revolutionary army brought treasures from its conquests in Europe; paintings as well as magnificent classical statues were seized in Rome and Venice. The museum became a showcase of imperial power. The emperor, who lived at the Tuileries, made improvements and additions.

GLORIOUS PROCESSION WITH THE SPOILS OF WAR
The great classical marbles of the Vatican can be seen on these Sèvres vases, pulled on chariots ▲ *164*: the Apollo Belvedere, the *Cnidian Aphrodite* and the Laocoön (above, top, from left to right). The procession also honored the victorious soldiers in their ornate uniforms (left). The Laocoön was exhibited at the far end of the new museum of antiquities, and Napoleon came to see it lit up by torches, the predecessors of today's spotlights (above).

VICTORY CELEBRATIONS
The procession bringing the works of art seized in Italy was part of the victory celebrations commemorated on this magnificent Sèvres vase.

> "Only what is big is beautiful;
> size and scale can disguise many failings."
>
> Napoleon I

THE ROTONDE D'APOLLON
The works seized in Europe were exhibited in the Rotonde d'Apollon in 1807 (above ▲ 126), alongside the bust of Napoleon. Vivant Denon, the museum director, can be seen here guiding visitors.

IMPERIAL WEDDING
In April 1810, Napoleon married Marie-Louise of Austria (left). To reach the Salon Carré where the ceremony was to be held, the nuptial procession passed through the Grande Galerie ▲ 130 which displayed paintings from all over Europe.

MUSÉE NAPOLÉON
After it had presided over the new acquisitions, the huge bust of Napoleon (cast in bronze by Lorenzo Bartolini) was placed by the entrance to the museum. Today it can be seen in room 1 of the gallery devoted to the History of the Louvre ▲ 122.

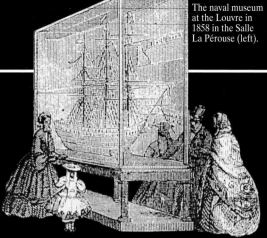

The naval museum at the Louvre in 1858 in the Salle La Pérouse (left).

When the Empire fell, the museum lost those pieces which were restored to France's allies. However it found a new lease of life, dedicating itself to the full range of artistic creation and exploring distant worlds. Champollion exhibited the masterpieces of ancient Egypt to brilliant effect and the discovery of the Assyrians followed in 1847. A series of new museums opened at the Louvre: of ethnography, America and China. As the collections grew, some sections had to be moved to other buildings.

THE MUSEUM OF ETHNOGRAPHY
The museum of ethnography (opposite page, top) was established under the Second Republic to display oriental and African works in the Cour Carrée next to the naval museum. In 1878 these collections moved to the Musée du Trocadéro. The pre-Colombian antiquities of the American museum followed the same route.

NAVAL MUSEUM
This museum (above and left) was created at the Louvre in 1827 under the name Musée Dauphin, to exhibit models of ships (but subsequently contained many ethnographic pieces). It was moved to the Palais de Chaillot in 1943.

A museum of distant worlds

In 2003 an eighth department, dedicated to the Islamic arts ▲ 146, was opened. This massive collection will eventually be housed in the modern space planned in Cour Visconti in 2010.

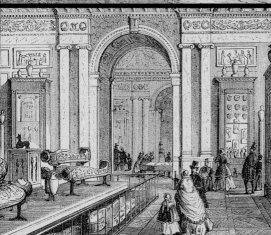

THE MUSEUM OF LOST CIVILIZATIONS

Initially the collections of classical sculpture formed the nucleus of the Louvre's collection of antiquities; however, other areas gradually caught up. The Egyptian museum was established by Champollion under Charles X, in ornate rooms decorated by the architect Fontaine on the second story of the Cour Carrée (left, center). The Musée Charles X, as it was called, opened in 1827 ● 128. In 1847 the Assyrian museum was created. Under the Second Empire it was transferred to the first story of the Colonnade, where the rich decorations of the palace of Khorsabad could be displayed, including the huge winged bulls ▲ 140, arranged face to face and not in parallel as they should have been (left, bottom). In 1863, the Etruscans made their début at the Louvre, when the museum paid a vast sum for the collection of Marquis Campana, bankrupt former director of the Mont-de-Piété in Rome. The new museum of antiquities, named Musée Napoléon III, consisted mainly of ceramics ▲ 174 and jewelry, and was enriched by the proceeds of official archeological expeditions to Greece and the Eastern world. Gradually the museum opened up to the Far East and to Islam. Islamic arts have occupied a large area of the museum ever since ▲ 146, while the Asian collections were transferred to the Musée Guimet in 1945.

● The Commune: 1871

MAY 1871
Barricades were set up in the streets of Paris (Rue de Rivoli to the right ▲ 287), to hold back the advance of government troops from Versailles.

The Second Empire had just collapsed. Artists elected Gustave Courbet to the head of the Committee of Arts and he took action to protect important works of art, while declaring the Vendôme column to be a "monument devoid of all artistic value . . . alien to the spirit of modern civilization and the union of universal fraternity". The Commune, proclaimed on March 28, pulled it down on May 16. On May 23, government troops entered Paris and *La Semaine Sanglante* (Bloody Week) began. Communards set fire to the Ministry of Finance, the Tuileries, the Palais-Royal, the Louvre library and the headquarters of the Beaux-Arts.

THE VENDÔME COLUMN: A SYMBOL DESTROYED
It was rebuilt in 1873 at the expense of the painter Gustave Courbet, leader of the Committee of Arts (▲ 284).

THE TUILERIES IN RUINS
The overall structure of the palace stood until 1882, when the government took the decision to erase all memory of discredited regimes and demolished the blackened ruins (right). "The ruins have neither beauty nor grandeur, they are merely ugly and sad", argued Jules Ferry, Minister for Public Education, who carried through the vote for demolition. The stones of the building were dispersed ▲ 276.

THE FIRE
On May 23, 1871, in the middle of Bloody Week, the Communards systematically set fire to major institutions, among them the Tuileries. The Louvre was saved from burning thanks to its curators, led by Barbet de Jouy and to the government troops, but the Tuileries fell victim to the flames (right).

**PAINTERS OF
THE RUINS**
Jean Louis Ernest
Meissonier (1815–91)
painted the chariot
on top of the Arc
de Triomphe on the
Carrousel ▲ 275
through the ruins
of a hallway (above).
In the painting by
Italian artist De
Nittis (1846–84),
ordinary people pull
their carts past the
burnt ruins of the
palace (right).

● The Louvre in packing crates

The masterpieces which had been evacuated during World War One were taken to safety once again in 1938. Their second exodus took place from August to December 1939, heading first for Chambord, and from there to nine other châteaux including Sourches, Courtalain, Valençay, Brissac and Cheverny. As the Germans advanced, everything that could be transported was sent toward the southwest, to Loc-Dieu, and from there to Montal and the neighboring châteaux. The Resistance told the English of these sanctuaries and the BBC announced "The Mona Lisa is smiling", and "Van Dyck thanks Fragonard.".

PAUL JAMOT (1863–1939)
This brilliant Greek scholar joined the department of classical antiquities in 1902 but later turned to painting as his chief passion. He was entrusted with supervising the works evacuated from the Louvre to Toulouse during World War One. He painted the loaded lorries (left) and the crates piled up in the Augustine church at Toulouse (below).

A. Durandeau (1854–1941) was also fascinated by the contrast between the Gothic architecture and the crates: his interior view of the Jacobin church at Toulouse (above) dates from 1918.

"The Gioconda is smiling"
"Van Dyck thanks Fragonard"

On the Quai du Louvre

In 1939, the director of the museum, Henri Verne, and Jacques Jaujard (below), its general secretary, organized the evacuation of the works of art, assisted by the museum curators. The plan was in place even before the Munich agreements (1938) and some works had already left for Chambord. By September 1, 1939, two days before the declaration of war, all the works had left Paris.

Transportation in Secret

Thousands of crates were ordered, each marked only with the package's department of origin. Most works were transported in crates, except for inlaid woods (too fragile) and sculptures that were too heavy to move. The Louvre had only one truck, so the vehicles of the Samaritaine store were requisitioned.

One of the museum entrances in the Flore wing is named after Jacques Jaujard.

A Remarkable Career

When Paul Jamot returned to Paris in 1919, he was appointed curator of the department of paintings. His energetic promotion of Impressionism and the painters of realism marked a turning point in the history of art between the two wars.

Trials and Tribulations of Moving

The *Raft of the Medusa*, too fragile to be packed in a crate, was evacuated in a scenery transporter belonging to the Comédie Française. From Chambord works were transferred to other locations under the supervision of curators.

● Origin of the name "Louvre"

The name "Louvre" or *Lupara* in Latin, appeared relatively late at the end of the 12th century, and was used at first to designate the surrounding district. A great deal of effort has been expended to discover the word's origin and many interpretations have been proposed based on distortions of the word or similar words. These include: leper-house, Saxon fortress, kennels for wolf-hunting, watchtower, red place and place planted with small oak trees. The enigma must remain unsolved, but there are a number of fascinating expressions which originated at the Louvre and the Tuileries palace.

THE SALON
The Academy of Painting and Sculpture exhibited its members' works at the Palais-Royal (1672), then in the Grande Galerie of the Louvre (1699). After 1725 it used the Salon Carré. From this point on the exhibition became known as the "Salon", and the critics were called *salonniers*.

THE "GUICHETS" OF THE LOUVRE
A *guichet* is a hole or opening in a doorway, especially in the gateway to a town. The word is still used of any passageway through the Louvre (one of the *guichets* of the Cour Carrée, right).

COURT SIDE AND GARDEN SIDE
From 1770 to 1782 the Comédie Française used the Salle des Machines in the Tuileries as a theater. The stage was between the Tuileries gardens on one side, and the court in front of the palace on the other, hence the French habit of referring to stage left and stage right as "court side" and "garden side".

Arts and traditions

● The Louvre on paper

In the 18th century stalls selling paintings and prints took over the archways (*guichets*) of the Cour Carrée, which became a popular place to stroll.

Paper as the vehicle of knowledge and memory, as a source of income and an instrument of power, has always played a major role in the life of the Louvre and its surrounding district – the Bibliothèque Nationale is just minutes away. The Louvre became the official center of intellectual life because of the Academies, and it housed the Ministry of Foreign Affairs archives for a time at the beginning of the 18th century. The Royal Press was founded in the galleries of the Louvre in 1640 and grew steadily up to the Revolution. Under the influence of the royal collections, and with the presence of dozens of artists living at the Louvre, paper became important in the form of engravings. The printing press has been central to the life of the Louvre quarter for the last two centuries since freedom of the press was established in 1789.

THE ROYAL PRESS
The quantity and variety of characters used made this the most important typographic workshop in Europe in the 18th century. On the eve of the Revolution the Royal Press was operating some twenty presses and employed over a hundred workers. Rétif de la Bretonne worked here as a printer from 1761 to 1764. Today's Imprimerie Nationale (National Printing Office) is its direct descendant.

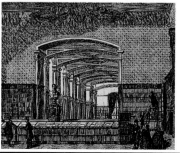

THE IMPERIAL LIBRARY
This was established in the north wing of the Louvre built in 1857.

THE SECONDHAND BOOKSELLERS
The stalls between Pont Royal and Pont Henri IV are the descendants of the 18th-century print dealers.

> **"**This expensive and idiotic craze for paintings and drawings, which are bought at ridiculous prices, is quite unbelievable. No other luxury, except diamonds and china, is more trivial and incredible.**"**
>
> L.-S. Mercier

PRINT DEALERS

In his *Tableaux de Paris*, Louis-Sébastien Mercier protests against the invasion of the Louvre and its quarter by a horde of small traders. Foremost among these were the print sellers who plied their trade under the arches of the Cour Carrée (above).

THE BIBLIOTHÈQUE NATIONALE

Paper still plays a vital role today, as is confirmed by the transfer of France's Bibliothèque Nationale (left, the former Print Room) to the larger Tolbiac site. This will leave the historic building in Rue de Richelieu free to house the future Centre National des Arts, bringing together collections and specialist archives in the field of art history.

The Louvre's location between the Seine and the Tuileries Gardens and the appeal of its buildings and its collections, have made it a natural setting for festivities and celebrations. This tradition was established under the last of the Valois dynasty and the Bourbons who celebrated births and marriages here; it continued under the Empire and the Restoration, culminating with Napoleon III. The Louvre was the centerpiece of the "Grands Travaux" in the 1980's and is once again the scene of many important official events.

Festivities ● at the Louvre

THE CARROUSEL OF 1662
An equestrian display, carnival and tournament combined, the Carrousel of 1662 took over the Cour des Tuileries for two days ▲ 276. The procession consisted of five equestrian quadrilles, with riders dressed in costumes designed by Henri Gissey. Louis XIV at the head of the quadrille of Romans, is surrounded by thirteen hundred courtiers dressed as dancers and acrobats. Leading court figures headed the quadrilles of Persians, Turks, Indians and Americans.

NAPOLEON'S MARRIAGE
In April 1810 Napoleon was married for the second time, to Marie-Louise, Archduchess of Austria. The reception was held at the Louvre. After crossing the court the procession, preceded by pages and chamberlains, paraded through the museum's Grande Galerie ▲ 130.

LADIES' SUPPER AT THE TUILERIES
A banquet for ladies was held in 1836 in the Salle des Spectacles at the Tuileries, on the site of the Salle de la Convention ● 39.

THE ARRIVAL OF MOHAMMED EFENDI
The procession of the Grand Turk's ambassador made a great impression on Parisians in 1721. Accompanied by royal troops on horseback he crossed the Tuileries Gardens on his way to the palace to meet the young Louis XIV.

● Fashion

THE FIRST COUTURIERS
Founded in 1891 at 3, Rue de la Paix, Paquin was one of the most famous couture houses (right, fashion workers leaving the workshops).

Since the 18th century the Louvre has been the Mecca of Parisian couture. Under the Directoire the dandies and fashion victims of their day strutted about at the Palais-Royal, starting one of the first fashion crazes. Dressmakers attached to the palace and the court prospered in the Saint-Honoré quarter. The oldest and most famous fashion names are linked with this district: Rose Bertin, Revillon, Paquin, Worth, Lanvin and Coco Chanel ▲ 283. This tradition continued in the 20th century with the establishment in 1982 of the Musée de la Mode, now in the Rohan wing in the Louvre ▲ 291, fashion parades in the Cour Carrée and, since 1994, in the Carrousel du Louvre.

LE NORMAND, PROSPER LE DUC, & COMPAGNIE,
Succeſſeurs de Monſieur BUFFAULT,
MARCHANDS DE TOUTES SORTES D'ÉTOFFES DE SOIE, D'OR ET D'ARGENT, ET MEUBLES,
RUE SAINT HONORÉ,

THE ROYAL TRADE
The first modern boutiques came into being in the palace arcades; the oldest of these is at the Palais-Royal ▲ 299. During the Directoire the fashion-conscious (left) found their most exquisite materials and loveliest finery here.

THE FIRST LADY OF COUTURE
Rose Bertin founded her couture house in 1774 at 26, rue Saint-Honoré ▲ 282, in a shop with glass windows, a novelty for the time. Her vanity was only equaled by her fame, and she was the first to impose her own taste on her clients, who included Queen Marie-Antoinette. In 1784 she moved to 96, Rue de Richelieu, remaining loyal to the Palais-Royal district.

Coco Chanel
in 1932.

eanne Lanvin created her couture house in
885, in Rue du Marché-St-Honoré ▲ 287
ut left in 1889 for Rue Boissy-d'Anglas.

**THE CARROUSEL
FASHION SHOWS**
The haute-couture fashion
shows have had a number of
homes including the Palais
des Congrès, the Palais de
Chaillot and the Musée
d'Art Moderne before
settling in the Louvre's
Cour Carrée in 1982.
Then, however, the
minister of culture
Jack Lang, decided to
give them the
Carrousel
(above).

● Walks around the Louvre

The Pyramide designed by architect I.M. Pei with its ornamental lakes and fountains has become a favorite meeting place. Bordered by the Seine to the south and close to the Pont-Neuf and the Pont des Arts footbridge, with the Palais-Royal Gardens to the north and the Tuileries Gardens to the west, the Louvre palace is a magnetic attraction, drawing in curious visitors and those who just want to take a stroll. Responsibility for the Tuileries Gardens, which passed to the museum in 2005, restored an aesthetic coherence to the entire complex, extending all the way from the colonnade of the Louvre to the gates in the Place de la Concorde.

OPEN-AIR MUSEUM

An integral part of the "Grand Louvre" project, the restoration of the Tuileries Gardens was completed in 2000. André Le Nôtre's original designs were renovated, and hundreds of trees and flowers were replanted. Finally, the restoration of statues by Rodin, Carpeaux, Coysevox and others together with the addition of works by such as Max Ernst, Giacometti and Henry Moore transformed the Gardens into an open-air museum.

THE PALAIS-ROYAL

Unlike the Tuileries Gardens which are open to the city, the Palais-Royal garden is enclosed, as though protected from its urban surroundings by a series of courtyards and buildings. To the south there is the Comédie Française and the Conseil d'État, while solid terraced buildings stand on the other sides, mostly dating from the Ancien Régime. The Palais-Royal garden is national property, open to the public throughout the year. To the stroller it offers serene shady avenues and a number of shops and restaurants to explore under the 180 arches of its arcades as well as the curious sight of the columns by contemporary artist Daniel Buren, which have been installed in the main courtyard ▲ 296.

The Palais Royal was fashionable from the 18th century onward. Its attraction lay not only in the variety of entertainments on offer, but also in the prostitution which flourished here, protected by a law forbidding police officers from entering the area.

● Cafés and restaurants

The Boeuf à la Mode,
Rue de Valois, around 1830.

The cafés and restaurants recently opened in the Louvre and the Carrousel are not mere concessions to fashion but a response to needs expressed by the public and museum visitors. In catering for these needs the Louvre is carrying on one of the district's strong traditions: it was here that the first restaurants and cafés were opened at the end of the 18th century as places for meetings and discussion during the Revolutionary era. The first establishments opened in the rue de Richelieu, round the Palais Royal and in the Tuileries Gardens, for example the Frères Provençaux restaurant shown below in 1846, or the Café des Aveugles (bottom) during the Revolution.

THE RESTAURANTS OF THE GRAND LOUVRE
The careful layout of the museum means that visitors can relax and have some refreshment between visiting the galleries without leaving the museum ◆ *323*.
All tastes are catered for with restaurants ranging from haute cuisine, to brasserie or simple bistrot.

THE MUSEUM'S CAFÉS
There are five cafés including the Café Richelieu (right), occupying the former offices of the Ministry of Finance now redesigned by three contemporary artists Buren, Raynaud and Giacobetti, and the Marly (far right) which has a breathtaking view of the Pyramid.

Behind the scenes

● In the wings

The Louvre is like a theater in that it stages a spectacle for visitors to see, but the actors are the works of art. In this performance, however, there is no room for improvisation even though it is the same every day. It is organized according to rules, traditions and rituals, time-honored customs and procedures. On both sides of the curtain, in the public areas and in the wings, nothing is left to chance. The world of the Louvre combines celebrity and anonymity, light and shadow. A secret hidden world exists behind the displays. This unseen side of the Louvre, the off-stage life which is vital for the performance, is astonishingly wide-ranging and diverse.

OF MASTERPIECES AND MEN
Large numbers of people are needed to find, acquire, store, catalog, restore, study, compare, communicate, manage, supervise, receive, present, maintain, air-condition, light, repair and feed. In order to carry out its twin tasks of research and receiving the public, the Louvre museum employs nearly 2,000 staff, active in forty different specialist areas.

THE CENTRE DE RECHERCHE ET DE RESTAURATION DES MUSÉES DE FRANCE
The center in the basement of the Louvre, carries out all the chemical, physical and

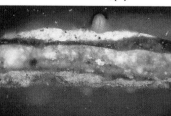

radiographic analyses necessary to understand and conserve the works of art (for example, dating and studying picture surfaces). It has an AGLAE particle accelerator, which permits examination and study of items without the need for taking samples.

THE RESERVE COLLECTION

As part of the Grand Louvre project the museum was given new store rooms, even larger and more functional than the old ones. Works are kept in reserve temporarily, for storage or conservation, arranged on sliding racks or in rows, as shown here. The museum's curators, responsible for the inventory of the Louvre's collections, do much of their work here.

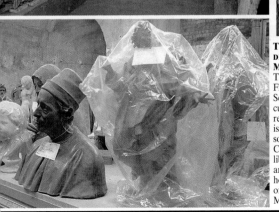

THE BIBLIOTHÈQUE DES MUSÉES DE FRANCE

The library of the French Museum Service open to curators and researchers only, is located in the south wing of the Cour Carrée. The library specializes in art history but also houses the archives of the French Museum Service.

● The Department of Graphic Arts

Over 126,000 works on paper make up the collection of this department, little known to the general public. Because of their fragility and the danger of exposing them to light for too long, the miniatures, engravings, drawings, watercolors, pastels and artists' sketchbooks are not on permanent exhibition. They can be seen on request in the consultation and documentation rooms (refitted in 1998) located in the Flore wing. The department regularly organizes temporary exhibitions in the French and foreign painting sections.

A MAJOR COLLECTION
The Department of Graphic Arts and the Edmond de Rothschild collection together constitute the largest collection of drawings in Europe. The collection is particularly rich in works of the 16th-, 17th-, 18th- and 19th-century Italian and French schœcools, especially those of the great masters like Leonardo da Vinci (*Drapery for a Seated Figure*, right) ▲ 262. The collection is the product of a traditional acquisition policy going back to the Ancien Régime and minor artists are less well represented than the major ones.

THE LOVE OF PEACE
This beautiful red chalk drawing by Edme Bouchardon is a study for a caryatid on the equestrian statue of Louis XV which stood on the site of the Place de la Concorde (▲ 280). It was commissioned in 1748, dedicated fifteen years later, and finally destroyed in 1792.

De Rembrandt, *Tête d'homme coiffé d'un turban*, et de Rubens, *Jeune femme agenouillée*.

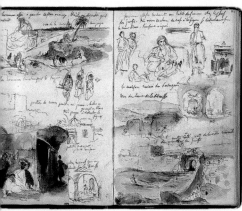

THE RANGE OF TECHNIQUES AND MATERIALS
This drawing entitled *View of Arco Valley in the Tirol* by Albrecht Dürer (above) demonstrates a variety of techniques: blue, brown, gray, ocher and green watercolors, black ink, brushwork and white highlights. The same is true of Leonardo da Vinci's drapery drawing (left-hand page), which has brushwork, white highlights and gray tempera on a primed canvas. The drawing by Rubens (below, left) is done in white pencil, black charcoal and red chalk. Rembrandt's drawing shows brown ink, brown wash, pen and white highlights; Raphael's uses charcoal, white highlights and metal point on beige paper; finally Claude Lorrain's uses graphite, sepia wash and China ink.

Self-portrait at Easel (left), pastel by Chardin; *Portrait of Mustapha* (above), by Géricault; (above this), *Shepherd by a Lake* by Claude Lorrain; *Woman's Head* (top left) by Raphael.

63

● Conservation and display

The new museum spaces are air conditioned in order to stabilize temperature and relative humidity; two humidity monitors (right).

Conservation ensures that as much as possible of the national heritage is passed on to future generations: this has been the responsibility of the curators since the museum was founded. The rehanging of the collections not only prompted major restoration work, it also inspired a rethink in other areas including lighting (the preference now is for natural light); colors used for display purposes; and museum furnishings which have always been entrusted to architects and designers and include display cases, pedestals and seats as well as the fixtures and fittings in cafés.

FRAMES

The museum has an exceptional collection of five thousand antique frames although paintings rarely have their original frames. In the 17th and 18th centuries great care was lavished on frames as works of art, providing sumptuous settings for the royal paintings. This tradition continued with varying degrees of success after the Revolution, with the influx of works to the central museum of art. Only in the 20th century, however, has the style of the frame been matched to the date and style of each painting.

The new display of the painting collections gave curators the opportunity to bring out their reserves of antique frames, to have them

restored, even to have new ones made, and to complete the collection through acquisitions.

THE MAGIC OF NATURAL LIGHT

Top lighting, the most suitable for exhibiting paintings, ensures an even distribution of light. This type of lighting has been adopted in the new painting displays designed by Italo Rota (Cour Carrée), I.M. Pei (Richelieu wing), or L. Piqueras (for the *Mona Lisa* and the *Wedding Feast at Cana,* Salle des États). A system of adjustable or fixed screens is used to filter the intensity of the light which can damage works of art, while at the same time giving views of the sky.

COLOR

The new spaces in the Richelieu wing provided curators and architects with an opportunity to study the colors best suited to the collections in each department (right and top of the page).

All the furniture in the Richelieu wing was designed by Jean-Michel Wilmotte, from some five hundred display cases to seats for the public and chairs for security guards.

The École du Louvre was created in 1882 to train curators; today its lectures are also open to the public. Equipped with a library and photographic collection, the school relocated to the newly restored Flore wing in 1998.

Once work had finished on the Grande Galerie, Henri IV allowed artists and craftsmen to move into the new building. This tradition of taking in artists continued with the Academies under Louis XIV, the Salon exhibitions after 1699 and then the more or less authorized proliferation of artists' studios in the abandoned palace up to the time of the Revolution. This tradition of fostering knowledge, teaching and the living arts continues through activities organized and encouraged within the Louvre: visits, workshops, conferences, copying and the École du Louvre.

THE ACADEMIES
After Louis XIV authorized the Academies to establish their headquarters at the Louvre they took over the palace: they included the Académie Française, the Académie des Inscriptions et Belles-Lettres, the Académie de Peinture et de Sculpture, the Académie d'Architecture and the Académie des Sciences. The royal apartments were divided up and the mezzanines were adapted to house studios and to accommodate the Academies' protégés.

An academician is received into the Académie Française around 1700 (engraving by Poilly after Delamonce, above).

"We made copies at the Louvre both to study the masters and to live with them, and also because the government would buy the copies" Henri Matisse

COPYISTS

For some it is a source of income, for others a means of study and apprenticeship: the tradition of copying great works of art is still alive although it has gradually become regulated by the museum. Permits are now granted only for a

limited period, and on condition that certain technical conditions are observed. The Louvre's most famous copyists include Turner, Delacroix, Degas, Cézanne, Vuillard, Matisse and Picasso.

Dominique Vivant Denon was director of the Musée Napoléon from 1802 to 1815. This allegorical portrait of him (left) painted by Benjamin Zix deals with only one aspect of the curator's work.

Some forty different types of specialist staff work in the Louvre. They include curators, technical and artistic specialists, engineers and architects, reception and surveillance staff, security and emergency teams, warehouse staff, archivists, cleaners, administrators, sales assistants, cashiers, cooks and waiters, who all do their job with the same respect for the buildings, the works of art and the visitors. The large team of curators, which was first established under the Revolution, is divided among the eight departments of the Louvre. There are around sixty curators. Between them they are responsible for the 35,000 works that are permanently exhibited and the hundreds of thousands of other works that are kept in the museum.

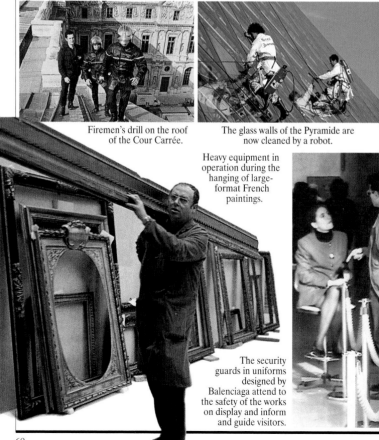

Firemen's drill on the roof of the Cour Carrée.

The glass walls of the Pyramide are now cleaned by a robot.

Heavy equipment in operation during the hanging of large-format French paintings.

The security guards in uniforms designed by Balenciaga attend to the safety of the works on display and inform and guide visitors.

Moving large-scale paintings is a masterpiece of organization in itself . . .

Madame Récamier by David gets a final touch of the duster before being hung in the new display of French painting.

. . . often requiring the use of large specialist teams.

On Tuesdays, when it is closed, the museum is given over to cleaning staff, electricians, painters, photographers and curators.

Sophisticated equipment specially adapted to the building, like this electricians' scaffolding (right), is used for restoring, repainting, repairing and replacing the museum's fittings.

Upholsterers, framers, restorers – many skilled specialists are needed in order to ensure that the museum fulfils its role.

● Souvenirs

Copy of an Egyptian papyrus knife from the New Empire.

Bronze reproduction of a limestone tablet from Lower Mesopotamia (end of the 4th millenium BC).

Beneath the Pyramide the museum offers its visitors the chance to take away with them a reminder of the pleasure and inspiration they found in the museum whatever their tastes and means. Some of the profits generated by the shops that sell these souvenirs, administered by the Réunion des Musées Nationaux, are devoted to the acquisition of works for national collections.

The Department of Graphic Arts has 13,000 engraved copper plates dating from the 16th century up to the present day.

Floral earthenware bowl (17th century).

Moroccan kohl bottle (early 19th century).

Iranian disk-shaped pin (8th–7th century BC).

(Above) Iranian earrings, a French seal ring (6th–7th century), an eye pendant from ancient Egypt.

The Louvre's cast workshop has a collection of some 5,000 pieces. Reproductions are made using materials such as resin, plaster, bronze and earthenware. *Study for the "Marseillaise"* by François Rude (far left), and the Egyptian cat goddess Bastet (left).

70

Architecture

● The medieval Louvre

Work on the Grand Louvre provided an opportunity to undertake extensive archeological excavations in both the Cour Carrée and the Cour Napoléon.

The fortress built by Philippe Auguste around 1200 to the west of the capital outside the city walls was not just a stronghold. Indeed the Great Tower which housed the treasury and also served as a prison was a symbol of royal supremacy over all the kingdom. A circular keep surrounded by a quadrangle of walls set with towers, was the perfect model of a "philippian" fortress and was imitated throughout Europe. It was not until the 14th century under Charles V that the Louvre became a royal residence. This educated monarch had the austere fortress converted into an elegant residence.

MEDIEVAL REMAINS

The medieval Louvre ▲ *122* had already been excavated in the 19th century, but it was not until 1989 that the moats of this period were opened to the public (a).

The lower hall (b) is the onl[y] part of the medieval buildin[g] which survives today; it is called Salle Saint Louis ▲ *124* because its decoratio[n] dates from this king's

a

b

GOTHIC REVIVAL
The 19th-century painter Hoffbauer attempted to visualize Charles V's Louvre. The result was a Romantic vision of an idealized fortress (above).

ST-GERMAIN, PARISH CHURCH OF THE LOUVRE
This church is dedicated to Saint Germain, bishop of Auxerre, who died in 448. It dates back to the 7th century, although the present façade dates from the 15th century ▲ 310.

BEFORE HAUSSMANN
Medieval buildings (like the house, above) could still be seen around the Louvre until the 19th-century construction projects ▲ 310.

PALACE OF THE SCHOLAR KING
Philippe Auguste's castle was transformed under Charles V. He had new windows set into the walls and added gargoyles, statues and high roofs crowned with chimneys.

Renaissance
palace of the Valois

CLASSICAL SCULPTURE
Caryatids (columns in the form of female figures) by Jean Goujon (around 1550).

François I was used to an itinerant court life, staying in the châteaux of the Loire, Blois and Chambord, and later in castles of the Paris region (St-Germain, Villers-Cotterêts and Fontainebleau). However, in 1527 he decided to build a palace in his capital city. The Great Tower was pulled down in 1528 and then Charles V's west wing was demolished to make way for a new residence in the contemporary style. The Louvre became a favorite royal palace and the setting for court celebrations under the Valois dynasty. Henri II and his sons, including Charles IX, continued the work on the palace which they entrusted to architect Pierre Lescot. Catherine de' Medici decided to have Philibert Delorme build a palace outside the city walls with a garden in the Florentine style. This was to become the Tuileries, a few hundred yards away from the old Louvre but separate from it.

Court façade of Lescot's wing with decorations by Jean Goujon.

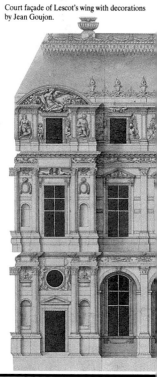

POMP AND CIRCUMSTANCE
The new palace of the king of France was intended principally as a setting for demonstrations of royal power. It was with this purpose in mind that Pierre Lescot built a new wing over the medieval foundations (right), with a large ceremonial room in the first story (the Salle des Cariatides, ▲ *125*). The room had a raised section for the throne and a gallery for musicians. The wide richly decorated staircase connecting it with the guards' room was completed under Henri II.

THE TUILERIES PALACE

Philibert Delorme had planned a huge quadrangle but was only
able to complete one section of it, dominated
by a pavilion, in collaboration with
Jean Bullant (below).

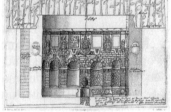

PIERRE LESCOT AND JEAN GOUJON

The architect and sculptor worked together
on the Louvre, collaborating on the façade of
the Cour Carrée and allegorical reliefs (below
and bottom of page). They also worked
together on the loggia of the Fontaine des
Innocents (which has now been converted into
a public convenience at the Halles, below).

A FLORENTINE GARDEN

The main attraction of Catherine de' Medici's
Tuileries Palace seems to have been its
Italian-style garden. Here Bernard Palissy
▲ 205 created a grotto covered with imitation
rockwork, shells and animals, all made of
terracotta (similar to the
grotto in this drawing).

● Henri IV's Grand Plan

The Louvre as we know it today is the product of Henri IV's imagination and energies; his reign (1589–1610) was a time of intensive construction work at the palace. He completed a façade on the Cour Carrée (and dreamed of making this court four times larger), finished the Petite Galerie and carried out Charles IX's plan to join the Louvre and the Tuileries with an immense gallery along the Seine (which he would have liked to match with a second gallery to the north). Classicism, a new architectural style, developed during work on these projects. Alternating vertical pavilions and horizontal wings, simple forms tempered by elegant decorations, columns in the French style with fleur-de-lys ornamentation, curved and triangular pediments and carved monograms of the reigning monarch, were all to become typical of French Classical architecture. Louis XIII and his architect Le Mercier continued Henri IV's work, extending the west wing of the Cour Carrée and building the Pavillon de l'Horloge.

PALACE BY THE RIVERSIDE
Clearly visible in this painting (above) are the Pavillon du Roi and the Renaissance façade with a medieval tower, as well as the Petite Galerie overlooking a garden and the beginnings of the Grande Galerie. The Grande Galerie (top of the page) was built by two architects: Métezeau (the town end) and Androuet (the Tuileries end). At its western end is the riverside pavilion now called the Flore pavilion, forming the southern tip of the Tuileries Palace.

THE PAVILLON DE L'HORLOGE
This square pavilion built by Le Mercier between 1624 and 1640 was to serve as a model for Napoleon III ● 82.

JESUIT ARCHITECTURE
The first stone of the Oratoire, a chapel in the Jesuit style, was laid by Louis XIII in 1621. Clément Métezeau and then Le Mercier were the architects ▲ 305.

THE CARDINAL'S PALACE
Cardinal Richelieu's magnificent palace, the future Palais-Royal ▲ 294 was the perfect example of a private residence.

THE PONT-NEUF.
The first stone was laid by Henri III in 1578 and Henri IV opened the bridge in 1607.

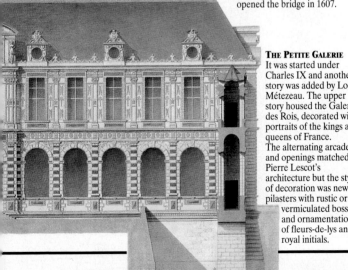

THE PETITE GALERIE
It was started under Charles IX and another story was added by Louis Métezeau. The upper story housed the Galerie des Rois, decorated with portraits of the kings and queens of France.
The alternating arcades and openings matched Pierre Lescot's architecture but the style of decoration was new: pilasters with rustic or vermiculated bosses and ornamentation of fleurs-de-lys and royal initials.

Palace of the Sun King

THE TUILERIES
The palace was finally completed following a perfectly symmetrical design reflected in the layout of the gardens.

The young Louis XIV wanted to demonstrate his power so undertook substantial improvements to the Louvre before leaving Paris for Versailles. He finished the Cour Carrée and the Tuileries palace with a garden designed by Le Nôtre and a theater (the Salle des Spectacles). He created apartments in the Tuileries and built a façade (the Colonnade) on the town side. This masterpiece was part of a program of improvements to the town, which included adding a number of royal squares.

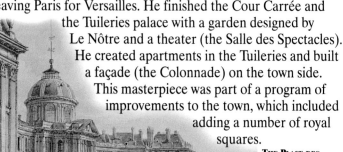

THE PLACE DES QUATRE-NATIONS
Le Vau's college (later the Institut de France) lies opposite the Louvre on the left bank.

THE ROYAL SQUARES

Henri IV created the triangular Place Dauphine and the square Place Royale (now Place des Vosges); Louis XIV created the almost circular Place des Victoires (above, right) and Place Vendôme (above). Jules Hardouin-Mansart built the latter (formerly Place Louis-le Grand) in 1699. It is surrounded by private residences, all with identical façades.

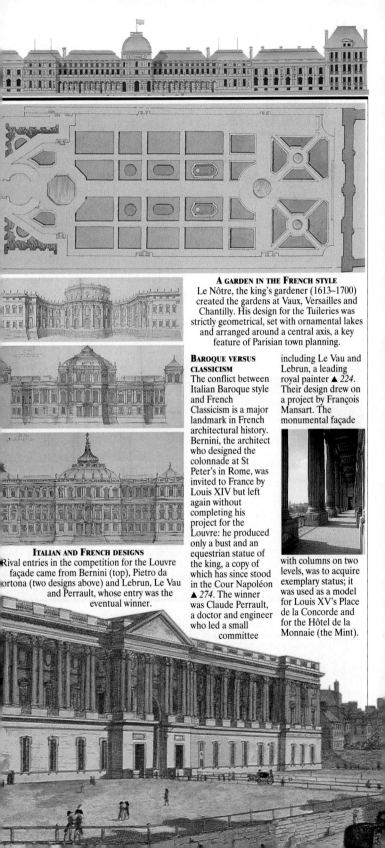

A GARDEN IN THE FRENCH STYLE
Le Nôtre, the king's gardener (1613–1700)
created the gardens at Vaux, Versailles and
Chantilly. His design for the Tuileries was
strictly geometrical, set with ornamental lakes
and arranged around a central axis, a key
feature of Parisian town planning.

ITALIAN AND FRENCH DESIGNS
Rival entries in the competition for the Louvre
façade came from Bernini (top), Pietro da
Cortona (two designs above) and Lebrun, Le Vau
and Perrault, whose entry was the
eventual winner.

**BAROQUE VERSUS
CLASSICISM**
The conflict between
Italian Baroque style
and French
Classicism is a major
landmark in French
architectural history.
Bernini, the architect
who designed the
colonnade at St
Peter's in Rome, was
invited to France by
Louis XIV but left
again without
completing his
project for the
Louvre: he produced
only a bust and an
equestrian statue of
the king, a copy of
which has since stood
in the Cour Napoléon
▲ 274. The winner
was Claude Perrault,
a doctor and engineer
who led a small
committee

including Le Vau and
Lebrun, a leading
royal painter ▲ 224.
Their design drew on
a project by François
Mansart. The
monumental façade

with columns on two
levels, was to acquire
exemplary status; it
was used as a model
for Louis XV's Place
de la Concorde and
for the Hôtel de la
Monnaie (the Mint).

Neoclassicism

The Place Louis XV, later renamed Place de la Révolution and finally Place de la Concorde (on the map, opposite) was completed in 1772.

The final flourish of French Classicism: the façade of the church of St-Roch (1738–9).

The key event at the Louvre in the period between 1750 and 1850 was the establishment of the museum in 1793. Major architectural work was abandoned since political instability meant that the reigning powers had no time to plan large projects let alone to complete them. Neoclassicism was to find political expression in the Republic and the Empire as well as in architecture. The ideas of the Enlightenment gave rise to town planning projects: new squares were created (Place de la Concorde), main roads were constructed (Rue de Rivoli), and public monuments and buildings were completed.

LA MONNAIE (THE MINT)
This building (above) was completed in 1775, echoing the colonnade of the Louvre. Its style of decoration is neoclassical ▲ 306.

BIRTH OF THE PARISIAN APARTMENT BLOCK
The Palais-Royal buildings completed by Victor Louis in 1784 mark the birth of the Parisian apartment block (a) ▲ 296. Percier and Fontaine picked up on the idea in 1802 for the Rue de Rivoli (b) ▲ 286, as did Jules de Joly for no. 4, Rue d'Aboukir, around 1820 (c) ▲ 302.

ELEVATION   CROSS-SECT

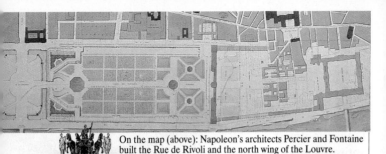

On the map (above): Napoleon's architects Percier and Fontaine built the Rue de Rivoli and the north wing of the Louvre.

IMPERIAL ARCH

The triumphal arch (left) on the Carrousel by Percier and Fontaine marked the entrance to the Tuileries palace. It is typically neoclassical in the most literal sense of the term, being an imitation of an arch from classical antiquity, the arch of Septimius Severus in Rome.

MUSÉE DES ARTS

First conceived under Louis XVI, the museum was finally opened under the Revolution. The project gave rise to several designs. Left, an entrance designed by Wailly; below, another design for the Grande Galerie.

MUSÉE NAPOLÉON

Percier and Fontaine designed the corridors and staircases for the museum. The entrance had a staircase and a vestibule, of which only the latter survives ▲ *128*; the large south and north staircases of the colonnade (above) also feature huge columns and vaults richly decorated with sculptures, stuccowork and paintings. The palace-museum became a backdrop for imperial ceremonies.

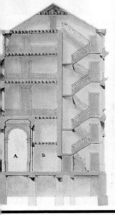

81

● The Louvre under Napoleon III

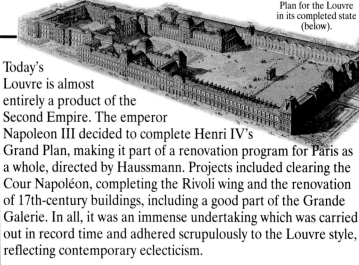

Plan for the Louvre in its completed state (below).

Today's Louvre is almost entirely a product of the Second Empire. The emperor Napoleon III decided to complete Henri IV's Grand Plan, making it part of a renovation program for Paris as a whole, directed by Haussmann. Projects included clearing the Cour Napoléon, completing the Rivoli wing and the renovation of 17th-century buildings, including a good part of the Grande Galerie. In all, it was an immense undertaking which was carried out in record time and adhered scrupulously to the Louvre style, reflecting contemporary eclecticism.

BUILDING WORK IN PROGRESS

This photograph shows the façade of the Cour Napoléon just before it was given its facing by Lefuel. On either side is the scaffolding for the new buildings which were to form the court as we know it today, composed of alternating wings and pavilions as in the 17th century.

HISTORICISM

Napoleon III's architects Lefuel and Visconti made a point of copying the Louvre's traditional style which was in keeping with the historical eclecticism of their own century, drawing both on medieval sources (Viollet-le-Duc) and on the Renaissance style which preceded French Classicism. The Denon pavilion (right) is the best example of this: it follows the structure of the Pavillon de l'Horloge which Le Mercier built two centuries earlier; the façades of the wings themselves show a similar structure of arcades and columns.

82

CARVED RELIEFS
The style of the Denon wing
matches that of earlier
centuries, but the
ornamentation is thoroughly
contemporary, featuring a
locomotive on the pediment.

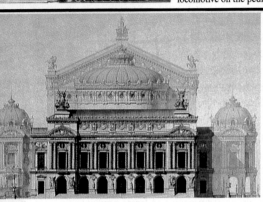

NAPOLEON III STYLE
When Empress
Eugénie asked:
"But what style is
that? It's not Louis
XIV, nor Louis XV,
nor Louis XVI!",
Charles Garnier
architect of the Opéra
(left) is supposed to
have replied:
"Madame, the style is
Napoleon III. So how
can you complain?"

THE "GUICHETS"
Although the Louvre formed an
enclosed whole, the *guichets*
(archways) ● *48* made it
accessible to traffic.

PAVILLON DENON

● The Grand Louvre

The Louvre's final transformation took place under President François Mitterrand's Grand Louvre scheme (1981–95). Architect Ieoh Ming Pei was entrusted with the architectural redevelopment of the Louvre, which was completed on the eve of the 21st century with the restoration of the Tuileries Gardens. The palace with its eight hundred years of rich architectural history now has at its center a symbol both of permanence and of contemporary creativity: the Pyramide which marks the museum entrance. The Pyramide was highly controversial at first; now it is considered a shining example of how to introduce new buildings into a historical context.

THE SECOND AND THIRD PHASES
In 1993 the Richelieu wing and the Carrousel gallery were opened in the former Ministry of Finance buildings, marking the completion of the project's second stage. The first phase culminated in the opening of the Pyramide in 1989 (above, left). The shopping center, with its inverted pyramid, (above, center) and large escalators gives access to the rooms of the Richelieu wing (right). The third and final phase of the work, on the Sully and Denon wings, was completed in 1997 and 1998.

IEOH MING PEI
This American architect of Chinese origin had previously been given the job of redeveloping Washington's National Gallery.

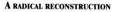
A RADICAL RECONSTRUCTION
The renovation of the Louvre observed two basic principles: to respect the old buildings and show them to their best advantage while at the same time making a resolutely contemporary contribution, free of pastiche, in the Richelieu wing and the underground areas, the Hall Napoléon and the Carrousel gallery. The Pyramide is just a tiny, visible part of Pei's work which encompasses all the underground areas of the Cour Napoléon and the Carrousel, including the reserves, the laboratory, shopping center and car park. These same principles governed the design and lighting of museum rooms (above, an openwork ceiling).

FORM AND FUNCTION
This geometrical shape was chosen not only for its timeless character but also for technical reasons; the glass Pyramide helps provide light and space to the Hall Napoléon, the vast crossroads and reception area for the public.

THE 20TH CENTURY
The large, distinctive buildings of the Samaritaine department store ▲ *308*, from 1910 and 1930, stand out in the Louvre district as does the Georges-Pompidou center (Beaubourg), which was built in the 1970's.

The inverted pyramid (left and below, while under construction) is held together by a system of cables, as is the Pyramide which points skyward.

LEITMOTIF
Attentive observers will note that the square with its diagonals marked, the basic single form of which the Pyramide is constructed, is featured on all surfaces, even on ceilings and elevators.

A technological challenge

The Pyramide is an extraordinary technical achievement: 70 ft high on a base of some 100 ft square, it is made of 793 glass diamonds and triangles fitted together with pinpoint accuracy and mounted on an aluminium framework supported by 93½ tons of girders and stainless steel joints. The French company Saint-Gobain developed an entirely new kind of glass for it which is both lightweight and strong, transparent but with minimum reflectivity. The same attention to technological detail governed the design of the many staircases, elevators, windows and ceilings.

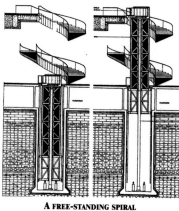

A FREE-STANDING SPIRAL
Alongside the simple, austere materials used in the Hall Napoléon (white Burgundy stone, glass, concrete glistening with crystals), the architect allowed himself a more personal touch in the staircase which surrounds the hydraulic elevator.

A UNIQUE TYPE OF GLASS
The iron oxide was removed to make this glass perfectly clear; it was drawn vertically for perfect smoothness and then polished in the traditional way in England.

THE CABLE CONSTRUCTION
The connecting joints on the Pyramide (above, a drawing by Pei) were cast by Eiffel Constructions, using the lost wax casting technique, rarely employed on an industrial scale.

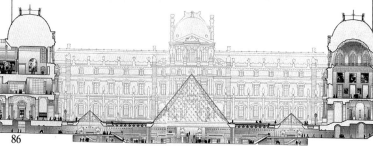

The Louvre
as seen by painters

Hubert Robert, curator: The Grande Galerie

The artist Hubert Robert (1733–1808) was entrusted with the royal painting collections intended for the future museum between 1784 and 1792. Between 1795 and 1802 he was put in charge of the nation's paintings in the newly renovated Grande Galerie ▲ *130*, and showed himself to be an imaginative curator. He lived at the Louvre in close contact with the buildings and works; here he painted and drew images of the museum's daily life, as well as visionary plans for its future development. To begin with his depiction of the reality (**1**): in 1794–6 the Grande Galerie was a long dark corridor, lit from the side by high windows. Paintings were tightly packed on the picture rails, while exhibits in the middle of the gallery were few in number and widely spaced out (including Giambologna's *Mercury* and a large Sèvres vase). In 1796 the gallery closed: the floors were renovated, the walls were painted green and statues were installed (some of these had been looted on military campaigns. In 1798 the new museum was ready to open its doors to the public (**2**). Such was the quiet, unremarkable day-to-day reality – a strong contrast to Hubert Robert's imaginary visions. He idealized the Louvre as a temple of art, imagining a wide gallery partitioned by columns (**4**). He dreamed of setting the masterpieces of classical antiquity alongside paintings of the great monuments in this gallery and his dream was indeed to become reality under Napoleon. The painter exhibited his plan for lighting the gallery in the Salon of 1796 (**3**): roof lights flood the gallery with light and the bays are separated by elegant pillars.

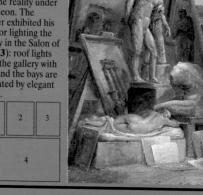

1	2	3
4		

"Plan for lighting the museum gallery through the roof, and for dividing it up without removing the view along the length of the building."

Hubert Robert (1796)

Hubert Robert, visionary:
The Grande Galerie in ruins

Hubert Robert exhibited this *Imaginary View of the Grande Galerie in Ruins* at the Salon of 1796, as a counterpart to his plans for improving the Grande Galerie. He projects the viewer into the distant future when this glorious plan will itself, like the Roman monuments, be no more than a picturesque and melancholy ruin. The picture is a reflection on the passing of time, on the cycle of lost civilizations. It is also a homage to antiquity; the *Apollo Belvedere* stands intact with a bust of Raphael at its feet. On the ground is Michaelangelo's *Dying Slave* ▲ 195.

In addition to the
Grande Galerie and
the Salon Carré,
painters have always
been attracted by the
apartments of Anne of
Austria which housed
the Musée des
Antiques from 1799
onward. They relished
the red walls, the long
view opening in the
distance through the
riverside window with
the midday light
flooding in, the
brilliant marble floors
and the imposing
pedestals ▲ 126. In
earlier years visitors
like this solitary lady
(2) had to look upward
to see the great
marbles. Madeleine
Goblot (19th century)
(1) emphasized the
profusion of statues
and busts, the
confusion of pillars
and plinths, depicted
in dim light. Around
1885 Guillaume
Larrue (1851–1935)
painted the Salle de la
Colonnade (4) which
was devoted to the
large Egyptian
monuments. He played
on the opposition of
the hieratic pink
Sphinx of Tanis (now in

the Crypte du Sphinx,
▲ *148*) and the worldly
elegance of the
visitors, in order to
emphasize the contrast
between this time-
defying masterpiece
and the transient
fashions of the day,
between the strong
lines of the stone and
the frail silhouettes of
the living people. In
1946 the Musée d'Art
Moderne acquired a
number of small
reportage paintings by
Paul Hugues
(1891–1972) depicting
scenes during the
reinstallation of
collections after
World War Two ● *46*.
Sarcophagi, packing
crates and works of art
(**3**) are here piled up
in a passageway in the
Musée Charles X
▲ *128*.

The Salon Carré ▲ *130* was intended as the Holy of Holies of high art, an arena for painting of all periods and all countries, like the Galleria degli Uffizi in Florence. However, up to 1914 paintings of all formats were packed in together with no concern for chronological or even geographical order. Many artists painted it, some conferring on the room a hushed, intimate atmosphere. Through the black-framed door of the Salle Duchâtel (**1** and **3**) part of the *Wedding Feast at Cana*, a huge painting by Paolo Veronese ▲ *264*, can be seen against the far wall on the Seine side. Alexandre Brun (1853–1941) also painted the Salon with some accuracy (**2**), showing that the works were still hung closely together in his day. However he does not show the gold and stucco work on the ceiling, commissioned by Duban during the Second Republic.

High black plinths and walls of a shade variously described as purple or chocolate contribute to a particularly somber atmosphere. High barriers with brightly polished brass protect the works behind a row of red seats. The room has two entrances, one from the Salle Duchâtel devoted to the early masters, and the other from the Grande Galerie where the majority of paintings were carefully ordered according to school and date. The entire space is given over to paintings: even the windows looking over the Seine are filled. The room is lit only by the roof light. The doorways are low, allowing for two paintings to be hung over the lintel (Hyacinthe Rigaud's *Portrait of Bossuet* and Jacob Jordaens' *Jupiter and Antiope* can be seen here). Cut-off corners in the room allow large-format works to be fitted in: Leonardo da Vinci's *The Virgin*

> "At the heart of this immense capital, the museum is
> like a cameo containing a bracelet set with precious stones.
> Art has made its supreme hallmark here."
>
> Théophile Gautier (1867)

and Child with *Saint Anne* ▲ 262 is seen below a large Guercino, for example. The far wall offers a typical example of the way paintings used to be hung. The higher section of the wall is used for large paintings (Jean Jouvenet's *Descent from the Cross*, Philippe de Champaigne's *Portrait of Richelieu*, and Valentin de Boulogne's *Concert*); the lower section features symmetrical arrangements of similar works, such as Raphael's *The Virgin and Child with Saint John the Baptist*, known as *La Belle Jardinière* ▲ 266, with oval landscapes by Claude Lorrain on either side, as well as Andrea da Solario's *Virgin with the Green Cushion* and a picture by Bernardino Luini.

1

2

3

95

Louis Béroud

"The product of this proximity of dead visions is something senseless and indefinable. They quarrel jealously for the eyes that give them life." Paul Valéry (1867)

Although Louis Béroud (1852–1930) did produce ordinary paintings of the Louvre (above), from time to time he gave free rein to his imagination. Here (right) he imagines Rubens being welcomed in the room of the *History of Marie de' Medici* series arranged by Gaston Redon in 1900 (shown in its brand new state in top painting). In a joyous confusion all the figures descend from their frames to pay homage to their creator ▲ *250*. In another picture (bottom), the most famous paintings of the Salon Carré where the masterpieces are hung, leave the walls to join in Veronese's *Wedding Feast at Cana* and Rubens' *Hélène Fourment*, the *Mona Lisa*, Titian's *Man with a Glove*, and other figures by Raphael and Correggio all invite themselves to the feast.

The Louvre through visitors' eyes

● The Louvre through visitors' eyes

Visitors from around the world

*F*ree entry to all, collections consisting entirely of original works from all over the world and an administration which held steady through times of political instability: these were some of the qualities which made the 19th-century Louvre an exemplary institution in the eyes of visitors from England, China and Spain.

Tcheng Ki Tong (1851–1907), a Chinese general and diplomat was sent to France in 1877 to become secretary of the Chinese embassy in Paris. After holding the post of military attaché in various European capitals he returned to Paris in 1883 and wrote a number of humorous works about the French in their own language.

❝What is called a museum in Europe is a sort of large building which houses masterpieces of the arts and sciences, or simply objects which can tell us about the life, customs and ideas of different peoples.
Among all collections of this type, the Louvre is one of the finest. It contains treasures collected from nearly all corners of the civilized world and allows us to review at a glance the history of nations and their various destinies. It is an admirable institution and I regret that we have nothing like it in China. Of course we too have wonderfully rich collections, but they relate to China alone and are not concerned with the arts of other countries. Furthermore they belong to individuals, the ordinary people have no access to them; unlike the lucky Parisians they cannot go and see them every day and learn from them free of charge.❞

TCHENG KI TONG,
PARISIANS DESCRIBED BY A CHINESE, PARIS, 1891

Mirza Aboul Taleb Khan was born in 1751 of a Persian father exiled to India. In 1799 he moved to Europe and lived in London for two years. He spent three weeks in Paris in 1802 before returning to Calcutta.

❝The Louvre is a very large and very lofty building: the entire ground floor is filled with statues and other objects, whose beauty I was entirely unable to judge. On the first floor there is a magnificent room, more than three hundred feet square and over fifty feet high, lit from above using mirrors placed at an angle: this method has the double advantage of increasing the intensity of light while keeping out snow and rain as effectively as a slate-covered roof. Several thousand magnificent paintings are displayed across the entire expanse of the walls. The collection is immense, its value incalculable: some of the paintings are 70 ft long and 30 ft high. After seeing the building and the treasures it holds I considered what I had seen in London and

Dublin and realized that these two cities have mere trifles by comparison with these wonders. The museum is funded by the public who are admitted without charge: the aim is to encourage a taste for the fine arts, to keep a shrine for them in France's capital and to give the government a popular appeal.**

MIRZA ABOUL TALEB KHAN,
*VOYAGES OF THE PERSIAN PRINCE MIRZA
ABOUL TALEB KHAN IN ASIA, AFRICA, AND
EUROPE*, PUB. CHARLES MALO,
PARIS, 1819

Visitors of all classes

*O**rdinary people crowded into the museum from its first
years onward. Under the Consulate and the Empire foreign visitors noted the
presence of "rough commoners" and the poorest citizens of Paris among the Louvre's
public. People of all social classes and conditions rubbed shoulders at the Louvre. The
only condition was that they should be "decently dressed", except for old and invalid
soldiers who sauntered about in tattered uniforms.*

*Norbert Truquin, who came from the Somme, described himself as a proletarian and
related his life's adventures as a series of experiences scarred by exploitation and
inequality. At the time of the 1848 revolution he was living in Paris. In 1850 he left for
Argentina and then Paraguay, where he wrote his memoirs.*

**After arriving in Paris I has spent the whole time visiting the sights of the capital.
Sometimes in the evening I bought the petit *Lazari* for a few centimes. I was able to
visit the main buildings, museums and public gardens but this was because I was
wearing a frock coat: people wearing overalls were not allowed in which meant that
many young people grew old
without knowing Paris.

In the museums it was the
paintings that interested me
most. I would try to guess at
their subjects and often pestered
other visitors with questions.
Some turned away in disdain;
others by contrast responded to
my request for explanations with
good grace. At this time I began
to observe the people there. I
noticed that those with a full
beard and a straight nose rarely
refused me information whereas
I could get nothing out of those
with flat or beak-shaped noses.**

NORBERT TRUQUIN,
*MEMOIRS AND ADVENTURES OF A
PROLETARIAN IN 1848*,
PUB. MASPERO, PARIS, 1977

● The Louvre through visitors' eyes

One Saturday in July 1850 a wedding party decided to go to the Louvre because it was raining and to fill in the time before dinner. It was the wedding party of Coupeau and Gervaise, characters in the novel "L'Assommoir" by Emile Zola (1840–1902).

❝M. Madinier politely asked if he could lead the procession. The Louvre was very big and they might get lost there; furthermore he knew all the best places because he had often come with an artist, a very intelligent young man, whose drawings were bought by a large cardboard box company to adorn their products. Downstairs, when the party reached the Assyrian museum, a little shiver passed through it. Goodness! it wasn't exactly warm down here, the place would make a magnificent cellar. And slowly the couples advanced, chins lifted, eyelids fluttering, between the stone pillars the silent gods of black marble with their hieratic rigidity, the colossal beasts, half-cat and half-woman, with cadaverous faces, thin noses and bulging lips. They found all this quite unpleasant. Stone carving nowadays was a jolly sight better than that . . .

Then the wedding party set off down a long gallery which contained the Italian and Flemish schools. Yet more paintings, nothing but paintings of saints, of men and women with faces they couldn't understand, landscapes with nothing but black, animals which had yellowed with age, a chaos of people and things in a violent din of colors which was starting to give them a terrible headache. M. Madinier was no longer speaking and slowly led the procession which followed in an orderly manner, necks twisted and eyes in the air. Whole centuries of art passed before their stupefied ignorance, the exquisite dryness of the early masters, the splendors of the Venetians, the luxuriantly and beautiful light-filled world of the Dutch. What interested them more was the copyists with their easels set up among the crowd, painting away unabashed; an old lady struck them particularly, standing at the top of a large ladder, moving her brush through the soft sky of a huge canvas.

> "From now on art was to satisfy everyone's thirst for culture and fulfil their dreams of sovereignty."
>
> Lawrence Gowing

Gradually however, the rumor must have spread about that a wedding party was visiting the Louvre. The painters hastened towards them grinning from ear to ear; curious onlookers took advance seats on the benches to see the procession pass in comfort while the attendants with pursed lips held back their witty remarks. And the wedding party, weary already and less polite, dragged their studded slippers and tapped their heels on the echoing floors with the stamping of a herd let loose, unleashed amidst the bare, contemplative neatness of the museum rooms.**

ÉMILE ZOLA,
L'ASSOMMOIR (1877), VOLUME 2 IN THE *ROUGON-MACQUART* SERIES,
PUB. GALLIMARD, PARIS, 1961

The working public came on Sundays: traders, factory workers and clerks. So did Eugène Delacroix with his old servant, and Charles Baudelaire (1821–67), who bumped into them in the Assyrian museum.

One day, a Sunday, I spotted Delacroix at the Louvre accompanied by the old servant who has cared for him for thirty years. This elegant, refined, erudite man did not consider it beneath him to show and explain the mysteries of Assyrian sculpture to the excellent woman who listened to him with simple earnestness.

CHARLES BAUDELAIRE,
THE WORK AND LIFE OF DELACROIX (1863), IN *ESTHETIC CURIOSITIES*,
BORDAS, PUB. CLASSIQUES GARNIER, PARIS, 1990

Jeanne Baudot, a pupil of Renoir, often worked at the Louvre in the last years of the 19th century. Her book of reminiscences was published in 1949 after the Louvre had become "less accessible"; no doubt she was referring to the introduction of entrance charges in 1922. Here she records to great effect how the museum, open to all comers, was brimming with life.

During the time when we were working at the Louvre, the museum was brimming with life – it has been robbed of this by the new regulations which made it less accessible, less democratic. I knew it when it was open to anyone. The only condition was to be suitably dressed. Sometimes tramps would thread their way through the crowds, warming themselves by the stoves or sitting on the benches. If they were unfortunate enough to doze off and fall over a frightened guard would rush over, glancing at the pictures for fear of an accident or theft and recovering only once the cause of the panic had fled. Nearly every day, always at the same time, a particular man would appear for his daily constitutional, walking straight ahead without pausing before any of the masterpieces. You could also see lovers, waiting in vain for their Dulcinea: others, happier, in couples, reminiscent of the *Embarcation for the Isle of Cythera*. And finally, a bourgeois Eros set marriages in motion through introductions made here!

JEANNE BAUDOT,
RENOIR, HIS FRIENDS AND HIS MODELS,
PUB. ÉDITIONS LITTÉRAIRES DE FRANCE, PARIS, 1949

Alfred de Musset (1810–57) considered that knowledge and explanations were by no means necessary to appreciate masterpieces: a naive sensibility was, to his mind, far better. Proof was supplied by a beautiful young peasant woman who happened to pass by.

**I am definitely one of those people who goes to the museum without

a guidebook. . . . Yes it occurred to me that when you visit, for example, the old gallery at the Louvre, you might as well fold your arms behind your back. What can any explanation teach you?

Stubbornly convinced of this I rubbed my hands, deprived of their guide book. I paused by a railing just below a patriotic painting. I don't know what particular subject it depicted but a large crowd had gathered there and was gaping at it.

"Well," I said to myself, "what a typical holiday crowd," but suddenly I noticed in the middle of these gawping nonentities, the sullen, indifferent head of a beautiful young peasant woman whose uncle was nudging her in admiration of the picture, while she was looking the other way!

She was wearing a lace bonnet and a pair of earrings as big as six-franc pieces; she had a pensive, stupid air, eyes gazing into thin air; she heard nothing and took no interest in anything her uncle called upon her to admire.

"Truly," I said to myself, "I am a fool if I don't follow this girl and see what captures her interest." I fancied I saw in her whole being the appearance of naive sensibility. I set off on her heels . . .

In this manner we went round the Salle Carrée, the uncle crying out in admiration, the young girl stifling her yawns; all of which led me to think that I was probably wasting my time, that the girl was a complete fool and as nothing interested her, I had better leave. And so I moved away and, chancing upon Henri, threw myself into a furious debate, denouncing everything as worthless . . .

A few paces away I caught sight of my beautiful peasant girl. Her large black eyes were fixed on a canvas quite high up; an expression of deep sensibility and a faint smile convinced me that I had not been wrong about her after all.

But what painting was she looking at? What had caught her attention? I took a few steps forwards and saw clearly that it was *The Flood* by Schnetz. What satisfaction I felt! . . . It is clear that this young girl knows nothing about it and here she is gazing at a masterpiece (for I must confess that this is my opinion of the work) . . . And what did I say then? What do we all say, all we demented artists who dare to claim that we are misunderstood? . . . Condemn and praise, argue and intrigue as you will, one day all of it will fall before the weak, ignorant gaze of a young girl.**"**

ALFRED DE MUSSET,
FANTASTIC REVIEWS, LE TEMPS, MAY 9, 1831,
IN *COMPLETE WORKS*, PUB. LE SEUIL, PARIS, 1966

Apprenticeship in art

*M*any artists came to copy at the Louvre, in order to study the masters. It was through drawing Classical works that Auguste Rodin (1840–1917) fell in love with sculpture. Alberto Giacometti (1901–66) came to the Louvre every Sunday during his first years in Paris. Henri Matisse (1869–1954) frequently spoke about the copies he made at the Louvre: "I studied in the studios in the morning and copied at the Louvre in the afternoon. This lasted for ten years." He started at the École des Beaux-Arts in 1892, in Gustave Moreau's studio. Paul Cézanne (1839–1906) reverted to a more sensible opinion after having wanted, like many others, to "burn down the Louvre".

❝I used to come here so often then, when I was only about fifteen years old. Initially I wanted passionately to be a painter. I was fascinated by color. I often went upstairs to see the Titians and Rembrandts. But alas! I didn't have enough money to buy canvas and tubes of color. To copy the Classical works, by contrast, I only needed paper and pencils. So I was forced to work only in the rooms downstairs and I soon fell so passionately in love with sculpture that I no longer thought of anything else.❞

AUGUSTE RODIN,
ART: CONVERSATIONS COLLECTED BY PAUL GSELL (1911)
PUB. GRASSET, PARIS, 1986

❝I have nearly the whole of the Louvre in my head: room by room, painting by painting . . . I copied a great deal . . . Nearly all the works, going all the way back . . . By trying to copy you get to see the thing better. I questioned each work in turn, intensely and at length.❞

ALBERTO GIACOMETTI,
IN *PIERRE SCHNEIDER, DIALOGUES OF THE LOUVRE* (1972), PUB. ADAM BIRO, PARIS, 1991

❝Moreau took an interest in my work. He was an educated man, who encouraged his pupils to look at all types of painting while other teachers could only think of a single period or style – their own, that is, contemporary academicism, a mish-mash of all the conventions. We made copies at the Louvre, both to study the masters and to live with them, and also because the government would buy the copies. However for the government the copies had to be executed with minute exactness, faithful to the letter of the work rather than its spirit. It was because of this that the works most favored by the buying committee were those done by the mothers, wives and daughters of museum attendants. Our copies were only accepted through charity or sometimes when Roger Marx pleaded our cause. I would have liked to make literal copies like the attendants' mothers, wives and daughters, but I was incapable of doing so.❞

HENRI MATISSE,
"CONVERSATION WITH TÉRIADE", *ART NEWS ANNUAL* (1952),
IN *WRITINGS AND REMARKS ON ART*, PUB. HERMANN, PARIS, 1972

❝I want to be a true classicist, to become classical again through nature, through feeling. Before my ideas were confused. Life! Life! This was the only word I could utter. I wanted to burn down the Louvre, poor cretin that I was! You have to go to

● The Louvre through visitors' eyes

the Louvre through nature, and return to nature through the Louvre.**

PAUL CÉZANNE,
QUOTED BY JOACHIM GASQUET, *PAUL
CÉZANNE* (1921), AS CITED IN *CONVERSATIONS
WITH CÉZANNE*, PUB. MACULA, PARIS, 1978

A forest of easels

A longside the artists who worked at the Louvre on commission – some of them only ever worked as copyists – and those who studied the masters, there was a whole community of copyists who set up their easels there too. These were the students, especially female students (hardly any art schools in the 19th century admitted women) and elderly toilers who were a favorite subject for caricaturists. Edmond Duranty, in his novella "The Painter Louis Martin", described the Louvre as "a forest of easels and ladders". This is the Louvre that Jeanne Baudot (1877–1957), Renoir's pupil, knew at the very end of the 19th century.

**At the Louvre, Renoir had me copy the right-hand group in Poussin's *Rape of the Sabine Women*. I wasn't yet twenty years old and I was worried at the prospect of painting in public. Renoir reassured me, saying that if the daubers bothered me he would come to my defence. He didn't have to intervene. My whole attitude let my colleagues know that I had come there purely to work ....

At the same time Matisse was copying Chardin's *The Furrow*; Flandrin was copying Ingres' *Odalisque* and Marquet, Poussin's *Arcadian Shepherds* ....

Another year I found Matisse and his friends at the Louvre, Matisse was copying Philippe de Champaigne's *The Dead Christ* in the hope of selling it to the committee to feed his large family. He was working conscientiously and unremittingly, and so well that looking at his copy you would have thought Philippe de Champaigne had just finished working at it. But the committee was inexorable, demanding a reproduction which was identical to the original, with the patina of age; Matisse, in order to achieve this, did not hesitate to cover his copy with "brown sauce" as he called it, two days before it was to be sold, to take off its freshness ....

Ah! it was good to be at the Louvre then, with the Old Masters who seemed to lift you up to the Infinite. What a privilege to hear the modern painters – a Renoir, or a Degas – speaking of the shock they always felt before their predecessors! ...

Daubers of all countries and all schools came to learn their trade by copying paintings. Others still, old men and women, painted unceasingly, although their hands were trembling and their eyes worn out. Like shipwrecked sailors they clung to the art which had destroyed

them! Many of them were still copying the same work, knowing from experience that it would be bought. A vicar could not fail to be charmed by Murillo's *Virgin*, or an American by the *Mona Lisa*.**

JEANNE BAUDOT,
RENOIR, HIS FRIENDS AND HIS MODELS,
PUB. ÉDITIONS LITTÉRAIRES DE FRANCE, PARIS, 1949

It was in Paris that Henry James (1843–1916), the English writer of American origin, put the final touches to his novel "The American". After this he settled in London where he wrote most of his works. "The American" contains several descriptions of the Louvre.

As the little copyist proceeded with her work, she sent every now and then a responsive glance toward her admirer. The cultivation of the fine arts appeared to necessitate, to her mind, a great deal of by-play, a great deal of standing off with folded arms and head drooping from side to side, stroking of a dimpled chin with a dimpled hand, sighing and frowning and tapping of the foot, fumbling in disordered tresses for wandering hair-pins. These performances were accompanied by a restless glance, which lingered longer than elsewhere upon the gentleman we have described. At last he rose abruptly, put on his hat and approached the young lady. He placed himself before her picture and looked at it for some moments, during which she pretended to be quite unconscious of his inspection. Then, addressing her with the single word which constituted the strength of his French vocabulary, and holding up one finger in a manner which appeared to him to illuminate his meaning, 'Combien?' he abruptly demanded.

HENRY JAMES,
THE AMERICAN, 1877,
PUB. HERON BOOKS, LONDON 1976

Women painters, however, even the young ones, were not always regarded with goodwill. In 1844, Jules Fleury (1821–89) who later used the name Champfleury, described them as a "calamity".

**The dauber is merely a nuisance; women painters are a calamity . . . At ten o'clock they arrive at the Louvre and get themselves ready – that is, they put on their sleeves, an apron and a gown, and climb up on their high stools. The

The Louvre through visitors' eyes

young ones love ladders: they are happiest at the top of the steps, copying a high painting. If this is coquetry then she is rather high up and poorly placed for it. At midday the young woman painter addresses the question of food: three or four companions meet up, eating bread and fruit with unshakeable self-assurance in front of the astonished visitors. Their tolerance is hard to understand: I have never seen men eating in libraries.❞

JULES FLEURY, "A VISIT TO THE LOUVRE",
L'ARTISTE, DECEMBER 1, 1844

With Edmond de Goncourt (1822–96) and Jules de Goncourt (1830–70), we rediscover the same copyists, only poorer . . . and seen through the eyes of a more bitter narrator. "Manette Solomon", one of the novels co-written by the brothers, describes the artistic scene under the Second Empire.

❝At the Louvre in the afternoon, he hardly worked any more. His mind, his eyes were quickly tired of looking at the colors and the design of the old canvases he was copying; and his attention soon wandered from the paintings to the baroque world of the copyists, men and women, who inhabited the galleries. He indulged his scorn on all these living ironies, thrown to the feet of masterpieces by hunger, poverty, need and the relentless pursuit of a false vocation; a population of paupers, so funny you could cry at them, picking up the crumbs of art from the feet of the gods! The old women with their grey ringlets, bent over copies of Bouchers – all pink and nude – looking like Alecto illuminating Anacreon; ladies with an orange complexion, in dresses without sleeves, a grey apron across their chest, perched, glasses on the bridge of the nose, at the top of ladders draped with green serge to preserve the modesty of their thin legs; the unfortunate china painters with their haggard eyes, squinting through a magnifying glass to copy Titian's *Entombment of Christ,* small old men in small black tunics, their long hair parted in the middle, each one like some fifty-year old baby Jesus preserved in brandy – all this world with its pitiable comedy, amused Anatole and made him laugh delightfully inside.❞

EDMOND AND JULES DE
GONCOURT, *MANETTE
SALOMON* (1867),
PUB. UNION GÉNÉRALE
D'ÉDITIONS, PARIS, 1979

A dream world

*I*t is a common desire to have access to the museum at night, to see the masterpieces in a stranger or more intimate context. Kings have had this privilege but only with a large escort. Security guards have the same experience, more intimately, every day. Others enjoy it, boldly and without restriction, through their imagination. At night, as we all know, the characters descend from their paintings. The painter Louis Béroud, in the last years of the 19th century and at the beginning of the 20th, was very successful at the Salon with his paintings combining the most famous figures of the Louvre, liberated from their frames. It was a spectacle of this kind that Roland Dorgelès (1885–1973) stumbled upon before being unmasked by Molière: the scenery of the "Wedding Feast at Cana" deserted by the banqueters, the Salon Carré full of guests, shipwrecked sailors from the "Medusa", gazing bright-eyed at a still life by Snyders . . .

❝Molière unmasked me; suddenly he realized. 'It's a man from the present, he shouted out . . . an attendant! watch out, everyone!'
Panic broke out. The alarm spread from the classical antiquities to the Salle

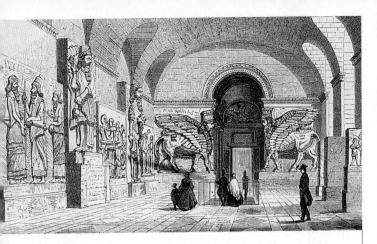

Camondo, fear caught on like fire, everyone running, shouting, jostling, like some shady midnight party invaded by the police.

In a spin I saw saints go by, kings, naked women, prelates, moors, lute players. I was thrown against the wall, knocked over . . . . A Troyon herd passed over my body, all Delacroix's crusaders, Dutchmen in clogs, Corot's nymphs uttering sharp cries and that immense fellow Saint Michael who nearly poked my eye out with his lance . . . Under the huge frame of the *Wedding Feast at Cana*, crazed characters jostled, clambered, gave each other a leg up – Don't push, there are children here! Hey you, the man with the glove, you're in the wrong painting! And where is the Mona Lisa? gone off again . . . And suddenly, in the twinkling of an eye, nothing is moving, everything is back in place . . . . They have all found a place, somehow, haphazardly. However some of them have got into the wrong pictures. Saint Bruno, looking irritated, turning his nose up at the seraglio of Algerian women. Degas' laundress has left her attic and thrown herself, puffing and blowing, at the foot of Queen Elizabeth's bed (the latter regarding her with some distaste); with a single leap Velasquez's dwarf has leapt onto the Raft of the Medusa where he seems somewhat out of place, while Decamps' three bell-ringers, drunk as lords, are standing respectfully behind Napoleon who, still rather shaky from running, is crowning the Empress in front of a motley assembly in which I spotted the two thieves, Colbert, the gentlemen from the *Burial of Ornans* and a young martyr looking so terribly respectable despite her soaking wet dress.**"**
ROLAND DORGELÈS,
"THE PALACE AWAKENED",
VIE PARISIENNE, MAY 25, 1918

Sigmund Freud (1856–1939), visiting the Louvre during his stay in Paris in 1885, did not need a fiction like this to discover, as he wrote to his fiancée, "a dream world" (literally and in Freudian terms "a world as in a dream").

"I just had time enough left to look briefly at the Assyrian and Egyptian rooms, which I shall have to return to several times. There were Assyrian kings as tall as trees, holding lions in their arms as if they were toy dogs, winged bulls with human faces and magnificent curly hair, cuneiform inscriptions as clear as if they had been carved yesterday, Egyptian bas-reliefs painted in bright colors, colossal kings, real sphinxes, a world as in a dream (*eine Welt wie im Traum*).**"**
SIGMUND FREUD,
LETTER TO MARTHA BERNAYS (OCTOBER 19, 1885),
IN *CORRESPONDENCE*, PUB. GALLIMARD, PARIS, 1979

A visit to the Louvre can inspire dreams of ownership. Napoleon asked his architect Fontaine if there was any way of moving his apartments in the Tuileries next to the museum, so he could have the Grande Galerie in his home . . . Michel Tournier (born in 1924) for his part, sees things less simply.

"The magic of the archaic Apollo of the Island of Paros! . . .I imagine what my life

would be like if this god was in my home, owned by me night and day. And to tell the truth, no, I cannot imagine how I would bear the incandescent presence of this meteor landing by me, after twenty centuries of falling."

MICHEL TOURNIER, *KING OF ALDERS*,
PUB. GALLIMARD, PARIS, 1970

Profusion and chaos

T oo many objects, of too many different types: the Louvre risks distracting the visitor's eye with the "indiscernible chaos" of its many juxtaposed works. Although the buildings and collections have been rearranged and reorganized at regular intervals, visitors still come up against a profusion of masterpieces, as well as the complexity of the museum itself. Regular visitors grow fond of this very abundance, even of the juxtapositions which are like those of a dream world.

This is not the case with Paul Valéry (1871–1945) who has here just entered a sculpture room and attacks the very idea of a museum with such extreme criticism that it is impossible to imagine any progress which could alleviate his displeasure at this "combination of separate beauties".

"I am in a commotion of deep-frozen creatures, each one of them demanding, but not obtaining, the inexistence of all the others. And I am not referring here to the chaos of all these sizes without a common measure, to the inexplicable mixture of dwarves and giants, of the perfect and the incomplete, the mutilated and the restored, of monsters and men ...

With a soul ready for suffering I move toward the paintings. Before me in the silence a strange organized disorder unfolds . . . This combination of separate but conflicting beauties is a paradox; even when they seem most alike they are in fact the greatest of enemies.

Only a civilization without a sense of pleasure or reason could have set up this house of incoherence. The product of this proximity of dead visions is something senseless and indefinable. They quarrel jealously for the eyes that give them life. My undivided attention is called for in all directions, throwing into turmoil that internal magnet which draws the whole machine of the body towards what attracts it . . . No ear could bear to hear two orchestras at once. The mind cannot follow or conduct a number of different operations at the same time and there are no simultaneous thought processes. But the eye in the aperture of its optical angle and at the moment of perception, is obliged to take in a portrait and a seascape, a still life and a triumph and characters of the most diverse states and sizes; furthermore it is supposed to absorb completely incompatible consonances and styles of painting.

Just as the sense of sight is assaulted by that abuse of space which is called a collection, so the intelligence is no less insulted by the proximity of important works. The more beautiful they are, the more they are exceptional products of human ambition, the more separate they should be. These are rare objects, whose authors would want them to be unique. This painting it is sometimes said, just KILLS all the others around it . . .

I believe that neither Egypt, China nor Greece, all of them wise and refined cultures, had this system of juxtaposing works which consume each other. They did

● The Louvre through visitors' eyes

not arrange incompatible units of pleasure according to reference numbers and abstract principles.**"**

PAUL VALÉRY,
THE PROBLEM OF MUSEUMS (1923) IN *OEUVRES II*, PUB. GALLIMARD, PARIS, 1960

The juxtapositions, the abundance and the chaos themselves become attractions for regular visitors to the Louvre. This is the view of Václav Vilém Štech, a Czech art historian, a professor of the Prague Academy of Arts from 1930 to 1945 and a student at the Sorbonne from 1912 to 1914. Among others of this opinion is Kenneth Clark, former director of the National Gallery and Surveyor of the King's Pictures in Great Britain.

"The Louvre has always been a chaotic museum. It grew for a long time without a plan for its development and without unity. But it is probably this anarchic abundance – so different from the synthetic character of the collections in Berlin, for example – that accounts for the living, unsettling attraction exercised by this testimony to humanity and humans. Here you can wander, compare, discover new visions and new worlds.**"**

VÁCLAV VILÉM ŠTECH,
ZA PLOTEM DOMOVA (BEYOND OUR FENCES), TRANSLATED BY
A. NOVOTNA GALARD, PUB. ČESKOSLOVENSKÝ SPOSOVATEL, PRAGUE, 1970

"Not only is the Louvre the largest collection of works of art in the world, but even its imperfections are endearing. The ordinary gaping tourists who are out of their depth in any art gallery must feel completely lost at the Louvre. However once you have become used to its extraordinary juxtapositions (a spiral staircase takes us from the early Egyptians to French 19th-century painting), these excite your affection. To adopt a French custom, you could say that the Louvre is a very feminine institution – complex, unpredictable, sometimes exasperating, and always enchanting.**"**

KENNETH CLARK,
THE OTHER HALF: A SELF-PORTRAIT, PUB. JOHN MURRAY, LONDON, 1977

Élie Faure (1873–1937) called it an "irreducible chaos"; Julian Gracq (born 1910) described it even more cruelly as a stage-scenery merchant. How could this be remedied? More weeding out? Ingres had already called for this, in the name of his ideal of beauty. Baudelaire, more open-minded and generous, considered the profusion good and necessary, as without it there would be only general beauty, while the minor artists, with their particular beauties, "have good, sound and delightful qualities".

"A deep stupefaction, an immense confusion where shapes and colors fought it out in a comical, irreducible chaos, stayed with me after all my visits and often nearly discouraged me. I nearly dropped the Louvre, I nearly dropped painting . . .**"**
ÉLIE FAURE, *EQUIVALENCES: CONFESSIONS OF A SELF-TAUGHT PAINTER*
(FIRST EDITION, PUBLISHED POSTHUMOUSLY IN 1951),
IN *OEUVRES COMPLÈTES*, PUB. J.J. PAUVERT, PARIS, 1964

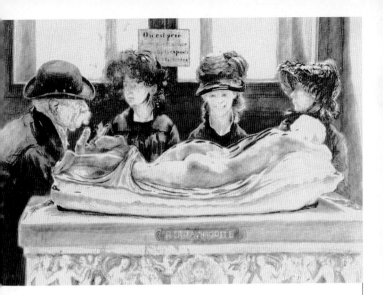

EROS

S *ome visitors are uneasy seeing figures and scenes which appear to be indecent.*
Their modesty is offended by the nudity on display. "The Louvre Museum: to be
avoided by young girls" notes Gustave Flaubert in his "Dictionary of Received Ideas".

Perhaps it should also be avoided by children suggests Julien Green (1900–98),
thinking of the visits his mother took him on around 1910.

"From time to time my mother took us to the Louvre, sometimes dragging us to
the sculpture displays. She did not know what she was doing. She could not suspect
that I came out of there in a sort of sexual intoxication which tortured me all the
more because I did not know its precise cause. Nudity, criminal nudity, why was it
permitted to see it like that, exalted, dominant, perched on pedestals and seeming
to trample us underfoot? 'These are works of art' explained my mother, 'statues of
false gods. Come on, let's go, don't stay there. We'll get the Passy-Hôtel de Ville bus
to go home. If there aren't any spaces we'll go up to the Imperial.' Why do we take
children to museums?"

JULIEN GREEN,
LEAVING BEFORE DAYBREAK, PUB. GRASSET, PARIS, 1963

Sergei Eisenstein (1898–1948) stayed in Paris in 1930 as part of a visit to France while
shooting the film "Sentimental Romance". In his "Memoirs", he shudders at the
memory of the Louvre and the dreams suggested by its "pernicious atmosphere".

"I cannot remember the Louvre without shaking. It was reorganized during the
pre-war years. But I still remember it, with all the suffocating splendor of its brightly colored rooms, and the turbulence of the indifferent multitude, somehow halfway
between an opera foyer and a post office.
The walls were so closely packed with masterpieces it was as if they had been
papered with postage stamps.
The women in the pictures seemed to be warming themselves on the animal heat of
the sweaty herds of visitors.
The construction of the canvases seemed to highlight their bodies, whether these
were plump, or ascetic in the early masters. And it seemed that in this pernicious
atmosphere these Venuses, Dianas or Europas were ready to slide down from their
frames, just as the cruelly spineless women of Degas' caustic pastels climb from
their bathtubs, to grab the visitor with the big nose by the sleeve and draw him to
them behind the flimsy olive-, puce- or cherry-colored curtains of the "foreground"
where their drapery is abandoned. Ah, if these ladies of the past were not protected
from visitors' eager hands by a lock and a grille . . .

● The Louvre through visitors' eyes

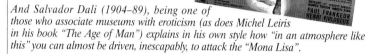

Such was the fate of the *Mona Lisa* after the infamous adventures of this illustrious mystery woman in the hands of international fraudsters. The grille and the lock suggest a chastity belt put on her for the next series of escapades.**

> SERGEI EISENSTEIN,
> *MEMOIRS* (1964),
> PUB. JUILLARD, PARIS, 1989

And Salvador Dali (1904–89), being one of those who associate museums with eroticism (as does Michel Leiris in his book "The Age of Man") explains in his own style how "in an atmosphere like this" you can almost be driven, inescapably, to attack the "Mona Lisa".

**To explain the 'naive aggression' directed against the *Mona Lisa* with reference to the Freudian discovery of Leonardo's libido and his subconscious erotic visions relating to his mother, we would require the genius of Michelangelo Antonioni (unique in the history of the cinema) who would film the following sequence: a son, simple and innocent, unconsciously in love with his mother and ravaged by the Oedipus complex, visits a museum. For this more or less Bolivian innocent the museum is the equivalent of a public house, in other words a brothel; the resemblance is reinforced by the multitude of erotic objects he finds here: nudes, scandalous statues, Rubens. Amidst such sensual and libidinous promiscuity, the oedipal son is dumbfounded to find a portrait of his own mother resplendent in the epitome of idealized femininity. His own mother, here! And what is worse his mother is smiling at him in an ambiguous way which can only appear suggestive and shameful in this context. Aggression is the only possible response to a smile like that; unless he were to steal the painting to rescue it from the scandal and shame of being exhibited in a public house.

If anyone can offer any other explanations with reference to the attacks suffered by the *Mona Lisa*, let them cast the first stone at me. I shall pick it up and continue my work as builder of the Truth.**

> SALVADOR DALI,
> "WHY THE MONA LISA WAS ATTACKED", *OUI 2*,
> PUB. DENOËL, PARIS, 1971

In 1933 a Japanese pair, unsettled and oppressed by the cruelty in the pictures, experience nausea at the sight of the Rubens. Sanki Ichikawa is Professor of English Literature at the University of Tokyo.

Going to the Louvre was quite a shock for me. It seems to me that I lack the ability to appreciate painting, almost as if I had an illness of some sort: therefore I shall say no more on this subject . . . But, for example, taking that Saint Sebastian whose body and neck are pierced with arrows: if people do not see the ecstasy in his face, turned towards the sky, they are considered as abnormal. For my part I can only see a stupefied expression . . . It is not that I am putting on airs and affecting a distaste for cruelty (I do sometimes get excited about bullfights), but this is a lost cause: not only do I not like this type of painting, it horrifies me to the point of giving me a migraine. The women painted by Rubens whose bodies would be nothing but sticky fat if you put them in a press, make me feel nauseous. I thought I would at least like a little the young girl painted by Greuze, but her eyes are like overripe fruit, beginning to go mouldy.

> SANKI ICHIKAWA, "PARIS, CITY OF FLOWERS",
> *OBEI NO SUMIZUMI (IN THE FOUR CORNERS OF THE WESTERN WORLD)*, JUNE 1933

Itineraries within the Louvre

▲ Finding your way around the Louvre

You can proceed through the museum in any of three directions: the **Denon**, **Richelieu** or **Sully** wings. Works are spread over four floors, and organized by department which are easily identifiable as they are color coded.

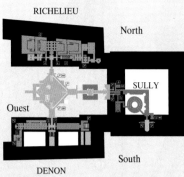

RICHELIEU

North

Ouest

SULLY

DENON

South

ENTRESOL

Oriental antiquities	Decorative arts
Egyptian antiquities	Islamic art
Greek, Etruscan and Roman antiquities	Graphic arts (prints and drawings)
Painting	History of the Louvre and medieval Louvre
Sculpture	

RICHELIEU

Islamic art

French sculpture
Cour Marly, Cour Puget, 17th-18th c.

SULLY

History of the Louvre and medieval Louvre
Egyptian antiquities
The Sphinx Crypt.

DENON

Egyptian antiquities
Roman and Coptic Egypt.

Greek, Etruscan, and Roman antiquities
Preclassical Greece.

Sculpture
Northern European (12th–16th c.), Italian and Spanish (11th–15th c.) sculpture.

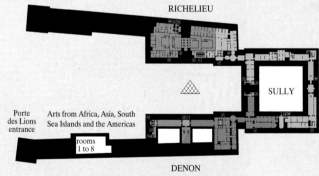

RICHELIEU

SULLY

Porte des Lions entrance

Arts from Africa, Asia, South Sea Islands and the Americas

rooms 1 to 8

DENON

GROUND FLOOR

You will find on the ground floor most of the antiquities collections and part of the sculpture exhibits. The collections from from Africa, Asia, South Sea Islands and the Americas, which came to the Louvre in 2000, are exhibited in the Pavillon des Sessions.

RICHELIEU

Sculpture
French sculpture
Cour Marly (5th–18th c.); Cour Puget, (18th–19th c.).

Oriental antiquities
Cour Khorsabad, Mesopotamia.

SULLY

Oriental antiquities
Iran and the Levant.

Egypt
Pharaonic Egypt, thematic circuit.

Greek, Etruscan, and Roman antiquities
Greek antiquities.

DENON

Greek, Etruscan, and Roman antiquities
Etruscan and Roman antiquities.

Sculptures
– Northern European (17th–19th c.);
– Italian (16th–19th c.).

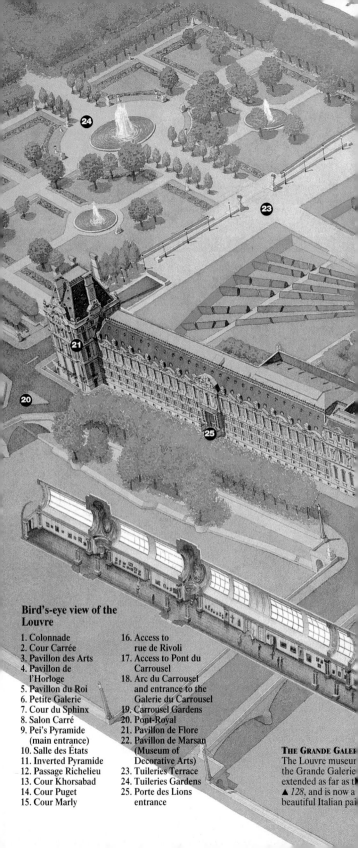

Bird's-eye view of the Louvre

1. Colonnade
2. Cour Carrée
3. Pavillon des Arts
4. Pavillon de l'Horloge
5. Pavillon du Roi
6. Petite Galerie
7. Cour du Sphinx
8. Salon Carré
9. Pei's Pyramide (main entrance)
10. Salle des États
11. Inverted Pyramide
12. Passage Richelieu
13. Cour Khorsabad
14. Cour Puget
15. Cour Marly
16. Access to rue de Rivoli
17. Access to Pont du Carrousel
18. Arc du Carrousel and entrance to the Galerie du Carrousel
19. Carrousel Gardens
20. Pont-Royal
21. Pavillon de Flore
22. Pavillon de Marsan (Museum of Decorative Arts)
23. Tuileries Terrace
24. Tuileries Gardens
25. Porte des Lions entrance

THE GRANDE GALER
The Louvre museu
the Grande Galerie
extended as far as t
▲ *128*, and is now a
beautiful Italian pai

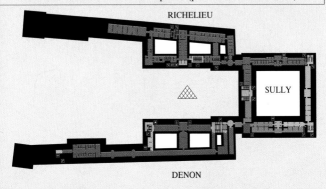

RICHELIEU

SULLY

DENON

FIRST FLOOR

RICHELIEU

🔲 **Decorative arts** From the middle ages to the 19th century; Napoleon III's apartments.

SULLY

🔲 **Greek, Etruscan, and Roman antiquities** Bronzes, precious metals, terracotta, silverware, Greek ceramics.

🔲 **Egyptian antiquities** Pharaonic Egypt, chronological journey.

🔲 **Decorative arts** 17th–18th c.

🔲 **Painting** English painting (18th–19th c.).

DENON

🔲 **Decorative arts** Galerie d'Apollon and the Crown's Jewels.

🔲 **Painting** – Italian painting (13th–18th c.); also on this floor is the Salle des États (rooms 6-7), which contains Leonardo da Vinci's *Mona Lisa*, Veronese's

Wedding Feast at Cana and Venetian painting from the 16th century; – Spanish painting (16th–19th c.); – Large-scale French painting.

🔲 **Prints and drawings** Italian drawings. 🔲 **Current events** Room 33.

RICHELIEU

SULLY

DENON

SECOND FLOOR

A floor is dedicated to Northern European painting (Richelieu wing) and French painting. The latter is hung chronologically, and exhibits take you from the Richelieu to the Sully wing, which they fill entirely. Go down one floor to view the large-scale French paintings.

RICHELIEU

🔲 **Painting** – Northern European painting from Flanders, Holland, Belgium, Germany, Austria Russia and Switzerland (18th–19th c.); – German, Flemish and Dutch painting

(15th–17th c.); – French painting (14th–17th c.).

🔲 **Prints and drawings** German, Flemish and Dutch drawings, room 12.

SULLY

🔲 **Painting** French painting (17th–19th c.).

🔲 **Prints and drawings** French drawings, rooms 41, 42, 44.

Le Grand Louvre ▲

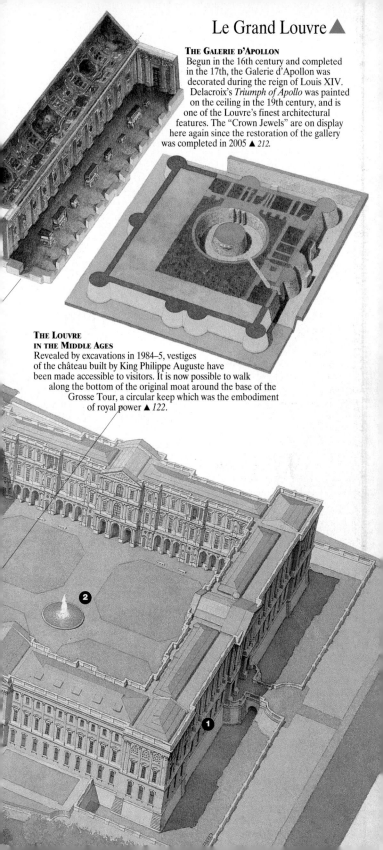

THE GALERIE D'APOLLON
Begun in the 16th century and completed in the 17th, the Galerie d'Apollon was decorated during the reign of Louis XIV. Delacroix's *Triumph of Apollo* was painted on the ceiling in the 19th century, and is one of the Louvre's finest architectural features. The "Crown Jewels" are on display here again since the restoration of the gallery was completed in 2005 ▲ *212*.

THE LOUVRE IN THE MIDDLE AGES
Revealed by excavations in 1984–5, vestiges of the château built by King Philippe Auguste have been made accessible to visitors. It is now possible to walk along the bottom of the original moat around the base of the Grosse Tour, a circular keep which was the embodiment of royal power ▲ *122*.

The Louvre and
its history

▲ The Louvre and its history

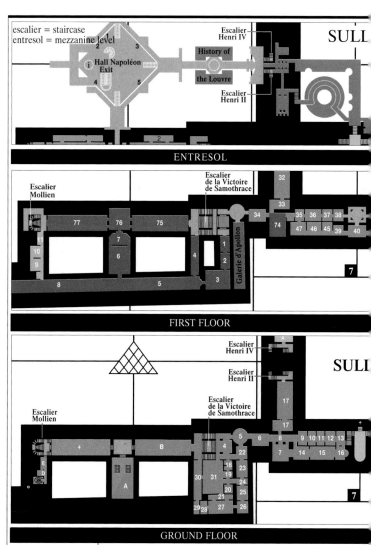

escalier = staircase
entresol = mezzanine level

Escalier Henri IV

SULL

History of the Louvre

Hall Napoléon Exit

Escalier Henri II

ENTRESOL

Escalier Mollien

Escalier de la Victoire de Samothrace

Galerie d'Apollon

FIRST FLOOR

Escalier Henri IV

SULI

Escalier Henri II

Escalier de la Victoire de Samothrace

Escalier Mollien

GROUND FLOOR

REPOSITORY OF MASTERPIECES
This itinerary gives an idea of the history of the museum and of its great decorative wealth and diversity – from the moats of the medieval Louvre to the modern Pyramid. It also offers an initial overview of how the collections are displayed which is developed more fully in the other itineraries.

THE MEDIEVAL LOUVRE

THE MOAT OF CHARLES V adjoins the Carrousel shopping area entrance to the Louvre. Originally fed by the waters of the Seine, it formed Paris' eastern defense line. The 14th-century earthworks were begun here by Étienne Marcel and completed by Charles V; the vestiges of the walls date from the early 16th century when the medieval fortifications were adapted to accommodate long-range artillery. The west wall was rounded by a low tower with an artillery platform on top. Note the long, well-preserved wooden beams on which the masonry rests and the traces of the water which once lapped at the stone foundations. To the west, the wall of the counterscarp served to retain the earth of the new gardens which were laid out for Henri IV in front of the Tuileries

122

Palace. In the reign of Louis XIII the surrounding walls were pulled down and the moat was filled in.

THE HALL NAPOLÉON under the Pyramide, leads into the museum. Walk toward the Sully wing and you will reach the areas concerned with the Louvre's history (Entresol). At the

entrance are four powerful figures in relief which originally decorated the attic story of the Renaissance Louvre ● *74*. They illustrate Charles IX's motto "piety and justice" and were sculpted at the workshop of Goujon. In the subsequent rooms, paintings by Hubert Robert form a coherent series of studies and meditations on the Louvre museum he loved so much. His illustrations of the Grande Galerie and the changes it underwent, and the antiquities rooms where the copyists worked, offer fascinating insights into the huge effort made to create a museum here at the time of the Revolution. There is also a group of preparatory sketches for the museum's giant ceiling paintings.

THE BOSSAGE WALL which you pass as you make your way toward the medieval Louvre, formed the facing for the moat; this was spanned by a bridge leading across to the Pavillon de l'Horloge. Built by Louis le Vau, this wall was discovered during the 1984–5 excavations. Not far away, in the Sully crypt a block of masonry and an outline on the ground indicate the position of the library tower where Charles V's library was located ● *35*.

MOATS OF PHILIPPE AUGUSTE'S CHÂTEAU. The sloping wall base in finely cut stone originally ran down to the water of the moats, through which visitors can now pass dryshod. The round towers dating from the time of Philippe Auguste ● *72* continue at regular intervals; there is also a massive square one built by Charles V. Only the north and east sides of the quadrilateral were exposed during the 1984–5 excavations, the other wings being covered over by later construction.

THE KEEP (*donjon*), accessible via a recently opened passage through the wall, is perfectly circular. It can be skirted by way of the moat here, which was always dry. At the end of it is a molding of the ground covered in potsherds, a reconstruction of

what the archeologists discovered. To the right is an overhang indicating the base of the great spiral staircase built in the reign of Charles V. A passage continues from here beneath the Renaissance wing.

THE SALLE SAINT-LOUIS (ROOM 7). Having passed through a vestibule in which ceramics discovered during the excavations are displayed, you enter the low room known as the Salle Saint-Louis. The perimeter walls here date from the time of Philippe Auguste. In the mid-13th century, these were altered: bases with grotesque masks sculpted into the masonry support the arches which rest on stout columns in the center of the room. In 1546 Pierre Lescot retained these substructures, but divided them up with walls and arcades (visible at the rear) to support his own construction, especially the stairway he had planned. This area is now used to display the pieces discovered in a well during the excavations, including plates with the arms of the dauphin and a gilded helmet. Described in a 1411 inventory, this helmet was probably stolen and scraped for its gold before being broken in pieces. By dint of careful work, its original shape and encircling crown of fleurs-de- lys have been restored. Note the winged

THE SALLE SAINT-LOUIS
This low room was found completely by chance under the Renaissance wing in 1882 in the course of work to install a heating system. It was subsequently opened to the public and for many years was the only visible part of the medieval Louvre. For a while it was called the Salle Philippe Auguste but was eventually renamed after Saint Louis because its capitals date from that king's time. Under Charles V there was already a Salle Saint-Louis in token of the dynasty's reverence for Louis IX. But his room must have been a large reception room, not a little-used basement area such as this one.

stags, heraldic emblems of Charles VI and Charles VII and their motto *"En bien"*.

THE RENAISSANCE

ESCALIER HENRI II.
Leaving the Salle Saint-Louis by way of the mezzanine of the Sully crypt, climb the staircase designed by Pierre Lescot to the end of the new Renaissance wing ● 74. The sober proportions of the banisters to the right are enlivened by a stone ceiling with strictly delineated compartments containing satyrs, dogs and a rendering of Diana the Huntress, the whole forming an elaborate allegory of Nature and the Chase.

THE SALLE DES CARIATIDES (GROUND FLOOR, ROOM 17), the next room, is a huge reception area constructed under Henri II for official and religious ceremonies and entertainments ● *74*. At one end marked off by columns is the *tribunal*, a kind of throne room framed by two hemicycles. At its entrance is a musicians' gallery held up by four gigantic caryatids sculpted in white stone by Jean Goujon in 1550 ▲ *186*. The body of Henri IV lay in state here after his assassination by Ravaillac and the room remained in use until the reign of Louis XIV who came to see Molière act here. But from 1692 until the Revolution it became the Salle des Antiques, a repository for the royal collection of sculptures including antique originals, contemporary pieces commissioned by the government and casts. The original room which had a ceiling of plain wooden beams was arched over in the 17th century. After serving as the earliest venue for the Institut de France (1796–1806), it was entirely redecorated by Percier and Fontaine before being turned over to the museum

PIERRE LESCOT'S DESIGN
In the vaulting over the Henri II staircase (above), as in the celebrated musicians' gallery which is supported by caryatids, Pierre Lescot ● *74* gave sculpture a pre-eminent role in his architectural design (in this he was probably abetted by Jean Goujon). Lescot knew how to offset the highly wrought plasterwork which covers the ceiling surface with monumental figures inspired by texts of Vitruvius, which Goujon illustrated. The caryatids may have been modeled on Roman originals; the work is exclusively sculptural without a trace of color to relieve the whiteness of the stone.

as a gallery for its ancient sculptures. The great marble fireplace was also built at this time by Belloni, who re-used two figures by Goujon (1551) for the purpose. Turn right after the exit.

THE 17TH CENTURY

THE ROTONDE DE MARS (ROOM 5) begins the series of apartments used by Anne of Austria which were decorated in 1654–8 on the ground floor of the Petite Galerie and converted into a museum of antiquities following the arrival of works of art looted by the French armies in Italy in 1799 ● *40*. After the return

SALLE DES SAISONS
The ceiling frescos of the painter G.F. Romanelli (c. 1610–62) are framed by large atlas figures in stucco by Michel Anguier. The former was Roman by birth; the latter learned his art in Rome. The result is typical of Roman Baroque in the sober, rhythmical classical style which characterized the beginnings of the grand style under Louis XIV. The King's function as a protector of the arts is extolled on the pediment of the Cour du Sphinx by an image of the sun illuminating the emblems of the arts and sciences.

to Rome of the celebrated Vatican marbles *Laocoön* and the *Apollo Belvedere*, the room was turned over to Roman antiquities. The rotunda itself is a mixture of décors from several different periods: grandiose 17th-century stucco, early 19th-century medallions in relief (by Chaudet, Lange and Lorta) and a fresco by Blondel.

THE SALLE DES FLEUVES which comes next is even more eclectic with 1799 stucco medallions featuring the rivers of antiquity side by side with thoroughly kitsch paintings by Biennoury, typical of the Second Empire.

QUEEN MOTHER'S APARTMENTS. The main rooms have frescos by the Roman painter Romanelli, combined with lively stucco work by Michel Anguier. The Salle des Saisons precedes the vestibule whose walls were replaced in 1799 by columns removed from the rotunda of Charlemagne at Aix-la-Chapelle. Note the stucco figures of the four great rivers of France. Next comes the antechamber, which is decorated with scenes from Roman history, recounted in assorted frescos (*Mucius Scaevola*)

and medallions (*Romulus and Remus*). Last is the queen's bedchamber which was enlarged in 1799 to include the vestibule leading on from it toward the Seine. The period décor (paintings by Hennequin, stuccos by Dejoux) is combined with compositions by Romanelli which show outstanding women in history framed by allegorical figures symbolizing the virtues of royalty. The Salle d'Auguste, which under Henri IV was the first Salle des Antiques, is a successful pastiche of the apartments of Anne of Austria. Its architect Lefuel employed the painter Matout (*Assembly of the Gods*) and the sculptor Duchoiselle (*Imperial Victories*) to produce decoration in the spirit of the 17th century.

COUR DU SPHINX. This covered courtyard may be entered by way of the Salle des Etrusques (Etruscan Room, room 31). On its east side is Louis Le Vau's façade for the Petite Galerie built in 1662. Take the broad staircase (unfinished by Lefuel during the Second Empire and only completed in 1934), and turn to the left past the *Winged Victory of Samothrace* ▲ 165 toward the Rotonde d'Apollon.

THE ROTONDE D'APOLLON, OR SALON DU DÔME (DENON, FIRST FLOOR). Built by Le Vau, this room was decorated with frescos in 1818–21. It opened onto the Galerie d'Apollon.

THE GALERIE D'APOLLON is closed off by an iron grille which originally came from the Château de Maisons.

A long room lit from the east, it was designed under Louis XIV by Le Vau and Lebrun in exaltation of Apollo. This sumptuous room, which is one of the earliest manifestations of Louis XIV style, owes its preservation and renewal to its occupation by the Académie Royale during the 18th century. The Académie commissioned several of the paintings here before the museum allocated the Salle d'Apollon for its collection of treasures and gemstones ▲ *212*. The vaulting stuccos are original. Girardon and the Marsy and Regnaudin brothers executed the muses, the regions of the earth, the seasons and the signs of the zodiac. There is also a heavily restored *Triumph of Neptune* by Lebrun on the tympanum nearest the Seine. The other paintings date from 1766–80 (by Taraval, Callet, Durameau and Lagrenée) and 1850–51 (by Müller and Guichard) when the architect Dubau installed the Delacroix's *Triumph of Apollo* (1849). Under the Second Empire, Gobelins tapestries were

THE TRIUMPH OF APOLLO
The Galerie d'Apollon was restored under the Second Republic which commissioned Delacroix, the most celebrated Romantic painter of the era, to execute its central panel (top). Delacroix made the connection with the ceiling perspective and lyricism of Lebrun by using a light-filled central panel with the chariot of the Sun bursting forth from a darker garland of bodies. Thirty years earlier, Blondel had used another solar theme for his *Fall of Icarus* (above) in the Rotonde d'Apollon. The Galerie was again beautifully restored in 2004.

127

hung on the walls featuring the artists and kings who contributed to the Louvre. **THE SALLE DES BIJOUX** (Jewel Room) is to the right of the gallery exit. This former vestibule to the apartment of Louis XIV was completely redecorated during the Restoration.
THE SALLE DES SEPT CHEMINÉES (ROOM 74) The Room of the Seven Fireplaces originally included the Pavillon du Roi where the royal bedrooms were. An enormous salon was installed here which was converted by the architect Duban in 1851 and subsequently became the center of French painting. The stucco is by Duret.

SALLE DES BIJOUX
During the Restoration, quantities of precious objects were displayed here in ill-lit, rather tall cases. The other rooms of the Musée Charles X stretch away into the distance.

PERCIER AND FONTAINE STAIRCASE
This retrospective painting (below) shows the former entry staircase to the museum, with Napoleon reviewing his architects' plan. The main stairwell no longer exists, but one can still see the vaults of the landing which overlooks the Cour Carrée.

THE MUSEUM IN THE 19TH CENTURY

THE MUSÉE CHARLES X (SULLY, FIRST FLOOR) inaugurated in 1827 occupies the south wing of the Cour Carrée. The former apartment of the queen, it was reorganized by Fontaine to exhibit the antique vases and the Egyptian collection assembled by Champollion. The walls covered in stucco, the fireplaces by the mosaic craftsman Belloni and the tall windows by Jacob Desmalter go together to create a neoclassical ensemble of very high quality. Various painters were commissioned to execute scenes on the ceilings connected with the collections below. Ingres' *Apotheosis of Homer*▲ 232 used to hang in the first room. Note the ceiling paintings on Egyptian themes by Picot and Pujol.
THE COLONNADE STAIRCASE at the far end of the Musée Charles X was designed by Percier and Fontaine as the access to the imperial apartments ● 81. On the left are the rooms which formed the Musée des Souverains under the Second Empire, which was devoted to relics of the French monarchy and empire. The first of these is a reconstruction of the council chamber at the Pavillon de la Reine at Vincennes; the rest contain woodcarvings from the Pavillon du Roi, relocated here in 1827. In the ceremonial bedchamber of Henri II, the ceiling by Scibecq de Carpi (1558) is characteristic of the School of Fontainebleau, while Gilles Guérin introduced classical themes on the ceiling of Louis XIV's bedchamber (1654). From the window the façades of the Cour Carrée offer a fine demonstration of stylistic continuity: opposite is the Henri II wing built by Pierre Lescot; to its right is the Pavillon de l'Horloge and the wing designed by Le Mercier (1639–43); and to the rear are the wings by Le Vau, with their Empire pediments and circular Restoration *oeil-de-boeuf* windows.
THE GALERIE CAMPANA (ROOMS 39 TO 47) running parallel to the Musée Charles X bears the name of the collection acquired by Napoleon III in 1863, for which the

huge showcases were specially made. The ceiling paintings are by Alaux, the younger Fragonard, Steuben, Heim and Schnetz; they date from the reign of Louis-Philippe and their theme is the state's patronage of the arts.

THE HENRI II VESTIBULE (ROOM 33). At the end of the Galerie Campana retrace your steps to the Salle des Sept Cheminées and turn right into the hall where Braque's *The Birds* (1953) is painted on the wooden ceiling. This was the first contemporary work to be incorporated into the Louvre. The other compartments are by Scibecq de Carpi (1557).

THE FORMER SALLE DES GARDES, adjoining, was used for royal audiences under the Restoration. Part of the column arrangement installed here by Fontaine still exists. From here, turn back to the staircase of the *Winged Victory of Samothrace* and after a quick look at the Cour Napoléon through the window, continue through the series of rooms awaiting you to the right of the *Winged Victory*.

THE SALLE PERCIER AND THE SALLE FONTAINE occupy the

THE SALON CARRÉ
This room has no windows. A strong light from above illuminates the white and gold stucco of the ceiling, evoking palatial magnificence. Hanging on sober colored dados above black wooden paneling, the paintings are densely packed. At the center of the room is an immense circular seat which one critic compared to a

landing of a staircase built by these two architects then demolished during the Second Empire when most of the work on the present stairs was carried out. On the ceiling of the third room, known as the Salle Duchâtel, the Restoration painter Meynier executed his *Triomphe de la Peinture Française,* which surrounds the bend of an arch: France's principal painters are represented here in a series of medallions. This glorification of national achievement acted as a counter-balance to the Salon Carré into which these rooms lead.

catafalque. All in all, this holy of holies of painting has a religious, quasi-mystical atmosphere which is quite unique.

THE ORIGINS OF THE MUSEUM

THE SALON CARRÉ (DENON, FIRST FLOOR, ROOM 3) is actually rectangular not square. It has been devoted since 1914 to masterpieces of all schools of painting irrespective of nationality or period. This room has always been one of the

THE GRANDE GALERIE Before 1861 the Grande Galerie was much larger than it is today, extending as far as the Pavillon de Flore. In sections demarcated by massive columns paintings were arranged according to school, with larger canvases above and smaller ones below. Views such as the exquisite watercolor by Nash, the English landscape painter (above), or else the meticulous record by Benjamin Zix (1810) of the wedding cortège of Napoleon and Marie-Louise of Austria (below), give an idea of this now vanished décor.

kernels of the Louvre. Under the Ancien Régime, it gave its name (Salon) to the exhibition of works by painters belonging to the Académie; later, it became a kind of judgement hall for painting, like the Uffizi in Florence. Duban decorated it lavishly in 1850–1; its white and gold stucco ceiling, sculpted by Simart, perpetuated the tradition of Anguier as seen through the prism of 19th-century eclecticism.

THE GRANDE GALERIE now looms ahead of you. There is no trace of Nicolas Poussin's *Labours of Hercules* painted on the vaulted ceiling for Louis XIII. Under the Ancien Régime the Grande Galerie became little more than a repository for relief maps of France's principal strongholds, used when teaching military tactics. Later, under Louis XVI, the room was earmarked as a museum, finally opening to the public on August 10, 1793. The paintings of Hubert Robert give an idea of the sheer austerity of the revolutionary museum: it was an immensely long vaulted corridor crammed with virtually every European masterpiece ● *29*. The classical exuberance of Percier and Fontaine (the architects of the Empire who added columns, arcades and a coffered ceiling) can also only be visualized by looking at old illustrations. In 1862 the gallery was again modified by Lefuel, who added skylights and reduced it to half its former size. To the section he rebuilt over the broad *guichets* (archways) fronting the Pont du Carrousel, he added two ornate rotundas. Here Rodin's master, Carrier-Belleuse, fashioned a bacchanal of white stucco against a background of gold. It was not until 1950 that the gallery acquired its present sober aspect inspired by the compositions of Hubert Robert. From the windows of the Grande Galerie there is a remarkable view across the Place Napoléon and the Place du Carrousel, at the center of which stands the Triumphal Arch of the Grand Army, erected in 1806. To the same era belongs the colossal wing opposite, which contrasts strongly with the highly

decorative, ornate façades built by Lefuel under Napoleon III. Also visible is the Jardin du Carrousel designed by Jacques Wirz, with box hedges radiating outward from its center. Halfway along the Grande Galerie, turn right into the suite of small rooms built under Napoleon III to house the minor French masters such as Lesueur and Vernet. From the window one can also see the inner courtyard, called the Cour Lefuel. Opposite, the wing constructed by the same architect contained the imperial riding school; of this there remains nothing but a splendid horseshoe staircase. The right-hand façade is that of the Grande Galerie: the lower floor still retains the elevation and the type of décor that characterized the era of Henri IV but the upper levels are Lefuel at his most lavish.

L'ESCALIER MOLLIEN, the bulk of which was completed in 1857, makes a pair with the staircase of the *Winged Victory of Samothrace*. It originally served as an entrance to the picture galleries and was used by the imperial cortèges making their way to the Salle des États, the focus of the alterations made to the Louvre under Napoleon III. It was endowed with a richly decorated ceiling in 1868–70 under Lefuel's supervision; the side walls and the banister were completed by Gaston Redon in 1910. At the center, Müller was

commissioned to paint an allegory of *Glory*, framed by stucco compartments representing painting, sculpture, architecture and engraving by Sanson, Janson, Duchoiselle and Hiolle. The atlas figures and caryatids of the tympana by Cavelier and Duchoiselle bear a resemblance to Anguier's stuccos.

THE SALLE MOLLIEN (ROOM 77) ▲ *234,* the next room you enter turning eastward, is broadly decorated in red, with interlacing gilt on the ceilings (painted by Denuelle). It was designed especially for Napoleon III's museum (1863).

THE SALON DENON (ROOM 76) occupies the entire area of the pavilion fronting the Cour Napoléon. It was originally designed as a vestibule for the Salle des États, in which Napoleon III received his administration (the room still bears this name, but its original décor has entirely vanished). The vault was painted by Müller in1864. After a look through the window at the Cour Napoléon, take the elevator to the ground floor.

THE COUR DES ÉCURIES
This stableyard was surrounded by stables and lodgings for the grooms and the Master of the Horse. It led through to the riding school which the horses entered by way of a gently inclined staircase copied from the Cour des Adieux at Fontainebleau (above).

THE SALLE DES ÉTATS (Denon, first floor, rooms 6 and 7)
Renovated between 2001 and 2005 to exhibit Veronese's *Wedding Feast at Cana* and Da Vinci's *Mona Lisa,* it was used for meetings of the joint assemblies (above). Its lavish décor by the painter Müller was destroyed in 1883. Under the Restoration the sessions took place in the present Salle des Bronzes (Sully, first floor) ▲ *172.*

▲ The Louvre and its history

LARGE PAINTINGS

LARGE PAINTINGS
The Salle Daru
(room 75, above
right, in 1906) is one
of the three rooms in
which large-scale
French paintings are
displayed ▲ *234*.

THE STABLES
Now used to display
the collection of
Italian paintings

▲ *194*, this area was
originally designed to
house the emperor's
horses (above). The
vaults are of brick, a
reference to the style
of Henri IV.

**THE SALLE
DU MANÈGE**
The huge riding ring
(right) was used by
the Prince Imperial;
Empress Eugénie
often came to watch
him here. The tall
columns which
support the brick
ceiling have stone
capitals sculpted with
the heads of various
animals: horses,
donkeys, wolves, dogs,
bears and birds. These
were the work of the
best animal sculptors
of the time (Fremiet,
Rouillard,
Jacquemard); again
their subject is the
hunt, which is a theme
found everywhere in
the décor of the
Louvre.

**THE SALLE DU MANÈGE
(DENON, GROUND FLOOR,
ROOM A)** was built by
Lefuel for the Prince Imperial's
riding lessons. Since 2004, a redesigned layout now houses
classical sculpture, mainly copies executed in the 17th and
18th centuries, arranged according to the taste of their former
owners such as the Borghese family, and Richelieu and
Mazarin, as well as the royal collections.
THE DENON VESTIBULE, a few steps higher, served for many
years as the principal entrance to the museum. The view of
the two galleries which lead away from it
to the respective staircases is
characteristic of the vast scale on which
Napoleon III's new palace-museum was
conceived. From here take the elevator to
the Pyramide mezzanine.
THE HALL NAPOLÉON, Ieoh Ming Pei's
magnificent brainchild, was opened in
1989. This area of the museum is all too
often overlooked by visitors who tend to
concentrate more on the spectacular
glass pyramid which illuminates it. The
same blend of technology and absolute
simplicity, at once innovative and traditional, may be seen in
the new Richelieu wing inaugurated in 1993. The light bathing
the covered courtyards filters through a metal structure which
is specially designed to soften its effect; the escalator leading
to the upper levels is also a fine stroke of contemporary
architecture with its great circular oculi. The Louvre is above
all a museum of staircases and this applies especially to the
Richelieu wing: here the Lefuel staircase is the most
ambitious with its multiple flights and stone décor. An
alternative route is by way of what is known as the Ministers'
staircase, richly decorated with paintings by Daubigny,
marbles and ornate banisters. From here you can proceed to
the Napoleon III apartments (formerly used by the Ministry
of State) ▲ *210*, whose lavish rooms illustrate the decorative
richness of this stately palace, and conclude the tour of the
Louvre's collection of paintings and *objets d'art*.

Oriental antiquities

RICHELIEU

Figurine of a woman (above) in painted terracotta (Halaf, c. 3000 BC).

The Louvre's collections of oriental antiquities cover a broad geographical area between North Africa and the Indus, and they date back as far as 7000 BC. Their origins are threefold: Mesopotamia, around the Tigris and the Euphrates (in the Richelieu wing), Iran, and the Levant (in the west and north wings of the Sully building). Finally, the collection of Islamic arts is on the entresol level. This has been the eighth department of the Louvre since its inception in 2003. Created in 1874, the Musée Assyrien has been considerably enriched by excavations carried out by French archeologists.

ANCIENT MESOPOTAMIA

THE BIRTH OF THE MESOPOTAMIAN CIVILIZATIONS (ROOM 1A). The neolithic revolution of the 7th millennium BC (in today's Iraq and Kurdistan) entailed the organization of the inhabitants into sedentary stable communities, and the invention of the ceramic process. One of these civilizations, the Hassuna, was known for the quality of its ceramics and its stoneware. With the civilizations of Samarra and Halaf in the 6th millennium, ceramics developed more sophisticated forms and decoration. In the 3rd millennium BC the Obeid civilization produced very fine terracotta figurines.
THE PRE-URBAN ERA (c. 3700–2900 BC) was characterized by the birth of city-states, especially Uruk, which secured the growing power of Mesopotamia. Toward 3300 BC,

Sumerian tablet (above) covered with cuneiform inscriptions.
Sumerian priest-king (right), limestone, c. 3300 BC.

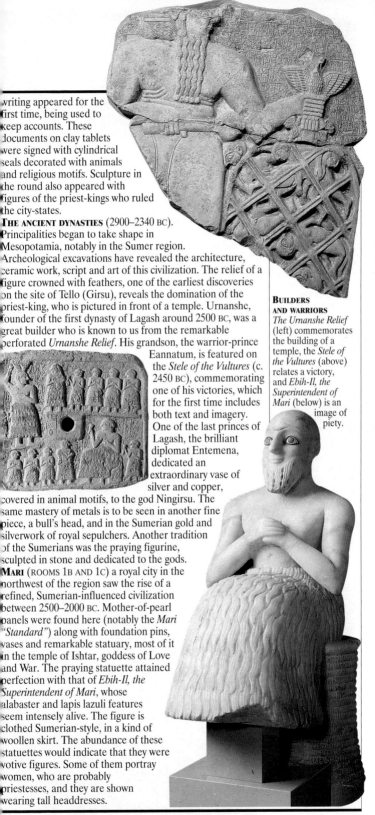

writing appeared for the first time, being used to keep accounts. These documents on clay tablets were signed with cylindrical seals decorated with animals and religious motifs. Sculpture in the round also appeared with figures of the priest-kings who ruled the city-states.

THE ANCIENT DYNASTIES (2900–2340 BC). Principalities began to take shape in Mesopotamia, notably in the Sumer region. Archeological excavations have revealed the architecture, ceramic work, script and art of this civilization. The relief of a figure crowned with feathers, one of the earliest discoveries on the site of Tello (Girsu), reveals the domination of the priest-king, who is pictured in front of a temple. Urnanshe, founder of the first dynasty of Lagash around 2500 BC, was a great builder who is known to us from the remarkable perforated *Urnanshe Relief*. His grandson, the warrior-prince Eannatum, is featured on the *Stele of the Vultures* (c. 2450 BC), commemorating one of his victories, which for the first time includes both text and imagery. One of the last princes of Lagash, the brilliant diplomat Entemena, dedicated an extraordinary vase of silver and copper, covered in animal motifs, to the god Ningirsu. The same mastery of metals is to be seen in another fine piece, a bull's head, and in the Sumerian gold and silverwork of royal sepulchers. Another tradition of the Sumerians was the praying figurine, sculpted in stone and dedicated to the gods.

MARI (ROOMS 1B AND 1C) a royal city in the northwest of the region saw the rise of a refined, Sumerian-influenced civilization between 2500–2000 BC. Mother-of-pearl panels were found here (notably the *Mari "Standard"*) along with foundation pins, vases and remarkable statuary, most of it in the temple of Ishtar, goddess of Love and War. The praying statuette attained perfection with that of *Ebih-Il, the Superintendent of Mari*, whose alabaster and lapis lazuli features seem intensely alive. The figure is clothed Sumerian-style, in a kind of woollen skirt. The abundance of these statuettes would indicate that they were votive figures. Some of them portray women, who are probably priestesses, and they are shown wearing tall headdresses.

BUILDERS AND WARRIORS
The *Urnanshe Relief* (left) commemorates the building of a temple, the *Stele of the Vultures* (above) relates a victory, and *Ebih-Il, the Superintendent of Mari* (below) is an image of piety.

THE AKKADIAN EMPIRE 2340–2200 BC (**ROOM 2**). Sargon was the first monarch to forge an empire by uniting Sumer, Akkad and northern Mesopotamia. His sons Rimush and Manishtusu and his grandson Nâram-Sin managed to hold this empire together, creating favorable conditions for a politicized form of art whose chief concern was the image of the all-powerful monarch whose palace was at Agade. The actual site of this town has yet to be discovered, but royal workshops were established here to produce monumental statuary – mostly in diorite, a hard black stone. The oldest steles dating from the reign of Sargon illustrate victories and battles, in a still-traditional archaic style which nonetheless shows early signs of the realism which was to characterize the sculpture of succeeding reigns. A fragment of a stele shows King Rimush in single combat with an enemy. Later with the reign of Manishtusu, more realistic lifesize royal figures were sculpted and installed in various towns of the empire. These statues, seated or standing, show the king wearing a long skirt with a shawl over his shoulders. The high point of the art of Agade was attained during the reign of Nâram-Sin. His victory stele in pink sandstone offers a striking glimpse of the king,

followed by his army, climbing a mountain which is crowned by divine symbols. The delicacy of the relief, the expressions on the faces and the presence of a text commenting on Naram-Sin's victory over a tribe of mountain people from the Zagros region, make this stele one of the great masterpieces of the museum. After the fall of the dynasty, a century of instability followed. The display cases of ROOM 2 illustrate the importance of written text in the Akkadian civilization; eventually Akkadian became the principal language of the area, eclipsing Sumerian and annexing its ideograms. Numerous texts bear witness to contracts, treaties and historical events, but there are very few literary texts. The art of seal-making complemented the iconography of major sculpture by featuring the Akkadian pantheon in its entirety: the god of the Sea, the Sun god surrounded by flames, the god and goddess of Vegetation, the two gods of the Storm – and lastly Ishtar herself, the goddess of Love and War.

THE SECOND DYNASTY OF LAGASH (2150–2100 BC) managed to stem the tide of "barbarians" from the mountains and preserve in its southern capital a civilization which we know as neo-Sumerian. This civilization was famous for its literature, and has bequeathed us the longest poems written in Sumerian. The princes of Lagash are also familiar to us: diorite votive statues of Ur-Ba'u, Gudea and his son Ur-Ningirsu have come down to us. By now the realism of gade sculpture had given way to a limited academic approach. Warrior kings were replaced by builders, and the inscriptions tell of labors of construction instead of military victories. In all there are about twenty statues of Gudea, seated or standing, with hands crossed, wearing a headpiece. One of these shows him carrying a fountain of water, clearly godlike. There are also a number of very beautiful female statuettes, among them the *Lady from Tello*, a libation vase of Gudea, and figurines of bulls with human heads. Most of this superb sculpture was found at today's Tello, the ancient site of Girsu. A certain number of objects evoke the architecture and construction of temples, the principal activities of the princes of Lagash.

There are also the *Cylinders of Gudea*, with text describing the construction of the temple of Ningirsu, foundation pins bearing figurines, and brick landfill used for seating four-cornered columns.

THE THIRD DYNASTY OF UR founded by Ur-Nammu, was distinguished for its political organization, as described in several texts.

GUDEA, KING OF LAGASH
Among the vestiges of the reign of Gudea, two statues bearing the name of the king show him seated (left) and bearing a vase that spouts water (below). The very similar *Lady from Tello* may have been his wife (below, left). A foundation figurine (above) evokes Gudea's achievement as a builder.

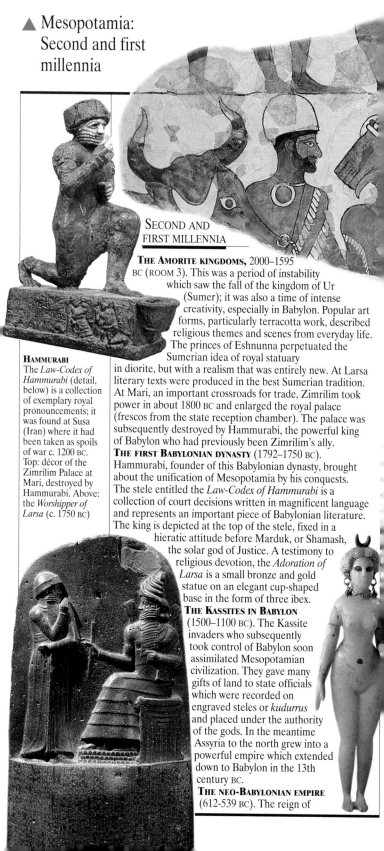

▲ Mesopotamia: Second and first millennia

SECOND AND FIRST MILLENNIA

THE AMORITE KINGDOMS, 2000–1595 BC (ROOM 3). This was a period of instability which saw the fall of the kingdom of Ur (Sumer); it was also a time of intense creativity, especially in Babylon. Popular art forms, particularly terracotta work, described religious themes and scenes from everyday life. The princes of Eshnunna perpetuated the Sumerian idea of royal statuary in diorite, but with a realism that was entirely new. At Larsa literary texts were produced in the best Sumerian tradition. At Mari, an important crossroads for trade, Zimrilim took power in about 1800 BC and enlarged the royal palace (frescos from the state reception chamber). The palace was subsequently destroyed by Hammurabi, the powerful king of Babylon who had previously been Zimrilim's ally.

THE FIRST BABYLONIAN DYNASTY (1792–1750 BC). Hammurabi, founder of this Babylonian dynasty, brought about the unification of Mesopotamia by his conquests. The stele entitled the *Law-Codex of Hammurabi* is a collection of court decisions written in magnificent language and represents an important piece of Babylonian literature. The king is depicted at the top of the stele, fixed in a hieratic attitude before Marduk, or Shamash, the solar god of Justice. A testimony to religious devotion, the *Adoration of Larsa* is a small bronze and gold statue on an elegant cup-shaped base in the form of three ibex.

THE KASSITES IN BABYLON (1500–1100 BC). The Kassite invaders who subsequently took control of Babylon soon assimilated Mesopotamian civilization. They gave many gifts of land to state officials which were recorded on engraved steles or *kudurrus* and placed under the authority of the gods. In the meantime Assyria to the north grew into a powerful empire which extended down to Babylon in the 13th century BC.

THE NEO-BABYLONIAN EMPIRE (612-539 BC). The reign of

HAMMURABI
The *Law-Codex of Hammurabi* (detail, below) is a collection of exemplary royal pronouncements; it was found at Susa (Iran) where it had been taken as spoils of war c. 1200 BC. Top: décor of the Zimrilim Palace at Mari, destroyed by Hammurabi. Above: the *Worshipper of Larsa* (c. 1750 BC)

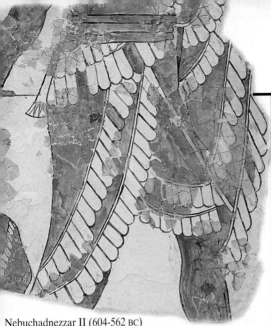

ANATOLIA
This *Rython in the Shape of a Lion* (c. 1900 BC, below), is representative of art at the time of the Assyrian colonies of Cappadocia. A small *Pendant in the Shape of a God* (above) dates from the Hittite period which followed.

Nebuchadnezzar II (604-562 BC) marked the apogee of this empire. While it lasted Babylon created its own sumptuous decoration; the Louvre now possesses fragments of this in the form of reliefs on terracotta bricks. Later the capital fell into the hands of the Persians followed by Alexander the Great. Hellenism blended with local traditions to produce a refined form of art including alabaster statuettes of women, one of which has retained its garnet-stone eyes and elegant golden jewelry (the goddess Ishbar, below left).

ANATOLIAN CIVILIZATIONS (ROOM 5). Anatolia was another early seat of civilization, especially the neolithic site of Catal Huyuk. Here ceramics, bronzes and sculptures were extraordinarily refined. At the beginning of the second millennium colonies of Assyrian merchants established themselves in Cappadocia where they introduced cuneiform script; their ceramics show this in highly elaborate forms. Subsequently Anatolia passed into Hittite domination (1650 BC) before becoming the center of the empire of the Great Kings, who were patrons of an imperial form of art characterized by statuettes made of bronze and gold.

THE ASSYRIAN EMPIRE (ROOMS 4 AND 6) reached its high point in the first millennium under the great monarchs Ashurnasirpal, Sargon, Sennacherib and Ashurbanipal: these kings even subdued Egypt for a while, before their defeat by the Medes and Babylonians in 612 BC. The Louvre also possesses reliefs from the palaces of Khorsabad ▲ *140*, Nimrod, Niniveh and other regional capitals.

ASSYRIA
The royal capitals of Nimrod and Nineveh, like the regional capitals, have left numerous reliefs dominated by the features of the king and peopled by protective spirits. The high point of this art came with the building of the palace of Ashurbanipal II at Nineveh, a hymn to the glory of the conqueror of Elam. Among the most beautiful portraits is one of the king standing in his chariot, directing strategy (left).

The Louvre possesses a remarkable collection of decorative architectural fragments from the palace of Sargon II, King of Assyria, at Khorsabad. Discovered in 1843 by the French consul at Mosul, Paul-Emile Botta, this site revealed a forgotten civilization to the world. On May 1, 1847 King Louis-Philippe opened the Musée Assyrien at the Louvre. The bulls with human heads and the many murals were moved in 1993 to a new courtyard covered over with glass, with a view to displaying this Assyrian architecture in something like its original scale.

BOTTA AND PLACE
Paul-Emile Botta quickly understood the importance of his discovery but his identification of it was incorrect. He had found the remains of Dur-Sharrukin, one of the capitals of the Assyrian Empire, not Nineveh. His successor Victor Place (above) continued excavating after 1850, but the collection he assembled was lost in a shipwreck in 1855.

THE SITE OF KHORSABAD
The painter Eugène Flandin sent to Mosul to assist Paul-Émile Botta with his excavations, made a scale drawing of the throne room (above). This shows the bulls which are now in the Louvre.

Among the reliefs on both the inside and the outside walls, those of the north walls (above, displayed in the Cour Khorsabad) form a fairly complete ensemble. Note the figures of Sargon and one of his dignitaries (left) and servants (right). *Transportation of Timber from the Lebanon* (top) is on the north wall of the courtyard.

Moving the remains from Mosul to Paris was by no means simple. In 1993 they were moved again, this time from the Cour Carrée to the Richelieu wing.

Photographs by Gabriel Tranchard show the various stages of the discovery.

RECONSTRUCTION
This attempt at a reconstruction of Sargon II's palace entrance was drawn by the architect Félix Thomas.

▲ Iran

Ibex goblet of painted
terracotta from Susa's
foundation in about 4000 BC.

Female statuette
in chlorite and
white limestone
(Bactria, c. 1800 BC)

Circular standard
from Luristan with
four figures radiating
from its center (early
2nd millennium BC).

This ensemble
of molded brick
called the *Panels
of the Temple of
Inshushinak*
(below), shows
the influence of
Mesopotamian
architectural
ornamentation
on the brickwork
of Iran, particularly
in Susa.

IRAN

Major civilizations flourished in Iran,
enriched by exchanges with neighboring
Mesopotamia and the Orient. Susa and the
mountain sites have yielded some important
archeological remains dating back to the 4th
millennium BC. During the Iron Age a neo-Elamite
renaissance took place, which ended in the 6th century BC
with the Achemenid Persian domination and the heyday
of Susa under Darius I. After the conquest of Alexander
the Great in 331 BC, the Seleucids, the Parthians and finally
the Sassanids, made their mark in Iran. The collections
are displayed in Rooms 7 to 16, in the Richelieu wing
and in the north wing of the Cour Carrée.

SUSA AND THE IRANIAN PLATEAU 5TH TO THE 3RD MILLENNIUM BC (ROOM 7).

This room features items dating from the urban revolution
in Susa, particularly ceramics decorated with geometric
patterns or animal motifs. Sculpture, metallurgy, and adding
machines were developed in the Uruk period under
Mesopotamian influence.

SUSA IN THE 3RD MILLENNIUM BC (ROOM 8).

During the Akkad period, Susa became a Sumerian
dependency and commercial center, but nevertheless
retained much of its individuality. Under the influence of
the king Puzur-Inshushinak, a contemporary of Gudea,
monumental sculpture and religious architecture developed.

IRAN AND BACTRIA (ROOM 9).

In the 3rd millennium BC
and at the start of the 2nd millennium BC, Luristan
and Bactria were notable for the emergence of dynamic
craft workshops. Objects carved from
chlorite and metalwork in copper,
from the province of Kerman and the
Lut desert, were much admired. Luristan
produced remarkable metalwork dating
from the 3rd millennium BC. Bactria
adopted the whole Iranian repertoire
with a spectacular decorative exuberance. This
room also features beautiful neo-Sumerian
craft objects from Susa, in particular bitumen
bowls and rich creations in gold.

IRAN IN THE MEDIO-ELAMITE PERIOD (ROOM 10).

From 1500 to 1100 BC, the kingdom of Elam once
again enjoyed autonomy and power, as may be
demonstrated by the royal monuments looted in
Mesopotamia.
The most remarkable
pieces, apart from the
royal statues from the
reign of Untash-Napirisha,
are the religious objects
found in the holy center of
Tchoga Zanbil. Fragments
of architectural adornments
from 12th-century BC temples,
dating from the reign of
Shilhak-Inshushinak, are
among the museum's most

valuable treasures. When Nebuchadnezzar, king of Babylon, destroyed Susa, he put an end to this golden era.

IRAN IN THE IRON AGE AND THE NEO-ELAMITE RENAISSANCE IN SUSA (ROOM 11).
From the 14th to the 6th century BC, the inhabitants of this region were affected by a number of events, in particular the arrival of the "Iranians", who spoke Indo-European, from east of the Caspian Sea. The displays in this room trace the evolution of ceramics, glyptics and gold work, as well as that of metallurgy, architectural decoration and funerary art. Luristan is again characterized by the flourishing of metalwork.

THE ACHEMENID PERSIAN EMPIRE (ROOMS 12 TO 15).
The Persian empire in Elam was founded by Cyrus II the Great (559–530 BC). Darius I (522–486 BC) brought the empire to the height of its powers, dominating the entire region, from the Indus to the Aegean sea and Egypt. Rooms 12 and 13 are devoted to the glazed bricks of the palace of Darius I in Susa, which surrounded one of the 36 capital monuments of the Apadana. Friezes depicting archers, lions, griffins and sphinxes reflect a fusion of the cultures conquered by the empire. The displays focus on sculpture, glyptic, coins, and the decorative arts of the Achemenid court. Room 14 concentrates on the second capital of the empire, Persepolis.

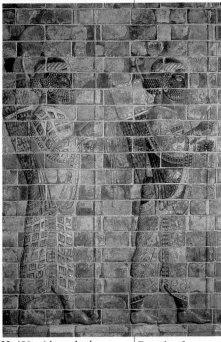

SELEUCIDS, PARTHIANS AND SASSANIDS (ROOM 16).
Alexander's empire was divided up on his death. The Seleucids, who gained Syria, were enemies with the Parthians, who dominated the area east of the Euphrates. The Romans took over from the Seleucides when in the 3rd century BC the Sassanides made an attempt to restore the Persian empire to its original size. Hellenism also began to filter in, bringing with it a new wave of Western ideas and techniques.

Examples of Achemenid Persian art and of the decoration of the palace of Susa (c. 520–500 BC): the frieze of the *Archers of Darius*, called "the immortals" (above), and the monumental capital of the Apadana (audience chamber) of the palace (center). Below, a vase handle in the shape of a winged ibex (c. 500 BC) in the zoomorphic tradition of metalwork in Iran.

143

▲ The Levant

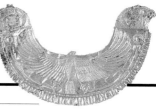

Falcon Pectoral (c 1750 BC), gold ornament discovered at Byblos, modeled on an Egyptian original.

This Mycenian-influenced *Fertility Goddess,* was carved for the lid of a Phoenician ivory cosmetics box (below, late 13th century BC). It was found at Ugarit on the Syrian coast.

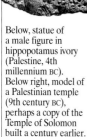

Below, statue of a male figure in hippopotamus ivory (Palestine, 4th millennium BC). Below right, model of a Palestinian temple (9th century BC), perhaps a copy of the Temple of Solomon built a century earlier.

THE LEVANT

The Mediterranean shore of the Near East, the Levant, has been a cradle of civilization since the paleolithic era. The smaller kingdoms of the Levant provided a link between Mesopotamia and Egypt, and later between Mediterranean civilizations such as Greece. Rooms A to D, in the east wing of the Cour Carrée, cover the periods to the early 1st millennium; the late Orient is presented in rooms 17 to 21, in the Sackler wing, on the north side of the Cour Carrée.

CYPRUS FROM ITS ORIGINS TO THE IRON AGE (ROOM A). The island of Cyprus, off the coast of Syria, produced ceramics and metalwork that illustrate daily life in the 2nd millennium BC.

THE SYRIAN-LEBANESE SHORELINE (ROOM B). French excavations in Byblos and in ancient Ugarit were the source of the Louvre's splendid collection. Jewelry from the 2nd millennium BC, influenced by Egyptian art, bears witness to the wealth of this commercial port. In Phoenicia at the end of the 2nd millennium BC, the alphabet was perfected as an alternative to the Akkad syllabic system and Egyptian hieroglyphs. The worship of gods is reflected in steles, particularly those of Ugarit. The decorative arts (ivory, works in gold, earthenware) are comparable in their sophistication to those of the Aegean world.

THE SYRIAN INTERIOR (ROOM B). This region comprises the plain of the Oronte river and the oasis of Damascus, in addition to the Euphrates, which links the area with Mesopotamia. Of particular interest here are the stylized terracotta idols, the copperplated figurines from the Sumerian period and the terracotta models of houses (right), which suggest home worship, and the statuettes of Syrian gods made from bronze or from stone, wearing crowns.

PALESTINE FROM ITS ORIGINS TO THE PERIOD OF THE JEWISH DYNASTY (ROOM D). The southernmost region of the Levant, Palestine has enjoyed fertility, rich soil and a strategic geographic position since the neolithic era. Painted ceramics, basalt vessels and objects in hippopotamus ivory reflect the cultural influence of neighboring Egypt. Toward 1200 BC, non-Semitic populations, the "sea-people", settled in Palestine. Among them were the Philistines, who gave their name to Palestine where David and the Israelites were said to have entered the land of Canaan. Solomon unified the country and built, in the 10th century BC, the Temple of Jerusalem.

PHOENICIA IN THE 1ST MILLENNIUM BC (ROOM 17).

Byblos, Sidon and Tyre were the main cities of Phoenicia (present-day Lebanon), neighbors to the Hebrews and the Arameans. Ernest Renan, in his 1860–1861 trip, assembled the core of this rich collection of stone sarcophagi, which clearly demonstrate the influence of Egyptian and Greek art.

CARTHAGE AND CARTHAGINIAN NORTH AFRICA
(ROOM 18).

Founded in 814 BC by Dido, Carthage was a Phoenician colony in the western Mediterranean. It was an enemy of Rome, who destroyed it in 146 BC during the Punic wars. The remains of this civilization come from the tombs and *tophets* – open-air sanctuaries with steles dedicated to the gods Baal and Tanit.

ARABIA (ROOM 19).

The southern part of the Arab peninsula, present-day Yemen, was notable for its wealth of incense and of myrrh; it was thanks to the trade in these products that the smaller kingdoms of the 1st millennium BC prospered. The displays in this room present objects from the temples, their offerings and amulets. The oases of the desert area of Arabia, places such as Teima and Petra, constituted vital trading posts.

THE CARAVAN STOPS OF ARABIA : PALMYRA AND DURA EUROPOS
(ROOM 20).

Built on the trade route between the Greco-Roman world and the Parthian empire, Palmyra enjoyed a golden era before it was conquered by Rome in 272 BC. The sculpture in this cosmopolitan city is remarkable, and its funerary art offers vital clues to the life of its inhabitants. Dura Europos, "city of all religions", was destroyed by the Sassanids in 256 AD.

FROM ANCIENT CYPRUS TO THE 1ST MILLENNIUM BC (ROOM 21).

Following on from room A, this room displays beautiful votive sculpture and numerous figurines, grouped around the huge Vase of Amathonte.

THE ART OF PALMYRA
Palmyra was a crossroads between east and west, and its art was profoundly influenced by Greece and Rome. Above, the *Trio of Gods* – the Sky, the Moon and the Sun – are dressed as Roman officers (2nd century AD). Below, this 2nd-century AD stele bears witness to the continuing vitality of the religion of Carthage during the Roman occupation. The dedicatee, in the center, is placed under the sign of the goddess Tanit.

ENTRESOL

RICHELIEU

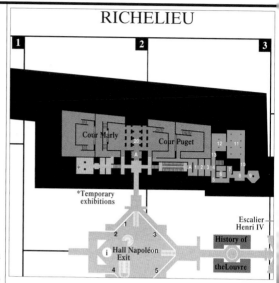

IVORY IN SPAIN
A masterpiece of 10th-century Cordoba sculpture on ivory, the *Pyx of Al-Mughira*, son of Caliph Abd-el-Rahman III, was cut from a single elephant's tusk (right).

CERAMIC PANEL IN THE FORM OF A MIHRAB (sacred wall of a mosque) is actually a funerary stele (Iran, Kashan, 13th century, below right).

THE BAPTISMAL FONT OF SAINT LOUIS
The large bowl (1320–1340) below is one of the masterpieces of the Louvre's collection of Mameluke art. It is made of a single sheet of hammered brass with gold and silver inlay.

These rooms display one of the world's biggest collections of Islamic art, and cover a broad panorama from the 7th to the 19th century. In 2009, a new space in the Cour Visconti will allow some ten thousand works to be permanently exhibited.

THE BEGINNINGS OF ISLAMIC ART (ROOM 1).
The Umayyads, founders of the first Islamic dynasty (AD 661–750), chose Damascus as their capital. Fragments of architecture, pots, lamps show a variety of influences such as Christian, Hellenistic and Iranian.

THE ABBASSIDS (ROOM 2). The art of this period (8th–10th centuries) blossomed thanks to the patronage of the caliphate of Baghdad (the new capital): it included palace decoration, art objects and ceramics with white opaque glazes and metal luster decoration.

THE FATIMIDS AND THE MUSLIM OCCIDENT 10th–15th centuries **(ROOM 3).** The Fatimids (909–1171) set up their capital in Cairo in 969. They excelled in the crafting of rock crystal and wood. Their ceramics tended to be covered in luster decoration featuring

Ceramic lusterware was one of the finest products of the Fatimid period.

animal motifs. After the conquest of Spain in 711, the Umayyad emirs of Cordoba reigned over the region until the 11th century, at which time sculpture in ivory, as well as bronze and ceramic work, reached their highest levels.

THE IRANIAN WORLD in the 10th–12th centuries (**ROOM 4**) produced a style of ceramic with a creamy white background and marbled engraved decoration.

IRAN DURING THE SELJUK PERIOD 11th–13th centuries (**ROOMS 5 AND 6**) saw a number of innovations, represented here by scientific objects. The ceramic work and calligraphy produced at this time were remarkable. The art of metalworking, especially in Khurassan, produced inkstands, metal ewers, candlesticks and perfume-censers.

EGYPT, THE NEAR EAST AND ANATOLIA in the 12th and 13th centuries (**ROOM 8**) produced extraordinary treasures: decorated ceramics, enameled and gilded glass objects, metal bowls and ewers and miniatures.

THE MAMELUKES (**ROOM 9**) covered the years 1250–1517. They perpetuated the lavish traditions of the Fatimid caliphs, evolved a very elegant style of calligraphy and initiated the use of blasons on lamps of gilded and enameled glass.

MONGOL IRAN 13th–14 century (**ROOM 10**). This period is illustrated by ceramic wall coverings with geometrical and cruciform patterns, metal objects and fine ceramics. The Mongol school of miniatures is justly famous.

THE TIMURIDS, SAFAVID IRAN, QADJAR IRAN AND MOGUL INDIA (**ROOM 11**). Iranian carpet weavers reached high levels of perfection during the 16th century. One of the showcases here is devoted to the arms and armor of the Islamic world (10th–17th century). The works of Mogul artists – metal, glass and carpets – are distinguished by the superb detail in the craftsmanship.

THE OTTOMAN WORLD 14th–20th centuries (**ROOM 12**). The Ottoman Empire, founded in the 13th century, reached its zenith under Suleyman the Magnificent in the 16th century. The ceramic pottery of Iznik is especially remarkable, with its cups, dishes and wall-panels. Also displayed are carpets and metal work from this period.

ROOM 13 is devoted to a rotating exhibition of splendid miniatures.

Rose-patterned cup, ceramic, luster decorations against a blue glaze (Syria, early 12th century).

MANTES CARPET
A detail of this asymmetrical weave, woolen carpet (below) from the collegiate church of Mantes-la-Jolie (Iran, late 16th entury).

Hanap with floral décor (Iznik pottery, Turkey, 16th century, right); *Lamp from a mosque with the name of Sultan Hassan*, in enameled and gilded glass (Egypt or Syria, 14th-century, center); *Horse-head dagger* of jade, inlaid with gold, rubies and emeralds; steel blade (India, 17th century, left).

147

▲ Egypt

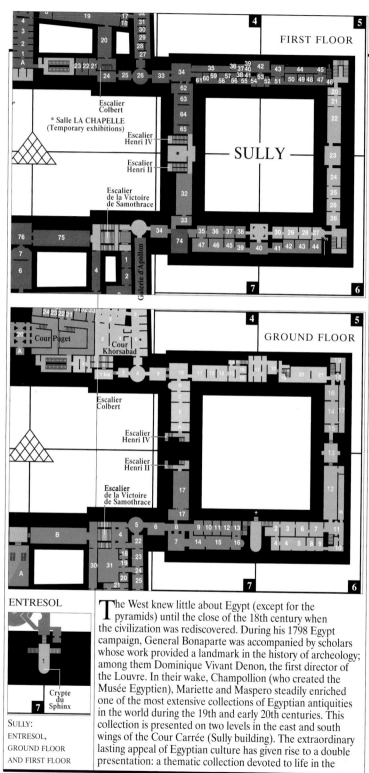

FIRST FLOOR

Escalier Colbert

* Salle LA CHAPELLE
(Temporary exhibitions)

Escalier Henri IV

Escalier Henri II

SULLY

Escalier de la Victoire de Samothrace

Galerie d'Apollon

GROUND FLOOR

Cour Puget

Cour Khorsabad

Escalier Colbert

Escalier Henri IV

Escalier Henri II

Escalier de la Victoire de Samothrace

ENTRESOL

Crypte du Sphinx

SULLY:
ENTRESOL,
GROUND FLOOR
AND FIRST FLOOR

The West knew little about Egypt (except for the pyramids) until the close of the 18th century when the civilization was rediscovered. During his 1798 Egypt campaign, General Bonaparte was accompanied by scholars whose work provided a landmark in the history of archeology; among them Dominique Vivant Denon, the first director of the Louvre. In their wake, Champollion (who created the Musée Egyptien), Mariette and Maspero steadily enriched one of the most extensive collections of Egyptian antiquities in the world during the 19th and early 20th centuries. This collection is presented on two levels in the east and south wings of the Cour Carrée (Sully building). The extraordinary lasting appeal of Egyptian culture has given rise to a double presentation: a thematic collection devoted to life in the

Nile valley is displayed in rooms 2 to 19 of the ground floor; and a chronological collection is held in rooms 20 to 30 on the first floor. Key works line a brief route through the collection, while further displays encourage those who wish to extend their knowledge in the field of their choice. The presentation starts with the Sphinx Crypt (right, ROOM 1), on the entresol of the Cour Carrée's south wing, accessed via the medieval Louvre.

THE NILE CIVILIZATION

GROUND FLOOR, ROOMS 2 TO 19 (▲ *150, 157*).
Room 2 provides an introduction to this section. Rooms 3 to 10 are devoted to daily life on the banks of the Nile: work in the fields, animal husbandry, hunting, fishing, writing materials and techniques, home and furniture, jewelry and leisure pursuits. The many objects found in tombs have added greatly to our knowledge of the life and customs of the people. Rooms 11 to 19, which constitute the Colonnade wing, focus on the spiritual and cultural aspects of Egypt: the architecture and decoration of temples and tombs, funerary rites, mummies, the Book of the Dead, gods and magic, sacred animals and their mummies.

EGYPTIAN ART

FIRST FLOOR, ROOMS 20 TO 30 (▲ *158, 161*).
In these rooms you can experience more than three thousand years of a culture whose artistic expression is still of prime importance. From the dawn of the Egyptian dynasties in around 3000 BC, to the last pharaohs, the Ptolemys subjugated by Alexander the Great and finally by Roman domination, all of these works – some realistic, some idealistic – are very powerful. These masterpieces range from the *Seated Scribe* (Old Kingdom, ROOM 22 ▲ *152*) to the effigy of Akhenaten (New Kingdom, ROOM 25 ▲ *155*), or graceful female figures such as that of Karomama. The final rooms (27 to 30) are housed in the Musée Charles X ▲ *128* whose adornments evoke the rediscovery of Egypt. The portraits of Fayoum and the Coptic collections ▲ *161, 162* are housed in the entresol of the Denon building.

LARGE SPHINX
Standing guard in the crypt (ROOM 1), on the way into the rooms holding the Egyptian collections, the *Large Sphinx* from Tanis (Middle Kingdom) is one of the 4,000 pieces that make up the Salt collection, acquired by Champollion in 1826.

THE PAINTINGS OF LÉON COGNIET (Galerie Charles X, 1st floor) These illustrate some of the characteristic features of Egyptology: most of the discoveries involved tombs, as death and immortality were overriding preoccupations for the Egyptians.

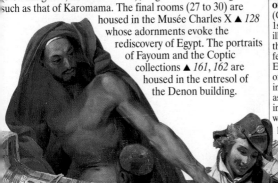

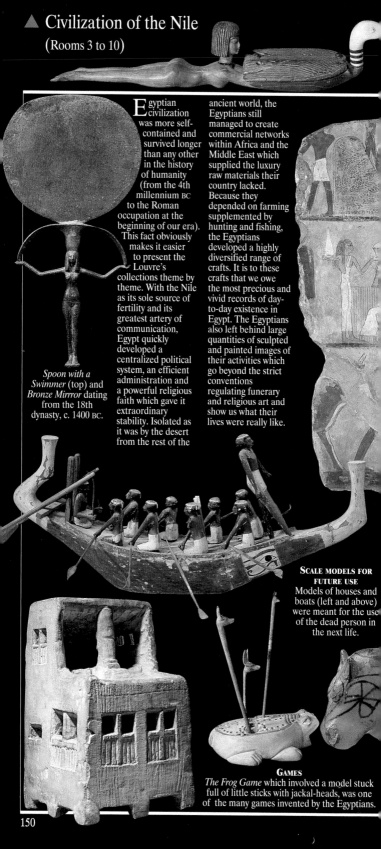

Egyptian civilization was more self-contained and survived longer than any other in the history of humanity (from the 4th millennium BC to the Roman occupation at the beginning of our era). This fact obviously makes it easier to present the Louvre's collections theme by theme. With the Nile as its sole source of fertility and its greatest artery of communication, Egypt quickly developed a centralized political system, an efficient administration and a powerful religious faith which gave it extraordinary stability. Isolated as it was by the desert from the rest of the ancient world, the Egyptians still managed to create commercial networks within Africa and the Middle East which supplied the luxury raw materials their country lacked. Because they depended on farming supplemented by hunting and fishing, the Egyptians developed a highly diversified range of crafts. It is to these crafts that we owe the most precious and vivid records of day-to-day existence in Egypt. The Egyptians also left behind large quantities of sculpted and painted images of their activities which go beyond the strict conventions regulating funerary and religious art and show us what their lives were really like.

Spoon with a Swimmer (top) and *Bronze Mirror* dating from the 18th dynasty, c. 1400 BC.

SCALE MODELS FOR FUTURE USE
Models of houses and boats (left and above) were meant for the use of the dead person in the next life.

GAMES
The Frog Game which involved a model stuck full of little sticks with jackal-heads, was one of the many games invented by the Egyptians.

WORK
Agricultural scenes are shown in tomb paintings (here, from the tomb of Ounsou, a grain accountant and scribe, New Kingdom).

c. One of the reliefs on the mastaba of Akhethep (ROOM 4) from the Saqqara burial ground shows harpists, flute players and singers.

Ceremonial chair of wood encrusted with ivory, and *Hippopotamus* of blue porcelain, evidence of great refinement.

Hieroglyphs and scribes
(Room 6)

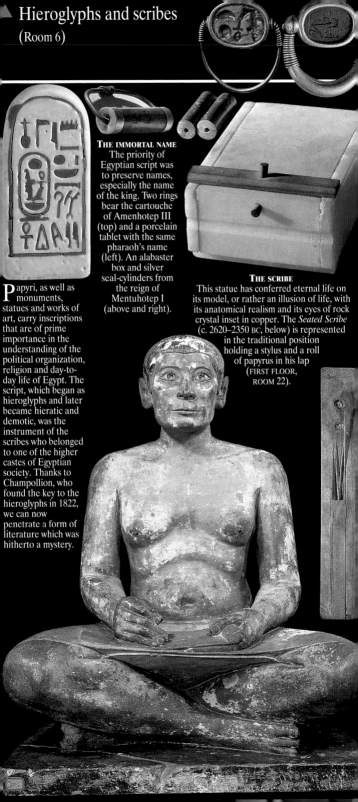

THE IMMORTAL NAME
The priority of Egyptian script was to preserve names, especially the name of the king. Two rings bear the cartouche of Amenhotep III (top) and a porcelain tablet with the same pharaoh's name (left). An alabaster box and silver seal-cylinders from the reign of Mentuhotep I (above and right).

THE SCRIBE
This statue has conferred eternal life on its model, or rather an illusion of life, with its anatomical realism and its eyes of rock crystal inset in copper. The *Seated Scribe* (c. 2620–2350 BC, below) is represented in the traditional position holding a stylus and a roll of papyrus in his lap (FIRST FLOOR, ROOM 22).

Papyri, as well as monuments, statues and works of art, carry inscriptions that are of prime importance in the understanding of the political organization, religion and day-to-day life of Egypt. The script, which began as hieroglyphs and later became hieratic and demotic, was the instrument of the scribes who belonged to one of the higher castes of Egyptian society. Thanks to Champollion, who found the key to the hieroglyphs in 1822, we can now penetrate a form of literature which was hitherto a mystery.

HIEROGLYPHIC AND HIERATIC
The Egyptians used several forms of writing derived from hieroglyphs such as hieratic script (room 4).

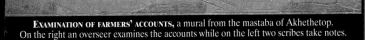

EXAMINATION OF FARMERS' ACCOUNTS, a mural from the mastaba of Akhethotep. On the right an overseer examines the accounts while on the left two scribes take notes.

THE ROSETTA STONE (original in the British Museum). Discovered in 1790, the year of Champollion's birth, the Rosetta Stone is engraved with the same text in hieroglyphic and demotic script with a translation in Greek. It became the key to the comprehension of Egyptian writing.

JEAN-FRANÇOIS CHAMPOLLION
Born in Figeac and the son of a librarian, Champollion studied both living and dead languages from a very young age. In 1826 Charles X put him in charge of a new section of the museum devoted to Egyptian and oriental monuments.

THE SCRIBE'S EQUIPMENT
A wooden tablet, a double inkwell in porcelain, a papyrus-cutter and a sheet of papyrus (above), a wooden palette with rush-stems and two cups for color blocks (left) make up a scribe's tools.

A PRECIS OF EGYPTIAN GRAMMAR
Published after his death, the third work by Champollion entitled *An Egyptian Grammar, or General Principles of the Egyptian Language* completed his discovery. The page (left) shows equivalent words in hieroglyphic, hieratic and demotic Egyptian along with their translations into Greek and French.

153

COLOSSI
The origins of this statue (left), which is inscribed with the name of Ramesses II, are unknown. The 14-foot colossus of Sety II was found at Karnak (right).

Long forgotten, buried in the sands or transformed into dwellings, Egypt's temples have been the object of intense archeological interest since the 19th century. Most have now been unearthed, notably at Thebes (Luxor and Karnak). Whether they were funerary temples or religious sites dedicated to the gods, they were always richly furnished with narrative bas-reliefs and monumental statues of gods, pharaohs and private individuals. Capitals and columns, the principal features of Egyptian stone architecture, have survived thousands of years into our own time. Although the Louvre can offer no complete ensemble, its collection of monumental sculpture and architecture in the Galerie Henri IV affords a good introduction to the subject.

BULL-GOD
This statue of the god Apis (ROOM 19) comes from the Serapeum of Memphis, the burial ground of the sacred bulls. During their lives these bulls were revered as incarnations of the god Ptah.

FALSE DOOR
False door steles were symbolic passage-points between the worlds of the living and the dead. This one of limestone was dedicated by Queen Hatshepsut to her father, Thutmose I; it evokes the huge masonry columns which marked temple entrances.

Lines of sphinxes and other animals generally marked the approaches to the temples (above, a lion from the Serapeum at Memphis).

An effigy of Amenhotep IV (Akhenaten, ROOM 25), in the crossed-arms pose of Osiris, illustrates the artistic canon of the Amarnian period.

The goddess Hathor's features adorn "Hathoric" capitals, such as this one (above) from the temple of Bubastis.

PILLARED INTERIORS
The interiors of temples were veritable forests of columns, often monolithic in type, and made of granite, limestone or schist. Those of the funerary temple of Unis at Saqqara (left) had elegant palm-leaf capitals.

Death and the gods

(Sully, ground floor, rooms 13 to 19; first floor, room 29)

This amulet in the form of an "oudjat" eye was placed in the mummy's wrappings to ensure the integrity of the body in the next world.

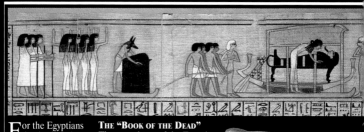

F or the Egyptians death offered not an end to life, but the promise of resurrection. This was one of the basic tenets of a religion whose pantheon of gods was remarkably diverse. Around the principal gods Re (or Amun) the Sun god, revolved Thoth, Anubis, Osiris, Isis and Horus. Creatures such as ibis, cats, rams, bulls, snakes, scarabs, falcons and crocodiles were sacred.

THE "BOOK OF THE DEAD"
The sacred text of the Egyptian religion is a collection of hymns to the gods, magic formulae to ensure the survival of the deceased. It was generally inscribed on papyrus (above).

RUSSIAN DOLL
The multipl sarcophagi of the riche tombs are spectacularl decorative. That of th Lady Madja (below and those o Tamutnefret, a singer o Amun (right) are i painted, stuccoe wood. The sarcophag of pharaohs might eve be in gold

THE SACRED IBIS
This bird which still haunts the banks of the Nile, was revered as one of the incarnations of Thoth, the god of scribes.

THE EGYPTIAN PANTHEON
This group of divinities is represented in the *Book of the Dead* of Khonsu (left). From right to left, Re-Hsrakhti, the principal god in the hierarchy crowned with the solar disc which is his symbol; Osiris, wearing the tall white crown of Lower Egypt is the resurrected god who protects the dead; Osiris' wife Isis who brought him back to life; and Nephthys. On the opposite page, from left to right, Bastet, the cat-goddess venerated at Bubastis; the god Bes; the lioness-goddess Sekhmet and Anubis, the jackel-god (ROOM 29).

FUNERAL RITES

The dead were embalmed then carefully wrapped in linen bandages incorporating protective amulets. The mummy was then "dressed" in cardboard packaging and placed in one or more sarcophagi and put in a stone tank deep within the tomb. Above is the mummy of Pachery with its cardboard packaging; on the left is a funeral cortège from a *Book of the Dead*.

It was only later that animals were sacrificed and mummified like humans. Right, a mummified cat.

▲ Egyptian art
From the origins to the Middle Kingdom
(Sully, first floor, rooms 20 to 23)

PRE-DYNASTIC EGYPT: THE NAGADA PERIOD
(ROOM 20) The civilization which appeared on the banks of the Nile in the 4th millennium had not yet mastered the art of writing, but is known to us through the first fruits of its art: figurines of men (left), stone vases (right) and schist tablets with animal motifs (below left). The Louvre possesses a masterpiece from this period, the *Guebel el-Arak Dagger* covered with wonderful carved relief (right).

Egypt entered recorded history around 3000 BC, when writing appeared and the pharaonic civilization was founded. The first two dynasties, established at this time gave their name to the Thinite period. The *Stele of the Serpent King* (right, ROOM 21) is remarkable from every point of view: it not only shows the image of a vanished palace, but also carries one of the first indications of a form of script, the serpent hieroglyph representing the pharaoh's name which is placed by convention above the palace. The falcon Horus, god of royalty, protects the pharaoh.

Plaque, of carved schist, used for grinding kohl, c. 3200 BC (ROOM 20).

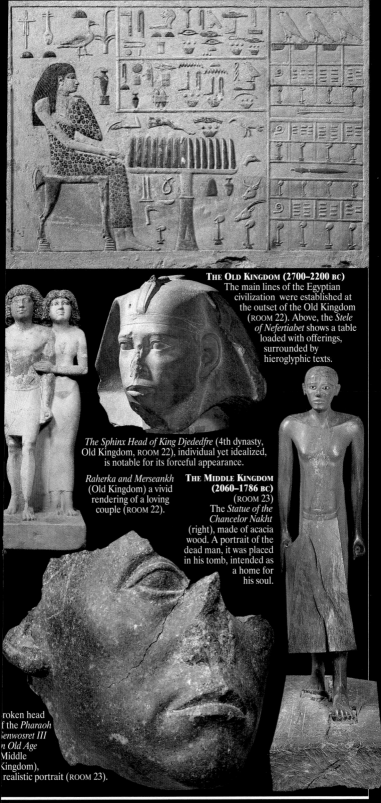

THE OLD KINGDOM (2700–2200 BC)

The main lines of the Egyptian civilization were established at the outset of the Old Kingdom (ROOM 22). Above, the *Stele of Nefertiabet* shows a table loaded with offerings, surrounded by hieroglyphic texts.

The Sphinx Head of King Djededfre (4th dynasty, Old Kingdom, ROOM 22), individual yet idealized, is notable for its forceful appearance.

Raherka and Merseankh (Old Kingdom) a vivid rendering of a loving couple (ROOM 22).

THE MIDDLE KINGDOM (2060–1786 BC)
(ROOM 23)
The *Statue of the Chancelor Nakht* (right), made of acacia wood. A portrait of the dead man, it was placed in his tomb, intended as a home for his soul.

roken head f the *Pharaoh Senwosret III n Old Age* Middle Kingdom), realistic portrait (ROOM 23).

TUTANKHAMUN?
This little head in *pâte de verre* could be that of Tutankhamun, the last pharaoh of the 18th dynasty, whose tomb was discovered inviolate. Its treasures are now at the Cairo Museum (ROOM 26).

QUEEN TIYI
This royal statuette of enameled schist (New Kingdom) is one of many Egyptian figures typifying a feminine ideal.

THE NEW KINGDOM (1555–1080 BC)
ROOMS 24 TO 28

Thebes was capital of a powerful Egyptian empire and the 18th and 19th dynasties marked a high point of Egyptian civilization and a period of intense artistic activity. A series of pharaohs called Amenhotep, Thutmose, Sety and Ramesses were among the greatest monarchs. Above, a painted limestone relief of Sety I and the goddess Hathor (ROOM 27).

RAMESSES II

(ROOMS 27 AND 28) One of the greatest pharaohs of the 19th dynasty, Ramesses II reigned for 67 years. He is shown (below) on a relief being embraced by the god Amun (Re). A sumptuous pectoral of electrum, colored glass and turquoise (left) bears his name written in a cartouche.

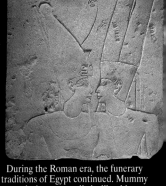

During the Roman era, the funerary traditions of Egypt continued. Mummy portraits became realistic, like this one of a man (2nd century AD, below).

THE LOWER EPOCH

(1000 BC to the Roman occupation) (ROOMS 29 AND 30) Egyptian civilization and religion resisted Greek and later Roman occupation for many centuries. Above, the *Osorkon Group* (reign of Osorkon II, 889–866 BC) in gold and lapis lazuli, shows Osiris, Isis and Horus.

Funerary Mask of a Woman in painted plaster: Roman era, from Antinoe.

Detail of the *Sabine's Shawl*: Cupid figures ride on the backs of crocodiles.

The roots of Coptic Egypt date back to the end of the Ancient World. The Copts (a distortion of the Greek word *aegyptos* meaning Egyptian) submitted to the Greeks of Byzantium and the subsequent triumph of Christianity renewed the iconography of their art. After the Arab conquest in AD 641, those Copts who did not convert to Islam turned to Byzantine forms. Eastern Mediterranean collections from the Roman (ROOM A) and Byzantine periods (ROOMS B AND C) are shown in the entresol of the Denon wing. Mosaics, fabrics, decorative sculpture and painting attest to an inventive civilization which found itself completely isolated within the Islamic world.

COPTIC WEAVING
Most Coptic fabrics were of linen and wool, decorated with brightly colored motifs. Their designers worked out an original formal language of their own, with strange proportions that owed nothing to perspective, but relied on graphic schematization and flat colors.

Among the many tapestries which illustrate the originality of Coptic art in the 5th century is this fragment showing the head of a dancing girl (left) and another highly graphic piece with geometrical, vegetable and figurative motifs (below, left).

THE SABINE'S SHAWL
Having abandoned the practice of mummification, the Christians buried their dead in rich fabrics decorated in the oriental style. The *Sabine's Shawl* (5th century, details left, right and top of page) was discovered in a tomb at Antinoe; it combines scenes from Greco-Roman mythology with Nilotic ones.

The *Birth of Aphrodite*
in limestone relief, 5th–6th century AD.

The Copts built
churches with
highly original
decoration: this
capital from Baouit
(left) blends
vegetable motifs with
the Christian cross.

CHRIST AND THE ABBOT MENA
The head of one of Egypt's
many monasteries is shown in
this painting on wood
(6th–7th century AD).

VIRGIN OF THE ANNUNCIATION
This Virgin carved of fig-wood
(late 5th century) may have
been part of a piece of
furniture illustrating scenes
from the life of the Virgin,
whose iconography was
spreading through the
Christian world at
that time.

MOUNTED HORUS
Christian art
assimilated some
Egyptian motifs.
This Saint George
has Horus's falcon
features and the
dragon is a
crocodile.

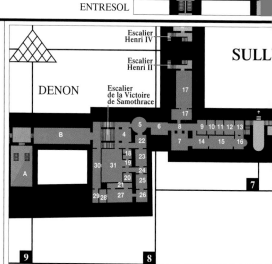

ENTRESOL

DENON

(ABOVE) GROUND FLOOR

(ABOVE) FIRST FLOOR

IDOLS AND KORES
Two millennia
separate the Cycladic
idols (below left)
from those of the
geometric period
(right). At the
center of the page,
the female statue
called the *Dame
d'Auxerre*, and the
Kore of Samos, are
two major landmarks
in the development
of archaic Greek
sculpture.

The collection of Greek, Etruscan and
Roman antiquities came from the
former French royal collection, enriched
by those of Cardinals Richelieu and
Mazarin. In 1795, before the arrival
of the marbles looted from Italy
by Bonaparte ● *40*, the antiquities
section was created. It grew
considerably during the first Empire,
notably thanks to the Borghese
collection bought by Napoleon from
his brother-in-law in 1808. But
the masterpieces in the Louvre
at that time, which included
Laocoön and the *Apollo
Belvedere*, were restored
to the Vatican in 1815.
Throughout the 19th
century other collections,
either left in wills or
purchased, enriched this
section of the museum. Start in
the entresol (Denon building)
in the former royal stables.

GREECE BEFORE THE PARTHENON

The rooms devoted to the origins of art in the Aegean world, from the 4th millennium BC and the Cycladic period, are beneath the Galerie Daru on the entresol. Especially noteworthy are the marble Cycladic idols of the Bronze Age (3200–1100 BC), as well as items from the rich Minoan (Crete) and Mycenean civilizations (3500–1100 BC, mainland Greece).

GEOMETRIC ART AND THE ORIENTALIST STYLE. The geometric style was dominant from the 11th to the 6th century BC; it was softened in the 7th century by oriental influences, which created what we know as the orientalist style. This change is particularly evident in the decoration of ceramic vases painted with funerary scenes (amphoras and loutrophoroi), dating from the archaic period ▲ 174, notably the *loutrophoros of the painter of Anatolos.* Archaic Greek sculpture is characterized by two themes: that of the Kouros, the nude male of athletic build, and that of the Kore, a young girl, clothed. These two types are typically depicted with the body set in the frontal, walking position, with the left leg slightly in front of the right. The female statue known as the *Dame d'Auxerre* is a prelude to the great Greek statuary in the exactness of its proportions and the sense of volume it displays. This piece probably came from Crete, c. 630 BC.

The figure stands in an attitude of worship, with one hand raised to her breast. A few traces of color remain on her dress, but none on that of the *Kore of Samos* (Samos, c. 570 BC), found in the shrine of Hera. This was one of the very earliest kores. She wears a ceremonial costume with a long skirt or *chitra;* her right shoulder is draped with a shawl or *himation.* A kouros from the same period seems to be a portrait of Apollo, since it was discovered in his sanctuary at Action. This piece shows the extraordinary care Greek sculptors took in the rendering of anatomical detail. The *Rampin Horseman* (Athens, c. 550 BC) consists of an original head and a body that is a cast of the original in the Museum of the Acropolis in Athens. The hair and beard have beautifully sculpted tight curls. The smile is also an archaic convention. In the 1st century BC sculptors developed a taste for representing sacred images in the archaic manner (*Piombino Apollo* ▲ 172).

THE SEVERE STYLE (ROOM 3, on the landing) The *Miletus Torso* (Miletus, c. 480 BC) marks the shift toward the Classical style; the figure is still frontal like the *Kouros of Actium*, but the hips are looser and more natural and the contours more slender.

In the same room, the funerary stele, known as *Exaltation of the Flower,* lies midway between Archaism and Classicism.

THE ERGASTINES
This was the name given to the young girls who were chosen from the best Athenian families to embroider the tunic offered to the goddess Athena in the Panathenaic procession (right, the Ergastines and two leaders of the ceremony on the Parthenon frieze).

IDEALS OF BEAUTY
The canons developed by the Greek sculptors of the Classical era are models of perfection which artists have striven to equal ever since. They were mainly invented by Polykleitos (below right, *Male Torso of an Athlete at Rest*) and Praxiteles (below, the *Cnidian Aphrodite*). These two sculptures are Roman copies of Greek originals.

CLASSICISM AND THE APOGEE OF ATHENS

THE OLYMPIA ROOM (DENON, GROUND FLOOR, ROOM 4). The exceptional sculpted decoration of the Temple of Zeus at Olympia, built c. 460 BC, is evident in the metope of *Hercules and the Cretan bulls*.

THE PARTHENON (SULLY, GROUND FLOOR, ROOM 7) was the most significant archeological achievement of the age of Pericles (5th century BC). At that time Athens was the dominant city of the Greek world, emerging with redoubled confidence from the Medic Wars against the Persians (480 BC). Phidias and Polykleitos created sculptures that blended observation of the real with artifice in which ideal beauty was achieved by the approximation of forms to ideas. The *Frieze of the Panathenaic Procession*, whose subject is the great feast held by the Athenians in honor of their tutelary goddess, adorned the walls of the Parthenon's peristyle gallery. Most of this work is in the British Museum in London; designed by Phidias it marks a high point in the progress of Classical sculpture. The Louvre has a fragment showing the slow, rhythmic march of the procession, notable for its attractive draperies. Also visible are the small holes used for attaching bronze accessories. This room also contains the *Laborde Head*, a fragment of the decoration of a Parthenon pediment. Return to room 8.

SCULPTURE (ROOMS 8 TO 16). From room 7, the route divides into two parallel galleries: on the right, the Galerie de la Melpomène (ROOMS 14 TO 16) displaying copies – mainly Roman – of Greek Classical sculpture (5th and 4th centuries BC); on the left, the Galerie de la Vénus de Milo (ROOMS 8 TO 13), with original Greek sculpture (4th to 1st century BC).

The rooms of Greek antiquities (Sully, ground floor, rooms 7 to 16) are undergoing refurbishment to improve access within the areas leading to the Venus de Milo. The new chronological arrangement shows sculptures in materials such as bronze, glass, wood and terracotta, from the 5th to the 1st century BC.

ORIGINALS AND COPIES.

The old texts describe cities embellished with thousands of statues in bronze, but the only ones which have come down to us are marbles, most of them late copies of vanished pieces. Bronze ▲ *172–3*, which was much used by artists who found it a more pliable material than marble for the representation of movement, was melted down during the barbarian epochs. The marbles were frequently smashed and mutilated as well, but fortunately they were reproduced during the Roman era and resculpted from plaster casts of their originals. It should be noted that the Roman sculptors, who were much concerned with solidity, often contrived to modify the positions of the arms of sculptures, and added supports such as the one that links the thigh and wrist of the *Borghese Ares* (ROOM 17, ▲ *168*) to maintain the equilibrium of bodies which were originally of much lighter bronze. In any case, these Roman copies have contributed greatly to our understanding of Greek art.

THE CANONS OF CLASSICAL GREEK SCULPTURE. ROOMS 14, 15 and 16 (Galerie de la Melpomène) offer an overview of the developing canons of Classical Greek sculpture, from the austere style of Polykleitos to the more delicate, feminine manner mastered by Praxiteles at the end of the 5th century, which we mostly know from copies. The *Diadumenos*, after Polykleitos, the *Apollo* and *Athena* after Phidias and the *Aphrodite (Venus Genitrix)* after Callimachos, a late 5th century Athenian sculptor who made the link between Phidias and Praxiteles, represent the canons of the Classical style, both masculine and feminine (ROOM 14). The *Cnidian Aphrodite* (Roman copy, ROOM 16), all sweetness and modesty, is the prototype of the feminine figure evolved by Praxiteles in the 4th century. The *Arles Aphrodite* (ROOM 16) which was similarly copied from Praxiteles' lost original, has caught forever the suppleness of Phryne, a courtesan who was the sculptor's mistress and favorite model. The *Apollo Sauroctone* by the same sculptor

APOLLO
The graceful masculine type developed by Praxiteles (above, *Apollo Sauroctone*) may be compared with that of Polykleitos a century earlier (facing page).

OFFICIAL AND PRIVATE ART
Athena, the tutelary goddess of Athens (below) is a Roman replica of an original attributed to Alcamenes (late 5th century). Below left, funerary stele in the 4th-century Attic style showing a reunited family.

(ROOM 16) contrasts with the powerful athletes of Polykleitos: the subject here is a soft adolescent. The Classical art of the 4th century seems dominated by a gentler sensibility, perhaps more individualistically inclined, than that of the 5th century, hence the proliferation of portrait paintings. There is greater realism, and the athletes and divinities are engaged in precise actions which the sculptors' handling of anatomy seeks to reflect.

THE HELLENISTIC PERIOD

The sculptor Lysippos, the creator of the *Borghese Gladiator* (GALERIE DARU), was working at the end of the Classical and the beginning of the Hellenistic periods. He was clearly mindful of the lessons of earlier masters; his *Gladiator* (c. 100 BC) is in fact a Hellenistic work, much influenced by Classicism. It depicts a gladiator in combat; the shield strapped to the left arm and the sword in the right hand are left to the imagination. The Hellenistic period began at about the time of Alexander's death in 323 BC. It is characterized by a much greater emphasis on movement and by interpretations of elements such as childhood, old age, ugliness, suffering and fear. The Hellenistic sculptors also favored picturesque scenes, such as a child playing with a goose or a child perched on a centaur.

THE VENUS DE MILO ▲ *170–1* is surrounded with works attesting to a period of Classical renewal (*Head of Aphrodite*, called the *Kaufman Head*); in addition, some Hellenistic works here echo a more severe earlier style. The sinuous rhythm and rendering of the body, the elaborate folds of the garment and the realism of the bust make it clear that the *Venus de Milo* is an original sculpture from the 2nd century BC; while the pose and facial expression remind us of Praxiteles and Lysippos.

THE SALLE DES PORTRAITS LAGIDES (ROOM 11) evokes the Ptolemaic dynasty to which Cleopatra belonged.

THE SALLE DES CARIATIDES (ROOM 17) houses sculpture of the Hellenistic period. A bust of Alexander stands at its entrance. Note the Roman replicas of lost works by Lysippos (4th century BC), one of the sculptors who represents the

THE CARYATIDS OF THE LOUVRE
The caryatids which support the gallery are a direct reference to Greek and Roman antiquity as reinterpreted by the Renaissance. This room (above right) is ideal as a showcase for the Louvre's collection of Hellenistic sculptures. *Artemis*, also called the *Diana of Versailles* (above), and the *Bust of Alexander* (below). To the right is the *Borghese Gladiator* (in ROOM 13) and on the facing page *Sleeping Hermaphrodite*, a replica of a (probably Alexandrian) original.

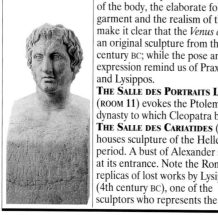

rejection of Classicism. Of the 1,500-odd masterpieces he
sculpted which were cast in bronze, only copies remain.
Marsyas, by an unknown sculptor, hangs from a tree
waiting to be flayed alive on the command of a
wrathful Apollo. In the same vein as the famous
Cnidian Aphrodite is the *Aphrodite of the
Capitol,* the modest gesture of whose right
hand echoes the hand of the lost Eros resting
on the shoulder of the *Seated Aphrodite.*
Diana the Huntress which was copied
many times over, is itself a Roman
replica of a 2nd century BC adaptation of
an original by Leochares
(4th century BC). At the far end
of the gallery lies the exquisitely
formed *Sleeping Hermaphrodite,*
discovered at the beginning of the
17th century in Rome. The
marble mattress was supplied
by Bernini. Behind the
caryatids, the Escalier Henri II
staircase (▲ *125*) leads back to
the first floor, to the rooms
containing bronzes and
ceramics (▲ *172–5*).

(▲ *125*) ... (▲ *172–5*).

EXPRESSION
Hellenistic sculpture
is distinguished by its

ability to express
passion. Above,
the tortured face of
Marsyas (Roman copy
from a Pergamon
original).

169

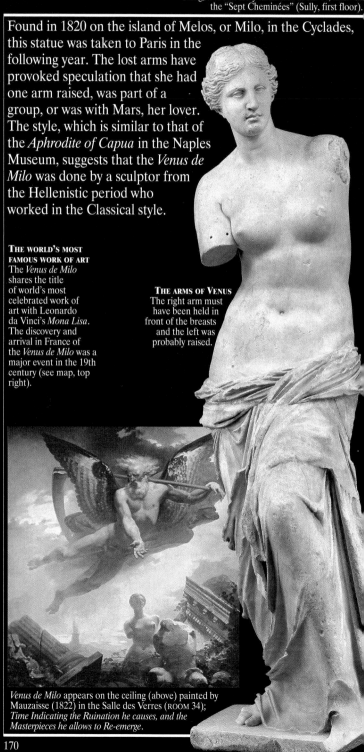

▲ Aphrodite or the Venus de Milo

The rooms of Greek antiquities (Sully, ground floor, rooms 7 to 16) are undergoing refurbishment to improve access within the areas leading to the Venus de Milo, which will eventually be on show in room 7. For the time being, it is currently housed in room 74, know as the "Sept Cheminées" (Sully, first floor).

Found in 1820 on the island of Melos, or Milo, in the Cyclades, this statue was taken to Paris in the following year. The lost arms have provoked speculation that she had one arm raised, was part of a group, or was with Mars, her lover. The style, which is similar to that of the *Aphrodite of Capua* in the Naples Museum, suggests that the *Venus de Milo* was done by a sculptor from the Hellenistic period who worked in the Classical style.

THE WORLD'S MOST FAMOUS WORK OF ART
The *Venus de Milo* shares the title of world's most celebrated work of art with Leonardo da Vinci's *Mona Lisa*. The discovery and arrival in France of the *Venus de Milo* was a major event in the 19th century (see map, top right).

THE ARMS OF VENUS
The right arm must have been held in front of the breasts and the left was probably raised.

Venus de Milo appears on the ceiling (above) painted by Mauzaisse (1822) in the Salle des Verres (ROOM 34); *Time Indicating the Ruination he causes, and the Masterpieces he allows to Re-emerge*.

170

Dumont d'Urville, then a ship's ensign, was one of the first to see the statue; he reported its discovery to the Marquis de Rivière, the French ambassador in Constantinople.

After negotiating with the Greek authorities of the island of Melos, the Marquis de Rivière (left) purchased the famous Venus along with all the other pieces found with it. He brought it back to France and presented it to Louis XVIII who immediately passed it on to the Louvre in May 1821.

LA *VENUS DE MILO* EST TRANSBORDÉE DU NAVIRE *LE GALAXIDI* A BORD DE LA GOÉLETTE *L'ESTAFETTE*.

MALE AND FEMALE
The statue of *Mithridates VI Eupator*, which belongs to the same period as the *Venus de Milo*, may also be by the same sculptor.
It too shows the return to classical style inspired by Phidias and Praxiteles (Hellenistic period, 2nd–1st century BC).

VISITORS FROM ALL OVER THE WORLD
The *Venus de Milo* is a star feature of tours of the Louvre, both today and in the past. Above, a press engraving entitled *Nasser-Ed-Din at the Museum of Antiquities* in 1873.

Great statues were cast in bronze, but also in gold-plated wood and ivory (chryselephantine statues); few of these have survived. This is why we know Greek sculpture mainly from copies, most in marble but some in bronze and on a smaller scale. In Greece, as in Etruria and Rome, a rich tradition of metalwork evolved, of which one of the richest sources known to us is the treasure found at Boscoreale near Pompeii.

THE PIOMBINO APOLLO
The date of this bronze Apollo (left) has long been disputed; it is characteristic of the 5th century return to Classicism that marked the close of the Hellenistic period.

BRONZE
Bronze was also used to make everyday objects: (above) a 5th-century BC mirror-holder; (left) a gladiator's greave found a Herculaneum (1st century AD) and (below) a sconce from the 6th century BC.

GOLD

Gold was used to make coins, statues and jewelry as well as ritual vases like this sauceboat dating from the 3rd millennium (above). The treasure of Boscoreale (1st century BC), most of which was of silver, also included a gold bracelet in the form of a serpent (right).

BOSCOREALE

The destruction of the Campanian towns by the eruption of Vesuvius in AD 79 preserved quantities of evidence of a refined way of life. The magnificent treasure of silver discovered in a buried villa close to Pompeii includes (among other things) 109 pieces of tableware, mostly of gold and silver. The treasure was purchased by Baron de Rothschild who presented it to the Louvre.

One of the most beautiful pieces from Boscoreale was a partly gilded silver goblet decorated with skeletons (above).

VICTORIOUS ATHLETE

This bronze head of an athlete in the Classical style and manner of Polykleitos, dates from the 1st century BC.

The statue of Apollo found at Lillebonne, Normandy, is of gilded bronze.

Greek ceramics

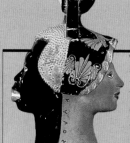

Perfumed oil flask in the form of a double head (6th century BC).

The collection of Greek ceramics in the Louvre, the most extensive of its kind in the world, is exhibited in the Galerie Campana on the first floor (rooms 39 to 47). Here the visitor can trace the development of forms, techniques and images. From the great funerary urns of the 8th century BC, which were geometric in style, to the masterpieces of Classical art and magnificent kraters signed by the finest painters, the Louvre has an extraordinary variety of pieces on display. Greek terracotta figurines are exhibited in the adjacent gallery of the Musée Charles-X (rooms 35 to 38).

CHALICE-SHAPED KRATER AND BELL-SHAPED KRATER
Left, *Hercules and the Argonauts* by the "painter of the Niobides" (Attica, c. 460 BC); right, *Massacre of the Suitors by Ulysses and Telemachus* (Campania, c. 310 BC); both are red-figured kraters.

AMPHORA (RITUAL VASE)
Attributed to the "painter of Analatos", c. 700–680 BC. Transition period between the geometric and oriental styles in Athens.

THE LEVY OENOCHOE (WINE JUG)
Rhodes, c. 850 BC. Oriental style of decoration with dark figures against a clear background, animal and vegetable friezes.

HYDRIA (WATER JUG)
By a painter of the Archippe group, c. 550 BC. Black figures against an ocher background.

–470 BC:
c ceramics,
figures on
k, austere in
e, created by
potter
okides.

470–320 BC:
Attic ceramics,
red figures,
Classical style.

**320 BC–1ST
CENTURY AD:**
Hellenistic
ceramics.

THE PAINTER EUPHRONIOS

Among the painters whose names we know,
Euphronios is one of the masters of the late
6th century BC, and one of the first to use
the red figure technique. The other side of
the krater featuring *Hercules and Antaeus*
(below) represents a music contest.

HE APOGEE F CERAMICS

his krater in the
ape of a chalice is
the great painter
uphronios, and is one
f the masterpieces of
e Louvre's collection.
ade in about
0 BC, it dates
om the period
mmediately after
e abandonment of
lack figure painting. Red figures
stand out
against the
black backdrop.
The anatomical
details, the force of the
gestures, and the terrified
expressions of the young
women watching the struggle
between the hero and the
giant show the
virtuosity of the
painter, who made
full use of the shape
of the vase to suit his purpose.

**HYDRIA
c. 520–510 BC**
*Achilles and Ajax
Playing Dice,*
black figures on red
background.

LECYTHE (FUNERARY VASE)
By a painter of the "R" group,
last quarter of the 5th century.
Offering with Stele and *Charon
the Boatman,* red figure on
white background.

**RHYTON
(DRINKING HORN)**
shaped like a
donkey's head, c.
440–430 BC. Red
figure, Classical style.

ETRUSCAN ORIGINALITY
On the way out of ROOM 20, note the small classical and Hellenistic bronzes, among them a classically-inspired vase in the shape of a young man's head (Gabies, late 4th century to early 3rd century BC, below) and the filiform Aphrodite (Nemi, c. 350 BC, right), with a beautifully proportioned face and elongated body.

UNITED FOR ALL TIME
The *Sarcophagus of a Married Couple* (far right), a masterpiece of Etruscan statuary, was discovered at Ceveteri (Caire in antiquity) in 1845. This piece came to the Louvre in 1863 with the Campana collection, to which the Louvre owes not only the greater part of its Etruscan objects, but most of its Greek vases as well. Above, facing page right, a cinerary urn with the same motif of a figure reclining for a banquet.

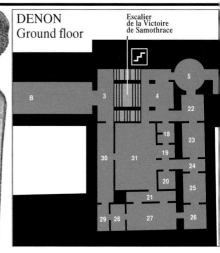

DENON
Ground floor

Escalier de la Victoire de Samothrace

ETRUSCAN ART

The Etruscan civilization, the most brilliant of pre-Roman Italy, blossomed in the region between the valleys of the Arno and Tiber, and the Tyrrhenian Sea. At its zenith in the 6th century BC it extended as far as the plain of the Po and into Campania. Strongly influenced by Greek art, whose development it broadly followed, Etruscan art was faithful nonetheless to its Italic roots. It evolved an original language of its own, excelling in terracotta, laminated bronze and goldwork.

ROOM 18 (9th–6th centuries BC). Villanovian culture supplied the prologue to Etruscan civilization. Characterized by the ritual of incineration, bronzework and geometrical decoration, it was distinctive for its *impasto* (rough clay) cinerary urns, vases and weapons. The history of ceramics between the 7th and the mid-6th century BC is illustrated in the Louvre collection by impasto ceramics and painted ceramics of Greek inspiration and, from the 7th century onward, by the appearance of *bucchero* ceramics (made with black clay, a typical feature of local production). The *Sarcophagus of a Married Couple* shows a man and a woman making the gestures of a perfume offering. This beautiful piece has the smiling grace of Ionian statuary whose influence was very strong in the late 6th century. The motif of the

reclining banquet is itself borrowed from Greek art. Etruscan terracotta is represented by a series of painted panels and by a series of architectural elements which were once colored. Two display cases contain small archaic bronzes made in Etruria.

ROOM 19 (6th–4th centuries BC). Another pair

METALWORK
The Etruscans who excelled in metalwork (*Achelous*, above), also applied their peculiar manual dexterity to the imitation of it. The 7th-century *bucchero sottile* (below), with its delicate outline, has the glint of metal.

cases in this room show some of the loveliest creations of ruscan silversmiths and goldsmiths. Note the pendant in e form of a head of Achelous (the River god), with hair d beard skillfully detailed in filigree and granulation. The rger display cases follow the evolution of Etruscan ceramics tween the mid-6th and 4th centuries (decorated with first ack, then red figures). In the course of the 6th century, the rms of *bucchero* vases grew more ponderous. In one display se are some cinerary urns called *canopes* by association th the canopic jars in which the Egyptians placed the scera of their dead. A lid in the shape of a head and ndles that sometimes had moving arms, give these pieces anthropomorphic character of their own. They are typical the Chiusi region, as are the bas-reliefs, decorated with enes of banqueting, dancing and exposure of the dead nich adorned Etruscan *cippes*, the small monuments that arked their tombs.

ROOM 20 (4th–1st centuries BC). This room contains veral sarcophagi, some in rracotta and others in stone, ong with terracotta and abaster urns. The art of rtraiture, another field in nich the Etruscans celled, is presented by e head of a oung man in onze, from esole (c. 200).

177

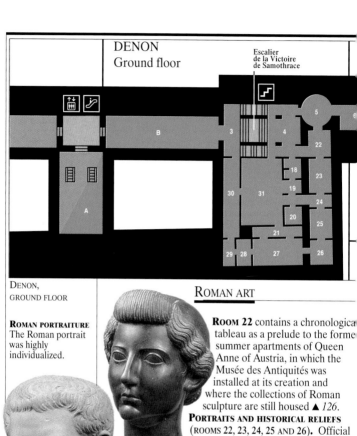

DENON
Ground floor

Escalier
de la Victoire
de Samothrace

DENON,
GROUND FLOOR

ROMAN PORTRAITURE
The Roman portrait
was highly
individualized.

A basalt head
of *Livia*, wife of
Augustus (right); the
Emperor *Caligula* and
Agrippina, mother
of Nero, in marble
(above). Far right,
a statue of Augustus
whose head and body
were sculpted at
different times.

ROMAN ART

ROOM 22 contains a chronologica
tableau as a prelude to the forme
summer apartments of Queen
Anne of Austria, in which the
Musée des Antiquités was
installed at its creation and
where the collections of Roman
sculpture are still housed ▲ *126*.
PORTRAITS AND HISTORICAL RELIEFS
(ROOMS 22, 23, 24, 25 AND 26). Official
Roman art appeared at the end of the
first century BC, its ground having
been prepared in advance by a long
Italic tradition inherited in part
from the Etruscans and
influenced by the Greeks.
As a manifestation
of political power
its goal was to
serve the gods,
the state and
the emperor.
Its two principal
concerns were
portraiture and
historical relief.
On one of the most
beautiful reliefs
of Republican Rome, the *Altar of Domitius
Ahenobarbus* (c. 100 BC), shows census-taking
and a sacrifice to the god Mars. *Marcellus*, a
great nude statue in the Classical tradition
(commissioned by Augustus in honor of his
nephew and son-in-law who died in 23 BC),
carries the signature of Cleomenes the Athenian.
The figure is both Greek and ideal, and a

thoroughgoing Roman portrait. The many
busts offer an unexpected opportunity
to study Roman coiffure: sophisticated
bandeaus for the women and fine tresses
and fringes for the men. This abundance of
portraiture is linked to the cult of household
gods, near whom the effigies of the principal
members of a family would be placed. It was
also linked to the deification of the emperors whose faces
could be seen everywhere in public places. The new style
introduced by each successive emperor had its effect on
private sculpture: neoclassicism under Augustus (1st
century BC), exaggerated expressionism under Nero (1st
century AD), and realism in the second century, from Hadrian
to Marcus Aurelius. A time of great diversity, it produced
official and private portraits.

ROOM 27: the four columns of the *Incantada*, decorated
with figures from mythology, come from a two-storey
portico that formed part of a large
monument built on the Roman agora
of Thessalonika. In the same room
are portraits and reliefs from the
beginnings of Christian art.

CHRISTIAN GAUL, ITALY AND SYRIA
(**ROOMS 28 AND 29**). A provincial
funerary art emerged with the Roman
Empire's conversion to Christianity.

THE GALERIE DES MOSAIQUES (ROOM 30)
illustrates the growth of private art: a
few examples of very rare, fragile painting
(*Winged Spirit* from Boscoreale near Pompeii,
and vine branch decoration) as well as the
most beautiful mosaics of antiquity, the
celebrated *Triumph of Neptune and Amphitrite*. The superb
Phoenix shining out from its bed of roses, a late mosaic
(5th century) discovered in Antioch, capital of Roman Syria,
is composed like a carpet. This piece is very different from the
ordinary run of 2nd-century mosaics which were conceived
like paintings (for example, the *Judgement of Paris*, a dining
room decoration that is similar to Pompeiian paintings).

THE MOSAIC OF THE CONSTANTINE VILLA (COUR DU SPHINX,
ROOM 31). The floor of this immense room, which was
originally a courtyard, is covered with a mosaic from a Roman
villa dating from the last years of antiquity (4th century). The

AFTER CHRIST
Roman art had a
prolonged period
of creativity in the
first centuries of
our era, during
which it kept up its
tradition of
portraiture –
witness the busts
of *Juba I* (left)
the Numidian
king who allied
himself with
Pompey against
Caesar in the 1st
century BC, and of
Hadrian in the 2nd
century (above).
Above left, *Portrait
of a Young Prince*, a
2nd-century marble
sculpture found at
Annaba in Algeria.

SACRIFICIAL ANIMALS
The relief below
shows a sacrifice
to Mars.

▲ Roman antiquities

PAINTING IN MOSAIC
The great Roman mosaics are frequently paintings transposed into this form. Above, a fresco from Pompeii (1st century AD); below, a mosaic from Antioch of the *Judgement of Paris* (2nd century AD). At the top of the page, detail from the border of the *Phoenix* mosaic (5th century AD).

Achilles and King Lycomedes, sarcophagus relief, (3rd century AD, above right).

villa was situated at Daphne close to Antioch, a city famed for its attractive gardens and springs. The decoration features the four seasons (in the corners) and hunting scenes (in the large trapezoidal panels). On the walls, the *Frieze of the Temple of Artemis Leucophryena* from Magnesia dates from the early 2nd century. Likewise, spectacular fragments from the

Temple of Didymian Apollo give a clear indication of the proportions of the columns. From here, turn left.
SARCOPHAGI (GALERIE DARU, ROOM B). These works from Roman workshops (at the beginning of the 2nd century, burial supplanted cremation in Rome) carry fine mythological friezes. At first there was no specific choice of subject (*Apollo and Marsyas, The Nine Muses*); later themes touched on

bereavement (*Phaedra and Hippolyte, Achilles and Penthesilea*). There are also illustrations of mortals saved by the gods, as in *Ariana and Dionysos, Selene and Endymion*.
In the **SALLE DU MANÈGE (ROOM A)** are pieces from the Borghese and Albani collections: a wild boar, a lion, alabaster basins, statues in which the bust alone is antique, and an *Old Fisherman* (also called *Dying Seneca*), a Roman copy. From the Daru vestibule, containing Piranesi's *Candelabra*, you can return to the Pyramid by the escalators, or continue through the rooms devoted to Italian sculpture ▲ *194*.

Sculpture

▲ French sculpture
The Middle Ages

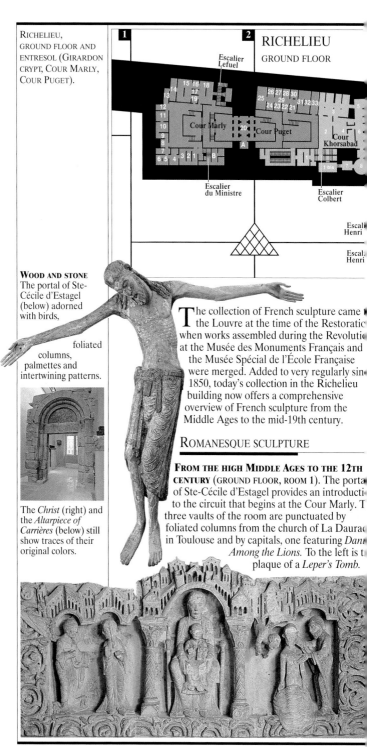

RICHELIEU, GROUND FLOOR AND ENTRESOL (GIRARDON CRYPT, COUR MARLY, COUR PUGET).

RICHELIEU
GROUND FLOOR

Escalier Lefuel

Cour Marly

Cour Puget

Cour Khorsabad

Escalier du Ministre

Escalier Colbert

Escali Henri

Escal. Henri

WOOD AND STONE
The portal of Ste-Cécile d'Estagel (below) adorned with birds, foliated columns, palmettes and intertwining patterns.

The *Christ* (right) and the *Altarpiece of Carrières* (below) still show traces of their original colors.

The collection of French sculpture came the Louvre at the time of the Restoratic when works assembled during the Revolutic at the Musée des Monuments Français and the Musée Spécial de l'École Française were merged. Added to very regularly sin 1850, today's collection in the Richelieu building now offers a comprehensive overview of French sculpture from the Middle Ages to the mid-19th century.

ROMANESQUE SCULPTURE

FROM THE HIGH MIDDLE AGES TO THE 12TH CENTURY (GROUND FLOOR, ROOM 1). The porta of Ste-Cécile d'Estagel provides an introducti to the circuit that begins at the Cour Marly. T three vaults of the room are punctuated by foliated columns from the church of La Daura in Toulouse and by capitals, one featuring *Dan Among the Lions.* To the left is t plaque of a *Leper's Tomb.*

SALLE CLUNY, 12TH-CENTURY ROMANESQUE SCULPTURE (ROOM 2). The vestiges of color on the Christ figure in the *Descent from the Cross* remind us that these pieces were mostly polychrome to begin with, as is the elongated *Virgin and Child* from the Auvergne, behind glass nearby. *Saint Michael Killing the Dragon* was originally part of the tympanum of a chapel. The capitals – *Abraham's Sacrifice*, the *Combat of David and Goliath*, and scenes of grape harvesting – are placed higher up.

THE SALLE ST-DENIS, EARLY GOTHIC IN THE ÎLE-DE-FRANCE, SECOND HALF OF THE 12TH CENTURY (ROOM 3). The *Altarpiece of Carrières* is one of the oldest in France; the figures are almost completely detached from their background. The two statue-columns here, which come from Notre-Dame-de-Corbeil, apparently show *Solomon* and the *Queen of Sheba*.

GOTHIC SCULPTURE

CHARTRES, THE TRIUMPH OF GOTHIC (ROOM 4). The two principal sculptures here are *Saint Geneviève* from the church of the same name in Paris (c. 1230), and *King Childebert* from the old abbey of St-Germain-des-Prés (1240), which is more alive and natural in its gestures and in the way the clothing is handled. There is a similar elegance in the relief from the rood-screen of Chartres representing the *Angel Dictating to Saint Matthew the Evangelist*. Smiling like the angels at Reims are some wooden angels behind glass which used to perch on the colonettes around medieval altars. If you look up you will see a set of gargoyles used to channel away the rainwater from the roofs of Gothic churches and cathedrals.

SALLE MAUBUISSON, 14TH-CENTURY ALTARPIECES (ROOM 5). The altarpiece of the Ste-Chapelle illustrates four scenes from Christ's passion; the one from the Abbey of Maubuisson, commissioned by the king in about 1340) is devoted to the Eucharist. The relief of *Canon Pierre de Fayel* from the tower of the choir of Notre-Dame-de-Paris, marks a trend toward individualizing images of people and a clear break with the frozen manner of religious art.

SALLE BLANCHELANDE, THE MADONNAS (ROOM 6). The wide variety of attitudes and styles displayed in this room shows the importance of the cult of the Virgin in the Middle Ages. The largest piece, from the Sens region, is a figure from a portal; here the Virgin is seen trampling underfoot an asp with a human head and a basilisk, another mythical reptile. *The Virgin of Blanchelande* with a hint of a sway in her hips, her delighted smile responding to the child's hand caressing her cheek, was the first medieval work purchased by the Louvre (in 1850). The *Virgin of la Celle* still shows traces of its original colors and inlaid *pâte de verre*. Also exhibited in this room are several marble Madonnas, a still more precious *Virgin of the Annunciation* made of alabaster, and an effigy of a child. This lovely piece is from the tomb of a daughter of Charles IV in the Abbey of Pont-aux-Dames.

GOTHIC MASTERWORKS
Major sculptures (like *King Childebert*, above) developed alongside the more mannered *Maubuisson Altarpiece* (below) and grotesque gargoyles (above left).

The white and polychrome Madonnas in the Salle Blanchelande.

183

▲ French sculpture
From the Gothic period to the Renaissance

ETERNAL REST
The *Effigies of the De Dormans Brothers* and of *Charles IV and Jeanne d'Évreux* have open eyes anticipating resurrection.

EFFIGIES. In the half-light of this tiny ROOM 7 lies a group of effigies. The effigies of the *De Dormans Brothers* have faces of marble and bodies of ordinary stone. On the left is the *Tombstone of Jean Casse, Canon of Noyon.* Clothed in his rich priestly vestments the cleric holds a chalice in his right hand; above his head is a rendering of the Last Judgement including his patrons the two Saint Johns. On the sides are other saints and two lay figures who may have been relatives.

THE TYMPANUM WITH A HEAD OF LEAVES (ROOM 8). Here the transition from the human face to vegetation is achieved imperceptibly.

SALLE JEAN DE LIÈGE (ROOM 9). The *Tomb of the Entrails of King Charles IV and Jeanne d'Évreux* (1372) is one of several separate tombs containing body, heart and intestines, which were customary at the time for important people. The statue of Charles V and his wife Jeanne de Bourbon (c. 1365–80) probably framed the east gate of the Louvre ● *34*; Charles V was one of the first kings to have himself portrayed by his own sculptor. The diminutive *Angel with Cruet*, *Saint Michael Killing the Dragon* and, above all the *Virgin and Child* are representative of the International Gothic style of the early 15th century.

THE PORTRAITIST'S ART
The face of *Jeanne de Bourbon* (above), Queen of France and wife of Charles V, is a delicate masterpiece.

ROOM 10 is arranged around the spectacular *Tomb of Philippe Pot* (made in 1480 during the subject's lifetime). Philippe Pot was the

FUNERAL CORTÈGE
The eight mourners of the *Tomb of Philippe Pot* (right and above) are a life-size transposition of the statuettes which were a feature of earlier tombs.

...rand marshall of the Duke of Burgundy
...ntil his death in 1493. His monument is
...xtraordinarily daring in conception. The
...om displays other notable pieces of
...urgundian art such as the *Altarpiece of Nolay* and the *Virgins*
f Plombières and Dijon and great funerary art like the *Effigy*
f Anne of Burgundy by Guillaume Veluton. The coiffure and
...naments give an idea of mid 15th-century costume.

*Saint George Fighting
the Dragon* by Michel
Colombe.

THE EARLY RENAISSANCE IN FRANCE

...ALLE MICHEL COLOMBE (ROOM 11). In the Loire Valley
...here Fouquet's art blossomed ▲ *215,* forms grew softer
...hile remaining sculptural; witness the statue of *Saint John*
n Calvary, in the rapt attitude of a figure at the foot of the
...oss. The group in the *Education of the Children* shows the
...alian influence spreading into France. Between the candid
...mplicity of the *Virgin of Olivet,* and that of Ecouen which is
...ore elegant, the contrast is clear. Michel Colombe, the great
...culptor of the turn of the 15th century executed a marble
...ltarpiece of *Saint George Fighting the Dragon* between 1504
...nd 1509 for the first great Renaissance building in France,
...e Château de Gaillon. Also in this room are several tombs,
...mong them that of Renée d'Orléans Longueville, who is
...tended by the Virgin, saints and heraldic unicorns.

...HE CHAPEL OF PHILIPPE DE COMMYNES, councillor and
...iplomatic agent of Louis XII, was built for the Couvent des
...rands-Augustins in Paris. Dismantled during the Revolution
...is evoked in diminutive ROOM 12; on the left, painted stone
...nages of the dead man and his wife adorn a sarcophagus;
...nderneath is stretched the *Effigy of Jeanne de Penthièvre,*
...eir daughter. The decoration of the chapel is a blend of
...religious themes (Samson, the Tree of Jesse, the
symbols of the Evangelists) and profane ones,
such as Orpheus with mythological monsters.

OBSESSION WITH DEATH is the theme of the
Dead Saint Innocent (ROOM 13).
Behind glass is a
*Christ in His Crown of
Thorns,* and an
Entombment, episodes
from the Passion which were
common features of churches
allowing the faithful to see
Christ's agony. The funerary
high-relief of *Jeanne de
Bourbon* offers the appalling
image of worms infesting a
semi-decomposed corpse.
The blackened alabaster
statue known as the *Dead
Saint Innocent* shows an
unreal-looking skeleton
clothed in tatters of flesh. The
*Altarpiece of the Resurrection of
Christ* shows the Nordic ▲ *196*
and Italian influence on
sculpture in the Champagne
region in the 16th century.

IMAGES OF DEATH
*Jeanne de Bourbon,
Comtesse d'Auvergne*
(above); the *Dead
Saint Innocent*
(below), which until
1786 stood in the
Cimetière des
Innocents in Paris.

THE FRENCH RENAISSANCE

Goujon introduces Mannerist art (ROOM 14). His style was
one of great fluidity, as we can see not only from the reliefs
he executed for the Fontaine des Innocents (1549), but also
in the draperies of his five reliefs for the rood-screen of
St-Germain-l'Auxerrois ▲ 310. Pierre Bontemps, an artist
trained by Primaticcio at Fontainebleau specialized in
funerary art; his *Charles de Maigny*, the captain of the Guard
at the Porte du Roi protects his sovereign from beyond the
tomb. Sculptors of the period liked to represent their dead
subjects in everyday poses a bronze attributed to Rosso of
Albert Pius of Savoy, Comte de Carpi shows him leaning on
one elbow leafing through a book. On his effigy executed by
Bontemps, the king's Chamberlain Jean d'Humières is also
seen leaning on one elbow sleeping. The same insistence on
sleep appears in the effigy of *André Blondel de Rocquencourt*
who holds a poppy bouquet (attributed to Ponce Jacquiot).
GERMAIN PILON (ROOM 15A) begins with careful observation
of reality and reinterprets it graphically and bitterly. On his
Tomb of Valentine Balviani, he contrasts two effigies of his
subject; in one she is alive, elegantly dressed and sculpted in
the round, and in the other she is dead, emaciated and
rendered in bas-relief. Pilon's *Resurrection of Christ* was
sculpted for the Rotonde des Valois, a chapel built by
Catherine de' Medici at St-Denis for Henri II and his
descendants. Here the utterly bereft *Virgin of the Sorrows*
expresses in her face all the anguish of the Passion.
BARTHÉLEMY PRIEUR (ROOM 15B). The simplicity of line is
classically elegant in the *Monument for the Heart of Anne
de Montmorency* and in the effigies of Montmorency and
his wife. Prieur's contemporaries were not all as
austere: the female nude was becoming a major theme.
Diane the Huntress of Anet (1558–9 anon.) which is
the oldest garden sculpture remaining in France, is a
triumphant and unashamedly voluptuous figure.
Near the window is the
Thorn-puller by Ponce Jacquiot, a rare example
of small sculpture from the French Renaissance.

The coming of the Bourbon Dynasty

SALLE FRANCQUEVILLE (ROOM 16).
The monument which Marie de' Medici sought to raise on the Pont-Neuf ▲ 308 to her husband Henri IV smacks of propaganda for the monarchy. Of the original ensemble, only the *Captives* which adorned the corners of the plinth of the king's equestrian statue have survived: these were sculpted by Francqueville and cast by his son-in-law Bordoni. Also in this room are two marbles by the same artist, *Orpheus* and *David*. ROOM 17, not yet completed, will display the works of the greatest sculptor of the Renaissance in Lorraine, Ligier Richier.

THE ANGUIER AND SARAZIN BROTHERS (ROOM 18).
Fame by Pierre Biard is still powerfully Mannerist in tone. In contrast François Anguier brought back from Rome a more classical approach which is manifest in the four figures of the Virtues in his *Monument or the Hearts of the Dukes de Longueville.* This obelisk contained the hearts of Henri I who died in 1595 and Henri II who died in 1663. The *Monument for Jacques de Souvre* dissociates the dying body, naked in its shroud, from its useless breastplate. Other funerary monuments even more imposing in style occupy this room. That of the Duke and Duchess de la Vieuville expresses both the pride of the aristocracy (the figures have the ribbon of the Order of the Saint-Esprit around their necks) and Christian humility (expressed in their faces and attitudes). The same expression of radiant faith shines out of the Baroque statue of *Cardinal de Bérulle* by Jacques Sarazin.

THE MONUMENT OF PONT-AU-CHANGE
ROOM 19). This masterpiece by Simon Guillain was completed in 1647. The three statues represent Louis XIII, his wife Anne of Austria and their son Louis XIV. Formerly a statue of *Fame* crowned the Dauphin and the plinth was embellished with dolphins. Opposite stands a bust of Louis XIII by Francois Bordoni which is more realistic than respectful. Emerging in the Cour Marly you are met by *Children with a Goat* by Sarazin (1640). This group purchased in 1667 by Louis XIV and placed in the park at Marly on a Rococo pedestal, prepares the visitor for the majestic courtyard which celebrates the royal residence at Marly and the sculptures which once adorned its gardens ▲ 189.

BRONZES
Two *Captives* by Francqueville (above and top left) and a fine head of Henri IV by Mathieu Jacquet (center). One of the builders of the Louvre, Henri IV commissioned the Grande Galerie among other things ● 76.

THE "NOBLESSE DE ROBE" is very much present in the gigantic *Funerary Monument of Jacques Auguste de Thou*, president of the Parliament of Paris (below).

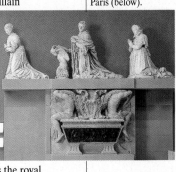

The glass roof which spans this former ministry courtyard avoids the inherent contradiction of displaying indoors those works that were made for the park of the Château de Marly. The Cour Marly is in the heart of the renewed Richelieu wing, the former ministry of Finance redesigned by the architect I.M. Pei. The most spectacular pieces here are the *Horses of Marly*: the two groups sculpted by Antoine Coysevox and Guillaume Coustou for the drinking-pond of Louis XIV's favorite château, are surrounded by marble figures.

ESCAPED HORSES
Guillaume Coustou received an order in 1739 for two groups of sculpture for the empty plinths at Marly. Out of gigantic blocks of marble he sculpted his *Horses Restrained by Grooms*.

Mercury Riding Pegasus (above) and its twin *Fame*, sculpted by Coysevox in around 1700, were transported in 1719 to the entrance of the Tuileries ▲ 281. The sculptures were replaced by casts.

THE ART OF MOVEMENT
Hippomenes (above) and *Apollo* (below) were once placed in the middle of large ornamental ponds, as the sumptuous *Album de Marly* commissioned by Louis XIV shows.

Installed during the Revolution in the Place de la Concorde, Coustou's *Horses* remained there until 1984 ▲ 281.

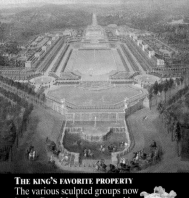

Other remarkable works by Coysevox in the Cour Marly (left) are *The Marne, Amphitrite* and *Neptune*, eroded by the salt-winds at Brest where they stood for many years; beside them *The Seine* which has been under cover since 1872 seems to be fresh from the sculptor's chisel. Much admired in the 17th century, the *Arria and Poetus* group is by Pierre Lepautre and the *Aeneas and Anchises* was even more famous. On the upper terrace Jacques Prou's *Amphitrite* combines the majesty of a classical face with Rococo curves.

THE KING'S FAVORITE PROPERTY
The various sculpted groups now in the Cour Marly once stood in the park at Marly (above) where they were centered on the king's pavilion. In the foreground, the drinking-pond and the *Horses* by Coysevox.

189

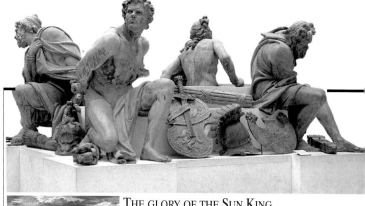

THE GLORY OF THE SUN KING

THE GIRARDON CRYPT (ENTRESOL, ROOM 20) exhibits the equestrian statue of Louis XIV, a smaller version of the monumental statue executed by Girardon for Place Louis-le-Grand (the present Place Vendôme ● 78). The king is dressed in Roman garb but wears a fashionable contemporary wig. The bust of the Prince de Condé by Coysevox is a work of great expressive force. Here also Puget's relief, the *Meeting of Alexander and Diogenes*, is enlivened by powerful Baroque undertones; despite the reference to the ancient world, the expressiveness of the attitudes and the diagonal composition somehow carry this scene.

ROYAL SQUARES
The group of sculptures in the Place de Victoires in the 17th century. Today they have been supplanted by an equestrian statue of Louis XIV by Bosio (19th century ▲ *300*). These colossal bronze

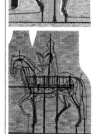

compositions involved the use of highly sophisticated techniques.

MILO AT VERSAILLES
Milo of Croton by Puget (right) was intended for the park at Versailles, the official residence of Louis XIV.

THE COUR PUGET. On the lower terrace are bronzes by the Dutch sculptor Martin van den Bogaert (who Frenchified his name to Martin Desjardins); these came from the Place des Victoires ▲ 300 where they complemented the pedestrian statue of Louis XIV (destroyed during the Revolution) and the *Chained Captives* representing the defeated nations at the Treaty of Nijmegen. On the wall at right are bronze reliefs entitled the *Precedence of France Recognized by Spain, The Crossing of the Rhine, The Conquest of Franche-Comté* and the *Peace of Nijmegen.* In contrast to this ensemble is *Hercules* by Pierre Puget.

The most famous work on the middle terrace is probably Puget's *Milo of Croton*. Its companion piece *Perseus and Andromeda* was brought to Versailles in 1685 and is the most Baroque piece in all the repertoire of French sculpture.

LOUIS THE WELL-BELOVED

Moving to the next terrace, in the Cour Puget, we pass from the reign of Louis XIV to that of Louis XV, whose favorite Madame de Pompadour had herself portrayed by Pigalle as *Friendship Offering Her Heart*. Her brother, the Marquis de Marigny, acquired *Two Children Playing with Flowers*. At the back of the courtyard above are reliefs by Clodion for the town mansion of the Princesse de Condé, *Scenes of a Childrens' Bacchanal*. At the top of the staircase is *Mercury Attaching His Heel Wings* by Bouchardon, a copy of an ancient statue.

Prince de Condé, bronze by Coysevox.

THE MARBLES OF THE ACADÉMIE
Among the reception pieces is Guillaume Coustou II's *Vulcan*, for his entry to the Academy in 1742.

THE GOLDEN AGE OF FRENCH SCULPTURE

TOMBS OF THE GREAT (GROUND FLOOR, ROOM 12). The funerary sculpture of the 18th century is represented by models for the tombs of illustrious men such as the Cardinal de Fleury, the *Mausoleum of the Comte d'Ennery* by Houdon, and the *Mausoleum of the Maréchal de Saxe* by Pigalle.

ÉTIENNE MAURICE FALCONET (ROOM 22). *Love's Threat* belonged to Madame de Pompadour ▲ 228 and the *Bather* to Madame du Barry. In the *Allegory of Music* is the score of *Aegle* by Pierre Lagarde, sung by the Marquise de Pompadour at the Théâtre des Petits-Appartements at Versailles in 1748.

BOUCHARDON (ROOM 23). This sculptor spent time in Rome and the influence of antiquity is clear. His *Love Carving a Bow from the Club of Hercules* (1750) inspired by an antique original, was judged vulgar because of its naturalism.

PIGALLE (ROOM 24). In this room is the statue of the unclothed Voltaire (1770) with its striking contrast between the inspired face and the scrawny body. Very much like this Voltaire is the bust of *Diderot as an Old Man* (1777) ▲ 229.

CLASSICAL NUDE
Pigalle's *Voltaire*, portrayed naked at the request of Diderot.

RECEPTION PIECES

ROOM 25. The Académie Royale de Peinture et de Sculpture was founded in 1648. Members had first to be accepted and then were asked to execute a reception piece on a predetermined subject. In the 18th century these pieces, mostly taken from mythology, tended to be less than half-lifesize and were usually isolated nude figures. Most are displayed here according to the manner adopted by the

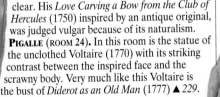

▲ French sculpture: Neoclassicism and Romanticism

Académie, whose headquarters was at the Louvre until the Revolution ● 28. The chronological succession emphasizes their stylistic evolution: the turbulence of Rococo at its apogee (*Neptune Calming the Waves* by Adam, or Slodtz's *Icarus*); the acme of feminine grace (*Leda and the Swan* by Jean Thierry): then the transition to neoclassicism in mid-century. Falconet's *Milo of Croton,* still in the Baroque mode, was coolly received in 1754 in contrast to the same piece by Dumont who was accepted in 1768. The panorama ends with pure classicism (Julien's *Dying Gladiator*). Behind glass are some studies in terracotta.

Two Americans
Benjamin Franklin (right) and *George Washington* (sculpted from life in the United States, seen here in profile); both portraits by Houdon.

The Republic
Among the rare works surviving from the Revolution is this allegory of the *Republic* by Chinard, holding the tablets of the Law. The piece illustrates one of many attempts by artists to embody the French people in one individual. They have included Hercules, the Republic and finally France herself in the person of Marianne in her Phrygian bonnet. *La Marseillaise* by Rude (right), a study for the Arc de Triomphe.

IN HONOR OF GREAT MEN AND THE PEOPLE

CAFFIERI (ROOM 26). Many of Caffieri's busts (done between 1770 and 1790) are displayed here, among them the jovial *Canon Alexandre-Gui Pingré.*

PAJOU (ROOM 27). To the left is a fine bust of *Madame du Barry,* Louis XV's mistress. Here also is his *Psyche Abandoned,* whose plaster cast caused a scandal at the 1785 Salon on account of its total nudity and dramatic facial expression. Behind glass is a small terracotta piece entitled *Ariana Abandoned*, a later variant on the theme.

HOUDON (ROOM 28).
A consummate portraitist Houdon earned a substantial income from his busts of the famous. He did likenesses of nearly every eminent man of his time including Diderot, George Washington, Benjamin Franklin, Buffon, Rousseau and Voltaire. In a display case are intimate works such as the children of the architect Brongniart, and the artist's own daughters. Houdon was also a fine monumental sculptor: see his *Mausoleum of the Comte d'Ennery* (ROOM 21) and *Diana the Huntress* (ROOM 29).

GALERIE DES GRANDS HOMMES (ROOM 29). In the center of the room are ten of the twenty-eight statues of great men commissioned in 1776 by the Comte d'Angiviller for the Grande Galerie which later became a museum ● 29.

CLODION'S work is exhibited in ROOM 20, notably the major reliefs in fine stone which once adorned the bathroom of the Baron de Besenval and some terracotta pieces, among them the *Comtesse d'Orsay,* who with her dying breath shows her husband the son she has borne him. *Egyptian woman at the Naos* recalls the late 18th-century vogue for ancient Egypt.

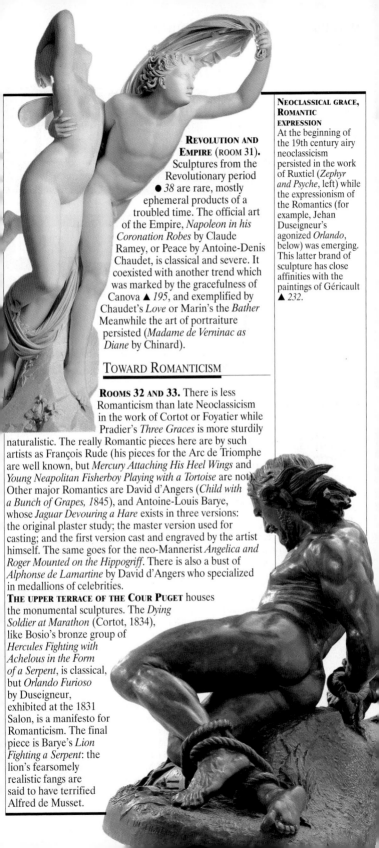

REVOLUTION AND EMPIRE (ROOM 31). Sculptures from the Revolutionary period ● *38* are rare, mostly ephemeral products of a troubled time. The official art of the Empire, *Napoleon in his Coronation Robes* by Claude Ramey, or Peace by Antoine-Denis Chaudet, is classical and severe. It coexisted with another trend which was marked by the gracefulness of Canova ▲ *195*, and exemplified by Chaudet's *Love* or Marin's the *Bather* Meanwhile the art of portraiture persisted (*Madame de Verninac as Diane* by Chinard).

TOWARD ROMANTICISM

ROOMS 32 AND 33. There is less Romanticism than late Neoclassicism in the work of Cortot or Foyatier while Pradier's *Three Graces* is more sturdily naturalistic. The really Romantic pieces here are by such artists as François Rude (his pieces for the Arc de Triomphe are well known, but *Mercury Attaching His Heel Wings* and *Young Neapolitan Fisherboy Playing with a Tortoise* are not). Other major Romantics are David d'Angers (*Child with a Bunch of Grapes, 1845*), and Antoine-Louis Barye, whose *Jaguar Devouring a Hare* exists in three versions: the original plaster study; the master version used for casting; and the first version cast and engraved by the artist himself. The same goes for the neo-Mannerist *Angelica and Roger Mounted on the Hippogriff*. There is also a bust of *Alphonse de Lamartine* by David d'Angers who specialized in medallions of celebrities.

THE UPPER TERRACE OF THE COUR PUGET houses the monumental sculptures. The *Dying Soldier at Marathon* (Cortot, 1834), like Bosio's bronze group of *Hercules Fighting with Achelous in the Form of a Serpent*, is classical, but *Orlando Furioso* by Duseigneur, exhibited at the 1831 Salon, is a manifesto for Romanticism. The final piece is Barye's *Lion Fighting a Serpent*: the lion's fearsomely realistic fangs are said to have terrified Alfred de Musset.

NEOCLASSICAL GRACE, ROMANTIC EXPRESSION
At the beginning of the 19th century airy neoclassicism persisted in the work of Ruxtiel (*Zephyr and Psyche*, left) while the expressionism of the Romantics (for example, Jehan Duseigneur's agonized *Orlando*, below) was emerging. This latter brand of sculpture has close affinities with the paintings of Géricault ▲ *232*.

▲ Italian and Spanish sculpture

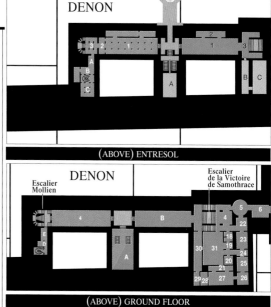

(ABOVE) ENTRESOL

(ABOVE) GROUND FLOOR

IN SEARCH OF ANTIQUITY
The marble *Head of an Empress* (Ariana?), the first piece of Italian sculpture on this circuit comes from Rome and dates from the early 6th century.

TUSCANY
Jacopo della Quercia (Siena, 1374–1438), a seated *Virgin and Child* (below right) and Donatello (Florence 1386–1466) *Virgin and Child* (below) were the most celebrated Tuscan sculptors of the Quattrocento.

The Louvre's collections of sculpture from other countries are displayed in the Denon building: in the Galerie Mollien, in the former vaulted stables of Napoleon III, and (in the case of the Northern schools) in the rooms adjoining. Though the collections are less complete than those of French sculpture, they nevertheless offer a wide variety of pieces ranging from the high Middle Ages to neoclassicism.

THE GALERIE DONATELLO (ENTRESOL, ROOM 1) contains Italian sculpture from the Byzantine era to the 15th century. The first bay is reserved for the Byzantine period, with among other things, a very fine *Head of an Empress*. The next three bays are filled with Roman and Gothic works, notably a 13th-century Umbrian *Descent from the Cross* and a *Virgin of the Annunciation* by Nino Pisano. The beginnings of the Renaissance are represented by Lucca della Robbia and the Sienese sculptor Jacopo della Quercia (look for his large polychrome wooden statue of a seated *Virgin and Child*). At the center of the gallery are works by Donatello and his school, in particular a *Virgin and Child* in gilded and painted terracotta: the background drapery which emphasizes the long graceful neck of the Virgin combines with the curves of the seat in the foreground to give this piece a remarkable illusion of depth. Certain other late Renaissance Italian artists are represented here including Mino da Fiesole (several Madonnas, a bust of the humanist *Dietisalvi Neroni* in antique dress, and a fragment of the tomb of Paul II);

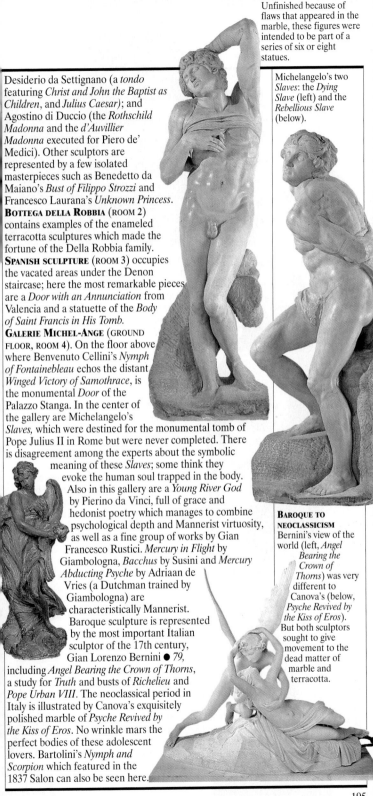

Desiderio da Settignano (a *tondo* featuring *Christ and John the Baptist as Children*, and *Julius Caesar*); and Agostino di Duccio (the *Rothschild Madonna* and the *d'Auvillier Madonna* executed for Piero de' Medici). Other sculptors are represented by a few isolated masterpieces such as Benedetto da Maiano's *Bust of Filippo Strozzi* and Francesco Laurana's *Unknown Princess*.

BOTTEGA DELLA ROBBIA (ROOM 2) contains examples of the enameled terracotta sculptures which made the fortune of the Della Robbia family.

SPANISH SCULPTURE (ROOM 3) occupies the vacated areas under the Denon staircase; here the most remarkable pieces are a *Door with an Annunciation* from Valencia and a statuette of the *Body of Saint Francis in His Tomb*.

GALERIE MICHEL-ANGE (GROUND FLOOR, ROOM 4). On the floor above where Benvenuto Cellini's *Nymph of Fontainebleau* echos the distant *Winged Victory of Samothrace*, is the monumental *Door* of the Palazzo Stanga. In the center of the gallery are Michelangelo's *Slaves,* which were destined for the monumental tomb of Pope Julius II in Rome but were never completed. There is disagreement among the experts about the symbolic meaning of these *Slaves*; some think they evoke the human soul trapped in the body. Also in this gallery are a *Young River God* by Pierino da Vinci, full of grace and hedonist poetry which manages to combine psychological depth and Mannerist virtuosity, as well as a fine group of works by Gian Francesco Rustici. *Mercury in Flight* by Giambologna, *Bacchus* by Susini and *Mercury Abducting Psyche* by Adriaan de Vries (a Dutchman trained by Giambologna) are characteristically Mannerist. Baroque sculpture is represented by the most important Italian sculptor of the 17th century, Gian Lorenzo Bernini ● 79, including *Angel Bearing the Crown of Thorns*, a study for *Truth* and busts of *Richelieu* and *Pope Urban VIII*. The neoclassical period in Italy is illustrated by Canova's exquisitely polished marble of *Psyche Revived by the Kiss of Eros*. No wrinkle mars the perfect bodies of these adolescent lovers. Bartolini's *Nymph and Scorpion* which featured in the 1837 Salon can also be seen here.

Michelangelo's two *Slaves*: the *Dying Slave* (left) and the *Rebellious Slave* (below).

BAROQUE TO NEOCLASSICISM
Bernini's view of the world (left, *Angel Bearing the Crown of Thorns*) was very different to Canova's (below, *Psyche Revived by the Kiss of Eros*). But both sculptors sought to give movement to the dead matter of marble and terracotta.

▲ Northern European sculpture

The *Altarpiece of the Passion* from the church at Coligny (right). In its center is the *Crucifixion* with the *Bearing of the Cross* on the left and the *Descent from the Cross* on the right. In the lower register are the *Nativity* and the *Adoration of the Magi*. An alabaster bust of Otteimrich, Count and Elector Palatine (1502–59) attributed to Dietrich Schro (above) is here also.

REPENTANCE Gregor Erhart's *Saint Mary Magdalen* (right) is portrayed nude with long fair hair. At far right is *Venus Holding an Apple* by Thorvaldsen.

The Louvre's collection of northern European sculpture has a number of gaps, but nevertheless the museum possesses many masterpieces in the field. Northern European sculpture occupies a suite of five rooms in the Denon building on two different levels.

ENGLAND (ENTRESOL, ROOM A) is represented by 15th-century alabaster reliefs.

THE SALLE DES BELLES MADONES (ROOM B) is devoted to the International Gothic style which dominated all of Europe around 1400. It contains a number of graceful, supple Madonnas and in particular a *Virgin of Piety* in alabaster by the pupils of the master altarpiece maker of Rimini.

LATE GOTHIC (ROOM C) contains sculptures of the late 15th and early 16th centuries from the Netherlands and the Holy Roman Empire. The *Virgin and Child* of Issenheim is a major example of the new style in German sculpture, with its tumultous drapery carved from limewood (a material which can be worked to a high standard of finesse). Tilman Riemenschneider's *Virgin of the Annunciation* illustrates the delicate lyrical art of this great master from Würzburg. But the unquestioned masterpiece of the German section is *Saint Mary Magdalen* by Gregor Erhart. Sculpture from the Low Countries is represented by the Antwerp altarpiece from Coligny, statuettes and reliefs from Malines, Brussels and Utrecht, and the monumental Nivelles *Calvary*.

ROOM D (GROUND FLOOR) is accessible by way of the former Grand Écuyer staircase and contains sculptures belonging to the northern European Baroque and Rococo schools of the 17th and 18th centuries.

THE GALERIE THORVALDSEN (ROOM E) completes this tour with works by the Swedish sculptor Johan Tobias Sergel and the Dane Bertel Thorvaldsen, characteristically neoclassical in inspiration.

Decorative arts

▲ Decorative arts

RICHELIEU AND SULLY

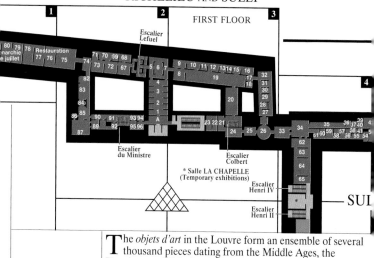

FIRST FLOOR

Escalier Lefuel

Escalier du Ministre

Escalier Colbert

* Salle LA CHAPELLE
(Temporary exhibitions)

Escalier Henri IV

Escalier Henri II

SUL

Below, pendant *"Bulle"* of Empress Maria.

Alpais Ciborium (Limoges, c.1200), gilt brass, chiseled and engraved, precious stones (right).

Serpentine Paten (below). Gold, precious stones and 9th-century cloisonné motifs; 1st-century saucer.

The *objets d'art* in the Louvre form an ensemble of several thousand pieces dating from the Middle Ages, the Renaissance (Richelieu building) and the 17th to 19th centuries (Sully and Richelieu buildings). They come from many sources: the treasury of the Abbey of St-Denis, bronzes from Louis XIV, the royal furniture collection, collections bequeathed by amateurs or purchased by the state, and bequests in lieu of death duty. The furnishings in the last rooms are reminiscent of the Tuileries Palace ▲ 276.

TREASURES OF THE MIDDLE AGES

SALLE CHARLEMAGNE, THE HIGH MIDDLE AGES.
ROOM 1 between the Cour Marly and the Cour Puget, introduces the high Middle Ages – from the last years of the Roman Empire (porphyry columns surmounted by the bust of an emperor) and the beginnings of Christian art (the *"Bulle"* of the Empress Maria, made in about AD 400, found in Rome in 1544). The *Chest Decorated with Rosettes*, made in Constantinople in the 10th century, shows the legacy of antiquity. The same richness is visible in several psalter-bindings and in the *Jewels of Queen Aregonde*, wife of Clothair. Ivory was much prized in Constantinople: examples are the *Barberini Ivory* (6th century) in honor of Justinian, and the *Harbaville Triptych* (10th century). The Carolingian emperors of the 8th and 9th centuries were also partial to ivory; in their time bindings were made of this material for the *Dagulf Psaltery* and the plaque known as the *Earthly Paradise*, in which imaginary animals are pictured with more familiar ones. The bronze *Equestrian Statuette of Charlemagne* was made in the reign of his son Charles the Bald, whose features it may have borrowed (the horse is a reused piece made in antiquity). This room also exhibits Western pieces

Detail from the *Barberini Ivory* (left) of Christ blessing Justinian.

(the *Serpentine Paten*), Byzantine objects like the *Reliquary of the Stone of the Holy Sepulchre*, mosaic-decorated pieces (*Icon of the Transfiguration*) and painted icons.

SALLE SUGER, 10TH–12TH CENTURY. ROOM 2 bears the name of the abbot who founded St-Denis, a building that heralded the birth of Gothic architecture. It contains fine ivories such as *Christ with a Child* and the *Feeding of the Five Thousand* (c. 968), along with ivory hunting horns, gaming counters, and other pieces of Limoges enamelwork. Gold items include a binding-case representing the *Crucifixion* with precious stones and gilded silver as in the *Arm-Reliquary of Charlemagne*. Gilded silver is shown combined with rock crystal, as in the *Vase of Eleanore*, or otherwise in the forms of a chalice and ewer which are typical of Fatimid art in the 10th and 11th centuries. There is also a masterpiece in porphyry, the famous *Suger's Eagle*, one of the abbot's many treasures. The hilt of the *Sword of Charlemagne* known as *La Joyeuse* is gold. Copper is combined with champlevé enamel on the *"Vermiculated Background" Reliquary*, and on the reliquary celebrating the *Assassination and Burial of Thomas à Becket*, the archbishop who was killed in 1170. However the high point of Limoges enamelwork in the Gothic style is the *Alpais Ciborium*. Alpais is one of the few artists of that period whose name has come down to us. The Salle Suger contains not only French pieces such as the *Apostle* carved from a walrus tusk, but also Italian (a superb plaque of *Cain and Abel*), Spanish (two magnificent ivory *Crosses*) and above all German pieces (*Reliquary of Saint Henry*, a memorial to the Emperor Henry II who was canonized in 1146). The final decades of the 12th century saw the blossoming of a new style, seen in the *Double Cross* made for Abbot Hugo, and a Limoges *Saint Matthew*.

SALLE JEANNE D'ÉVREUX, THE STYLE OF 1200 (ROOM 3). This room holds a number of important Limoges pieces, notably the *Reliquary of Saint Francis of Assisi* and the *Casket of Saint Louis*. In the reign of Louis IX the quality of ivory work improved considerably: the *Virgin and Child of Ste-Chapelle* is skillfully crafted around the naturally curving elephant's tusk. The groups depicting the *Descent from the Cross* and the *Coronation of the Virgin*, left, whose polychrome features lend emphasis to its perfect craftsmanship, represent the summit of the art of Parisian ivory carvers. This Parisian style spread throughout northern France (for example, the *Polyptych of Floreffe* probably came from the Ile-de-France). The metal *Arm Reliquary of Saint Luke* is made in the shape of the evangelist's arm and that of the *Finger of Saint Lawrence* depicts the saint on the gridiron of his martyrdom.

RICHNESS AND VARIETY OF MATERIALS Rock crystal and gilded silver for the *Arm reliquary of Saint Luke* (below left), porphyry and silver gilt for *Suger's Eagle* (above), ivory heightened with gold for the 13th-century Parisian *Descent from the Cross* (below).

199

▲ Decorative arts

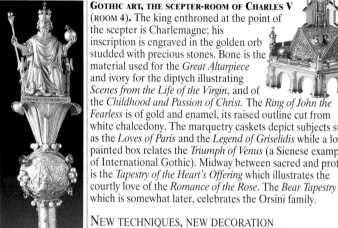

Salt-cellar which belonged to Louis XIV (right) and two *Angel Reliquaries*, which belonged to Anne of Brittany (center).

GOTHIC ART, THE SCEPTER-ROOM OF CHARLES V
(ROOM 4). The king enthroned at the point of the scepter is Charlemagne; his inscription is engraved in the golden orb studded with precious stones. Bone is the material used for the *Great Altarpiece* and ivory for the diptych illustrating *Scenes from the Life of the Virgin*, and of the *Childhood and Passion of Christ*. The *Ring of John the Fearless* is of gold and enamel, its raised outline cut from white chalcedony. The marquetry caskets depict subjects such as the *Loves of Paris* and the *Legend of Griselidis* while a lovely painted box relates the *Triumph of Venus* (a Sienese example of International Gothic). Midway between sacred and profane is the *Tapestry of the Heart's Offering* which illustrates the courtly love of the *Romance of the Rose*. The *Bear Tapestry* which is somewhat later, celebrates the Orsini family.

NEW TECHNIQUES, NEW DECORATION

Scepter of Charles V.

THE SALLE ANNE DE BRETAGNE (ROOM 6) between Valencia corridor (ROOM 5, left, Spanish ceramics) and the Faenza corridor (ROOM 7, right, Italian ceramics and metalwork) displays 14th and 15th century treasures against a backdrop of Flemish tapestries. These include a pair of *Angel Reliquaries*; a gold and agate *Salt-cellar*; and the *Self-portrait of Jean Fouquet* the first great name in French painting. In this piece, the earliest known self-portrait by a Frenchman, the copper support was first covered with black enamel, then with grey-brown enamel before being hatched with gold. The *Reliquary of the Flagellation* with its plinth in blue enamel covered with gilded embossed silver, has a vase of rock crystal and the same materials predominate in the *Chessboard of Saint Louis*.

Self-portrait by Jean Fouquet (above) and Reliquary of the Flagellation (below).

THE STORY OF SAINT ANATOLIUS (ROOM 8) is illustrated in three Bruges tapestries, which were part of a series ordered for the Cathedral of Salins in the Jura in homage to its patron saint.

MILLEFLEURS TAPESTRIES are displayed in ROOM 9 (turn left). The showcases contain pieces of German Gothic gold and silverwork along with the *Reliquary of the Hand of Saint Martha* by Leon of Cologne.

IN ROOM 10 are tapestries which once belonged to Thomas Bohier, Chamberlain

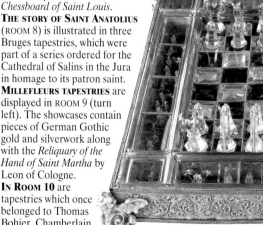

of Charles VIII who began building the Château de Chenonceaux in 1515.

SALLE LOUIS XII, PAINTED ENAMEL ON COPPER (ROOM 11). This technique was current at Limoges in the last years of the 15th century. The *Coronation of the Virgin* by the same master who did the triptych of Louis XII, is a fine example.

THE ITALIAN RENAISSANCE

THE ART OF BRONZEWORK (ROOMS 12 to 14). Donatello, though not himself a bronze-worker created a number of works for casting in that material, notably a *Crucifixion* exhibited in ROOM 12 beside pieces by his pupil Bartolomeo Bellano (*Saint Jerome and the Lion*). From the Padua studio of Andrea Briosco known as Riccio, came a number of small bronzes inspired by mythology and fables of antiquity, among them *Arion* (by the master himself), who is depicted enchanting the dolphins with the music of his lyre. One of Riccio's major works displayed in ROOM 13 is the tomb of Marcantonio della Torre (about 1511) who was a professor of medicine at the University of Padua: this explains the themes of some of the bas-reliefs. The medallions in ROOM 14 served as memorials to Italy's great families – d'Este, Gonzaga, Malatesta. Pisanello (c. 1380–1455) was the first to distinguish himself in this branch of decorative art.

THE SALLE DU MAÎTRE DE L'"ÉNÉIDE" (ROOM 15) presents an array of magnificent French enamels from the first half of the 16th century. The eleven *Aeneid Plaques* were made in about 1530.

ROOM 16, THE REIGN OF FRANÇOIS I (see on the door to the left, the king's salamander emblem). The *Tapestry of Saint Mammès* is a Parisian piece dating from 1544, after Jean Cousin. The furniture, dressers and caskets blend Gothic tradition and ornament with the Italian taste for arabesques and vegetable motifs.

GLASSWORK. After this cross the Passage des Nielles (ROOM 17) to visit the diminutive ROOM 18. Charles Sauvageot bequeathed to the Louvre his collection of Venetian and German glass.

THE ART OF THE EVERYDAY
A detail from a 16th-century French tapestry (above) *Fruit Pickers*. A *Feeding bottle* (left) made at Rheims c. 1500 is very much an everyday object. *Saint Jerome and the Lion* by Bellano shows how small sculptures can still have monumental overtones.

CRYSTAL
The *Chessboard of Saint Louis* (center, below) is in rock crystal, a material which was surpassed from the 15th century onward by Venetian glass (below, *Venetian Gourd* from the 16th century).

The *Curse of Rome*, a majolica dish by Xanto Avelli (Urbino, 1532).

Baroque pearl mounted as a dragon's breast (Spain, 16th century).

APOGEE OF PAINTED ENAMEL Objects in painted enamel became very fashionable in the 16th century. *Moses and Jethro*, a dish painted by Pierre Reymond in grisaille (above).

THE CENTURY OF CHARLES V

THE GALERIE DES CHASSES DE MAXIMILIEN (ROOM 19) is devoted to tapestries illustrating the twelve months of the year with twelve hunting scenes from the forest of Soignes near Brussels, the capital of Flanders and of the art of tapestry. At the center of the room is a display of majolica – faience from Italy or in the Italian taste – dating from the 16th century. *Istoriato,* majolica illustrating themes from history, originated in Faenza and Urbino; it is represented here by a dish from the *Service of Isabella d'Este* (1525) signed by Nicola d'Urbino. More ornamental is the style of Castel Durante, the rival of Urbino where grotesques, flowers, fruits and landscapes are all mixed into the equation. To this school was attached that of the portrait of the *Belle Donne* (Deruta), which produced plates of a yellowish, coppery sheen, as distinct from the dark blood-red of Gubbio.

THE EIGHT TAPESTRIES OF THE GALERIE DE SCIPION (ROOM 20) were woven in the late 17th century by the Gobelins factory, commissioned by Louis XIV to reproduce a series of 16th-century tapestries which were destroyed during the Revolution. They were inspired by Livy's history of the Second Punic War and the exploits of Scipio Africanus. Also in this room are some pieces of Limoges enameled porcelain painted in grisaille by Pierre Reymond (1513–84), a service by Pierre Courteys (who died c. 1581) and work by the Penicaud family (also shown in ROOM 15).

ENAMELS AND CERAMICS (ROOM 21). The enamel portraits executed by Leonard Limosin of Limoges who invented this genre, are amazingly vivid (to achieve the maximum finesse, Limosin applied his enamel with a thin brush). At the center are 13 pieces of rare St-Porchaire pottery, the largest collection of its kind in the world. Everything about these first Parisian experiments in French porcelain is original: the white, sonorous clay, the technique used for the decoration and even the shapes.

THE SALLE HENRI II (ROOM 22) contains various enamels (panels of altar-screens with portraits of François I and Henri II), tapestries and stained glass.

SALLE PAUL GARNIER, CLOCKS (ROOM 23). The watch was invented in the second half of the 15th century and very soon jewelers and clockmakers became obsessed with it. Miniaturized to an extreme degree the earliest watches were meticulously ornamented combinations of precious metals, enamel and rock crystal and were worn like jewelry around the neck or waist. The *Spherical Watch* by

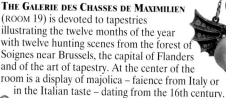

Anne de Montmorency, Constable of France by Leonard Limosin (1556).

Spherical Watch by Jacques de la Garde (1551, right). *Vermeil Basin with Reptiles, Frogs and Crayfish* (c. 1550), below.

THE IMPERIAL HUNT

March (top) is the first hanging in the series titled *Maximilian's Hunt* (at the time March was officially the first month of the year in Flanders). The city in the background is Brussels with the ducal palace on the left and the towers of the church of Ste-Gudule on the right.

The rider in red is Charles V. *December* (center and bottom, with detail and preparatory sketch by Bernard van Orley) shows a boar-hunting scene and the confrontation between the rider and the beast. A medallion at the top of each tapestry gives the signs of the zodiac.

A necklace decorated with scenes from the *Passion* (left) and a pendant of the *Annunciation* (below), are two treasures from the Rothschild collection.

Jacques de la Garde (1551) is the oldest in the Louvre. Several are displayed open, showing mechanisms of astonishing complexity. Some of the German and French table clocks are as delicate as the watches, while the Renaissance jewelry exhibited in the same room gives an idea of the sheer luxury of contemporary courts: crosses and enameled gold pendants with inlaid baroque pearls and precious stones. In one case there is a collection of *Busts of the Twelve Caesars* cut from gemstones.

SALLE CHARLES QUINT (ROOM 24). The tapestries here celebrate Hercules, an omnipresent character in the 16th and 17th centuries. A number of treasures demonstrate the wealth of the Renaissance Habsburg Empire (Flanders, Spain and Germany), most of which derived from the wealth of the Americas: the *Sword and Dagger of the Grand Master of the Order of Malta*, with golden knotwork; *Vermeil Basin with Reptiles, Frogs and Crayfish* by Wenzel Jamnitzer; *Ewer and Basin of Charles V* in enameled vermeil; and finally Hercules again, with the *Centaur Abducting Deianira* in vermeil and silver.

TOWARD CLASSICISM

ADOLPHE DE ROTHSCHILD bequeathed his collection of religious gold and silverwork to the Louvre (ROOM 25) in 1900 along with funds to display it. These funds made it possible to acquire and install a 16th-century coffered Venetian ceiling. Particularly admirable here is a pendant representing the *Annunciation* and a necklace made up of cartouches of the *Passion of Christ*; there is also an archbishop's crozier illustrating the *Annunciation to the Shepherds*. Behind glass are bronzes combining religious motifs (*St Francis of Assisi*) and pagan figures such as *Atlanta* or *Hercules*. The porcelains come from Florence. For centuries porcelain was imported from China but in 1575 Duke Francesco de' Medici established a factory in Florence. All the pieces were decorated in blue, to rival oriental porcelain.

THE BRONZES OF THE ROTONDE JEAN BOULOGNE (ROOM 26) were cast in Florence for the Medici family. The most famous is probably *Nessus and Deianira*. *Morgante* the celebrated dwarf-jester of the Florentine court is represented here as Bacchus astride a barrel.

Monkey from the collection
of small bronzes
by Giambologna
(Jean Boulogne).

SALLE HENRI III (ROOM 27; turn left past the corridor) displays the lavishness of the order of the St-Esprit (founded in 1578 by Henri III), the most important of France's royal Orders. A ciborium, some cruets, a holy water pail and various candlesticks are among the exhibits; all are made with rock crystal, gilded metal and precious stones. In the same room are the helmet and shield of Charles IX, the latter with the monogram K (Karolus) around the rim alternating with medallions in cloisonné enamel.

THE ORDER OF THE ST-ESPRIT

(ROOM 28). In an evocation of the Order's chapel, this room exhibits a collection of its *mantles* made of black velvet embroidered with gold flames. In the corridor to the right is a tapestry of the *Battle of Jarnac* which celebrates a victory of Henri III over the Protestant forces. **ROOM 29** displays typical furniture from the second half of the 16th century including a pair of armchairs and an English tapestry from Mortlake (c. 1630).

BERNARD PALISSY, MASTER OF FRENCH FAIENCE (ROOM 20). Here are displayed Palissy's dishes decorated with reptiles, shells and plants cast from life – fabulous schemes which refer to one of the great literary successes of the 16th century, Francesco Colonna's *Hypnerotomachia* (Venice, 1499). Palissy was inspired by this novel to build a grotto in the gardens of Catherine de' Medici's Tuileries, which he peopled with green creatures ● 75. Alongside these striking works are others celebrating the *Nymph of Fontainebleau,* the *Judgement of Paris* and the *Triumph of Galatea*. Among the figurines from the workshops of Avon is an *Equestrian Statue of Louis XIII*.

THE SALLE HENRI IV (ROOM 31), contains in addition to some beautiful choir-stalls, a wardrobe illustrating the *Seasons* and a casket with the arms of Marie de' Medici. There are also some bronzes, among them *Girl Drawing out a Thorn* and the *Milkmaid*, attributed to Bathélemy Prieur who also did a likeness of *Henri IV as Jupiter.*

THE SALLE D'EFFIAT (ROOM 32). Louis XIII commissioned the tapestry of *Moses in the Bullrushes* from Simon Vouet. The ebony cabinet displayed with it has bas-reliefs with religious, mythological and historical themes. The bed and the armchairs of the Château d'Effiat (in the Puy-de-Dôme) are typical of the mid-17th century.

THE SALLE MAZARIN (ROOM 33) on the far side of the rotunda, contains the *Deborah Tapestry*, painted on silk with gold and silver embroidery, which once belonged to Cardinal Mazarin. In the middle is a *Casket*, a masterpiece of the French goldsmith's craft. From here, continue through the Sully building, back into the Richelieu wing for a tour of the furniture and decorative arts of the 18th and 19th centuries (ROOMS 35 TO 81 ▲ *206*); this ends with the Napoleon III apartments (ROOMS 82 TO 96 ▲ *210*).

GLAZED EARTHENWARE
French potters of the 16th century made a specialty glazed earthenware, while the Italians concentrated on ceramics. The inspiration for the former came from Fontainebleau, as is shown by the dish called the *Nymph of Fontainebleau* (left) after a work by Rosso Fiorentino. The same movement affected French painting ▲ *218*.

THE BIRTH OF FRENCH CABINETMAKING
The ebony-veneered cabinet with an ivory interior is representative of German cabinets of the 17th century which inspired the first Parisian "ebenistes". A new rich era in the history of French furniture was about to begin.

Silver *salt-cellars* (1734–6) by
François-Thomas Germain.

The Louvre's collection of French furniture was assembled very late, at the fall of the Second Empire when the furniture from the Tuileries and St-Cloud palaces was moved to the museum and thereby saved from destruction by fire. After 1900 this basic collection was reinforced by pieces from the Mobilier National followed by sundry gifts, bequests and purchases. Today the collection offers a complete panorama from the 17th century to the 1830's, from Boulle to Jacob by way of all the greatest cabinetmakers of the 18th century.

The introduction into France in the early 17th century of the German "ebenisterie" technique (veneer) brought about a revolution. Paris cabinetmakers devised lavish polychrome decorative schemes, using wooden marquetry and even blending wood, tortoiseshell and metal, as in the work of André-Charles Boulle (1642–1732) who gave his name to this technique.

Eight-footed Table-console (c. 1715).
The use in furniture-making of gilded wood (here it is oak) was widespread in the reign of Louis XIV, in the second half of the 17th century. This table acquired by Napoleon III was frequently copied at the end of the 19th century.

Monkey Commode by Charles Cressent (c. 1745). The reign of Louis XV saw the triumph of the curve: Cressent, who was a trained sculptor, took special care over his bronze decoration (at center, children with a monkey on a swing).

Commode by Matthieu Criaerd (c. 1742) using the Martin veneer technique to imitate oriental lacquer. Created for the blue bedroom at the Château de Choisy, it was used in an apartment at Versailles under Louis XVI.

Mechanical Table by Jean-François Oeben (c. 1755) the royal cabinetmaker. A mechanism makes the top draw back, pushing forward a large drawer which in turn reveals other drawers and pigeonholes. Some parts are of mahogany, a type of wood then only just coming into use.

Cylinder Desk by Jean-François Leleu (c. 1768–70), with plaques of Sèvres porcelain. The cylinder desk was a new design that had been perfected ten years earlier by Oeben.

Surtout (1758) cast in silver and worked by François-Thomas Germain for Joseph I of Portugal. Appearing at the end of Louis XIV's reign, *surtouts* generally incorporated salt-cellars, oil-jugs etc. This one is purely decorative.

As the king's gold and silversmith, Germain was given lodgings at the Louvre but he did work for all the courts of Europe.

Wardrobe by André-Charles Boulle (c. 1700) allying polychrome flower-marquetry on a tortoiseshell background with Boulle marquetry in brass, tin and stained horn.

Armchair (1690–1700). From the 1650's onward, the Spanish-Flemish style of chair gradually assumed the name of "arm-chair" as its comfort increased.

Commode by Jacques-Philippe Carel (c. 1750) embellished with Chinese lacquer champlevé panels, called "Coromandel" panels. This piece has two doors, a rarity for the time.

Armchair by François-Simon Houlié (c. 1747–50). The wood, which became increasingly visible, is carved.

Commode by Leleu (1772), made for the Prince de Condé. In the 1760's the Greek style with straight lines and Greco-Roman bronze decoration became popular.

Armchair c. 1770–5 by oval-backed, Philippe Poirié.

Chair "en cabriolet" by Jean-Baptiste Séné (1787) for the Château de St-Cloud.

Chair by Georges Jacob (1776–7), then a little-known chair-maker, for the Turkish room of the Comte d'Artois.

Desk by Martin Carlin (c. 1780). The four mosaic panels in the fla... came from older pieces furniture, probably 17th-century Florentine.

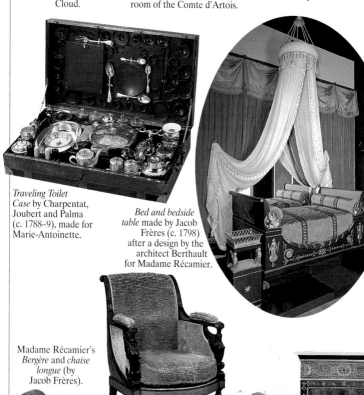

Traveling Toilet Case by Charpentat, Joubert and Palma (c. 1788–9), made for Marie-Antoinette.

Bed and bedside table made by Jacob Frères (c. 1798) after a design by the architect Berthault for Madame Récamier.

Madame Récamier's *Bergère* and *chaise longue* (by Jacob Frères).

The bergère is the one on which Madame Récamier sat for her portrait by Jacques-Louis David in 1800 ▲ *230*. The painter brought back drawings of antique furniture from Rome and the cabinetmaker used these as his model.

Lower section of a bookcase by Georges-Alphonse Jacob-Desmalter

Writing table by Adam Weisweiler (1784) for the inner cabinet of Marie-Antoinette at the Château de St-Cloud. The sides are of steel, the feet are of bronze adorned with caryatids, and the slender lines are characteristic of Weisweiler.

Cylinder desk by Jean-Henri Riesner (1784) furniture maker to the king from 1774 to 1784. At the center of the cylinder a trophy celebrates the attributes of poetry.

Above, *Athénienne* made by Martin-Guillaume Biennais (1800–4) for Napoleon I, a washbasin of yew wood and gilt-bronze which the Emperor took with him to St Helena. At right, the *jewel cabinet* (1809) of Empress Josephine designed by the architect Charles Percier and made by F.H.G. Jacob-Desmalter.

(1832). The shape is still in the Empire style, but a marquetry of hollywood and rosewood has replaced mahogany and gilt bronze.

Dressing table and chair from the shop "À l'Escalier de Crystal" which specialized in objects of crystal mounted in gilded bronze (c. 1819).

The Louvre, as completed by Napoleon III, was used for state receptions which were formerly given in the Tuileries Palace (now vanished) and in the apartments of the Ministry of State, which had been installed in the new north wing along the Rue de Rivoli, today's Richelieu building. Once occupied by the Ministry of Finance, this wing was opened to the public in 1993, displaying the restored apartments in all their glory (first floor, rooms 82 to 96). The paintings, the stucco, the gilded furniture with its silk coverings, and the marble and bronze of the fireplaces constitute one of the greatest achievements of the Napoleon III style, on a par with the Paris Opéra by Garnier.

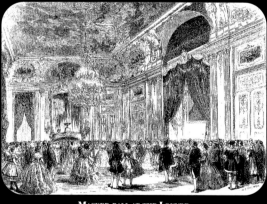

MASKED BALL AT THE LOUVRE
A masked ball was given for the inauguration of the Ministry of State apartments in 1861. This engraving emphasizes the colossal proportions of the Grand Salon which was designed to contain guests in very large numbers at official receptions.

"The brocade-style ornamentation of the vaulting, the vault itself and the walls of the orchestra decorated with trellis-work accented with gold, covered with flowers and foliage against a sky that gives the effect of night . . ."

Laurent-Jan, artist, 1861

DIFFERENT ROOMS, DIFFERENT FUNCTIONS Each room in the apartments corresponds to a precise function, a fact which distinguishes them from the undefined rooms of the 18th century. Below, the Galerie d'Introduction, and left the Grand Salon with furniture in the style of Louis XV. Below, left to right, the "niche" of the Petite Salle à Manger, the Salon-Théâtre and a detail of the décor of the Grand Salon, a homage to the builders of the Louvre, in this case François I, with a model of the façade designed by Pierre Lescot for the Cour Carrée.

▲ The Galerie d'Apollon

Diadem of Empress Eugenie (1853).

The Galerie d'Apollon (on the same floor as the Petite Galerie built by Henri IV) was completely refurbished between 1999 and 2004. Its decoration, first created by Le Vau and Le Brun for Louis XIV and with many later additions culminating in Delacroix's Triumph of Apollo of 1851, has been meticulously restored to the magnificence of former times.

It now houses the Crown Jewels, part of the Department of Decorative Arts.

THE CROWN OF LOUIS XV
This remarkable piece contains no fewer than 282 diamonds and 64 other precious stones.

Throughout history French monarchs accumulated gifts from foreign princes, spoils of war, ritual objects used for coronations along with emblems of monarchy. The oldest pieces are now in the Decorative Arts section of the Louvre ▲ 198 and the more recent ones are in the Galerie. In 2004 a set of jewels containing 38 emeralds and 1,246 diamonds, given to the Empress Marie-Louise by Napoleon I as a wedding gift, was added to the collection.

THE SANCY
A 56-carat diamond (below): one of the many crown jewels.

Vessel with a Statuette of Neptune in rock crystal and lapis lazuli with enameled mounting.

THE REGENT
This 140-carat diamond, bought in 1717 is considered to be the world's most beautiful diamond. It was part of Louis XV's personal crown (above) as well as that of his son Louis XVI; later it adorned Napoleon I's sword and the crown used for the coronation of Charles X.

European painting

▲ French painting

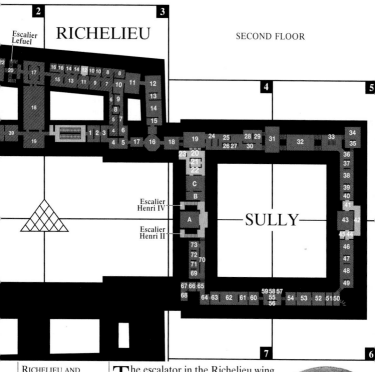

RICHELIEU

SECOND FLOOR

Escalier
Lefuel

2 3

4 5

Escalier
Henri IV

Escalier
Henri II

SULLY

7 6

RICHELIEU AND
SULLY, SECOND
FLOOR,
AND DENON, FIRST
FLOOR (LARGE-SCALE
PAINTINGS)

The escalator in the Richelieu wing leads to the second floor and the rooms assigned to French painting. Assembled from the time of Louis XIV, the royal collections form the kernel of this section; to these were added the works confiscated during the Revolution. In the 19th and 20th centuries acquisitions, bequests and donations helped complete this unique ensemble of pictures.

MEDIEVAL TRADITION TO THE RENAISSANCE

**INTERNATIONAL
GOTHIC**
Malouel's large circular *Pietà* (right) illustrates the style called International Gothic of which Burgundy was one of the most active centers.

**PORTRAIT OF
JEAN LE BON**
This picture is said to be the oldest French portrait in existence.

AT THE ENTRANCE (ROOM 1) is the portrait of *Jean le Bon* which is supposed to be the oldest French painting in existence (c. 1350). The portrait of the future king, then Duke of Normandy is a straightforward and unflattering likeness.
THE ALTARCLOTH OF NARBONNE (ROOM 2). A grisaille painting on silk made to decorate a Lenten altar faces a round *Pietà* by Jean Malouel in the International Gothic style.
ROOM 3 contains the *Saint Denis Altarpiece* by Henri Bellechose which combines

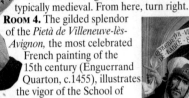

realism with the Gothic style. In the *Calling of the Virgin* the clumsily-handled perspective and the disproportion between the Virgin and the architecture are typically medieval. From here, turn right.

ROOM 4. The gilded splendor of the *Pietà de Villeneuve-lès-Avignon,* the most celebrated French painting of the 15th century (Enguerrand Quarton, c.1455), illustrates the vigor of the School of Avignon which emerged in the 14th century with the installation of the Papacy in that city. A diptych by Nicolas Froment evokes Provence and its "good king" *René of Anjou*, a lamentable politician but an intelligent patron of the arts.

ROOM 5 contains the richly expressive and dramatic *Three Prophets* assigned to the same Provençal school and is near the great *Boulbon Altarpiece* (c. 1450).

JEAN FOUQUET (ROOM 6). A native of Tours, Fouquet traveled to Italy in about 1445, where he discovered the painting of the Italian Renaissance and the techniques of perspective. His *Charles VII* with its diamond pattern of construction is a monumental royal portrait which reveals the man as much as it exalts the power of the prince. The Flemish Jean Hey (the "Master of Moulins") was a portraitist of great talent (see *Suzanne de Bourbon* and his picture of the Dauphin, *Charles-Orlant*, first floor, room A). The *Altarpiece of the Parliament of Paris* depicts the capital in the 15th century, with the Cité at right and the Louvre on the left, before the Pont-Neuf was built ▲ 308.

PORTRAIT OF FRANÇOIS I BY JEAN CLOUET (ROOM 7) was one of the rare French paintings owned by that king. During his Italian campaigns, François employed Italian artists, among them Leonardo ▲ 262 convincing them to come to France to stimulate the artistic renewal then underway at Fontainebleau. Clouet overshadowed other French portraitists of his time, who espoused the fashionable realism of the 16th century. Their work ▲ 216 is displayed in ROOM 8.

The *Three Prophets* (c. 1480, below, and detail above).

Guillaume Jouvenel des Ursins by Jean Fouquet, a painter of the French Renaissance.

THE SCHOOL OF AVIGNON
Avignon produced paintings of great austerity and emotion like the *Pietà de Villeneuve-lès-Avignon* by Enguerrand Quarton (c. 1455, left), but also with singular expressive force (as in the *Three Prophets* above). In the *Villeneuve Pietà* the canon who commissioned the picture is shown in prayer behind Saint John. At the time, the few portraits being done were of people who commissioned religious paintings and had themselves included in them.

▲ French portraiture in the 16th century

FATHER AND SON
From the studio of
François Clouet,
portraits of *Henri II*
(left) and *Charles IX*
(right), the husband
and the son of
Catherine de' Medici.

A ROYAL PATRON OF THE ARTS
François I, King of France by Jean
Clouet (perhaps in collaboration with
his son François?) painted c. 1530.
The king is richly dressed in the
Italian style and the composition
is not unlike that of Fouquet's
Charles VII.

Two trends emerged
in the art of
French portraiture in
the 16th century. The
first played on allegory
or mythology to flatter
its models (ROOM 9
▲ *218*). In ROOM 8
where the atmosphere
is intimate and
precious, are works
belonging to the
second movement:
realist portraits
painted by Jean Clouet
and his son François,
both of them painters
to the king, and by
Corneille de Lyon.
These are very
different from
Mannerist Italian
pictures and form a
definite French type of
small portrait. Shown
here are portraits of
the royal family: the
last of the Valois
dynasty up to Henri III
by François Quesnel,
and a picture of
Catherine de' Medici
(anonymous), all of
whose children came
to the throne but
failed to produce
direct descendents.
Opposite them, the
court is represented,
notably the Guise and
Lorraine families,
familiar through such
Dumas novels as
La Reine Margot and
Les Quarante-cinq.
There are also some
intriguing unknowns
whose faces alone
are familiar to us.

CORNEILLE DE LYON
Among the rare portraits definitely
attributed to Corneille de Lyon
are those of the poet *Clément Marot*
and *Jean de Bourbon-Vendôme*
(above). *Jean d'Albon, Seigneur de
St-André* (left) is the work of
several different hands.

> "Once the king of France
> was a lover of letters . . ."
> Pierre de Ronsard

Pierre Quthe, Apothecary by François Clouet, indicates a change of style.

A LITTLE-KNOWN QUEEN
The portrait of Elizabeth of Austria by François Clouet reveals a largely forgotten French queen, the daughter of Maximilian II and wife of Charles IX.

LAVISH FRAMES
The works of Corneille de Lyon were placed in frames originally made for mirrors, probably during the 19th century. His studio produced *Anne Stuart* (above) and he himself painted the *Portrait of a Young Man* and *Mellin de St-Gelais* (right).

Corneille de Lyon was a Dutch painter who settled in Lyon in 1547. He did a number of small portraits on panel, in which the subjects are represented half-length against a blue or green background. While his technique had much in common with that of the Clouets – realistic features, narrow framing of the bust, three-quarters or full face, single-toned background – Corneille's meticulous brushwork reveals his northern origin. A number of portraits which are probably by pupils are displayed alongside his work: among these is *Pierre Aymeric* painted in 1534 (above).

·EVA PRIMA PANDORA·

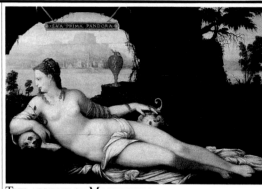

GALA AT THE TUILERIES
The *Sibyl of Tibur* (below) shows both Roman and Parisian monuments in the Tuileries Gardens, a royal spectacle mounted by Caron. At the center of the canvas is Catherine de' Medici (insert). The countryside depicted in Jean Cousin's *Eva Prima Pandora* (right) is also as much a vista of Paris as antiquity.

THE ADVENT OF MANNERISM

THE SCHOOL OF FONTAINEBLEAU (ROOMS 9 and 10) shows the influence on French painters of the period by artists from the other side of the Alps who were attracted by François I to Fontainebleau. Theirs is a delicate courtly art, full of references to Italian Mannerism. The theme of Diana is very much present, perhaps in homage to Henri III's mistress Diane de Poitiers: indeed Diana became a regular feature in paintings of courtly love. *Diana the Huntress* owes much to the idealized elegance which the French perceived in Italian art. The reference to mythology and history suggests a personality type more

than an individual likeness. *Eva Prima Pandora* was painted in about 1550 by Jean Cousin, one of the few Parisian painters whose name is well known to us even though he was relatively independent of the Court. Using a pose reminiscent of Cellini's sculpted *Nymph of Fontainebleau* ▲ *195,* the picture associates the biblical theme of original sin with the myth of Pandora. Her left hand rests on the vase she should never have opened. Fontainebleau remained

the center of French art throughout the second half of the century, which was scarred by the Wars of Religion ● *36.* The surreal, icy violence of Antoine Caron's work of great Mannerist refinement, the *Massacres of the Triumvirate,* evokes the killings perpetrated during the Second Triumvirate of Octavius, Antony and Lepidus (43 BC). But the real theme was the contemporary massacre of French Protestants. Very similar is the spatial arrangement of Caron's *Sybil of Tibur* in which the prophetess shows the Emperor Augustus the Virgin and Child and enjoins him to worship them. For Augustus read Charles IX, and for the Sybil, Catherine de' Medici. Nobody knows who painted the enigmatic double portrait of *Gabrielle d'Estrées and One of Her Sisters.* One of the women's delicately pinching the nipple of the other would seem to imply the illegitimate daughter Henri IV had with his beautiful mistress, while the theme of the bath legitimizes

"GABRIELLE D'ESTRÉES AND ONE OF HER SISTERS"
"A breast like new white satin/You who could make a rose blush/A breast more beautiful than anything/A firm breast, hardly a breast/More like a little globe of ivory," wrote the poet Clement Marot of this painting in about 1535 (above, details at top of page).

the sensuality of the two figures framed by the red folds of a curtain. Already the period was becoming embittered. In the anonymous *Funeral of Love* a funeral cortège featuring all the greatest poets mourning the death of Eros, mark the drowning of gallantry in the bloodbath of the Wars of Religion.

THE INFLUENCE OF CARAVAGGIO (ROOM 11). By about 1600, Caravaggio in Italy ▲ *267* was producing spectacular effects of chiaroscuro, with realistic dramatization of scenes that had nothing to do with the idealization then so prevalent in religious art. The painters who followed his lead, known in France as the "Caravagesques" included Claude Vignon, Valentin de Boulogne and even Simon Vouet at the outset of his career. The light which falls on the body of Nicolas Tournier's *Christ on the Cross* and on the faces of the women beneath him, blazes out dramatically from the shadowy background in which the colors of the draperies are barely visible.

CHIAROSCURO
Valentin de Boulogne who spent most of his life in Rome was one of the most faithful followers of Caravaggio – an artist who made a point of having no pupils. Above, *Concert* (c. 1622–5), a work of refined chiaroscuro in which the ordinariness of the figures and the perfection of the expressions pay homage to the great Italian.

French painting
In the era of Poussin

"I HAVE NEGLECTED NOTHING." (POUSSIN) On the tomb in his *Arcadian Shepherds* (left) are the words "Et in Arcadia ego", a reminder of the presence of death even in Arcadia. Poussin (below, detail from his *Self-portrait*) avoided official honors to devote himself entirely to his art. He preferred Rome to Paris and spent most of his life there, yet eventually he was attracted back to France by Louis XIII and Richelieu who wanted him to paint the Grande Galerie at the Louvre. This project never came to fruition.

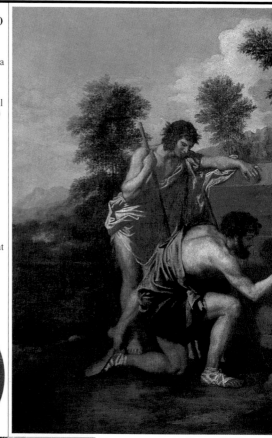

SUMMER
At the end of his life Poussin turned his attention to landscapes. In his *Four Seasons* the light seems to emanate from the countryside itself. *Summer* (above) is one of the four canvases displayed in the rotunda which bears Poussin's name.

THE PAINTERS OF LOUIS XIII

SIMON VOUET (ROOM 12), inspired by Caravaggio while visiting Italy, came back to France on the orders of Louis XIII. There he became the king's favorite painter and was loaded with commissions including the *Presentation at the Temple* and channeled French painting toward a clear, frank palette and broad, lyrical treatments; his canvases *Charity, Virtue* and *Wealth* seem to make yellow and blue fabrics glint with Baroque iridescence. In his time the Louvre was the palace of Louis XIII ● *76*, whose portrait was painted by Philippe de Champaigne for the Galerie des Hommes Illustres du Palais Cardinal (now the Palais-Royal ● *77*), the residence of Richelieu whose portrait upstages that of the king with its glorious purple.
NICOLAS POUSSIN (ROOMS 13 and 14), who was in Rome at this time, was building a reputation with paintings like the *Inspiration of the Poet* (1630, ROOM 12). Poussin found in his mythological sources (*Triumph of Flora, Echo and Narcissus, Bacchanals*) a pretext for the depiction of beautiful bodies as well as everything else to do with the pleasures of life: wine,

In the works of Poussin and Vouet there are similar harmonies of yellow and blue.

ROYAL DECORATION
Virtue and *Wealth* by Simon Vouet (above).

dance and music in particular. With his *Self-portrait* (ROOM 14) Poussin appears as a man with a character of his own, poised between the seductions of mythology (*Arcadian Shepherds*) and the austerity of the Bible (*Plague of Ashdod*).
WITH CLAUDE LORRAIN came the loveliest sunsets in all painting and the idea of landscape as a separate genre (ROOM 15). Claude's pictures are hymns to light, set in realistic Roman landscapes or imaginary ports of the ancient world. Titles include *Ulysses Restoring Chryseis to Her Father* (1644) and *The Disembarkation of Cleopatra at Tarsus* (1642).
THE ROTONDE POUSSIN (ROOM 16) shows Poussin's *Four Seasons* painted for the Duc de Richelieu between 1660 and 1664. *Winter* featuring the Flood is dramatic; *Spring* shows an earthly Paradise; *Summer* and harvest time is illustrated by the story of Ruth and Booz; while *Autumn*, replete with bunches of grapes evokes the Promised Land. On the right is an information and documentation room (ROOM 17); continue your circuit by way of the Salle Poussin (ROOM 18) and the *Love of Apollo and Daphne,* Poussin's final unfinished canvas.

SUNSET in the *Disembarkation of Cleopatra at Tarsus* by Claude Lorrain.

CHURCH DECORATION
The similar formats of Eustache Le Sueur's 22 paintings of the *Life of Saint Bruno,* founder of the Charterhouse Order, create an odd cartoon-like impression clearly intended for a public which seldom knew how to read. Above,

left to right, *Dream of Saint Bruno*, *Saint Bruno Taking the Monk's Habit*, *Saint Bruno Teaching Theology at Rheims*, and *Death of Saint Bruno*.

PRIVATE TOWNHOUSES
The building of many new private townhouses in Paris under Louis XIII meant an abundance of commissions for painters. Most of the décor of the Hôtel Lambert (above, the Cabinet de l'Amour) on the Île St-Louis has now been transferred to the Louvre: in particular, canvases and panels by Le Sueur. (Right, the *Birth of Eros*).

FROM ALLEGORY TO REALISM

The great altarpieces of the 17th century (ROOM 19) were the prerogative of the painters of the Académie Royale de Peinture et de Sculpture founded in 1648. Alongside the large canvases of Eustache Le Sueur (the *Sermon of Saint Paul at Ephesus*) are such works as *Virgin and Child* by Laurent de la Hyre and Poussin's *Saint François Xavier* which depicts the Jesuits in Japan. Most of ROOMS 20 to 23 exhibit the cartoons of Lebrun, preparatory drawings for ceremonial décors such as the Ambassadors' staircase and the Grande Galerie at Versailles; all exalt Louis XIV.

ROOM 24 holds the twenty-two paintings done by Eustache le Sueur to illustrate the *Life of Saint Bruno*. In his *Plan of the Charterhouse of Paris* you can pick out the Louvre, the Pont Neuf ▲ *306* opposite, and in the background, the spire of Ste-Chapelle and the towers of Notre Dame.

ROOM 25 has some of the canvases commissioned for private mansions in Paris, such as the Galerie

...les Muses and the Cabinet d'Amour at the Hôtel Lambert (Le Sueur).

CABINET PICTURES (ROOM 26). This type of painting was intended specifically for private collectors; it mostly consisted of genre scenes, still lifes and small landscapes. Examples here are by Claude, Patel and Jacques Stella.

STILL LIFES (ROOM 27) often involved food as in Lubin Baugin's *Still Life with Wafer Biscuits* but they were not devoid of sensuality, as in *Strawberries and Cherries* by François Garnier, *Grapes* by Pierre Dupuis and *Half-opened Pomegranates* by Jacques Linard. This tradition took hold during the 17th century under the influence of Flemish painters. The art of the still life sometimes allied itself with the theme of the *vanitas*, with such images as skulls accompanied by the symbols of vain hopes.

THE SALLE LA TOUR (ROOM 28). An artist from Lorraine who went unrecognized for many years, Georges de la Tour was much influenced by Caravaggio. His night scenes (*Saint Joseph*, the *Adoration of the Shepherds*, the *Mary Magdalen*, and *Saint Sebastian Tended by Irene*) are illuminated by candlelight; his daytime scenes are strikingly different, bathed by a colder sheen (*The Cheat*).

DAY AND NIGHT
The Cheat (above) and *Christ with Saint Joseph in the Carpenter's Shop* (below) by Georges de la Tour.

THE LE NAIN BROTHERS (Antoine, Louis and Mathieu) worked together often on the same canvases and signed them with their family name only. Their scenes of peasant life brought them special fame. ROOM 29 contains their principal works notably the *Peasant's Repast* and *Peasant Family*. The dignity of their subjects, the simplicity of their composition and the austerity of their palette show a deliberate rejection of the picturesque. Take seven steps down to ROOM 31.

Above left, *Peasant Family* by the Le Nain brothers.

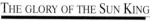

JANSENIST PIETY
The *Ex-Voto of 1662*
(below), the
masterpiece of
Philippe de
Champaigne.

THE GLORY OF THE SUN KING

PHILIPPE DE CHAMPAIGNE (ROOM 31). The seven steps from the previous room lead down to a harsher world peopled by great lords and ravaged by the religious warfare which shook France in the 1650's. Philippe de Champaigne who had lived among the Jansenists at the Abbaye de Port-Royal, painted the portrait of *Mère Angélique Arnauld*, the mother superior at the convent, along with *Arnauld d'Andilly* and above all the remarkable *Ex-Voto of 1662* His terrifyingly realistic *Christ on the Cross* and *Dead Christ* is a reminder of the austere faith of the Jansenists. In the portraits which made his reputation (*Portrait of a Man*, 1650) Champaigne showed his exceptional skill at making his models lifelike. The king and the church were the protectors of painters at that time: thus Lebrun, a pupil of Vouet, was successively employed by Séguier, Richelieu, Fouquet, Mazarin and Louis XIV. The accession of Louis in 1661 gave Lebrun primacy among his painter colleagues allowing him to impose a newer, less somber style of his own.

CHARLES LEBRUN (ROOM 32) ● *78*. This room houses the monumental canvases painted by Lebrun between 1665 and 1673 in celebration of Alexander the Great. The golden, sunlit sheen of the the young conqueror's armor makes it clear that the painter's rea

TRIUMPHS
Chancellor Seguier
(above) and
*Alexander the Great
Entering Babylon*
(right) by Charles
Lebrun.

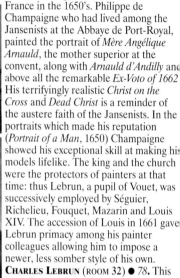

subject is the Sun-King himself, who enjoyed comparisons of himself with Alexander. In 1665, Racine dedicated his play of Alexander the Great to the young king. Lebrun painted these four pictures at the same time as his work on the Galerie d'Apollon at the Louvre (1665) ▲ *127* and on the Hall of Mirrors at Versailles (1673).

JEAN JOUVENET (ROOM 33). This artist, a Norman by birth, painted his *Raising of Lazarus* and the *Miracle of the Fishes* in 1706 for the Benedictine priory of St-Martin-des-Champs; for the latter painting he sketched Dieppe fishermen from life

PAINTERS OF LOUIS XIV (ROOMS 34 AND 35).

The paintings of Charles de la Fosse reveal a charming, innovative style which rejects the austerity of the later years of Louis XIV and ushers in the 18th century (*Moses in the Bullrushes*). In the *Arrival of Louis XIV at the Siege of Maastricht*, Adam Frans van der Meulen portrayed the king appearing on the battlefield where the musketeer d'Artagnan was killed. In his portrait by Hyacinthe Rigaud in 1701, the King is still in excellent form, his shapely leg clothed with silk: this is truly the apogee of the formal state portrait. Pierre Mignard became "premier peintre" in 1690; his *Self-portrait* contrasts with *Lebrun* by Nicolas de Largillierre. The portrait of *Bossuet*, the "Eagle of Meaux" also by Rigaud, seems to make a pair with that of the king: the two great powers of the century, temporal and spiritual, are seen in identical compositions. Nearby, the double portrait of *Madame Rigaud* (right profile and three quarters left) is ample proof that the official court painter was also a vigorous portraitist. By contrast Antoine Coypel's *Democritus* seems to mock at the instability of a world which he views as no more than a shifting mass of matter. As to Jean-Baptiste Santerre's *Susannah Bathing*, the flesh-tints of the central figure are of such porcelain loveliness that one can well understand the emotion of those old men in the Bible who were so little discouraged by her legendary chastity.

The King is surrounded by the symbols of monarchy: crown, scepter and golden fleurs-de-lys on the great mantle lined with ermine. He is also highly idealized: at 63 he was already ravaged by disease.

PILGRIMAGE TO CYTHERA (above)
Watteau's famous painting also called the *Embarkation to Cythera* is the masterpiece of the *peinture galante* of the 18th century; it is also the work which the artist produced on admission to the Academy in 1717.

CROSSING TO HADES
Charon Ferrying Souls Across the River Styx by Pierre Subleyras (below) contrasts in its melancholy subject-matter with the sensual surroundings of Boucher and Watteau.

THE REIGN OF LOUIS THE WELL-BELOVED

WATTEAU (ROOMS 36 AND 37). Jean-Antoine Watteau entered the Louvre in 1869 with a major donation from Doctor La Caze. In 1715 Louis XIV died and was succeeded by a Regent: the time had come, after the religious excesses of the old king's last years, to make a new start (with Philippe d'Orléans), epitomized by Watteau's *Pilgrimage to Cythera* (1717) – the island of Venus. With this painting Watteau gained admission to the Academy ● 66 at the age of 33, using a new approach to the idea of the *fête galante*. This theme originated with the theater and consisted of a meeting of honest folk in pastoral surroundings. *Nymphs and Satyrs* like *Diana Bathing* unveil and celebrate the female body. If Watteau's masterpiece *Pierrot* (which used to be called *Gilles*) appears grave and enigmatic this is because his role in the Commedia dell'arte is exactly so. The *Two Cousins* or the *Indifferent Lover* celebrates the voluptuousness of life; Watteau excels at suggesting the graceful line of a girl's neck, or the undulating movement of her dress. In the same room, note Coypel's *Young Negro* and *Young Girl*.

THE PAINTERS OF LOUIS XV (ROOM 38) embarked on the themes of lightness and gallantry: this was dubbed Rococo. Small paintings were commissioned in ever greater numbers by individuals. François Lemoyne portrayed his *Hercules* subdued by the distracted grace of Omphale, his club metamorphosed into a distaff. Nicolas Lancret celebrates the *Delights of the Bath* while François Boucher's *Diana Rising From Her Bath* is yet another pretext for a study of the female nude. With the contrast between the blue velvet and the flesh tints of the women's bodies, and the second contrast between the hunting trophy and the obvious sensuality of the pose, everything is in place for a celebration of the freeing of both minds and bodies. The hunting scenes and *déjeuners champêtres* of Jean-François de Troy or Carle van Loo depict the amusements of the court which have nothing in common with Subleyras' *Charon Ferrying Souls Across the River Styx* nor with

> " Chardin, what you mix on your palette is neither white, nor red, nor black; no, what you place on the tip of your brush and put to the canvas is the very substance of things. It is azure. It is light. "
>
> Diderot

CHARDIN'S ART OF THE ORDINARY
In paintings like his *Young Man with a Top* Chardin draws attention to ordinary objects which he raises to the level of sentient beings. He does this for cauldrons, pipes, glasses, copper fountains, cooking pots and pieces of porcelain which he traces with a deep love of form and shape, and with tender half-tones (left, his still life of a *Basket of Peaches, with Nuts, Knife and Glass of Wine*). Even more famous are his genre scenes such as *Grace* (1740, below).

Chardin's tragically realistic *Skate*, a forlorn triangular dead fish.

JEAN SIMÉON CHARDIN is exhibited in ROOMS 39 and 40 which contain his *Poor Meal* and *Rich Meal* framing an attentive *Young Draughtsman Sharpening His Pencil*. The painter's *Young Man with a Top* is equally absorbed with his toy while the *Dead Rabbit* confronts a similarly lugubrious *Dead Hare*. The still lifes are complemented by genre scenes, such as Boucher's the *Lunch*.

The new rooms for the French painting section were designed by the Italian architect Italo Rota.

PAINTINGS OF THE ENLIGHTENMENT

PASTELS AND MINIATURES. In ROOM 41 the Department of Graphic Arts ● *62* exhibits its finest pastels by rotation for conservation reasons. In the Couloir des Poules (ROOM 42) – the name probably comes from the Rue des Poulies and has no connection with chickens – there is a permanent display of miniatures. These are tiny portraits which girls give to their lovers in the plays of Marivaux. There are also mid-sized pastel portraits, mostly of artists and their close relatives. Two oculi here offer a view of Perrault's Colonnade ● *78*.

PENTECOST by
Jean Restout (right).

*La Marquise de
Pompadour*, a friend
to many philosophers
and artists by
Delatour.

❝What would you
have that artist put
on canvas? Whatever
he has in his
imagination. And
what can a man's
imagination contain
who spends his life
among the lowest
prostitutes?❞
     Diderot on the
subject of Boucher

The *Forge of Vulcan*
(right and details
above).

HISTORY PAINTING (ROOM 43) – in this case
religious in tone – was not abandoned;
indeed it maintained its position as the
noblest genre as Jean Restout's *Pentecost*
(1732) shows. Restout was a master of
great religious themes and royal or church
commissions were abundant in the 18th
century. *The Hermit* by Joseph Marie Vien
seems still to believe in a world freed from
the constraints of the flesh.

A FEW FINE PASTELS are displayed in ROOMS
44 and 45 in rotation; among these are two
portraits, *La Marquise de Pompadour* and
D'Alembert by Maurice Quentin Delatour.

RETURNING TO BOUCHER (ROOM 46) and
history painting (here the subject matter is
drawn from mythology) we find the *Rape of Europa*; never
was any rape accomplished in such an atmosphere of good
humor if the face of the girl astride the bull is anything to go
by. The same is true of the *Forge of Vulcan*: the subject is epic
the treatment idyllic. Two *Views of Naples* by Joseph Vernet,
one showing the smoking Vesuvius, illustrate the evolution of
landscape painting. And in a fine hunters' return scene by
Jean-Baptiste Oudry (*Bittern and Partridge Guarded by a White
Dog*) the painter has skillfully included a single shaft of light
coming from the background to strike the dog's white neck.

DIDEROT AS ART CRITIC

ROOM 47 contains the favorite painters of Diderot, the first art critic, grouped around his portrait by Louis Michel van Loo. Diderot liked still lifes, sentimental genre paintings and bourgeois pathos (as in Greuze's *Village Betrothal* of which he said: "one feels oneself touched by a gentle excess of emotion as one gazes at it". And he liked his paintings suggestive, as in *The Dead Bird* by Greuze which implies the loss of virginity. 'The subject of this small poem is so refined that many people have not perceived it: they thought this girl was weeping for no greater loss than that of her canary," he wrote about another picture with a similar theme.

ROOM 48. Greuze achieved the same effect with *The Broken Jug*, a pair to his *Milkmaid*. Diderot also liked Fragonard, his portraits above all (see *Diderot*, *Inspiration* and the *Abbé de St-Non*, the latter painted with brio "in one hour"). Fragonard's skies also found favor with Diderot (the *Storm*, the *Tivoli Cascade* and *Women Bathing*. To paint his *Port of Marseilles* Vernet went out in a boat to work, while Hubert Robert specialized in ruins (the *Pont du Gard*, the *Maison Carrée* and the *Arenas of Nîmes* ● 90).

ROOM 49. Jean Honoré Fragonard was also a painter of the triumph of the flesh as in his *Love's Oath*, the *Stolen Chemise* and *The Bolt*. "That is beautiful, very beautiful, sublime", said Diderot of the *Paternal Curse* by Greuze (ROOM 51).

LOST INNOCENCE
The Bolt by Fragonard graphically conveys the moment of temptation, through its bold diagonals. *Diderot* (center) by Louis Michel van Loo shows the writer in the dressing gown given to him by Catherine II, on which he never dared wipe his pens. Below *The Broken Jug* by Greuze.

229

▲ French painting
David and neoclassicism

NEOCLASSICISM

ROOM 52 contains the remarkably vivid portraits by Mme Vigée-Lebrun with works by other women painters such as Anne Vallayer-Coster and Adelaide Labille-Guiard. In *Night*, a canvas by Vernet the full moon seems to be a reflection in the sky of the fire lit by the men.

THE SO-CALLED GREEK STYLE (ROOM 53) was initiated by Joseph-Marie Vien in 1763 followed by François-André Vincent. The most beautiful example of this kind of neoclassicism is *Psyche and Eros* by François Gérard, a famous portraitist of the time. The inconstancy of love is symbolized by a buttterfly hovering above the girl's head.

DAVID AND HIS PUPILS. David was the principal painter of the years 1780–1820 and a master of neoclassicism and the quest for ideal beauty. His works are displayed in ROOM 54 (along with those of his pupils) and in the rooms for large-scale paintings (Daru, Denon and Mollien ▲ *234* to *237*). The extraordinary *Madame Trudaine* in ROOM 54 is noteworthy; as is the *Wounded Roman Soldier* by Drouais, David's favorite pupil who died in 1788 at the age of 25. Antoine-Jean Gros, a future baron of the Empire, is represented here by a study for the famous *Bonaparte at Arcole* as is Girodet by his portraits. Vincent, another founder of neoclassicism (*Zeuxis*, 1789, ROOM 53) who was also a painter of battle scenes has contributed a *Battle of the Pyramids* in grisaille.

Antoine-Jean Gros: already in 1796 the outlines of the Napoleonic legend were being drawn.

LANDSCAPES, GENRE PAINTINGS AND PORTRAITS. ROOM 55 has a rotating exhibition of the 125 *Studies of Italian Landscapes* by Pierre-Henri de Valenciennes, a fascinating repertoire of

> "Under his hands, which rival those of the gods,
> the canvas blazes into eloquent life."
>
> André Chénier, 1791

THE SALLE DAVID
The large-scale masterpieces of David are exhibited in rooms in the Denon building; nonetheless ROOM 54 is a preparation for these since it contains sketches for such pictures as *Belisarius*, and the *Oath of the Horatii*. There are also a number of portraits, notably *Madame Charles-Louis Trudaine* (left), painted about 1791 but unfinished, in which the patrician lady's silhouette is set against a strange red background.

skies and landscapes which is a reminder of how important it was for all these painters to travel to Italy. On the right, in ROOM 57, are genre paintings from around 1800, notably the *Convalescence of Bayard* by Pierre Révoil (exaltation of the troubadour style which haunted the first generation of romantics who had read Walter Scott). There is also a very rare piece by Daguerre, an *Interior of a Chapel* in which the consummate light effects remind us that this painter later became a photographer. The portraits and genre scenes of around 1800 are assembled in the Salle Boilly (ROOM 58) and include *Meeting of Artists in Isabey's Studio* (1798) by Louis-Léopold Boilly. Likewise, the *Rain Shower* gives us a glimpse of the streets of Paris, not yet paved in which pedestrians had to pay a toll to those who laid down planks for crossing the mud. ROOM 59 exhibits the landscapists of the same period, especially a fine *Interior of the Coliseum* by Marius Granet.
THE SALLE PRUD'HON (ROOM 56) is dominated by the theme of love (*Venus Bathing*); but Pierre-Paul Prud'hon was also a painter of portraits, who specialized in dignitaries of the imperial court such as *Empress Josephine,* the *King of Rome* and the Egyptologist *Baron Vivant Denon*, the first director of the Louvre under Napoleon ● *68*. The antithesis of David, Prud'hon found his inspiration in hellenistic Greece and Leonardo da Vinci ▲ *262*. He was one of the masters of early Romanticism.

THE ITALIAN REFERENCE
Villa Farnese: Two Poplar Trees, a composition by Pierre-Henri de Valenciennes.

GLORIFICATION OF THE FEMALE FORM
Bain turc (*Turkish Bath*) by Ingres (above) is constructed around a form consisting of a series of overlapping circles.

PORTRAITS
Ingres' portrait of *Louis-François Bertin*, (far right) is a realistic evocation of the character of the great press baron. Géricault's painting of *Louise Vernet*, daughter of the artist Horace Vernet, is more disturbing. The deformed body with its monstrous head and the kind of troubled gaze seen in monomaniacs betray the painter's own unease with the theme of childhood.

ROMANTICISM VERSUS ACADEMICISM

JEAN AUGUSTE DOMINIQUE INGRES. In the first half of the 19th century there was a controversy between the colorists whose champion was Delacroix, and the draftsmen whose leader was Ingres, a pupil of David, who said "Drawing does not mean simply reproducing contours; drawing is not merely line. Drawing is expression, the inner line; it is planes and reliefs." The works assembled in ROOM 60 display the relief and the line perfected by Ingres: the *Small Bather* and the larger *Valpinçon Bather* demonstrate the art of a painter who saw himself above all as a follower of Raphael. Baudelaire wrote very unkindly that Ingres' figures "looked like very

correctly shaped dolls, swollen with some kind of soft, dead matter entirely foreign to the human organism". On the contrary, these (bathers) are marvelous studies of the female body, and the rounded composition of Ingres' *Turkish Bath* is one of perfect harmony. Ingres was also a major portraitist of the new bourgeoisie in France; see his *Louis-François Bertin*, director of the *Journal des Débats* or *Edme Bochet*.

The *1821 Derby at Epsom* (left) by Theodore Géricault shows the vogue for horse-racing on the English model, and the contemporary state of research into the mechanics of movement. The unreal landscape and the fantastic atmosphere of this painting are a far cry from the realism of contemporary English painting.

THE PAINTER OF MADNESS. Géricault is best known for his *Raft of the Medusa* ▲ *238,* painted in 1819, a sketch of which is shown in ROOM 61. But he was also a painter of horses which were both his passion and his nemesis; he died at 33 as a result of a fall from a horse. The gliding thoroughbreds of his *Epsom Derby* are a striking example of this aspect of his art. In his portraits of human beings (the *Compulsive Gambler*) the people are handled like horse-portraits with the same sense of volume and the same nervous, flaring nostrils. And the smoke that rises above Géricault's *Plaster Furnace* is not unlike the disquieting clouds of the *Raft of the Medusa*.
EUGÈNE DELACROIX was the greatest of the Romantic painters; his major works are displayed with other large-scale canvases elsewhere, but otherwise he appears for the first time in ROOM 62 with a *Portrait of Frédéric Chopin, Self-portrait* and *Jewish Wedding in Morocco*. The dramatic *Assassination of the Bishop of Liège* reminds us that the younger generation in 1830 were captivated by the works of Sir Walter Scott, while *Hamlet and Horatio* is inspired by Shakespeare. The above painters are also present in ROOMS 71 and 72 (the Georges Thomy-Thiery and Étienne Moreau-Nélaton Collections ▲ *242*) and ROOMS 75 to 77 (Daru, Denon and Mollien ▲ *238*).

Self-portrait (above) and *Jewish Wedding in Morocco* (below) by Eugène Delacroix.

▲ David and neoclassicism

(Denon, first floor, rooms 75 to 77)

The large-scale canvases of French painters are displayed in the Salles Daru, Denon and Mollien (ROOMS 75, 76 AND 77) in the Denon building. They range from David to Delacroix by way of Ingres and Géricault, and from the 1780's, when the Revolution began, to the 1850's, which saw the coming of the Second Empire. Indispensable as they are to an understanding of this period, they more than complement the rooms where these schools are presented in detail; they are of outstanding quality and reputation. David's *Coronation of Napoleon I*, Géricault's *Raft of the Medusa* and Delacroix's *Liberty Leading the People* are prime examples. Most of the others are what the French call *grandes machines* in terms of their sheer scale, the hugeness of their themes and their theatrical approach; they depict male virility, female grief, glory personified by great men and abundant historical and dramatic narrative.

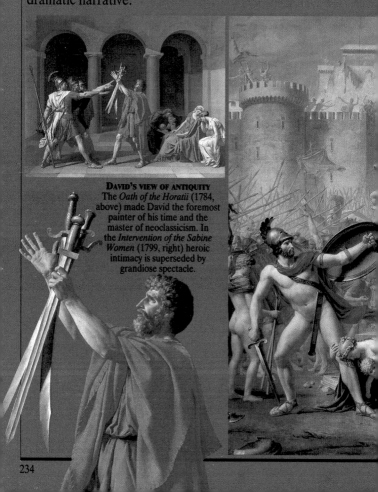

DAVID'S VIEW OF ANTIQUITY
The *Oath of the Horatii* (1784, above) made David the foremost painter of his time and the master of neoclassicism. In the *Intervention of the Sabine Women* (1799, right) heroic intimacy is superseded by grandiose spectacle.

A MANIFESTO FOR COLOR
The *Death of Sardanapalus* by Eugène Delacroix, painted in 1827 is one of the major works of French Romantic painting; it refers to the suicide of a king of Babylon who preferred this end to dishonorable surrender.

THE APOGEE OF LINE
Two works by Ingres, the strange *Roger Delivering Angelica* (right), commissioned to go above the door of the Throne Room at Versailles, and the *Great Odalisque* (right) painted in 1814 for Caroline Murat, Queen of Naples.

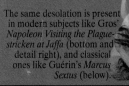

The same desolation is present in modern subjects like Gros' *Napoleon Visiting the Plague-stricken at Jaffa* (bottom and detail right), and classical ones like Guérin's *Marcus Sextus* (below).

> "I want to work in the purest greek style. I feast my eyes on the statues of antiquity, and I mean to imitate some of them."
>
> Jacques-Louis David, 1799

THE NEOCLASSICAL IDEAL

Neoclassical painting set out to illustrate the values of antiquity: integrity and respect for heroes (*Marius Imprisoned* by Germain Jean Drouais, above right), fidelity to death (*Entombment of Atala* by Anne-Louis-Girodet-Trioson, center right, with details) and justice (*Justice and Divine Vengeance Punishing Crime* by Pierre-Paul Prud'hon, right). The emotion of the *Return of Marcus Sextus* by Pierre-Narcisse Guérin (top) shows that neoclassicism was far from cold and insensitive as some have called it.

th. Géricault

Although Gros and Girodet were the first to free themselves from the influence of David, they could hardly have foreseen the revolution that the Romantics Géricault and Delacroix were to bring about. These two set themselves up in opposition to the partisans of classicism, led by Ingres (below right, his *Great Odalisque*, in strong contrast to Delacroix's *Death of Sardanapalus*, center). The Romantics stressed emotion, not virtue, and glorified the individual as opposed to the state. Once freed of the "antique" repertoire, they found new sources of inspiration such as contemporary history and the literature of the Middle Ages and the Renaissance. Nature found a place in their work which the neoclassicists had denied to her, preferring their theatrical decorative schemes. Stormy seas, misty horizons and jagged rocks were part of the new backdrop for Romantic drama. Two of the best-known paintings of the French Romantics were inspired by two pivotal events in the history of France: the *Raft of the Medusa*, (Géricault 1819, below) was prompted by the wreck of a frigate in 1816 and the subsequent abandonment of 149 sailors, who drifted off the coast of Africa for twelve days on a raft. This caused an international scandal and discredited the restored monarchy. *Liberty Leading the People* (Delacroix 1830, right), which evoked the *Trois Glorieuses*, the three days of Revolution in late July 1830 which precipitated the fall of Charles X.

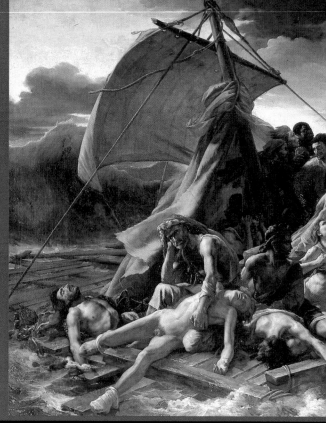

DANTE REREAD BY THE ROMANTICS
The *Souls of
Francesca da Rimini
and Paolo Malatesta
Appearing to Dante
and Virgil* (1855, right)
by Ary Scheffer is taken
from an episode in
Dante's *Divine Comedy*
(early 14th century).

THE MEDIEVAL VEIN
The Middle Ages and
the Renaissance along
with their tragedies
were rich sources for
the Romantics. The
Princes in the Tower
(1830) was inspired by
history and a play by
Shakespeare. Paul
Delaroche (right)
portrays the youthful
Edward V of England
and his brother
Richard who were
assassinated in 1483 by
their uncle Richard III,
himself the subject of a
Shakespeare play.

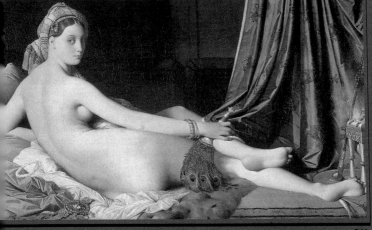

▲ French painting, the 19th century

(Sully, second floor,
rooms A, B, C and 50 to 73)

Rooms A, B and C conta
the collection of Carlos
Beistegui, the Princesse
Croÿ, and Hélène and Victo
Lyon, together with a numbe
of Impressionist work

The *Weir at Optevoz* by Charles-François Daubigny (1859, above).

Andromeda Chained to a Rock by the Nereids by Chassériau (1840, below) and *Young Man Sitting by the Sea* by Flandrin (1836, bottom).

TOWARD ECLECTICISM AND IMPRESSIONISM

LINE AND COLOR (ROOM 63), the two conflicting tendencies in French art, remained at odds as the 19th century wore on but sometimes they came together. A demonstration of pure form came with Hippolyte Flandrin's *Young Man Sitting by the Sea* which shows the legacy of Ingres. The supremacy of color was celebrated by orientalism with its realistic or idealized images of the East that was opening up to Western travelers: examples are Alexandre-Gabriel Deschamps' *Caravan* and Adrien Dauzat's *Convent of Saint Catherine on Mount Sinai.*

Théodore Chassériau's lines were bold enough but he was tempted by color contrast in his earlier paintings with their growing sense of movement: *Esther at Her Toilette*; *Andromeda*; and *Apollo and Daphne* in which the young girl is caught at the moment when her metamorphosis begins.

LANDSCAPE ART became a major genre in 19th-century France. The painters of the Barbizon School (ROOM 64) who took their name from a village near Fontainebleau, celebrated nature; Théodore Rousseau was the leading light among this new group of young artists. The *Chestnut Avenue* framed to accentuate its somber vaulting effect was refused by the 1841 Salon, but applauded by the Romantics. Rousseau's

subsequent *Way Out of the Forest at Fontainebleau*, a state commission, was enthusiastically received in 1850; his skies were thought especially remarkable. By contrast Narcisse Diaz de la Peña, a Barbizon painter and the future master of Renoir, enlivened his landscapes to emphasize their sensual side (*Folles Filles*, ROOM 65). Another major figure of the same school was Charles-François Daubigny (*Weir at Optevoz*, 1859, ROOM 66).

JEAN-BAPTISTE COROT AND HIS COLLECTORS (ROOMS 65 to 73).
The Louvre owes its Corot collection to two donors: Étienne
Moreau-Nélaton (1859–1927) and Georges Thomy-Thiéry
(1823–1902). Moreau-Nélaton bequeathed twenty-nine Corots
to the museum, covering the painter's entire career from his
first visit to Italy (*Castel Sant'Angelo and the Tiber*) to the
landscapes of the Île-de-France (*Bridge at Mantes*, the
Tower at Montlhery and the *Church at Marissel*, ROOM
69). There were also paintings by Delacroix: the *Taking
of Constantinople, Knights in Combat* and the *Orphan-
girl at the Cemetery*, a study for the *Massacre at Chios*.
Georges Thomy-Thiéry donated the works of 1830's
painters, including Ernest Meissonier and Delacroix
and some antique tragedies, among them the *Wrath
of Medea* which is simply a mouth, a silent shriek
and wild eyes staring through the darkness. Thiéry's
collection also included paintings by Decamps,
Millet and Daubigny in addition to Corot's *Woman
with a Pearl*, a study of the *Mona Lisa*, a pensive
Woman in Blue and *Souvenir de Mortefontaine* bought by
Napoleon III. This last comes very close to Impressionism.

▲ Northern european painting 15th to 17th centuries

Northern European painting, 18th to 19th centuries ▲ 272.

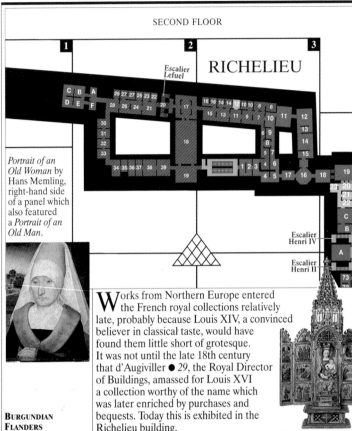

SECOND FLOOR

RICHELIEU

Escalier Lefuel

Escalier Henri IV

Escalier Henri II

Portrait of an Old Woman by Hans Memling, right-hand side of a panel which also featured a *Portrait of an Old Man*.

W orks from Northern Europe entered the French royal collections relatively late, probably because Louis XIV, a convinced believer in classical taste, would have found them little short of grotesque. It was not until the late 18th century that d'Augiviller ● *29*, the Royal Director of Buildings, amassed for Louis XVI a collection worthy of the name which was later enriched by purchases and bequests. Today this is exhibited in the Richelieu building.

BURGUNDIAN FLANDERS
Jan van Eyck was one of the first painters to get away from the International Gothic style (exemplified here by the *Chapelle Cardon*, early 15th century, far right) and to imagine an art much closer to reality, made possible by the technique of oil painting. His *Madonna of Chancelor Rolin* (right) was commissioned by the Duke of Burgundy's chancellor for his family chapel at the church of Notre Dame at Autun. Burgundy and Flanders formed a single political entity at that time.

THE 15TH CENTURY IN FLANDERS AND HOLLAND

INTERNATIONAL GOTHIC (ROOM 3). Cross the two first rooms of French painting to ROOM 3 where the *Chapelle Cardon* is displayed. The glass case to the left contains a Bohemian *Virgin and Child* (15th century).

VAN EYCK AND VAN DER WEYDEN (ROOM 4). Jan van Eyck c. 1400–41) so influenced his contemporaries that he was thought by them to have invented painting in oils. In the *Madonna of Chancelor Rolin*, one of his greatest works, van Eyck included a portrait of the donor himself; above the chancellor's head the capitals illustrate human weaknesses *Adam and Eve Driven from Eden, Cain and Abel,* the *Drunkenness of Noah*). Between Rolin and the Madonna is an empty space in which the prayer of the man and the blessing of the Christ-Child are exchanged against a background of a landscape and an idealized city divided in two by a river. In the left-hand glass case is a superb anonymous diptych, a *Saint John the Baptist* and a *Madonna and Child* in grisaille tone according to a technique which brings painting and sculpture close to one another. Quite as remarkable is Rogier van der Weyden's *Annunciation*; here everything has symbolic meaning with the three corollas of the blossoming lilies suggesting both virginity and the Trinity, the ewer and basin implying purity and the phial on the chimney piece transfixed by light evokes virginity and the approaching birth of Christ. The *Triptych of the Braque Family* by the same painter was a portable altarpiece used for the family's devotions when it was raveling. This is the first example in Flemish painting of half-length figures. If you view the triptych from behind, you see the *vanitas* on the reverse: on the back of the left panel is a skull – *Memento Mori* – and on the back of the right, the Cross.

HANS MEMLING (ROOM 6). The Louvre possesses an extraordinary *Portrait of an Old Woman* and the *Madonna of Jacques Floreins* painted by Hans Memling for a Bruges spice merchant in about 1490. On the wall to the left are several beautiful triptychs, along with the *Ship of Fools* by Hieronymus Bosch, a composition on the vices of gluttony and drunkenness heavily laced with anticlericalism.

THE STUDIOLO OF URBINO. ROOM 6 juxtaposes 14 of the 28 portraits of famous men painted in about 1475 for the *Studiolo* of Duke Federigo da Montefeltro at the Palace of Urbino (acquired for the Louvre by Napoleon III in 1861). These portraits are the work of the Flemish Justus of Ghent and the Spaniard Pedro Berruguete.

Triptych of the Braque Family (c. 1480). Center panel: Christ the Redeemer, the Virgin and Saint John the Evangelist; left panel, Saint John the Baptist; right panel, Saint Mary Magdalene.

A PANTHEON OF FAMOUS MEN
As though talent made great men part of a single family, all the great originators of the Renaissance in Italy feature in the *Studiolo* of Urbino, from Plato to Dante by way of Aristotle and Saint Augustine (above, Ptolemy and Plato).

SATIRE
The *Ship of Fools*, the only work by Hieronymus Bosch in the Louvre, was inspired by the book of the same name published in Basel in 1494 by the Alsatian Sébastian Brant. It shows the fools embarking for the land of folly, Narragonia.

**THE PORTRAIT,
A GENRE IN ITS
OWN RIGHT**
Above, left to right:
Erasmus Writing, by
Holbein, is caught in
profile engaged in his
intellectual calling
(Erasmus'
*Commentaries on the
New Testament*
epitomize the return
to the old texts then
championed by
humanism); Albrecht
Dürer *Self-portrait*
(the thistle in his
hand was a token of
fidelity from his
fiancée); Lucas
Cranach's
*Portrait of
Magdalena
Luther.*

GERMANY IN THE 15TH AND 16TH CENTURIES

In **ROOM 7** the Seine and the Louvre appear in the *Pietà*
painted (c. 1500) by the master of St-Germain-des-Prés ● *26*.
Bartolomaus Zeitblom was the painter of an altarpiece with
four panels centered on an *Annunciation* and Ulrich Apt the
Elder of another, centered on an *Adoration* scene which is a
fine example of late Gothic portraiture. The German schools,
without forsaking the Gothic tradition represented by the
great Flemish altarpieces and portraits of donors, were
heavily influenced by the Italian Renaissance. Iconographic
themes developed, spurred on by the Reformation, and the
isolated portrait became a genre in its own right.
THE TWO CABINETS IN ROOM 8 contain some breathtaking
marvels: Holbein's portraits of *Erasmus* and *Anne of Cleves*,
the fourth wife of Henry VIII of England; Lucas Cranach's
Portrait of a Lord of Kockeritz, Portrait of Magdalena Luther
(the daughter of the reformer Martin Luther), and the
celebrated *Venus in a Landscape* (1529) with her
transparent veil. A winged serpent concealed
in the décor holds a ring, the signature of
Lucas Cranach. Lastly there is the
extraordinary self-portrait of Albrecht
Dürer. *Christ Blessing the Children*
is attributed to the Master of the
Griffon's Head.

THE LOW COUNTRIES
IN THE 16TH CENTURY

ROOM 9 contains the *Banker and His Wife*
by Quentin Metsys. The figures have
nervous faces and hands that seem full of
life. Metsys was the first of a long line of
Antwerp painters; this picture is dated
1514 on the manuscript on the shelf
behind the couple. A Virgin by the same
artist known as the *Rattier Madonna*, has

a face reminiscent of Leonardo. There is also a *Madonna and Child* by Joos van Cleve which is noteworthy for its medieval background and for the Dominican monk, a witness of the purest faith who accompanies the Virgin. Saint Dominic in his 12th-century sermons had imposed the idea of austere virtue through his monastic Order (the Dominicans controlled the Inquisition at that time). The theme of religion had become a pretext for painting landscapes, a genre which acquired ever-greater importance; it also sanctioned portraits of women (the Madonna, Saint Barbara and Saint Catherine of Alexandria painted by Ambrosius Benson, an Italian who worked in Flanders. Heavily influenced by the Italian Renaissance is the *Carondelet Diptych* (1517) by Jan Gossaert known as Mabuse. The donor of this masterpiece who was doyen of the church at Besançon and a counselor of Charles V is shown praying beside the Virgin; on the back of the diptych is a magnificent trompe l'oeil of a skull, with a precept of Saint Jerome.

IN THE TWO SMALL CABINETS OF ROOM 10 are landscapes by Simon Bening rendered with an attention to detail that

ITALIAN INFLUENCES
The *Carondelet Diptych* (1517, top) by Mabuse, like the *Banker and His Wife* (above) by Quentin Metsys, show the influence of Italian art on the Northern schools. The *Banker* illustrates the tremendous economic development underway in Flanders, but it is also a kind of still life whose realism is illusory.

A PROTEST
Bruegel the Elder's *Beggars* (1568) with their fox brushes and carnival disguises represent a muted protest against the Spanish occupation of Flanders. On the back is written "Legless cripples, take heart, may your affairs prosper".

Left page, bottom, a *Vanitas* on the back of a mid 16th-century Flemish triptych.

NORTHERN MANNERISM
David and Bathsheba by Jan Massys from Antwerp (above), and *Perseus Rescuing Andromeda* by Joachim Wtewael, of Utrecht (below) are perfect illustrations of

betrays the miniaturist; *Saint Mary Magdalene Reading* by the master of half-figures; Pieter Huys' monster-filled *Temptation of Saint Anthony* (1547); and the elder Bruegel's *Beggars* (1568). *Lot and His Daughters* (School of Leyden) is a superb composition showing the wrath of God smiting Sodom.

IN ROOM 11 the splendors of the flesh dominate *David and Bathsheba* by Jan Massys. The subject is drawn from the Bible: Bathsheba in Hebrew means the "opulent one" who is noticed in her bath by the ageing David who will shortly become a sinner and a criminal (Samuel II, 11 and 12). The same room contains the *Dwarf of Cardinal Granvelle* who foreshadows Velasquez' degenerate buffoons and reminds us of Spain's long occupation of Flanders. The artist, Mor van Dashorst, went by the name of Antonio Moro when he worked for the Spanish court.

ROOM 12 consigned to the museum's Department of Graphic Arts, exhibits by rotation the designs for the *Hunt* tapestry by Jan van der Straet (1523–1605), commissioned for the Poggio a Caiano villa in Tuscany. The painter was a native of Bruges who came to live in Italy, and signed his works under the name of Giovanni Stradano.

16TH-CENTURY MANNERISM
Mannerism which came from Italy and spread throughout Europe. These paintings exemplify the curving lines, Baroque rhythms and refined materials of the genre to which Northern painters added sumptuous landscapes.

(ROOM 13). The second Italian Renaissance influenced by Mannerism ▲ *265* found echoes all over Europe. Line, stylization, affectation and rhythm were its principal characteristics. The foreground of Joachim Wtewael's *Perseus Rescuing Andromeda* contains a mass of shells whose tones echo the pearly flesh of the princess. In Paul Bril's *Diana and Her Nymphs* the surroundings also contribute to the narrative, as they do in Valckenborch's *Temptation of Saint Anthony*, where an overwhelming forest over which an imaginary monster soars, seems to crush the saint.

7TH-CENTURY FLANDERS

N ROOM 14 cabinet 1 are more
pictures by Paul Bril and some
beautiful landscapes (on the
right at the entrance), notably a
wonderful *View of a Seaport*
attributed to Anton Mozart and
Winter Landscape by Denys
van Alsloot. In cabinet 2 is the
Battle of Arbelles (in which
Alexander the Great crushed
Darius and the Achemenids)
painted with considerable dash
by Jan Bruegel (the Elder
"Velvet" Bruegel) to whom we
also owe a *View of Tivoli*. The
Italian landscape had by now
become an esential reference in
European painting.

"VELVET" BRUEGEL also
features in ROOM 15 with an
Earthly Paradise awash with wild
animals and nostalgia. In
addition to a *Church Interior* by Van Steenwyck, a portrait of
Queen Marie de' Medici (in whose portrait Frans Pourbus
seems more interested in the clothes than in the face)
foreshadows the Baroque extravagance of Rubens.

POURBUS reappears in ROOM 16, cabinet 1 with *Henri IV King
of France in Black Costume. Diana Discovering the Pregnancy
of Callisto* is more memorable for its landscape by Denys von
Alsloot than for its figures by Hendrick de Clerck.

RUBENS (ROOMS 17 and 18) was the most influential Flemish
painter of the 17th century, when his home city of Antwerp
was one of the world's greatest ports. A consummately
European artist, trained in Italy where he met with the first
glimmerings of Baroque, Rubens
worked for the courts of Paris,
Madrid and London. A first great
Rubens, among many others,
dominates ROOM 17: this is
*Tomyris, Queen of the Scythians,
Plunging the Head of Cyrus
into a Pitcher filled with Blood.*
The series of paintings
done by the artist
illustrating the history of
Marie de' Medici may be
seen in the Galerie Médicis
(to the left, ROOM 18, ▲ *250–1*).

JACOB JORDAENS (ROOM 19 at the end of the Galerie
Médicis) was Ruben's best pupil. This room contains
a number of his tumultuous, joyous canvases, notably
Jesus Evicting the Merchants from the Temple (nobody
in this picture seems too worried about what is
happening), the *King Drinks* and the *Child Jupiter* in
which the god is eclipsed by the goat Amalthea who
nourished him on Mount Ida. Go back to ROOM 17
to continue the circuit.

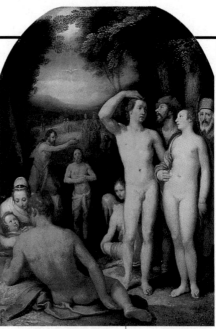

FLEMISH GRACES
In the *Baptism of
Christ* (above) by
Cornelis van Haarlem
the subject of the
picture is relegated to
the deep background
behind a group of
cunningly executed
Italianate nudes. Left,
an *Imaginary View* of
a landscape packed
with Italian
architecture by Jan
Bruegel the Elder.

*Tomyris, Queen of the
Scythians* (below) by
Rubens entered
Louis XIV's
collection in 1671.

The Coronation of M...
de' Medici at St-I...
(painting XIII, be...
which inspired Da...
Coronation of Napole...
two hundred years l...

The group of twenty-four canvases
painted by Rubens between 1622 and 1625 for
the Galerie Médicis in the Luxembourg Palace
constitute a phenomenal achievement; over 300
square yards of painting done by a single artist.
The work is a series of allegories on the life of
Marie de' Medici, wife of Henri IV, who was
regent after his death until her son Louis XIII
came of age. In this masterpiece of Baroque
art, realism and fantasy are blended in a series
of compositions which display wonderfully
fluent dynamism and unearthly light.

*Birth of Marie de' Medici
in Florence*
April 26, 1573 (painting V).

Education of Marie de' Medici
(painting VI).

*Marie de' Medici
Landing at Marseilles,*
November 3, 1600
(painting IX).

The Triumph of Juliers,
September 1, 1610
(painting XVI).

Happiness of the Regency
(painting XVIII).

The Majority of Louis XIII,
October 20, 1614
(painting XIX).

*The King Meets Marie de'
Medici at Lyons*
November 9, 1600
(painting X).

*Birth of Louis XIII at
Fontainebleau,*
September 27, 1601
(painting XI).

*Henri IV Goes to War in
Germany and Entrusts the
Government of His Kingdom
to the Queen ,*March 20, 1610
(painting XII).

*The Queen Flees from the
Château de Bois* on the night
of February 21–2, 1619
(painting XX).

The Treaty of Angoulême,
April 30, 1619
(painting XXI).

*Conclusion of the Peace at
Angers,* August 10, 1620
(painting XXII).

THE PAINTER'S FAMILY
The portrait of
*Hélène Fourment and
Her Children* (right)
by Rubens (husband
and father) was
bought in 1784 for
the collection of
Louis XVI.

**FROM THE HUMBLEST
TO THE GREATEST**
Joos van Craesbeeck's
Smoker may be a
lively self-portrait.
Charles I of England
by Antony van Dyck
(below) acquired by
Louis XVI in 1175,
shows the English
monarch at the hunt
in a simple
composition painted
with enormous
sensitivity. Charles
epitomizes the
elegant, enlightened
prince. The cane is
his symbol of royalty
along with his rich
costume which
contrasts vividly with
the landscape.

RETURN TO ROOM 17 and take time to look at the landscapes
of Bril, a *Cat Discovering Game* from an unexpected angle by
Jan Fyt and the *Holy Family During the Flight from Egypt*, a
lovely night landscape lit by the moon. The Lefuel staircase
(ROOM 20) leads on through to ROOM 21, which contains more
works by Rubens.

RUBENS APPEARS AGAIN in ROOMS 21 and 22. In ROOM 21 are
two portraits of *Hélène Fourment*, the
artist's wife. In one, she wears black with
a striking tonal contrast to the red
doublet of the child on her left. In the
other, she is in white. The cluster of fat-
bottomed *putti* surrounding the *Madonna
and Child* are echoed by the whirling
figures of the *Village Wedding*; all
Baroque art is here with its perpetual
motion and tumult of colors.

ROOM 22 contains a collection of Rubens
sketches, among them one for the *Raising
of the Cross* (this altarpiece is at Angers).
There is also a fine *Cavalry* by David
Teniers the Elder with some powerful
light effects.

TENIERS. There are more painting by this
artist in ROOM 23, notably caricatures,
along with Joos van Craesbeeck's
Smoker. The man depicted was the baker

at the prison in which Adriaen Brouwer was imprisoned for debt. Brouwer was Ruben's favorite painter; the prisoner so thoroughly won over the baker that he made him his disciple in both his paintings and his debauches. Tavern scenes were a frequent and well-worn theme of Flemish painters.

MONUMENTAL PORTRAITS BY VAN DYCK occupy ROOM 24. Here the atmosphere changes, with formal portraits of aristocrats such as a *Gentleman with a Sword* or the beautiful *Marquesa Geromina Spinola-Doria* from Genoa. The Flemish painter lived in England from 1632 until his death in 1641, shortly before the destruction of the world he had painted. Van Dyck's portraits of *Charles I* and *James Stuart* are full of life as well as being profound psychological studies.

IN ROOM 25 are two tiny church interiors by Pieter Neefs the Younger. Dutch painters were masters of the art of illustrating architecture because of their mastery and close application of the laws of perspective.

VAN DYCK IN ROOM 26. He reemerges with a double portrait of the *Dukes of Bavaria and Cumberland*. In *Rinaldo and the Enchantress Armida* the tangled bodies show how much Van Dyck owes to Rubens and Jordaens, his masters. *The Dessert* by Jan Davidsz. de Heem, illustrates the care taken by Dutch painters in rendering such things as fruits, dishes and silver.

THE 17TH CENTURY IN HOLLAND

ROOM 27. To the right are those favorite characters of Baroque writers, *Pyramus and Thisbe,* painted by Leonaert Bramer: their story formed the basis for the play of Romeo and Juliet. Beside them, the dress of the *Lady at Her Toilette* by Pieter Codde, is altogether admirable. In the second cabinet are the magnificent ruins of *Campo Vaccino,* among other Italian landscapes by Cornelis van Poelenburgh. There is also a superb *Ham* spiked all over with cloves (spices were then a supreme luxury in cooking) by Floris van Schooten.

ROOM 28 contains a series of remarkably detailed portraits – *Portrait*

Although his masters knew Italy, Rembrandt never visited that country; nevertheless he developed an art in Amsterdam which blended the magnificence of Baroque painting with an inward-looking somberness. This gave his work a tragic dimension. Everything in Rembrandt is absolutely unique, including his mastery of light, his dark glazes, his dull-golds and his brushwork, which began with great precision and later grew troubled. Always a reflective artist, he painted many self-portraits – the Louvre alone has three – illustrating the sense of deep introspection that he was to cultivate until his death in 1669 at the age of 63. Although he remained aloof and independent of official commissions, he won immediate fame: his influence on art was enormous, even in his own lifetime.

The Flayed Ox Carcass was bought very cheaply by the Louvre in 1857 because its subject matter offended the bourgeoisie taste. "The sordid butcher's cellar is illuminated with the gold and ruby sheen of the bloody carcass," writes Charles Sterling in his *The Still Life, from Antiquity to the 20th Century* (1985). Delacroix, Daumier and (in 1925) Soutine were all inspired by this provocative painting, which has parallels with Chardin's painting, *The Skate* ▲ 227.

The three *Portraits of the Artist* at the Louvre. Rembrandt painted the ones on the left and right when he was 27 and the one in the middle when he was 54.

Rembrandt Van Rijn ▲
(Richelieu, second floor, room 31)

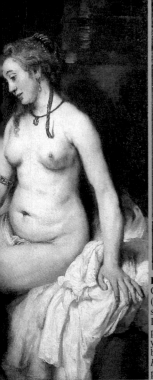

LIGHT ABOVE ALL THINGS Confronted by *Bathsheba* (1654, left) the spectator sees with the eyes of King David who is not in the picture; the beauty of the young woman is breathtaking. The *Philosopher* (top) with its pronounced chiaroscuro approaches the monochromatic. The *Archangel Gabriel Quitting Tobias and His Family* (above) seems to be sucked upward by the light, an impression that is strengthened by the dark void in the lower right hand corner.

255

SCENES OF DAILY LIFE
Despite their different ways of treating their themes, we find the same interest in ordinary existence and the same meticulous detail in the work of Adriaen van Ostade (*Portrait of a Family*, top of facing page, details above), Gerard Dou (*Self-portrait with Palette*, right) and Vermeer, two of whose most celebrated works the Louvre possesses. These are the *Lacemaker* (below) and the *Astronomer* (facing page, center right).

of a Man by Frans Hals, *Portrait of a Woman* by Pieter Soutman. The *Lady Musicians* by Gerrit van Honthorst, the *Gypsy Girl* and the *Clown with His Lute* by Frans Hals are characteristic of the influence of Caravaggio on Dutch painting in the first half of the 17th century: these are not so much portraits as subjects; the handling is broader and the brushwork similar to Caravaggio's.

FRANS POST (ROOMS 29 and 30) went to Brazil with Prince Maurice of Nassau's expedition between 1637 and 1648. He was the first European artist to paint these landscapes of the New World. A rodent in the estuary of the *Rio San Francisco*, cactuses, negros – Post was depicting something completely different, so much so that his works were eventually used as patterns for West Indies wall-hangings. Also in ROOM 29 is a *Church Interior* by Saenredam, a coldly geometrical piece; the same high finish may be seen in the portraits of Nicolaes Elias (called Pickenoy) with lace that is a pretext for an exercise in painterly virtuosity. In ROOM 30 there is a *Portrait of a Child of Twelve* by Wybrand de Geest, and a fine *Still life with a Silver Goblet* by Willem Clausz. Heda which clearly indicates that this genre – the allegory of passing time contrasted with human vanity – was a major feature of 17th-century Holland. Landscapes are also represented by the works of Nicolaes Berchem.

ROOM 31 is entirely given over to Rembrandt ▲ *254*. The most famous of the master's paintings to be seen in the Louvre is *Bathsheba*.

ROOM 32 contains *Bathsheba Receiving King David's Letter* by Willem Drost, a pupil of Rembrandt; more nudes in Nicolaes Maes' *Bathers* and dramatic light effects in Frans de Halst's *Castle*.

IN ROOM 33 a young *Dutch Prince Drawn in a Coach by Miniature Goats* is the subject of a canvas by Ferdinand Bol, one of Rembrandt's favorite disciples. Adriaen van Ostade who was a follower of Frans Hals, was the author of the fine *Portrait of a Family* displayed here: note also the beautiful portraits by Nicolaes van Helst (*Unveiled Woman Lifting a Drape*). Finally the simple *Bush* painted by Jacob van Ruisdael somehow has the motion of a flame. Note also a *Young Man and a Procuress* by Michael Sweerts.

THE OUDEKERK AT DELFT (ROOM 34) is the subject of a superb architectural study by Hendrick van der Vliet. Nearby, the *War Fleet Close to Shore* is rendered in dramatic black and white tones (Van de Velde), a reminder that Holland was a maritime nation (under attack in this case by the France of Louis XIV) and that for the Dutch the painting of seascapes was a genre in its own right.

GERARD DOU (ROOM 35). Apart from his *Self-portrait*, Dou's the *Gold-weigher*, the *Trumpet Player*, the *Cook,* the *Dutch Housewife* and the *Grocer's Wife* offer intriguing insights into the occupations and callings of ordinary people. The *Dropsical Woman* is fascinatingly realistic with scintillating fabrics, fine light and exquisite detail.

ROOM 36. The *Meal of Herrings* and the *Herb Market* by Gabriel Metsu (1629–67) give another glimpse of life in Amsterdam. The latter is remarkable in that it is an open air scene, combining the themes of love and the still life.

IN ROOM 37 hangs Jacob van Loo's *Half-clothed Woman* and a *Still life with Fruits* by Abraham Mignon.

TWO GREAT VERMEERS, the *Lacemaker* and the *Astronomer* occupy ROOM 38. Both protagonists are involved in their tasks, haloed in diffuse light. Here also is Pieter de Hooch's *Young Woman Drinking* with her striking scarlet skirt, and various Dutch landscapes – in particular Jacob van Ruisdael's superb *Ray of Sunlight*, seascapes (*Storm at Sea* by Aelbert Cuyp, the "Dutch Claude Lorrain") and city scenes (the *Herengracht in Amsterdam* by Jan van der Heyden).

THE DUTCH COUNTRYSIDE (ROOM 39) with its astonishing skies is represented in the paintings of Wouwerman (*Wooden Bridge over a Torrent*), in Adam Pynacker's *Landscape at Sunset* with the horn of a goat catching the last rays of the sun, and in Meindert Hobbema's *Watermill* and the *Farm*.

A MARITIME POWER
The wealth of the Low Countries was founded on trade in which the Dutch merchant fleet played the principal role. Seascapes were a genre in which Ludolf Backhuyzen was the outstanding figure (*Dutch Vessels off the Port of Amsterdam*, below).

▲ Italian painting

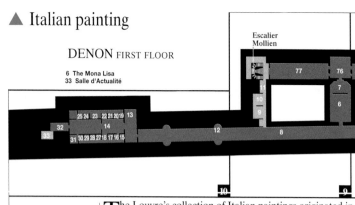

The Louvre's collection of Italian paintings originated in the royal collection, thanks to the acquisitions made by François I and Louis XIV. Its presentation, by period and by region (concentrating on the artistic centers of the peninsula traces the history of Italian painting from the 13th to the 18th century. The collection occupies the Grande Gallerie and its connecting spaces. The best way to start the visit, via the Escalier de la Victoire de Samothrace, is to pass through the Percier and Fontaine vestibules (ROOM 1), then into Salle Duchâtel (ROOM 2) where the frescos of Botticelli and Fra Angelico hang.

FLORENCE FROM THE 13TH TO THE 15TH CENTURY

THE GRACE OF THE RENAISSANCE
Linear rhythm and tender colors served the classical ideal of Botticelli in his 1483 frescos for the Villa Lemmi, near Florence. (Above, *Venus and the Graces Offering Gifts to a Maiden*).

THE SALON CARRÉ (ROOM 3, ▲ 129). This room houses the Florentine "primitives", including Cimabue and Giotto, contemporaries of Dante who were rediscovered in the late 1700's, and whose works were brought to the Louvre by Vivan Denon. They demonstrate an interest in realism that allowed them to move away from the rigorous traditions of Byzantine art. At that time Florence was a major artistic center, as evidenced by the *Virgin and Child in Majesty* by Cimabue (right, c. 1270), borrowed from Byzantine iconography but handled with a more supple sense of line. Thirty years later, Giotto's *Saint Francis of Assisi* (below, left) exhibited a totally new approach to figurative expression. This room also houses works by Fra Angelico, Uccello and Filippo Lippi, which mark the start of the Florentine Renaissance ▲ 260.

In the late 1430's, Paolo Uccello painted a group of three panels (one of which is at the Louvre) entitled *Battle of San Romano*, in which he put into practise his research on perspective. In addition to the sense of confusion demanded by the subject matter, the organization of the painting is entirely ruled by an obsession with depth.

Escalier de la Victoire de Samothrace

34

Galerie d'Apollon

1
2
3

FROM THE END OF THE 13TH TO THE 15TH CENTURY: INTERNATIONAL GOTHIC, SIENA AND VENICE

SALLE DES SEPT MÈTRES (ROOM 4)

8

Napoleon III's purchase of the Campana collection in 1863 gave the Trecento and Quattrocento (the 14th and 15th centuries) the distinction they now have in the Louvre. Florence was not Italy's only artistic center, even if Vasari concentrated on the city in his painting *Lives of the Artists,* and Siena, Venice, Bologna, Padua and Ferrara should be recognized for their original "schools". Despite its intense focus on religious themes, Italian painting of the 13th to 15th centuries offers clear insights into a contemporary society in which politics and art were changing radically. In the Salle des Sept Mètres are works by the masters Guido da Siena, Gentile da Fabriano, Pisanello, by the Venetian Giovanni Bellini and by Liberale da Verona: painters whose names evoke the cities, republics and principalities of this change. Also in this room is the *Carrying of the Cross* by Simone Martini, a work painted by this artist from Siena shortly before his entrance into the papal court of Avignon (1336–44).

MONUMENTALITY
In the *Portrait of Sigismondo Malatesta* (above, c. 1450), Piero della Francesca follows the formula of head and chest in profile borrowed from traditional Gothic style, but Francesca's style gives the portrait a monumentality.

APPLIED PERSPECTIVE
In the 1420's, Brunelleschi's perfection of perspective created a revolution in the painter's art, as may be seen in the *Martyrdom of Saints Cosmos and Damian*, by the Florentine artist Fra Angelico (1438, left) and, from the same period, in Paolo Uccello's *Battle of San Romano* (below, left): the alternating planes of color give the illusion of depth. These two paintings are on show in the Salon Carré (ROOM 3).

ITALIAN PAINTING
OF THE LATE 15TH CENTURY

THE GRANDE GALERIE (ROOMS 5, 8 AND 12, ▲ *129*) holds masterpieces from Tuscany and Northern Italy dating from the 15th century to the 17th century. The art of the *Quattrocento* (15th century, ROOM 5) is characterized by representations largely inspired by the revival of architecture and sculpture in Florence. Close attention to perspective, and a refinement of design and color characterize the works of such painters as Andrea Mantegna, Domenico Ghirlandaio and Perugino. The *Calvary* of Mantegna (c. 1459), is a masterpiece of the perspective perfected by Brunelleschi in Florence at the start of the century. New themes, both sacred and profane, came into vogue: the *Portrait of an Old Man and a Boy* by Ghirlandaio is far removed from the hieratic character and the still Gothic coldness evident in portraits painted by Pisanello in the Quattrocento. This change is particularly striking in painters such as Filippino Lippi (ROOM 3) or Sandro Botticelli: in the latter's fresco *Venus and the Graces Offering Gifts to a Maiden* (ROOM 1, ▲ *258*) the terrestrial world represented by a young girl contrasts in its simplicity

Above,
Christ by the Column,
by Antonello
da Messina.

> "Andrea Mantegna is so sure that his hard
> road leads to absolute reality, that he marches
> to the rhythm of a steel harp."
>
> Élie Faure

with the fluid outlines of the immortals. Venice also formed part of the early Renaissance: Giovanni Bellini's emotional *Virgin and Child with Saint Peter and Saint Sebastian* clearly echoes the works of his Florentine contemporaries.

Above, *Virgin and Child between Saint Peter and Saint Sebastian,* by the Venetian Giovanni Bellini.

Above left, *Portrait of an Old Man and a Boy* by Domenico Ghirlandaio (ROOM 5).

ABSOLUTE REALITY
Calvary by Andrea Mantegna (left), formed the central scene of the lower part of an altarpiece for a church in Verona. The details demonstrate the painter's skill, particularly in the rendering of perspective (ROOM 5).

261

▲ The Mona Lisa

Since 2005, the room formerly known as Salle des États displays the Mona Lisa opposite Veronese's *Wedding Feast at Cana*. Both pictures benefit from the overhead lighting, and are surrounded by about fifty 16th-century Venetian paintings

The *Mona Lisa* has had a checkered history: stolen in 1911, she was recovered two years later. Today she is as coveted and praised as ever and is closely protected.

The *Portrait of Lisa Gherardini,* also called *La Gioconda* or *Mona Lisa*, was the principal jewel of François I's collection and has long been the most celebrated painting in the Louvre.

Leonardo da Vinci was a painter, a scholar and a theoretician: his art marks the apogee of the Renaissance. He came to live in France in 1516, at the request of François I ▲ *215* and died there three years later. A mysterious poetry flows from his paintings, most of which contain

elaborate compositions, delicate reliefs, a serene misty light and enigmatic smiles. Above right, and shown in ROOM 5, the *Virgin and Child with Saint Anne* (above, a sketch for *Saint Anne* in the Department of Graphic Arts ● *62*), remarkable for its movement and the interaction between the figures. Right, *Saint John the Baptist,* ROOM 8; facing page, the *Mona Lisa*.

▲ Italian painting
Venetian painting

The restoration of the Salle des États, completed in 2005, has greatly improved the lighting on the works displayed, and also made it easier to relate them to the overall chronological presentation of Italian painting whose central avenue is the Grande Galerie

RENAISSANCE OF VENICE
Below, Vittore Carpaccio's *Sermon of Saint Stephen at Jerusalem* (1514), ROOM 5, in which the lucid palette of Bellini is used to depict Jerusalem filled with light and figures in sumptuous eastern dress.

"THE WEDDING FEAST AT CANA"
(above, right) Painted by Veronese in 1562–3 for the refectory of the monastery of San Giorgio Maggiore, this painting is about 21 feet by 30 feet. The huge canvas had to be restored in situ between 1989 and 1992: its sheer size made it impossible to move. The restoration uncovered the original colors under the various touchings-up and grime (far right, top to bottom, a detail of the steward before restoration, X-rayed and after restoration).

TITIAN AND GIORGIONE
Masterpieces by Titian, court painter to Emperor Charles V: *Christ Crowned by Thorns* (right) and *Concert Champêtre* (left), which for years was attributed to his master, Giorgione. Titian's motto was "Art is stronger than Nature".

VENETIAN PAINTING
OF THE LATE 16TH CENTURY

THE ROOM CONTAINING THE MONA LISA (SALLE DE LA JOCONDE), FORMERLY SALLE DES ÉTATS ▲ *131* (ROOMS 6 AND 7) demonstrates the extraordinary creative dynamism of Venice in the 16th century. At this time, patrician families, doges, churches, religious institutions and *scuole* ("schools") all employed many painters.

A merchant city and an international maritime power, Venice was a focus of creativity. In general, the Venetians favored coloration over the art of draftsmanship exemplified by the Florentines, and Venetian painting came to define a type of classicism whose influence was just as strong as its rival's. In the second half of the 15th century, Giovanni Bellini was the greatest exponent of the science of light, using a lucid, brilliant palette. A second generation of painters, centered around the artists Giorgione and Titian, were heavily influenced by Leonardo da Vinci's visit to Venice in 1501. They worked to soften outlines and use light and broad masses of color to give dramatic intensity to their compositions, portraits, religious and mythological works, and to major pieces commissioned for Venice's churches and religious institutions. Among the most famous of these pieces is Tintoretto's sketch for *Paradise*, which once decorated the Council chamber at the Doge's Palace but was destroyed in a fire. The works of Paolo Veronese, including the spectacular *Wedding Feast at Cana,* are prime examples of Venetian classicism. A group of musicians at the front of this picture are thought to depict the main Venetian painters of the artist's time, among them Titian (in red) and Veronese himself (in white). Also in these rooms are other works by Veronese, including *The Beautiful Nani, The Pilgrims from Emmaus* and *Jupiter Striking Down the Vices.* By Titian, in addition to *Concert Champêtre,* is the beautiful *Woman at the Mirror* and the portrait *Man with a Glove.* The artist Jacopo Bassano is also represented in this room, with the works *Deposition of Christ* and *Two Dogs.*

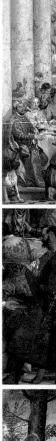

GRANDE GALERIE
(ROOMS 5 AND 8).
This magnificent gallery contains some priceless masterpieces from the Golden Age. If Michelangelo, the painter of the Sistine Chapel, is only represented in the Louvre by sculptures ▲ *195*, thanks to François I the museum contains several paintings by Leonardo da Vinci ▲ *262*, including the *Mona Lisa* (ROOM 6), *Virgin and Child with Saint Anne, the Virgin on the Rocks,* and the *Portrait of a Woman (La Belle Ferronnière)* and

"LA BELLE JARDINIÈRE"
Virgin and Child, with Saint John the Baptist (known as *La Belle Jardinière*, above) and the portrait of *Balthazar Castiglione* (below, left) – one of the painter's friends – are among the most famous of Raphael's works.

a number of sketches in the Department of Graphic Arts (● *62*). Opposite the works of Leonardo hang those Isabella d'Este collected in her *studiolo* (Mantegna, Correggio, Perugino, Costa), ROOM 5. The painter Raphael was born and did much of his work in the Marches, but also established himself in Florence and laid the groundwork for what was to become the classical style. He is well represented in the Louvre's collections, in particular by *La Belle Jardinière,* but also by many sketches. In the mid-16th century, Italian painting evolved in the direction of Mannerism, which sought to represent an ideal of beauty rather than a natural image of it. The sinuous lines, unreal light, strange proportions and meticulous refinement typical of this movement have been viewed as signs of a growing insipidity. However artists such as Pontormo (*Madonna and Child with Saint Anne and Other Saints*) and Bronzino (*Portrait of a Man Holding a Small Statue*, below right) achieved a balanced synthesis and

Below, right
Portrait of a Sculptor (Pierino da Vinci?), by Bronzino, ROOM 8.

roduced paintings of rare intensity. The
Venetian painter Lorenzo Lotto's *Saint Jerome*
s a poetical, nostalgic work in the manner of
Giorgione.

ITALIAN PAINTING OF THE 17TH CENTURY

GRANDE GALERIE (ROOMS 8 AND 12). The
Renaissance was followed, in the 17th century,
by several parallel movements, including
Baroque, classicism and Caravaggism, while
Venice and Florence yielded their primacy to
Rome and Naples. One dominant personality
emerged at the turn of the 16th century; this was
Michelangelo da Merisi, known as Caravaggio,
a tormented, violent painter who used ordinary
people as his inspiration and models. Though
he had no pupils and was always on the move, Caravaggio
achieved enormous influence throughout Europe ▲ *219*
and *271*. The revolutionary use of light and realism in his
paintings contrasted with the classicism of the brothers
Agostino and Annibale Carracci from Bologna, who moved

**REALISM
VERSUS THE ACADEMIC**
There is no similarity
between Caravaggio's
Death of the Virgin,
(ROOM 8) for which
he used the body of
a girl drowned in the
Tiber as his model
(1605–1606, below
left) and *Deianeira
and the Centaur
Nessus* (above, ROOM
12) by Guido Reni.
The first is about
grief and death,
a dramatic reality
peopled with grave
silhouettes; the
second presents
a female figure,
graceful but
unearthly. "For the
first time in the
history of painting,
the principle of
reality is immaterial:
it has substance, but
is not made flesh."
R. Longhi, on
Caravaggio.

ROME – ANCIENT MEETS MODERN
Romulus and Remus Recovered by Faustulus by Pietro da Cortona (c.1634, above) recounts an ancient legend using conventional figures, decorative colors and well-worn classical references.

The *Gallery of Views of Ancient Rome* by Giovanni Paolo Panini (1758, right, ROOM 14), which has a conterpart in the *Gallery of Views of Modern Rome*, represents an imaginary museum of architectural monuments in the guise of a gallery of paintings. It was in the 18th century that interest in archeology was born, with the discoveries of Pompeii and Herculaneum and the first excavations in Rome.

Mannerism toward a form of classicism that bordered on the academic. In the western part of the Grande Galerie, hang Caravaggio's *Death of the Virgin*, *The Fortune Teller* and the portrait of *Alof de Wignacourt*, as well as classical works by L'Albane, the Carrachi brothers, Pietro da Cortona, Domenichino, Guercino, and Guido Reni.

THE GRAPHIC ARTS: ITALY

THE SMALL SALLES MOLLIEN (ROOMS 9, 10 and 11).
These two rooms feature displays by the Department of Graphic Arts which include the collection of drawings (Drawing Cabinet), the Edmond de Rothschild collection, original engraved plates and 16th-century Italian cartoons on show in rotation.

LA SERENISSIMA
Venice in the 18th
century was in steep
decline, though
the prevailing
atmosphere there
was one of perpetual
carnival. The genre
scenes of Gian
Domenico Tiepolo
(The *Tooth Puller*,
left) and Guardi's
painting of the
carnival (*La Salute*,
c. 1770, below)
reflect this.

17TH AND 18TH-CENTURY NAPLES, GENOA, ROME, VENICE... AND SPAIN

THE SALLE SALVATOR ROSA
(ROOM 13). Works by Salvator
Rosa, Pietro da Cortona and
Luca Giordano, representing
17th-century painting in
Naples, Genoa and Rome.

THE SALLE PIAZZETTA (ROOM 13).
This room is devoted to 18th-
century painting in Venice, Rome and Naples. Eighteenth-
century Venetian art was extremely fashionable in the 19th
century and there are many examples here, but the Louvre
also has some very important Roman works in particular
Giovanni Paolo Panini's "Galleries" of views of Ancient
Rome and of Modern Rome (below left), as well as a series
of pictures depicting the celebrations held in Rome in honor
of the Dauphin, son of Louis XV. You will also find in these
two rooms superb paintings by Giambattista Piazzetta,
Antonio Pellegrini, Giuseppe Crespi and others.
THE SMALL "CABINETS". These rooms complete the survey
of 17th- (ROOMS 15 TO 18) and 18th-century Italian
painting(ROOMS 19 TO 25), the latter featuring important
works by Canaletto, Guardi and Tiepolo.
SPAIN AROUND THE TIME OF GOYA (ROOMS 26 TO 30 AND
32). Goya (1746–1828) dominated Spanish art between
1760 and 1820. He painted every genre, sacred as well as
profane, and his numerous portraits reveal the sharpness
of his vision and the vigour of his interpretation. Also in
ROOM 32 are works by two painters from an earlier
generation: Germany Llorente and Melendez, as well as
Velázquez. ROOM 31 displays Greek and Russian icons.

This Greek icon from
the 16th century
(below) depicts Saint
John the Baptist.

▲ Paintings of the Spanish school
(Denon, first floor, rooms 26 to 30 and 32
(Sully, second floor, room A)

*Still Life with F
by Luis Euge
Meléndez (1716–8*

The vogue for Spanish painting came late to France, impelled
by the Romanticism of the 19th century. The works "collected"
or rather looted by Napoleon I were restored to Spain after
the fall of the Empire; another collection assembled by Louis-
Philippe was unfortunately sold under the Second Empire.
The Louvre's acquisition policy and a number of major
donations have made it possible to reconstitute an ensemble
of paintings that is representative of Spanish art from the Gothic
period onward, from Martorell to Goya (late 18th century),
by way of Mannerism and El Greco. These works are on show
in rooms 26 to 30 and 32 of the Denon wing, after the Grande
Galerie, as well as in Room A of the Sully wing.

A GREEK IN SPAIN
Domenico
Theotocopoulos
called El Greco
(1541–1614), a nati
of Crete, moved to
Toledo at the end o
the 16th century.
Trained in Italy by t
Mannerists he was
the painter of agon
and ecstasy, sinuou
line and extreme
austerity of color as
exemplified by his
*Christ on the Cross
Adored by Donors*
(left).

THE MARTYRDOM OF SAINT GEORGE
The *Flagellation of Saint George*
(above) is one of four paintings by
Bernardo Martorell (c. 1427–52)
which formed the side panels of an
altarpiece centered on a portrayal
of *Saint George and the Dragon*.

THE RIGOR OF ZURBARÁN
Francesco de Zurbarán
(1598–1664) painted a four-part
series on the life of Saint
Bonaventura, the moral reformer of
the Franciscan order. Two of
these pictures are in the Louvre,
among them *Saint Bonaventura on
His Deathbed* (right). Austerity and
spirituality characterize this
"Caravaggesque" painter.

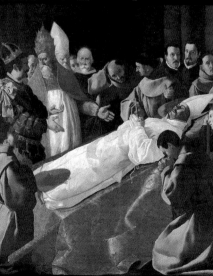

THE 17TH CENTURY IN SPAIN

Jusepe de Ribera (1591–1652) and Bartolomé Esteban Murillo (1618–82) were among the greatest painters of their age. Influenced by Caravaggio and Flemish painters their works have an astonishing realism which shows a darker aspect of the Spanish Golden Age. See Ribera's *Club-footed Boy* (1642, left) and Murillo's *Young Beggar* (above).

THE CARLOS DE BEISTEGUI COLLECTION

This rich collection was bequeathed to the Louvre in 1942 and is displayed in the Sully Wing. It includes a number of masterpieces of European painting, among them the portrait of the *Contessa del Carpio*, Marquesa de la Solana (above), by Francisco de Goya y Lucientes (1746–1828), the elegant and serious portraitist of the king and Madrid aristocracy.

▲ Northern European painting: 18th to 19th centuries

(Richelieu, second floor, rooms A to F)
(Denon, first floor, room 74)

Northern European paintings (Dutch, Flemish, Belgian, Scandinavian, Swiss, Russian, German and Austrian) from the 18th to 19th centuries are displayed on the second floor of the Richelieu wing. A selection of English paintings is temporarily exhibited on the first floor of the Denon wing. These works illustrate the development of Romanticism through canvases by Fuseli, Friedrich, Lawrence and Turner.

Lady Macbeth Sleepwalking (1784) by Henry Fuseli (1741–1825).

ROMANTICISM
The leader of the Romantic movement in German painting was Caspar David Friedrich. His *Tree of Crows* (left) shows a leafless oak which grows on the burial mound of a forgotten hero, a symbol of the vanity of human pretensions picked at by the crows. Even so, the light in the background lends an aura of hope.

ENGLISH PORTRAITS
Conversation in a Park (below) by Thomas Gainsborough, similar to the *fêtes galantes* of Watteau, shows the painter and his wife in a park in the year of their marriage (1742). The temple in the background would seem to be that of Hymen. The carefully depicted park shows the painter's love of landscape. Sir Thomas Lawrence gained fame for portraits such as *Mr and Mrs Julius Angerstein* (1792, below). Angerstein, art-lover and friend of Lawrence who did several portraits of him, was also one of the founders of Lloyds, the marine insurance company.

Itineraries around the Louvre Quarter

▲ The Carrousel

COUR NAPOLÉON

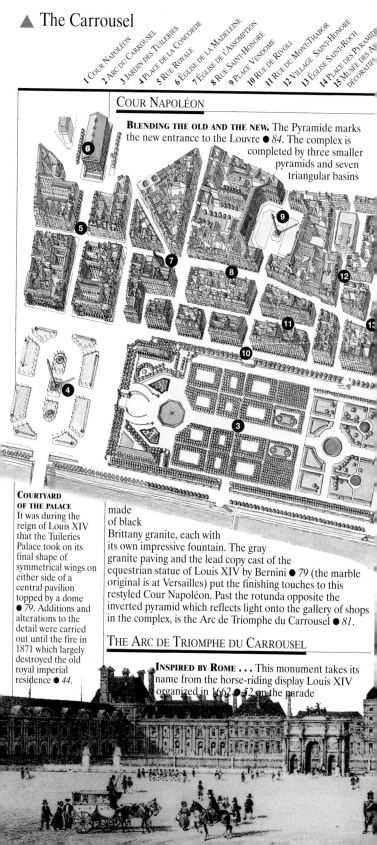

BLENDING THE OLD AND THE NEW. The Pyramide marks the new entrance to the Louvre ● *84*. The complex is completed by three smaller pyramids and seven triangular basins

COURTYARD OF THE PALACE

It was during the reign of Louis XIV that the Tuileries Palace took on its final shape of symmetrical wings on either side of a central pavilion topped by a dome ● *79*. Additions and alterations to the detail were carried out until the fire in 1871 which largely destroyed the old royal imperial residence ● *44*.

made of black Brittany granite, each with its own impressive fountain. The gray granite paving and the lead copy cast of the equestrian statue of Louis XIV by Bernini ● *79* (the marble original is at Versailles) put the finishing touches to this restyled Cour Napoléon. Past the rotunda opposite the inverted pyramid which reflects light onto the gallery of shops in the complex, is the Arc de Triomphe du Carrousel ● *81*.

THE ARC DE TRIOMPHE DU CARROUSEL

INSPIRED BY ROME . . . This monument takes its name from the horse-riding display Louis XIV organized in 1662 ● *52* on the parade

ground which had previously been the site of the Tuileries' old private garden. The architects Charles Percier and Pierre-François-Léonard Fontaine drew their inspiration for this monumental entrance to the Tuileries Palace courtyard from the Arch of Septimius Severus in Rome. This splendid example of Empire architecture built between 1806 and 1808 is flanked by eight Corinthian columns of red and white marble from the Languedoc. Six marble bas-reliefs depict victories by Napoleon. Over the cornices the arch is topped by eight soldiers dressed in the uniform of Napoleon's Grande Armée.

... WITH CONTRIBUTIONS FROM VENICE. A chariot driven by *Victory* and *Peace* bearing the *Emperor Napoleon I* was intended to crown the arch. The sculptor Frédéric Lemot carved the three figures, but the emperor vetoed the plan to erect the statue. The four antique gilded bronze horses on the Basilica of San Marco in Venice removed in 1797 as spoils of war, were then hitched to the chariot ● 40. The horses were handed back in 1815 and it was not until 1827 that the chariot in place today was rebuilt from a design by Percier with a copy of the famous chariot and four horses, along with a figure of the Restoration by

Bosio. On both sides of the arch on tall pedestals are the stone statues of *History* (on the left) and *France Triumphant* (on the right), carved in 1814 by Antoine Gérard. From the arch looking north can be seen the façade of alternating pilasters and pediments which Percier and Fontaine began to build in 1806, and the wing rebuilt by Lefuel in 1875 to match the one on the south side put up some ten years earlier. The Tuileries Palace stood between the Pavillon de Marsan to the north and the Pavillon de Flore to the south.

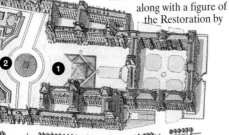

A TRIUMPHAL ENTRANCE
Until the Louvre was completed during the Second Empire, private houses occupied the area between the Tuileries courtyard and today's Cour Napoléon. The arch was a truly grand entrance of honor to the Tuileries Palace. The design for the decorative sculpture was put in the hands

of archeologist Dominique Vivant Denon, who was virtually Napoleon's minister for the arts since he occupied the post of director of the Musée Napoléon ● 68. When Napoleon's statue in a chariot drawn by its four horses was erected without his knowledge, Napoleon is alleged to have said, "It is not I who should be a figure in a statue, I leave that to others." In 1810, however, it was Napoleon himself who commissioned his huge effigy for the column in the Place Vendôme ▲ 284.

▲ Grandeur and decadence of the Tuileries

THE TUILERIES PALACE

A COUNTRY RESIDENCE. Catherine de' Medici commissioned Philibert Delorme to build a country residence on land occupied by a sewage outlet and factories producing tiles and bricks from the clay on the banks of the Seine. Work on the palace began in 1564. Between 1659 and 1666 Louis Le Vau completed the palace, preserving the original proportions between the main pavilions and the wings. The interior has undergone constant alterations over the centuries. The theater known as the Salle des Machines was built in 1659 and housed the first performance of an opera in France; in 1793 it was rebuilt as a meeting chamber for the Convention ● *39*.

SYMBOL OF THE MONARCHY. The palace was burned down by the Commune in May 1781 and stayed in ruins until 1883. Several plans for its restoration were drawn up but in spite of the sound state of the shell of the building, the Republic decided to get rid of this reminder of the monarchy for political reasons, destroying the "grand design" perfected by Napoleon III. The stone remains are scattered as far away as Saint-Raphaël, Corsica and Bulgaria. Bits of stone were even cut up into paperweights and given away to subscribers to the *Figaro* newspaper.

VIEW TOWARD THE ÉTOILE. From the terrace spanning the Général-Lemonnier underpass the eye stretches to the Arc de Triomphe at the Place de l'Étoile and beyond that to the Défense. Two massive urns mark the entrance to the Tuileries.

THE TUILERIES GARDENS

CATHERINE DE' MEDICI'S GARDEN.
Covering some seventy acres, the Tuileries are the largest, as well as the oldest gardens in Paris. Separated from the palace by a public pathway, the enclosed gardens designed by Catherine de' Medici in 1564 consisted of elaborate Italian-style flower-beds with basins, statues and pavilions. Excavations in the Carrousel courtyard have uncovered remains of enameled terracotta items used by Bernard de Palissy to decorate the garden's ornamental grotto ● 75 ▲ 205. The latter's naturalistic decoration included representations of mosses, aquatic plants, frogs, snakes and turtles. Major works carried out in the Louvre and the Tuileries also included the planting by Henri IV of mulberry trees along the edge of the present-day rue de Rivoli (which encouraged the breeding of silkworms) and the construction of silkworm houses inside the Orangerie. When the king was not there, the gardens were opened to the public.

A MASTERPIECE BY LE NÔTRE. In 1664 on the site of this first garden, André Le Nôtre designed an open garden running east to west ● 79. The main features of his classical layout can still to be seen today. Bordered to the north along the Rue de Rivoli by the Terrasse des Feuillants and to the south, facing the Seine by the riverbank terrace, the garden is laid out in three main sections. On the east side separated by a ditch are the private gardens of Louis-Philippe and Napoleon III, decorated with two symmetrical basins, then the Grand Carré where flower-beds surround the large round basin on which children hire and sail model boats in summer. The second section

THE GRAND STAIRCASE
Built by Fontaine in 1837, this staircase escaped the ravages of the great fire and, in spite of the narrow stairwell, looked imposing thanks to its three landings and connecting Corinthian columns.

CREATING A THROUGHWAY
André Le Nôtre (bust on left) was the amiable creative spirit behind the plan for a major east-west axis which thereafter decided the planning format for the extension toward the west of Paris.

The Tuileries
Gardens were laid
out to take full
advantage of the fact
that the Seine runs
alongside.

PLAN OF THE GARDEN
0. Louvre
1. Carrousel Gardens
2. Tuileries Terrace
3. Grand Carré
4. Grand Couvert
5. Octagone
6. Orangerie
7. Jeu de Paume
8. Terrasse des
   Feuillants
9. Waterside Terrace

includes the large shaded area (Grand Couvert) thickly
wooded with irregular rows of chestnut and lime trees around
the lawns. The third section is on the west side from the large
octagonal basin right up to the railings on the Concorde side
and includes two semicircular walkways leading up to the
Octagone where splendid views can be had from the terraces.
PLEASURE GARDEN. During the Ancien Régime the Tuileries
Gardens were the most colorful walk in Paris but also a mecca
for prostitutes and clandestine male encounters. Decorated
with a constantly changing array of designs fashioned out of
wood, plaster and painted canvas, and lit with lanterns and
firework displays, it was used as a venue for welcoming
dignitaries and for holding splendid receptions. During the
Revolution the flower-beds just missed being turned into
vegetable patches but the plan was never put into operation.
In 1794 Jean-Jacques Rousseau's ashes were kept on a small
island built in the middle of the large basin for a short time
before finally being taken to the Panthéon.
FLAVOR OF THE SECOND EMPIRE. A pavilion was built during
the Second Empire on both the esplanades which form the
western boundary to the gardens on the Place de la Concorde.
To the south, the Orangerie was built (1853) which today
houses the Walter Guillaume collection of Impressionist
paintings and the *Water Lilies* by Claude Monet; to the north
is the Jeu de Paume (1861), once the museum of Impressionist

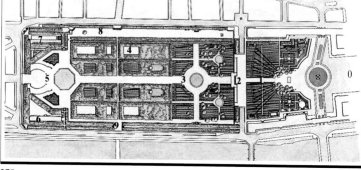

painting (1958–91); it was redesigned in 1991 by Antoine Stinco and is now devoted to exhibitions on photography in the 19th and 20th centuries.

OPEN-AIR MUSEUM. A large number of sculptures can be seen in the Tuileries Gardens. From the Ancien Régime right up to the 1980's new works have been continuously added. The variety of the pieces covering four centuries of creative output has made this collection into a veritable open-air museum of sculpture.

A NEW LIFE. Because of the dilapidated state of the Tuileries and Carrousel Gardens, the Louvre was given the task in 1989 of carrying out a complete renovation program. After an international competition, the designs submitted by Jacques Wirtz for the Carrousel Gardens and Pascal Cribier, Louis Bénech and François Roubaud for the Tuileries were approved. Restoration work, started in 1991, was completed in 2000. This huge undertaking has revived and given meaning to the gardens' history – the main avenues, the water basins and statues – while introducing contemporary ideas of landscaping. A wider variety of plants have been introduced as well as more recreation and refreshment facilities with tearooms and play areas.

MERCURY AND FAME. Opposite the Louvre you arrive onto the Place de la Concorde, one of the finest pieces of urban design and planning in the world. Above the gate on either side stand the equestrian statues of *Mercury* and *Fame* by Coysevox who

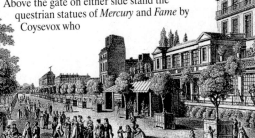

The Tuileries seen from the Left Bank at the beginning of the 19th century.

ON THE TERRACE DES FEUILLANTS
The 1990s beds (above) bring a contemporary note to these gardens whose layout had not been altered for a long time and which had become somewhat neglected.
At the beginning of the 19th century, tubs of orange trees set off the Terrace des Feuillants (left) beautifully.

originally designed them for the Château de Marly. They were replaced in 1986 by copies ▲ *188*.

PLACE DE LOUIS XV

PAVILLON DE L'ORANGERIE
Built during the Second Empire, it houses Impressionist paintings which complement the collections in the nearby Musée d'Orsay on the Left Bank.

PLACE ROYALE. The city of Paris wanted to contruct a square bearing the name of Louis XV. The king, mindful of financial problems, made a gift of a piece of land outside the capital and his architect Jacques-Ange Gabriel conceived this square as a wide open four-sided shape like the square in front of a palace surrounded by ditches. To the north (on the Rue Royale side) he drew his inspiration for the two palaces with their Corinthian colonnades built between 1757 and 1770, from the Colonnade du Louvre ● *78*. At the intersection of these two perpendicular axes of the square was placed the equestrian statue of Louis XV begun by Edme Bouchardon and finished by Jean-Baptiste Pigalle. In 1792 the statue was melted down (only the right hand survives and is on display in the Louvre) and the square, renamed the Place de la Révolution, was the setting for executions including those of Louis XVI and Robespierre.

EXORCIZING THE PAST. First given the name Concorde in 1795, under the July monarchy this name was fixed once and for all. As part of his policy of reconciliation Louis-Philippe decided to redesign the square in 1835 in order to remove the political implications and symbolic significance this square held for the opposing parties. The architect Jacques-Ignace Hittorff gave it the character of a central square with two huge fountains and eighteen raised gilt-painted decorative lampposts. He placed allegorical statues of the main towns in France as

lookouts in the ditches. The Strasbourg statue
carved by James Pradier has the features of Juliette
Drouet, muse and mistress of Victor Hugo; from
1870 to 1914 the statue was revered as a place of
patriotic pilgrimage and was draped in black.

A 46-FOOT-HIGH OBELISK AT THE CENTER. In 1836
no less than 200,000 spectators watched the obelisk
from the Temple of Amun in Luxor being erected.
These very complex operations are described on the
base of this monolithic structure which weighs 220
tons and celebrates Ramesses II. The square is used
for national celebrations and military parades and in
1934 also witnessed the bloody riots which almost
brought down the Third Republic.

TO THE WEST, THE MARLY HORSES. The entrance to
the Champs-Elysées has been guarded since 1795 by two
Horses Restrained by Grooms. The original works created by
Guillaume Coustou came from the drinking-pond at Marly
near Versailles, and were replaced in 1984 by copies;
the originals are in the Louvre ▲ *188*.

**TO THE SOUTH, THE PONT DE LA
CONCORDE.** Built in 1791 partly from
stones of the demolished Bastille,
the width of the bridge was more
than doubled in 1931. It leads to
the Palais Bourbon on the Left
Bank, whose façade in the style
of an ancient temple, dates
from the First Empire and
echos the front of the
Madeleine Church.

**TO THE NORTH, TWO COLONNADED
PALACES.** These palaces were
initially intended as residences for
special ambassadors. The palace on the
right was used as a depository for royal furniture and was for
a long time the headquarters of the French Naval Ministry.
The one on the left was quickly let to members of the
aristocracy, and part of it has now become one of the capital's
luxury hotels. The company which acquired the *Hôtel de
Crillon* in 1907 (it had previously been a private residence),
asked the fashionable architect Walter Destailleurs to make
it into an hotel for travelers. The hotel opened in 1912 and its
reception rooms have kept
their sumptuous 18th-
century décor.

**THE SENTRIES ON
THE PLACE DE
LA CONCORDE**
The architect Hittorff
borrowed from
Gabriel the idea of
erecting this series of
statues of women
symbolizing the major
towns in France:
Lyons and Marseilles,
Bordeaux and
Nantes, Rouen and
Brest, Lille and
Strasbourg (above).

Louis XV passing
in front of his own
equestrian statue
(left).

MARLY HORSES
At the instigation of
the painter Jacques-
Louis David, the
Marly *Horses* by
Guillaume Coustou
have stood over the
entrance to the
Champs-Élysées on
the west side of the
Place de la Concorde
since
1795.

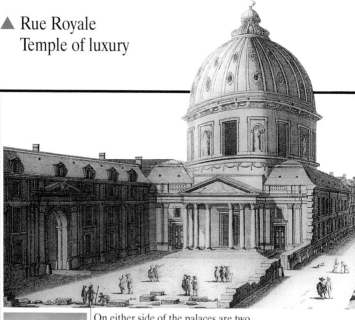

On either side of the palaces are two mansions set well back: the one on the left, built in the 1930's was modeled on the one on the right which belonged to Prince Talleyrand. Both buildings house the US diplomatic and consular offices. Go north up the Rue Royale.

AROUND THE RUE ROYALE

CHURCH OF THE ASSUMPTION
Crowned by a dome, the church is the last remnant of a convent of Augustinian nuns. On the site of the convent today stands the Audit Office. At the apex of the coffered dome is the *Assumption of the Virgin* by Charles de La Fosse (1676). It is the only piece of original decoration left since all the rest was either destroyed or scattered during the Revolution.

RUE ROYALE. From 1758 onward this prestigious thoroughfare was lined with identically fronted mansions following a design proposed by Jacques-Ange Gabriel to keep the harmony of the Place de la Concorde. The ground was the subject of speculation on the part of architects like Louis Le Tellier and Étienne-Louis Boullée. Some of the buildings have kept their neoclassical interiors from the late 18th century but since companies use them as offices today, it is difficult to visit them. Some of the world's leading names, however, still carry on business in this street including Christofle the silversmiths, the crystal houses of St-Louis and Lalique, Lachaume the florists and that world-famous restaurant Maxim's, whose windows and Art Nouveau interior date from 1899. The Ladurée tearooms at no. 16 which opened in 1862 has a 1890's décor and the reputation for fine macaroons.
THE MADELEINE CHURCH – TO THE GLORY OF NAPOLEON'S GRANDE ARMÉE. Recently cleaned and restored, it is impossible not to look in closer detail at the imposing façade of the Madeleine sitting at the end of the Rue Royale with all the air of an ancient temple. Building was begun in 1764 but the church remained unfinished for some time. In 1806 the church was dedicated to the glory of the Grande Armée and was finally finished in 1842 by Vignon the last architect to work on it. In the triangular pediment, there is a *Last Judgement* by Philippe-Henri Lemaire.

RUE ST-HONORÉ. To the right take the Rue St-Honoré, the only road which cuts across the Rue Royale. Until the Rue de

Rivoli was opened at the beginning of the 19th century, it was the only main east-west thoroughfare in Paris. Right up to the Place Vendôme there are numerous shops selling antique jewelry. At the first crossroads on the right, the Rue St-Florentin contains fine buildings which as far as the Place de la Concorde, make up a very impressive collection of urban architecture. At no. 263 bis a square opens up with the Church of Our Lady of the Assumption.

NOTRE-DAME DE L'ASSOMPTION. The church and its convent were the headquarters of the order of the Sisters of the Assumption (Dames de l'Assomption) known as the Nouvelles Haudriettes. It was built between 1670 and 1676 by the painter and architect Charles Errard who was director of the brand new Académie de France in Rome. The rotunda with its porticoes takes its inspiration from the Pantheon in Rome; the lack of symmetry might be attributable to the clumsy interpretation of the plans by the builder while the architect was away. Inside the dome is an *Assumption* painted by Charles de La Fosse (1676). Since 1850 it has been the parish church of the Polish community in Paris.

RUE CAMBON. On both sides of the Rue St-Honoré, the Rue Cambon is lined with buildings from the 18th and 19th centuries; banks and large business concerns, the offices of the Ministry of Justice and an annexe to the Ritz hotel. Rue Cambon owes its world-wide renown to the boutique opened at nos. 29–31 in the 1930's by Coco Chanel which still houses the famous couture house. Continue along the Rue St-Honoré as far as nos. 362–4. It was the architect Ventre who in 1934 designed the buildings whose private courtyard is used as a public walkway during the day. The whole is characteristic of the neoclassical revival of the inter-war period with its bas-reliefs and stylized capitals. The passage leads to the Place Vendôme.

LUXURY SHOPS
Toward the west end of the Rue du Faubourg-St-Honoré are the great names of haute couture and their boutiques ● *54* (Lanvin); on the Rue St-Honoré are jewelers, fine leather workers and perfumiers; on the Rue Royale are crystal and porcelain (Christofle, Lalique, St-Louis). The house of Chanel on Rue Cambon has kept its mirrored staircase designed by an exiled Russian grand duke and the apartment with the Coromandel lacquered screens belonging to Coco Chanel, who preferred to live in the Ritz hotel.
On the Rue Royale is Lachaume the florists, while Maxim's restaurant maintains the traditions and pleasures of the Belle Époque. This restaurant founded in 1891 is named after the person who created it and anglicized it to follow fashion. An identical copy of the original Paris décor can be found in an offshoot of the Paris restaurant – in Beijing.

VAN·CLEEF & ARPELS

PLACE VENDÔME

AN ENCLOSED SALON. The old Louis-le-Grand square occupie the site of the mansion belonging to the Duke of Vendôme. Minister Louvois initially planned a huge center for institutions like the Académies or the Mint. In 1686 Jules Hardouin-Mansart designed a square with three sides, the fourth being left open on the south side. To increase the area to be built on, the square gradually became octagonal from 1699 ● *78*, closed and completed with its two openings facing the convents of the Capucines and the Feuillants which have now been replaced respectively by the Rue de la Paix and the Rue de Castiglione. Designed as a sort of enclosed salon the square has arched windows with fantasy stone figure decoration at ground level, two upper stories joined by Corinthian pilasters and large attics with dormer windows. The sides are cut at angles and a forward section with a triangular pediment supported by columns is used to ornament the center of each of the main sides.

HISTORIC IRONY
The seventy-six bronze bas-reliefs (above) curl round the central stone body which hides a staircase leading to a spectators' platform. Carved by thirty-two sculptors, they represent the victories of Napoleon over the Austrians. The monument was unveiled very discreetly in 1810 because the emperor had just married an Austrian ● *41*. The parts damaged during the Commune were eventually recast. Ordered to pay the rebuilding costs from his own pocket, the painter Gustave Courbet was often caricatured as above: "Courbet sets about work on the Vendôme column himself so that he can employ one workman less. At least that's a little bit less to pay!"

THE VENDÔME COLUMN. The equestrian statue of Louis XIV dressed as a Roman emperor was designed by Girardon who began work on it in 1699 and it was sent for casting in 1792. Napoleon gave orders for it to be replaced by a monument to the glory of the victors of the Battle of Austerlitz. The architects Gondoin and Lepère, who based the design on Trajan's column in Rome put up the column between 1806 and 1810. It is made of stone, reaches a height of 145 feet and is covered with 425 bronze plaques weighing 251 tons altogether. These were made from the 1,250 pieces of artillery taken from the Austrians and Russians. The 850-feet bas-reliefs which rise in a spiral tell the story of 1805. Originally the statue of *Napoléon Imperator* made by Chaudet in 1810 sat at the top of the column, whereas the one currently there is a copy put up by Napoleon III in 1803. In 1871 under the Commune the pins were taken out of the column and it was knocked down at the instigation of the painter Gustave

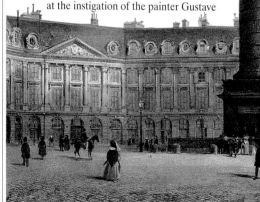

Courbet who called it *le mirliton* (carnival whistle). He was later made to rebuild it at his own expense ● *44*.

MECCA FOR JEWELRY. The public cannot see many of the interiors of the magnificent houses all round the Place Vendôme which include the Chancery or Ministry of Justice at no. 13, the famous Ritz hotel at no. 15, the Evreux mansion at no. 19, where the Crédit Foncier has offices and which moreover owns much of the property on the Place. World-famous makers of luxury goods, particularly jewelry, are still based at Place Vendôme and to the north along the Rue de la Paix as far as the Place de l'Opéra. Since 1992, the square (700 feet long and 405 feet wide) has been paved with gray granite flagstones in the shape of a checkerboard. Stone or steel posts show the demarcation areas for automobiles and pedestrians.

DETOUR THROUGH NEOCLASSICISM. The sightseer can go straight down the Rue de Castiglione as far as the Rue de Rivoli or on the left, go along the Rue du Mont-Thabor with its rows of buildings whose strict neoclassical style is a feature of the Restoration period. At no. 6 a plaque recalls that the poet and writer Alfred de Musset died in this building in 1857. Turning right after that into the Rue d'Alger leads back to the Rue de Rivoli with, in the distance, the Hôtel de Ville to the left and the Place de la Concorde to the right.

RUE DE CASTIGLIONE. The street which opened in 1802, was formed from the old walkway linking the Rue St-Honoré to the Tuileries Gardens and separated the convents of the Feuillants and the Capucins. It took in a part of the room known as the Salle du Manège where the First Republic was proclaimed in 1792 ● *39*. Here are the same buildings with their arcaded open sidewalks as in the Rue de Rivoli. At no. 3, the Intercontinental was one of Paris's first luxury hotels to offer all modern comforts. It was built in 1878 by the architect Henri Blondel for the Paris Universal Exhibition on the site of the Ministry of Finance which was burnt down under the Commune ● *44*. The reception rooms retain their rich Napoleon III décor; the Salles des Fêtes is a listed building.

RUE DE RIVOLI

A MODEL OF RESIDENTIAL PROPERTY. The Rue de Rivoli opened bit by bit between 1802 and 1835 from the Place de la Concorde to the Place du

▲ Rue de Rivoli, imperial urbanism

MOSAIC ARCADES
Many of the walkways in the arcades of the Rue de Rivoli are decorated with mosaic medallions and arabesques, seen here at the corner of the Rue de Castiglione.

Palais-Royal and was intended to be used as a main east–west thoroughfare to complement the old Rue St-Honoré.

The apartments, built only on the north side of the street facing the Tuileries and the Louvre, sit on top of colonnades designed by Percier and Fontaine ● *81*. The attics, rounded off in shape and made of zinc, were to become an architectural feature of residential apartments in Paris. Some of them have been heightened since then, breaking the line of the frontage. Between 1848 and 1850 the street was extended eastward to the Hôtel de Ville and then on into the Marais as far as the Rue St-Antoine, but with different façades.

ESSENTIAL STOPS ALONG THE WAY. Amidst the souvenir shops and travel agencies, is the Galignani bookstore at no. 224, the first English bookshop established on the Continent, in 1802. At no. 226 there is the Angelina tearoom (the old firm of Rumpelmeyer, founded in 1903) with its neo-Louis XVI white and gold décor. It is an institution among gourmands and is famous for its hot chocolate and its *Mont-Blanc* (whipped cream and chestnut purée).

HÔTEL MEURICE. At no. 228 the Hôtel Meurice, opened in 1907, has kept a magnificent series of 18th century-style reception rooms on the ground floor designed by Henri-Paul Nénot, architect of the new Sorbonne. At the time a sign of grand luxury was that each suite had its own private bathroom. The hotel was equipped with central heating and elevators designed to look like Marie-Antoinette's sedan chairs. The biggest novelty which brought it enormous success was its open-air roof garden restaurant with its incomparable view of the Tuileries Gardens and the Left Bank. The Meurice was a favorite with kings and princes between the two world wars and on June 14, 1940 was requisitioned to provide headquarters for the *Gross Paris*, the German chiefs of staff who commanded Paris.

VILLAGE ST-HONORÉ. Turning left into the Rue du 29-Juillet, so named after the last of the three days in July 1830 known as *Les Trois Glorieuses*) and then into the Rue du Marché-St-Honoré, the visitor goes into the Place du Marché-St-Honoré. Until mid-1990s, the heart of the square was occupied by a multi-level garage and fire station which in the 1950's replaced the old covered market. There are now a glass shopping arcade and office complex inaugurated in 1997. They are designed by Ricardo Bofill, the Catalan architect, born in 1939, who champions an up-dated version of neoclassicism. All round the square with its modest façades – witnesses to domestic architecture in the 18th century – have sprouted various restaurants, hip cafés and fashion houses like Philippe Model. On the corner of the Rue St-Hyacinthe, the Rubis is an attractive wine bar. Return to the Rue St-Honoré by way of Rue de La Sourdière which has kept something of the flavor of Paris during the Ancien Régime.

CHURCH OF ST-ROCH

PARISH CHURCH OF THE TUILERIES. A church was first built here at the end of the 16th century. In this area which owes its rise to the proximity of the Tuileries Palace, the church's reconstruction as one huge building was intended to mark its elevation to the status of parish church. Jacques Le Mercier, architect of the Sorbonne, drew up the plans but because of the lie of the land, was forced to change the positioning of the church; the chancel faces north rather than east as tradition normally dictates. Louis XIV laid the first stone in 1653. In 1690 the chancel, transept and nave were finished and in 1705 Jules Hardouin-Mansart was commissioned to complete the church. To the apse he added the Lady Chapel whose

287

A CHURCH WORTHY OF THE LOUVRE
The carved classical façade of the church of St-Roch, destroyed at the time of the Revolution, was partly restored between 1873 and 1943. The interior of the church is a veritable museum of 17th- and 18th-century religious and funerary sculpture from churches that no longer exist. The huge chancel has four barrel-vaulted bays with lunettes richly decorated in gilt. These have recently been cleaned. At the rear the Lady Chapel has a dome in which there is an *Assumption* painted in 1756, while a *God*

in Majesty, inspired by St Peter's in Rome decorates the vault behind the huge altar and completes the dramatic visual effect.

elliptical nave is surrounded by an ambulatory; a series of rather daring arches and a large amount of light give a definitely theatrical feel to the whole structure. In 1722 the financier John Law, inventor of the banking and financial system which proved a resounding failure, gave 100,000 livres to finish the nave.

BAROQUE AND CLASSICAL FAÇADE. Robert de Cotte drew up designs for the main façade onto the Rue St-Honoré which was built between 1738 and 1739 ● *80*. This façade has two levels with a set of Doric columns on the lower and Corinthian pillars with wide entablatures on the upper; it combines the principles of the Baroque with the heavier features of French classical architecture.

JEAN-BAPTISTE MARDUEL, CURATE OF ST-ROCH. During the second half of the 18th century, Fr. Jean-Baptiste Marduel undertook a large-scale program to enrich the church. In 1754 Étienne-Louis Boullée built a Chapel of the Crucifixion onto the north side which extends and connects to the interior of the church. In 1756 Jean-Baptiste Pierre painted an *Assumption* on the dome of the Lady Chapel. The sculptor Étienne-Maurice Falconet decorated the gallery behind the altar in the Lady Chapel with a *God in Majesty* inspired by Bernini's depiction of the same subject in St Peter's in Rome. The priest also had a pulpit built in 1758 and the transept was decorated with a series of paintings and sculptures from the best artists of the day which were completed in 1767. During this period Boullée redesigned the altars and reredos at either end of the transept.

MUSEUM OF RELIGIOUS ART. St-Roch houses treasures which make it a veritable museum of sacred art between the 17th and 19th centuries; some of these come from buildings previously destroyed and were brought here. A number of artists who were parishioners are buried here; in the chapels can be seen busts of *Mignard* by Lemoyne and of *Le Nôtre* by Antoine Coysevox. The church itself and St-Sulpice on the Left Bank are the finest extant examples of a major parish church built in the classical style.

UNDER ATTACK FROM NAPOLEON. The church is also famous for having undergone very heavy cannon and gunfire attack by order of Bonaparte on September 5, 1795. He was leading forces of the Convention whose aim was to dislodge the royalist rioters who had made it their stronghold. Continue along the Rue St-Honoré as far as the Rue des Pyramides which leads onto the square of the same name to the right.

PLACE DES PYRAMIDES

FROM SIEGE TO BATTLE. The square, opened in 1802 on the site of the royal mansion of the Grandes-Écuries, was called the Place de Rivoli until 1932. It echoes the theme of arcaded houses and identical frontages of the Rue de Rivoli. In the middle stands the gilt bronze statue of Joan of Arc by Emmanuel Frémiet. The place where the statue stands is the spot on which Joan is alleged to have been wounded during the fruitless siege of Paris. The Hôtel Régina, at no. 2, has kept the décor of the reception rooms as designed by the architect Armand Sibien; in the entrance lobby there are clock faces showing the time in the world's major capital cities. From the back of the square runs the Rue des Pyramides which opened in 1802 as far as the Rue St-Honoré and extended in 1877 as far as the Avenue de l'Opéra. Its name recalls the victory Napoleon won in Egypt in 1798 ▲ *148*. The Administration of France's museums (DMF) has its headquarters in the old annexe of the Hôtel Régina. Cross the Rue de Rivoli after that to reach the Musée de la Mode et du Textile or the Musée des Arts Décoratifs ▲ *290*, both housed in the Louvre in the Rohan and Marsan buildings.

JOAN OF ARC
The statue of Joan of Arc by the sculptor Emmanuel Frémiet was erected in 1874. Since then leagues, groups and parties involved in nationalist activities have used it for march pasts.
The saint represented resistance to the enemy and symbolized the spirit of revenge after the loss of Alsace-Lorraine (1870). The original gilding has been restored and its base still has hooks for hanging commemorative wreaths.

HÔTEL RÉGINA
This hotel which opened in 1903 was

one of the few decorated in Art Nouveau style; the smart set usually preferred "Louis-style" decoration.

PAVILLON DE MARSAN
This pavilion (left) was rebuilt from 1874 onward by the architect Lefuel who used a modern metal frame for the roof. Its monumental pediments are decorated with allegorical subjects.

▲ Musées des Arts Décoratifs

Founded by a group of collectors in the afterma of the Great Exhibitions of the 19th century, the Museum of Decorative Arts, in the Marsan wing the Louvre, is devoted to the technology and crafts manship involved in the production of art and design. It reopen in 2006 after restoration, with a complete panorama of decorati arts from the Middle Ages to the present day. Grouped by subje and by chronology, it is divided into ten departments are: Midd Ages, Renaissance, 18th & 19th centuries, Art Nouveau-Art Dec Modern Art, and Contemporary design including wallpapers, to glassware, and items from the Galerie des Bijoux, opened in 200

THE "PERIOD ROOMS"
These are designed to show works in their original surroundings. Above: "Le Berger", a tapestry in the Salle du Moyen Age (room of the Middle Ages)

THE 1900 EXHIBITION
The pavilion designed by Georges Hoenstche using wood as its theme has been reconstructed. Its display cases contain fine glass, porcelain and metalware from the 1900's

18TH-CENTURY POMP
The Salon Barriol contains, with the Louvre and the Musée Nissim-de-Camondo (part of the Musée des Arts Décoratifs), one of the finest collections of Louis XVI furnishings including wood paneling, furniture, *objets d'art*, silks, bronzes and chandeliers.

ART DECO treasures
Jeanne Lanvin's reconstructed bathroom shares center stage with works by Lalique, Gallé, Pierre Chareau, Charlotte Perriand, not to mention Percier and Fontaine, Delacroix, Guimard and a marvelous collection of old toys.

The Musée de la Mode et du Textile, founded by Jack Lang in 1982 under the name Musée des Arts de la Mode, opened in the Pavillon de Marsan in 1986 and since 1997 has been part of the Rohan wing. The "permanent gallery" shows a thematic selection from a collection 6,000 garments dating from the 16th century to today. There are also 35,000 accessories and 30,000 pieces of fabric. A documentary research center and a center for conserving pieces also form part of the museum.

ON PAPER TOO . . .
The museum conserves works of reference on the beginning of the 19th century, the souvenirs of daily life and the plans of designers of everyday objects such as cups (above).

Below left, a Persian dress from the 18th century.

AN ORIGINAL APPROACH
The collections of the Musée de la Mode et du Textile were originally part of the former textiles department of the Musée des Arts Décoratifs and of the collections of the Union Française des Arts du Costume. The museum's exhibition changes on an annual basis, in order to protect the fragile garments. The exhibitions, thematic or not, offer chronological routes into the collections. Left, a "persian" dress from the 18th century.

Formerly situated in the rue de Paradis, the Musée de la Publicité, reopen its doors to the public in the Rohan wing in autumn 1998. With 250 000 old and contempary posters, more than 100 000 filmed adverts from France and foreign countries, objects, the museum illustrate the main stages in the history of modern advertising which can be said to have begun in the mid-18th century.

DECORATIVE ARTS LIBRARY AND ARCHIVES
Since it was installed in the Pavillon Marsan in 1904, the library has become an important center of reference and research. It also has a valuable archive, which can be accessed via the internet. Above: Mucha's poster for Job cigarette papers (1895), and Villemot's for Perrier (1976).

▲ Place du Palais-Royal

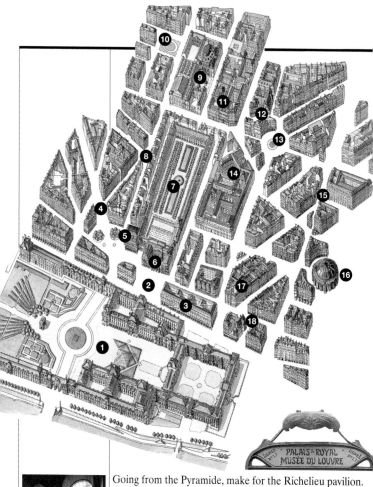

FROM PALACE TO TOWN
Cour Marly and the Pyramide seen from the Richelieu passage.

Going from the Pyramide, make for the Richelieu pavilion. At the entrance to the passage, on the left is the Café Marly, whose Second Empire décor sits well with contemporary furniture and evokes literary café society of the past. From the second room there is a view down onto the Cour Marly. **PASSAGE RICHELIEU.** The eye is drawn by both the richness of the decorative carvings in the vaults and the side bays opening up onto the Cours Marly and Puget ▲ *188*. When the Ministry of Finance took over this part of the Louvre, the Richelieu passage was reserved for the exclusive use of the minister and the two open-air courtyards were jam-packed with official cars. Cross the Rue de Rivoli to get back to the Place du Palais-Royal. The Metro station entrance with its cast-iron Art Nouveau decoration is one of the 141 public restrooms designed by Hector Guimard at the beginning of the 20th century. Today the ones which survive are officially listed

PLACE DU PALAIS-ROYAL

Originally built in 1648 the square was enlarged several times during the 18th century and on the south side even featured a decorative water tower which ironically burnt down during the 1848 Revolution. It was not until the Second Empire, however, that it acquired the appearance it has today. It owes its name to the Palais-Royal whose entrance is marked by the Cour de l'Horloge. The façade of the Palais-Royal built in 1763 by Moreau-Desproux was rebuilt to its original design after the devastation caused by the Commune ● *44*. To the right on the corner of the Rue de Valois and the Rue St-Honoré a plaque commemorates the site of the Petit-Cardinal theater where Molière and

his troupe of actors performed from 1661 onward. It was here on February 17, 1673 that Molière died while he was giving a performance of *Le Malade Imaginaire*. The Académie Royale de Musique then occupied the premises until 1780. On the east side of the square stands the Louvre des Antiquaires and on the west the façade of the Hôtel du Louvre. On the south the façade of the Louvre has a magnificent decorative sculpture with two pairs of caryatids supporting the front and several decorative symbols of imperial power.

THE SQUARE IN 1910
The Hôtel du Louvre and the Théâtre-Français from left to right and the Cour de l'Horloge on the right which leads to the Palais-Royal, seat of the Conseil d'État.

THE LOUVRE DES ANTIQUAIRES. This collection of buildings is bounded by the Rue de Rivoli, the Rue Marengo, the Rue du Faubourg-St-Honoré and the Place du Palais-Royal, and contains, apart from offices, three floors of antique shops which make up a commercial center unique in Europe. It is constructed along the same lines as the Rue de Rivoli with its arcaded freestone buildings as designed by Percier and Fontaine during the Empire. The brainchild of financier Émile Pereire, it initially housed the Grand Hôtel du Louvre which opened in 1855 for the first Universal Exhibition in Paris and subsequently, from 1878 onward, the large stores known as the Grands Magasins du Louvre. As early as the first decade of this century, they were the first shops to put up electric Christmas and New Year decorations. One of the founders of this temple to trading, Alfred Chauchard, donated his collection of paintings including Millet's *Angelus* to the Louvre .

The Metro station entrance designed by Hector Guimard.

HÔTEL DU LOUVRE. On the left of the square turn west and go along the side of the Hôtel du Louvre. On the ground floor, looking onto the Place Colette, are the Delamain bookstore and the Civette tobacco shop. At the crossroads, looking right to the far end of the Avenue de l'Opéra designed by Haussmann, can be seen the Palais Garnier, a perfect example of the Napoleon III style of architecture. It was built between 1862 and 1875 by Charles Garnier and until recently was the main home of the Paris Opéra ● *83*.

ORATOIRE DU PRINCE NAPOLÉON.
Cross over the Rue St-Honoré and pass beneath the

TEMPLE OF BUSINESS
The Louvre des Antiquaires (above) occupies buildings which were once the Grands Magasins du Louvre (below).

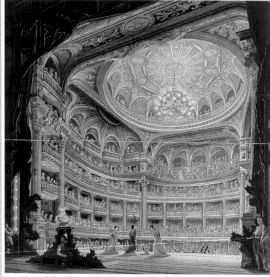

THE THÉATRE-FRANÇAIS
A large chandelier with fifty oil lamps lit the sumptuous interior of the theater designed by Victor Louis. The current decoration formed part of the reconstruction carried out by Julien Guadet after the fire in 1900.

THE BUREN COLUMNS
The black and white columns in the ceremonial courtyard of the Palais-Royal. Shown at night (below) lit from below by illuminated underground water and colored lamps; (below that) the columns by day.

arcades of the Comédie-Française to join the Nemours passage. The two first-floor windows on the left are decorated with stained glass; this is the neo-Gothic oratory of the emperor's cousin, Prince Napoleon (1822–91) and his wife Princess Marie-Clotilde de Savoie who took up residence in the Palais-Royal after their marriage in 1859.

THE PALAIS-ROYAL

THE DISSONANCE OF ANCIENT AND MODERN. The visitor comes out onto the ceremonial courtyard where there is series of black and white striped columns surrounded by a pattern of grilles through which can be seen an underground fountain. The whole is lit after dark by red and green lights. This contemporary work by Daniel Buren erected in 1986 gave rise to the same debate as the Pyramide by Pei ● 84.

THE PALAIS CARDINAL TO THE PALAIS-ROYAL. The façades of the buildings overlooking the ceremonial square reflect the complex history of the palace which was originally built in 1634 for Cardinal Richelieu by Jacques Le Mercier, the architect responsible for the Pavillon de l'Horloge at the Louvre ● 76. All that remains today is the Galerie des Proues on the east side where the maritime artefacts on display – rostrums, anchors, ropes and rigging – remind us that Richelieu was in charge of supervising navigation in 1626. It took the name of Palais-Royal in 1643 when Anne of Austria stayed there and in 1692 was given over to the exclusive use of the Orléans family who kept the whole property until 1848.

The Galerie d'Orléans covered with its glass roof as it was at the 19th century.

THE ARCADES OF THE PALAIS-ROYAL
The arcades (bottom, in a model) were designed by Victor Louis with the intention of taking maximum advantage of the piece of land. From the Duke of Orléans to Louis-Philippe, they contained gaming rooms and brothels, cafés and cabaret halls to which tourists from all over Europe flocked in pursuit of pleasure, helped by numerous and very explicit guides. Shops selling fashionable clothes and novelty items lived side by side in the gallery (below, in a model), whose use of a multicolored decoration was inspired by antiquity.

A CONTINUAL PROCESS OF EMBELLISHMENT. Louis XIV's brother, the Duke of Orléans and then his son the regent, commissioned the greatest artists of the day (architects Hardouin–Mansart, Antoine Lepautre and Gilles-Marie Oppenord and painters Noël and Antoine Coypel) to extend and make the palace more ornate. It was in his apartments that the Regent entertained his roué friends to grandiose supper parties which were the talk of the town. His son who succeeded him in 1723 retained the services of the cabinet-maker Cressent, the goldsmith Thomas Germain and the sculptor Slodtz. In the 1750's, Pierre Contant d'Ivry redesigned the apartments of the Duchess of Orléans. The elegant front pavilion with its wrought-iron balcony and façade looking out over the Rue de Valois dates from the period of these works.

REBUILDING. The fire at the Opéra on April 6, 1763 utterly destroyed the east wing of the palace and a part of the main building. The building was then completely rebuilt adjoining the Valois wing in 1770 by Pierre-Louis Moreau-Desproux, superintendent of buildings for the city of Paris. He also designed the new façade of the front courtyard on the Place du Palais-Royal. Contant d'Ivry rebuilt the frontage onto the ceremonial courtyard and decorated the new apartments. On the terraces stand four statues carved by Pajou (1766): *Military Talents*, *Prudence*, *Liberality* and the *Arts*.

THE COMÉDIE-FRANÇAISE AND THE GARDEN APARTMENTS. In 1780 the Duke of Orléans made a gift of the Palais-Royal to his son the Duke of Chartres, who for all his huge fortune was suffering from truly chronic debts. The area was short of places of entertainment after the fire at the Opéra de Moreau and the prince decided to build a theater west of his palace, which the Comédie-Française today uses as its base. The grounds surrounding the gardens were to provide the necessary space to extend the palace. Overseeing the work was put in the hands of the architect Victor Louis who had just finished the Grand Théâtre in Bordeaux. To give the gardens an attractive setting, he built sixty apartments for renting

▲ A garden in town

between 1781 and 1784, occupying the space of three arcades. The uniform façades featuring large Corinthian pilasters, balustrades and decorative urns make up a total of 180 arched arcades on the ground floor, with a mezzanine level of galleries and boutiques, a floor of commemorative windows, another mezzanine and a top-floor attic ● *80*. Streets called after members of the Orléans family, Valois, Montpensier and Beaujolais, were later opened up around the outside perimeter to the great displeasure of the occupants in the apartments who had formerly enjoyed an uninterrupted view over the gardens. Between these and the ceremonial courtyard was built the Camp des Tartares, huge temporary wooden and glass galleries given over to boutiques. Gaming clubs and brothels proliferated in the atmosphere of the Palais-Royal which acquired an international reputation for debauchery. This promenade, the most popular in Paris, was also a meeting place for revolutionary activists up to 1794.

RESTORATION. When he returned in 1815 Louis-Philippe Duke of Orléans, commissioned Fontaine to restore the palace. The architect added on the Galerie d'Orléans (1829–31) with a double portico separating it from the palace. During the inter-war years the gallery acquired its current layout and its two square basins were decorated in the early 1980's by steel spherical mobiles designed by Pol Bury.

THE GARDENS IN THE PALAIS-ROYAL

The gardens of the Palais Cardinal were in their day the biggest private gardens in Paris. Le Nôtre began altering them in 1674 to please the distinguished people who often visited them. His nephew Desgots, the king's architect undertook the task again in 1730: trellises with architectural themes surrounded the gardens which were decorated with statues. A large circular pond was dug in the center and, for the first time ever, hoses were used to water the huge flower-beds which had been laid out.

A HAVEN IN THE CITY. Having only just escaped road-building plans at the beginning of the 20th century, the gardens whose rectangular shape covers a around 2½ square acres, offers a haven of peace in the center of town. Always at the ready, facing the Galerie d'Orléans,

THE MIDDAY CANNON SALUTE The Palais-Royal's small cannon has recently been restored and tells Parisians the exact time.

The classic order of the galleries, and a chair designed by Wilmotte.

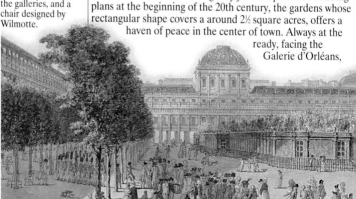

the famous cannon gun has gone off at noon every day since 1786. Four double rows of lime trees trimmed into a sort of tent offer visitors shade during the summer. The metal seats available for the public to sit on were designed by Jean-Michel Wilmotte ● 64. The two wide lawns on either side of the fountain have been newly planted with more colorful and attractive flower displays designed by landscape gardener Mark Rudkin. At night the galleries are closed to the public; only residents and owners have the key to the gates of this state-owned property.

THE GRAND VÉFOUR AND THE THÉÂTRE DU PALAIS-ROYAL. At the northern end of the garden in the Beaujolais gallery is one of the loveliest restaurants in Paris, the Grand Véfour. First called the Café de Chartres, it was opened in 1784 although the rich style of its decoration dates from the Restoration. Turn left in to the Rue de Montpensier and the Théâtre du Palais-Royal. Originally a puppet theater then a venue for fairground entertainment, it has been famous since it was rebuilt in 1830 for the light comedies that are put on there. Climb the steps of the Passage de Beaujolais to reach the Rue de Richelieu.

RUE DE RICHELIEU, A MEMORIAL TO MOLIÈRE. This road was opened by Cardinal Richelieu in 1634 in a straight north-south axis which was something new in Paris at the time. Keep to the left side of the street. At no. 37 the Molière fountain commemorates the great comic actor who died at what is today no. 40. The fountain was built in 1844 by public subscription and keeps alive the Parisian tradition of corner fountains set into houses. It was designed by Louis Visconti and decorated with an engraving of *Molière Seated* by Charles-Émile Seurre and of figures from *Serious Comedy* and *Light Comedy* by James Pradier. Go back along the Passage de Beaujolais and turn left toward the Rue Vivienne, crossing the Rue des Petits-Champs on the way. Go along the side of the garden railings to enter the Bibliothèque Nationale.

LE GRAND VÉFOUR
The old Café de Chartres which became the Véfour restaurant (above) at the beginning of the 19th century is famous for its beautiful painted panels fixed under glass. Café du Caveau at the time of the Revolution (left).

The metal fire escapes of the Théâtre du Palais-

Royal themselves form part of the decoration on the Rue de Montpensier. Colette and Jean Cocteau

made the Palais-Royal a haunt for intellectuals right up to the 1950's.

THE BIBLIOTHÈQUE NATIONALE

IN THE GARDENS. Set back and parallel with the street is the brick and stone building which formerly housed Cardinal Mazarin's treasures, displayed in two galleries sitting one on top of the other. Part of the original décor can still be seen in these galleries, which are now used for temporary exhibitions. The statue of a man leaning forward at the bottom left is philosopher Jean-Paul Sartre. Go through the door on the right to the Mansart wing and reach the famous Salle de Lectures des Imprimés on the left.

ONE OF THE RICHEST LIBRARIES IN THE WORLD. First the Royal and then the Imperial Library, the Bibliothèque Nationale covers an area of around 20,000 square yards bordered by the Rues Richelieu, Colbert, Vivienne and Petits-Champs. Since the removal of most of the collections of printed material to the new Bibliothèque de France Francois-Mitterrand at the Tolbiac site, designed by Dominique Perrault, the historical sections have retained most of the specialist material here such as visual arts, maps, prints and photographs, manuscripts, coins, medals, ephemera, and music.

THE SALLE DE LECTURES DES IMPRIMÉS. Set up in the Rue Richelieu in 1725, the library owes its basic structure to the architect Henri Labrouste. Its real gem is the reading room called the Salle de Lecture des Imprimés which can be seen through the glass door at the entrance. It opened in 1869 and can accommodate 360 people. Its rationalist architecture is shown in its nine metal domes, each crowned with a circular window and decorated with colored ceramic plaques set on eleven 30 feet-high slender cast-iron pillars. The walls covered in books on three-tiered shelving are decorated at their highest level with paintings and Sèvres medallions. The two caryatids at the back of the room stand guard at the entrance to the main repository. By crossing the main courtyard, access can be gained to the Square Louvois off the Rue de Richelieu, which occupies the site of the Opéra where the Duc de Berry was assassinated on February 13, 1820. He was second in line to the throne of France. Retrace the same walk to return to no. 2, rue Vivienne.

GALERIE COLBERT. This magnificent covered market, whose name reminds us that a private hotel on this spot was owned by Colbert, was designed in 1826 by the architect J. Billaud. The property company who commissioned it wanted to set it up as a rival to the adjacent Vivienne gallery and take advantage of the hustle and bustle of the nearby Palais-Royal. Today the complex houses annexes belonging to the Bibliothèque Nationale. Come out at no. 6, rue des Petits-Champs. On the opposite sidewalk the small passageway set at an angle to the Deux-Pavillons was arranged by the owner of the Galerie Vivienne in such a way as to waylay to his own advantage people coming from the Palais-Royal, in whose path lay the entrance to the Galerie Colbert. Turn left at

THE BIBLIOTHÈQUE NATIONALE Labrouste's rationalist architecture inside an historical exterior; the corner rotunda on the Rue des Petits-Champs (top) and the famous reading room (above). The Molière fountain (below) brightens up a congested part of town.

The Galerie Colbert with its columns of imitation marble and its neo-Pompeiian rotunda contains the statue of *Eurydice Being Bitten by a Serpent* (1822) by Charles Lebœuf-Nanteuil.

The Grand Café Colbert with its typical Paris brasserie décor is enobled by neoclassical friezes. The old bookstore in the passage links the Colbert and Vivienne galleries.

There is a restrained and yet bright quality to the various features of the Galerie Vivienne, making it an elegant setting for its luxury shops.

Marble, paintings, mahogany and bronze blend in the Galerie Véro-Dodat.

Notre-Dame-des-Victoires.

Statues of Louis XIV by Bosio (1822) and Desjardins (1686) demolished in 1792.

no. 4, rue des Petits-Champs to turn into the Galerie Vivienne.
GALERIE VIVIENNE. This glass-roofed shopping arcade designed in 1823 for a Paris lawyer, was laid out by the architect François-Jean Delannoy in the neoclassical style. Wands of Hermes, anchors and cornucopias, the mottos of trade, are found around the windows set in a half-moon on the mezzanine level with goddesses and nymphs in the rotunda. The gallery's success was short-lived and it was nearly demolished in the middle of the 20th century. Today the Institut de France, which owns the gallery, has restored it to its original elegance. The bookstore specializing in antique books remains as it was at the beginning of the century. A perpendicular passageway leads to the Galerie Colbert. Returning to the Rue des Petits-Champs, take the small passage which comes out onto the Rue de La Banque. Go into the passage of the Petits-Pères.

NOTRE-DAME-DES-VICTOIRES

THE PETITS-PÈRES. The Place des Petits-Pères keeps alive the memory of the barefoot Augustinian monks or *petits pères*, whose Order was established in 1628 and whose monastery stood on this site until the Revolution. The buildings were destroyed in 1859 with the exception of the chapel which is now the parish church. Its dedication records Louis XIII's gratitude for his battle successes, particularly at La Rochelle. **A CENTURY OF WORK.** The architect Le Muet built the chancel

between 1629 and 1632, Jacques Bruant the transept and the last bay of the nave between 1642 and 1666 and finally Sylvain Cartault crowned the whole building with vaulting and put in the main door between 1737 and 1740. Three doors on the lower level with Ionic pillars, an arched bay at the upper level with Corinthian columns and two inverted consoles cushioned by two

obelisks and a pediment decorated with the arms of France make up a façade whose classical style is echoed in the church's interior design and décor. From 1796 to 1809 the church was the headquarters of the Bourse (stock exchange).
PLACE OF PILGRIMAGE. On the right of the transept is the chapel of the Très-Saint-et-Immaculé-Cœur-de-Marie with its statue of the Virgin. Twenty thousand plaques and silvered metal hearts cover the walls of this place of pilgrimage instituted in 1836. The chancel's long shape is a reminder that the church was first used by a religious community. It contains seven pictures painted by Carle van Loo between 1748 and 1755 telling the story of Saint Augustine. This set of pictures is one of the few to remain in the place for which it was created ▲ 226. In the second chapel on the left stands the memorial to Jean-Baptiste Lully, superintendent of music to Louis XIV and composer of *Au Clair de la Lune*. His bust by Jean Collignon is surrounded by the figures of *Poetry* and *Music* by Pierre Cotton.
SHOPS FROM A BYGONE ERA. At no. 8, rue des Petits-Pères stands the last remaining shop (called Au Coeur Immaculé de Marie) to sell religious objects, a type of business that once flourished in the area. At no. 10 an old baker's shop has kept its late 19th-century decoration with its colored ceramic tiles.

PLACE DES VICTOIRES

A NEW MODEL FOR ROYAL SQUARES. The Place des Victoires was the first to be dedicated to Louis XIV and was to become the model for royal squares throughout France. Maréchal Duc de La Feuillade asked the principal architect to the king, Hardouin-Mansart, to devise an Italian-style circular area in 1685 which had not existed before in Paris. This type of town architecture was intended to highlight the statue of the king on a plinth commissioned as early as 1679 after the victory at Nijmegen from the courtier and sculptor Martin Desjardins. The huge statue whose very height determined the axis of the square's layout, was unveiled in 1686. Louis,

dressed in a coronation cloak, was portrayed crushing a three-headed dog symbolizing the Triple Alliance. A gilt bronze figure of *Winged Victory* was presenting him with a crown of laurels and at the base four male figures seated and in chains, represented the captive nations Holland, Germany, Spain and Turkey. At the corners four lanterns set atop columns decorated with medallions burned day and night. None of the streets running into the square was ever extended into another street in order to give the illusion of an enclosed area and thus make the royal effigy stand out against the buildings. The identical façades feature pilasters, the "court dress" of architecture in the Grand Siècle. At ground level there were walled arcades, which prevented pedestrians from looking upward.
FROM ONE STATUE TO ANOTHER. Louis

RUE DE LA BANQUE connects the Bank of France to the Bourse. At nos. 2 and 4 a 1905 apartment block was the headquarters of the Louis-Dreyfus Bank.

At no. 1 Legrand's (top of page), which keeps alive the tradition of gourmet groceries, was set up in a residential apartment block from the period of Louis XVI. Victor Ballard who built the metal market chambers in Les Halles also built the *Mairie* (town hall) of the 2nd arrondissement (1850) at no. 8 and the Hôtel du Timbre (1844) at nos. 9–13.

ROYAL COMMEMORATION A medallion featuring a copy of the royal equestrian statue decorates the corner of a shop which dates from the partial rebuilding of the Place des Victoires at the end of the 19th century.

AN ARTIST'S INTERIOR
Through the window of this *Artist's Interior* painted around 1810 by Martin Drolling, can be seen the west side of the unfinished Church of St-Eustache designed by the architect Pierre Patte (18th century).

COUR DES MESSAGERIES
Today the Rue Croix-des-Petits-Champs stands on the departure point for the coaches which carried mail and travelers to destinations throughout France.

XIV's statue was sent to be melted down under the Revolution. Today all that remains are the four slaves in chains which can be seen in the Cour Puget in the Louvre Museum ▲ *190*. The existing equestrian statue of Louis XIV by François-Joseph Bosio was erected in 1822. It replaced the statue of General Desaix, shown as a nude from antiquity which was melted down to make the equestrian statue of Henri IV at the Pont-Neuf!

SUCCESSFUL TOWN LANDSCAPING. Looking up the Rue Catinat, the visitor can see the front entrance of the Bank of France. In spite of excessive alterations and out-of-proportion reconstructions which have compromised the original harmony of the square, the Place des Victoires remains a successful piece of urban landscaping and the reputation of its high-class shops has been maintained since the end of the 19th century.

RUE DU MAIL FOR FURNISHING FABRIC. This street was opened in 1636 on the site of the croquet game set up along the old Charles V ramparts. Its main attraction lies in the large number of showrooms run by some of the best-known manufacturers of furnishing fabrics. Return toward the Place des Victoires.

RUE D'ABOUKIR, SOUVENIR OF EGYPT. The street partly occupies the site of the wall and ditches of the Charles V ramparts destroyed after 1634. It took its name in 1807, and like those of the other streets in the district (Cairo, Nile and Damiette) commemorates Napoleon's expedition to Egypt ▲ *148*. No. 4 is a fine example of neoclassical residential property from the 19th century ● *80*. Then go along the Rue Étienne-Marcel, opened in 1858 between the new Boulevard de Sébastopol as far as the Place des Victoires which opens up on the east side. The first main crossroad brings the visitor into the Rue du Louvre.

RUE DU LOUVRE

TRIUMPH IN METAL AND CONCRETE. The road was built in sections between 1854 and 1906 from the Quai du Louvre as far as the Rue Montmartre. It is in typical Haussmann style and cuts right through the traditional

THE NEW POST OFFICE
With its hydraulic lifts, its steam-powered machines to ensure the proper functioning of the pneumatic telegraph system and its generator room to supply electricity, the new Post Office building became *the* symbol of the modern

ownscape of the Palais-Royal and Les Halles districts. Lined on both sides with office buildings, it offers a omprehensive view of the various styles of architecture ossible with metal and concrete.

POST OFFICE, BEACON OF MODERNITY. This model of ationalist architecture (nos. 48–52) was built between 880 and 1886 by Julien Guadet on a small piece of and created by the opening of the Rue Étienne-Marcel and the Rue du Louvre. The building is four-ided with its longest side measuring some 425 feet and a urface area of some 10 acres. Its six stories rise around a teel structure partly built by the firm of Eiffel. Behind the lassically ordered façades the floors are laid out on very wide netal frames. Next door at no. 46 bis the old Paris telephone xchange built between 1890 and 1892 by the architect Jean-Marie Boussard, stands out thanks to its corner rotunda overed with pale-blue glazed bricks.

RUE COQUILLIÈRE. Take the second street on the right, the Rue Coquillière. At the corner of the Rue du Bouloi, the afé L'Imprimerie has kept part of its décor of glass paintings dating from 1913. From here you can see one of the wings of the Bank of France which goes onto the Croix-des-Petits-Champs, with its pediment decorated with an allegorical sculpture by Pierre Carrier-Belleuse.

COUR DES FERMES. At no. 15, Rue du Louvre behind a door surrounded by figures of Atlas, there is a complex of offices, shops and apartments. This is the Cour des Fermes built in 1889 by the architect Henri Blondel. A second entrance on the Rue du Bouloi opens onto an impressive metal frame with exposed rivets. Continue toward the south. At the next crossroad on the left is the Bourse du Commerce.

BOURSE DU COMMERCE. The

age at the end of the 19th century. With its attractive bright layout and pleasant airy atmosphere for both workers and clients alike, it was to become the model for post offices throughout France. The sorting office (above left) and a cross-section of the old Paris telephone exchange around 1893 (below left).

▲ The Bourse

Bourse (stock exchange) is circular in shape and occupies the site of the old Corn Exchange. It was built in 1767 and the wooden frame which covered the central courtyard was replaced in 1811 by an iron dome covered in brass leaf then glass panes. In 1887 Blondel reworked the building to make it into an exchange hall for commodities. The huge dome, painted in 1889, celebrates the virtues of trade. On the pediment at the front of the building the allegorical group by Onésime Croissy, *Town of Paris Protecting Commerce and Industry*, is characterized by its late 19th-century monumental sculpture. On the east side the fluted column, a relic of the mansion belonging to Catherine de' Medici, is reputed to have been used as an observatory by her astronomer Ruggieri. Cross the Rue du Louvre and take the diagonal Rue Jean-Jacques-Rousseau as far as no. 19 and the Passage Véro-Dodat.
PASSAGE VÉRO-DODAT. Built on the initiative of two butchers after whom it is named, this is one of the prettiest galleries in Paris. Inaugurated in 1826 the gallery caused a sensation thanks to the refinement of its decoration: checkered tiling, alternating glass and painted ceilings, copper window and door frames and panels of mirrors, wood painted to look like mahogany and small trompe l'oeil onyx columns. Its gas lamp

The buttresses on the apse and sides of the Oratoire, together with its gables make a very attractive building. The main façade onto the Rue St-Honoré, a French interpretation of the Jesuit style, saw its rich decorative sculptures dating from 1745 disappear during the Revolution.

were a great novelty. Today the gallery houses antique shops, art galleries, fashionable boutiques and the Café de l'Époque, famous in the 19th century. Take the Rue Jean-Jacques Rousseau again as far as the Rue St-Honoré and turn left.

ORATOIRE DU LOUVRE. The church was first built in 1621 as a chapel in the monastery of the Congregation of the Oratory of France, an Order of priests dedicated to preaching and teaching which was founded in 1611 during the Counter-Reformation. Designed by Clément Métezeau and Jacques Le Mercier ● 76, it was not finished until 1745 by Pierre Caqué. Louis XIII is reputed to have wanted to incorporate it within the Palais du Louvre which he was keen to extend. Bossuet, Massillon, Bourdaloue and Malebranche preached in this church.

A munitions' store under the Revolution and then the Opéra's costume storeroom, it became a Protestant church in 1811.

ART NOUVEAU ARCHITECTURE. Continue along the Rue St-Honoré as far as the crossroads with the Rue du Louvre where at no. 32 the Paris headquarters of the firm of Saint-Frères, previously the owners of the jute mills in Picardy was situated. Still in the Rue du Louvre at no. 16 is an example of late Art Nouveau built in 1912 by Frantz Jourdain, architect of the Samaritaine ● 85. Its bow-windows which go up to the fourth floor, its stylized decoration, wrought iron balconies and plaques of multicolored enameled tiles are typical of this period.

APSE OF THE ORATOIRE. Turn right into the Rue de Rivoli just by the apse of the Oratoire, to see the monument to Admiral Gaspard de Coligny. Cross the Rue de Marengo and go back via the arcades of the Louvre des Antiquaires until you are back in the Place du Palais-Royal.

The monument to Gaspard de Coligny, head of the Protestant party, assassinated during the St Bartholomew's day massacre in 1572, is the work of the sculptor Gustave-Alphonse-Désiré Crauk (1889).

305

THE PAVILLON DES GUICHETS

The pavilion was rebuilt in 1868 by Hector Lefuel. At the foot of the arcades are two groups of stone carvings, the *Merchant Navy* and the *Military Navy*, by François Jouffroy; on the pediment the *Spirit of the Arts*, a high-relief in beaten copper by Antonin Mercié (1877) has replaced an equestrian statue of Napoleon III by Antoine Louis Barye.

THE "GUICHETS" AND THE BRIDGE

Go in the direction of the arched gates of the Carrousel, pass beneath the pavilion called Lesdiguières which juts out on the left side then cross the Quai du Louvre toward the bridge. Below, a stroll along the river bank offers a splendid view across to the embankments on the Left Bank of the Seine.

A NEW BRIDGE. At the end of the 1930's the Pont du Carrousel replaced the metal bridge designed in 1834 by the engineer Antoine-Rémy Polonceau. With its reinforced concrete structure, stone facing and three arches stretched very low, the bridge looks a bit like a hunchback. The groups of sculptures carved by Louis Petitot in 1846 have been replaced at the four corners: *Industry* and *Plenty* on the Right Bank and *The Town of Paris* and *The Seine* on the Left Bank. At both ends the lampposts, which used to have variable heights of 40 feet during the day and 70 feet at night, were made by Raymond Subes a famous craftsman of wrought-iron objects active during the interwar years. Continue eastward along the Quai du Louvre.

GALLERY AT THE WATER'S EDGE

THE GRANDE GALERIE was built for Henri IV between 1595 and 1610 by Louis Métezeau to link the "Old Louvre" to the Tuileries ● *76*. On the first floor, the windows have been blocked to give prominence to overhead lighting. In 1848 Félix Duban restored the façades which have remained unchanged since then. Virtually all the decorative sculpture dates from that time. The mezzanine level was crammed with the studios of artists enjoying the king's protection but they were kicked out by Napoleon in 1806. The Lefuel door opens onto the courtyard with its double balustraded staircase in the riding school and the emperor's stables ▲ *132*.

PAVILLON DU SALON CARRÉ. The first and second floors house the Italian-style Salon ● *28* where exhibitions were periodically put on.

PETITE GALERIE. Coming back from the square, the Petite Galerie was originally a passage linking the Louvre to the Grande Galerie in which Louis Le Vau redesigned the first floor in 1661 to accommodate the Galerie d'Apollon. In 1849 Félix Duban restored the façades and at the far south end added the loggia decorated with Anne of Austria's monogram. The single-color decoration relieved with some gold embellishments

FOOTBRIDGE OF THE ARTS

Rebuilt in 1981 after the original design but in steel and with seven rather than nine arches, the bridge with its exotic wooden boards is used by strollers, artists and tourists who enjoy one of the best views along the Seine.

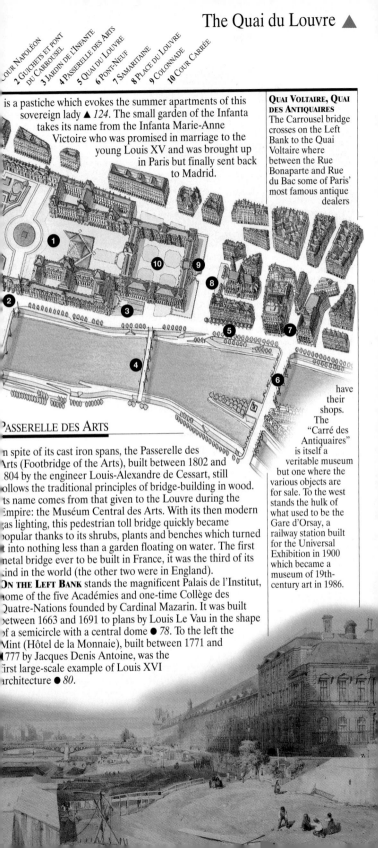

is a pastiche which evokes the summer apartments of this sovereign lady ▲ *124*. The small garden of the Infanta takes its name from the Infanta Marie-Anne Victoire who was promised in marriage to the young Louis XV and was brought up in Paris but finally sent back to Madrid.

QUAI VOLTAIRE, QUAI DES ANTIQUAIRES

The Carrousel bridge crosses on the Left Bank to the Quai Voltaire where between the Rue Bonaparte and Rue du Bac some of Paris' most famous antique dealers have their shops. The "Carré des Antiquaires" is itself a veritable museum but one where the various objects are for sale. To the west stands the hulk of what used to be the Gare d'Orsay, a railway station built for the Universal Exhibition in 1900 which became a museum of 19th-century art in 1986.

PASSERELLE DES ARTS

In spite of its cast iron spans, the Passerelle des Arts (Footbridge of the Arts), built between 1802 and 1804 by the engineer Louis-Alexandre de Cessart, still follows the traditional principles of bridge-building in wood. Its name comes from that given to the Louvre during the Empire: the Muséum Central des Arts. With its then modern gas lighting, this pedestrian toll bridge quickly became popular thanks to its shrubs, plants and benches which turned it into nothing less than a garden floating on water. The first metal bridge ever to be built in France, it was the third of its kind in the world (the other two were in England).

ON THE LEFT BANK stands the magnificent Palais de l'Institut, home of the five Académies and one-time Collège des Quatre-Nations founded by Cardinal Mazarin. It was built between 1663 and 1691 to plans by Louis Le Vau in the shape of a semicircle with a central dome ● *78*. To the left the Mint (Hôtel de la Monnaie), built between 1771 and 1777 by Jacques Denis Antoine, was the first large-scale example of Louis XVI architecture ● *80*.

PANORAMA ONTO THE LOUVRE
Designed by five architects including Jacques Androuet du Cerceau, the Pont-Neuf has two sets of arches, one with five spans and the other with seven joined in the middle by an artificial platform built on two small islands and today called Square du Vert-Galant. On the esplanade Lémot's equestrian statue of Henri IV (1818) has replaced that made by Giambologna which was destroyed during the Revolution.

Old-style grandeur at the Samaritaine. (facing page center right and cross-section above).

PONT-NEUF

THE OLDEST BRIDGE IN PARIS. The Pont-Neuf was built to make it easier for the king to cross from the Louvre Palace to the Abbey of Saint-Germain-des Prés; Henri III laid the first stone on May 31, 1578. Work was not completed till 1606 and it was Henri IV who gave it the name of Pont-Neuf. Spanning almost 900 feet it is still one of the longest bridges in Paris. Under the Ancien Régime popular sideshows were constantly held there. In the summer of 1985 the artist Christo wrapped it in white sheeting tied with ropes. For a period of two weeks hordes of people crowded onto the bridge to rekindle the spirit of traditional popular entertainment.

LA SAMARITAINE

Opposite the Pont-Neuf on the right bank stands the Samaritaine, one of the most famous department stores in Paris whose name evokes the pump installed on the bridge from 1603 to 1813. Its style is a catalog of industrial and commercial architecture from 1900 to 1930.
EVEN THE RIVETS CAN BE SEEN. Between 1905 and 1910 the architect Frantz Jourdain built a revolutionary building between Rue de la Monnaie, Rue des Prêtres-St-Germain-l'Auxerrois, Rue Baillet and Rue de l'Arbre-Sec. The metal structure with its exposed rivets supports large bay windows. Painted bright blue, it was decorated with

single-color strips: mosaic signs in flowered enameled tiles on an orange background. Inside it had glass tile floors and a central area covered in glass guaranteed maximum illumination for the interior.

AN ART DECO FAÇADE. The municipal council opposed the design for a building with a completely metal frontage and so Frantz Jourdain worked together with his young colleague Henri Sauvage to design the huge frontage onto the Quai du Louvre which they finished in 1928. The metal frame rising to eleven stories is hidden behind a stone facing decorated with bow windows and recesses. The Samaritaine thus joins the ranks of the "monuments" and is in fact the only large Art Deco façade in Paris.

RENOVATIONS. For safety reasons, however, the famous store closed for business in June 2005, but is scheduled to reopen after refurbishment which could take up to six years.

THE BELLE JARDINIÈRE. To the right of the Samaritaine, a number of old stores collectively known as the Belle Jardinière, were famous for their array of working clothes, particularly liveries for domestic servants.

THE QUAI DE LA MÉGISSERIE. Until the seventeenth century, tanners prepared skins along this quay which is well known today for its shops selling plants and domestic animals. Booksellers ply their trade on the Seine side of the road. Return to the Samaritaine and turn into the Place de l'École on the right and then on the left, the Rue des Prêtres-St-Germain-l'Auxerrois to reach the church of the same name on the Place du Louvre.

This painting from 1666 shows how busy the Pont-Neuf was even then.

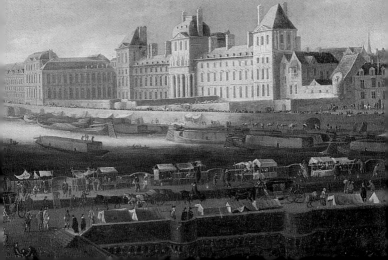

CHURCH OF ST-GERMAIN-L'AUXERROIS

Few monuments have undergone so many transformations in their history as this church, which became a royal parish church when the Valois settled in the Louvre in the 16th century. Founded at the end of the 7th century and rebuilt in the 12th, it was extended in the 13th century. It is from this period that the chancel, apse and main central door date. The nave and transept were built between 1420 and 1425, the porch between 1435 and 1439. During the night of August 24, 1572 it was the bells of St-Germain which announced the St Bartholomew's Day Massacre. In 1710, to make it easier for processions to pass, the central pillar with its statue of Saint Germain and the recessed pediment of the *Last Judgement* in the central door (13th century) were taken down. In 1728 the stained glass was replaced by clear panes of glass. In 1754, Claude Bacarit and the sculptor Louis-Claude Vassé adapted the central nave of the chancel to bring it in line with the taste for classicism; they knocked down the rood-screen of which five pieces can be seen in the Louvre ▲ *186*. The church was restored between 1838 and 1855 by Jean-Baptiste Lassus and Victor Baltard.

BURIAL PLACE OF ARTISTS. From the 17th century artists under the king's protection were buried here: the architects Le Vau, de Cotte, Gabriel; the sculptors Desjardins, Coysevox, Vassé, Coustou; the painters Coypel, Desportes, Restout, Boucher, Van Loo and Chardin. The link with the arts is kept alive today with the service of the Ashes offered for artists, the almshouse of the École des Beaux-Arts and the exhibition of current works of religious art.

MASTERPIECES. Notable are two early-Renaissance Flemish altarpieces, the royal family pew carved between 1682 and 1684 to designs by Charles Lebrun, *Christ* in the nave by Bouchardon and the Louis XVI organ case which came from Ste-Chapelle. The Lady Chapel is neo-Gothic; the architect and restorer Lassus designed the altar and reredos, Eugène Viollet-le-Duc designed *The Stem of Jesse* and the painter Eugène-Emmanuel Amaury-Duval decorated it with paintings inspired by the primitives.

PLACE DU LOUVRE

A HAUSSMANN CREATION. As early as 1660, some forty plans had been devised for a square between St-Germain-l'Auxerrois and the Louvre. Such a square was declared to be in the public interest in 1855 and it owes its creation to the program of decorative improvements headed by Baron Haussmann. In 1854 as a suitable frame for the new square on the clearing between the two monuments, Haussmann built two buildings on the Seine side of the Rue de Rivoli based on those Percier and Fontaine had designed for the Rue de Rivoli . Between 1857 and 1859 he added on the building which is Mairie of the 1st arrondissement. The architect Jacques Ignace Hittorff took his inspiration from the medieval outline of the neighboring church but drew on the architectural vocabulary of the Renaissance. To correct the misalignment of the church the architect thought of building a belfry on a street planned between the church and the Mairie. It was on this square in 1881 that the Town of Paris installed the first of around a hundred public restrooms, a worthy attempt at hygiene which continued with the famous public circular urinals (known somewhat more romantically in French as "vespasiennes") which have now been replaced by "superloos". At the corner of the square on the Seine side the Cadort teashop (founded in 1896) has retained its pretty gold and white decoration and Corinthian columns.

THE BELLS
The famous set of bells installed in 1878 and renovated in 1982, are in the belfry; thirty-eight bells cast in 1862 each give out a different sound; the heaviest weighs 2 tons and the lightest 35 lbs. At 11am the bells play pieces by Couperin and Rameau and a tune written by Marie-Antoinette.

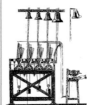

TRUE GOTHIC AND FALSE RENAISSANCE
The entry to the church is the only Gothic doorway in Paris, apart from that at Ste-Chapelle. It borrowed a certain flamboyance from Burgundian architecture, along with five unequal bays and a complex system

▲ Masterpiece of French architecture

THE WING ON THE COLONNADE

The wing was restored between 1756 and 1757 by Jacques-Ange Gabriel who took inspiration from it to build the palaces on the Place Louis-XV (Concorde). The surrounding area was cleared but a plan for a monumental square had to wait until the Second Empire. In 1808, Lemot carved on the pediment a *Minerva* surrounded by the *Arts* and *Victory* crowning Napoleon's bust, which the Restoration replaced with a bust of Louis XIV. Ditches planned were not finally dug till between 1964 and 1967. They are 80 ft wide and 25 ft deep and relieve the huge foundation area, setting the colonnade in its proper proportions. The bridge leading to the palace's main entrance was designed from 17th-century drawings with the foundation stones from the first plan made by Le Vau.

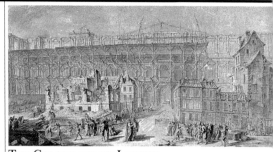

THE COLONNADE DU LOUVRE

A MONUMENTAL FAÇADE. Louis XIV wished the east side of the palace to have a grand entrance as part of an architectural east-west axis. A first design by Louis Le Vau, begun in 1661, was abandoned in 1664. A year later there was a design by Bernini which was considered too Baroque and then in 1667, a second design by Le Vau was put forward and accepted by the king. However the architect was so absorbed in building the château at Versailles that he was unable to see it through. Part of the work then passed to Claude Perrault. The most striking element in this 550 feet long façade is the range of Corinthian columns ● *78*.

THE COUR CARRÉE

THE HEART OF THE PALACE. The Cour Carrée is the result of extensions and decorative improvements carried out from the time of François I to Napoleon III. The west wing begun in 1546 by Pierre Lescot ● *74* is the oldest. His successors have respected the Renaissance architecture remarkably well. Recent restoration makes it easier to read the pediments. On the east side spirits support a cock surrounded by a serpent; on the north side the *Genius of France* with the features of Napoleon evokes the *Gods of Peace* and *Law*; on the south side, *Minerva* is accompanied by the *Sciences* and *Arts*. At night the courtyard is magnificently floodlit.

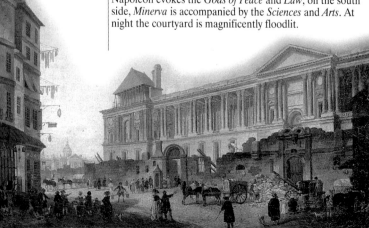

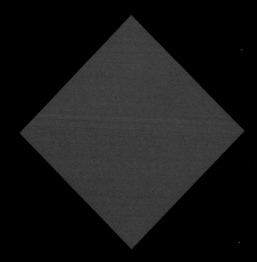

PRACTICAL INFORMATION

◆ Practical information

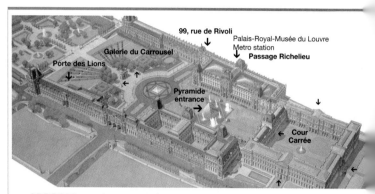

99, rue de Rivoli
Palais-Royal-Musée du Louvre Metro station
Passage Richelieu
Galerie du Carrousel
Porte des Lions
Pyramide entrance
Cour Carrée

ADDRESS

■ **MAILING ADDRESS**
Musée du Louvre
75058 Paris
Cedex 01 France
■ **PHONE NUMBERS**
Switchboard
Tel. 01 40 20 50 50
Information desk
Tel. 01 40 20 53 17
Daily (except Tue)
9am–6pm (9.45pm
Wed and Fri)
www.louvre.fr
■ **DISABLED VISITORS**
Tel. 01 40 20 53 17
or 01 40 20 59 90

GETTING TO THE MUSEUM

→ **BY METRO AND RER**
■ **METRO STATIONS**
Palais-Royal/Musée du Louvre
(Metro lines 1 and 7);
this station is the
closest to the
Pyramide.
Louvre-Rivoli (Metro
line 1); entrance via
the Cour Carrée.
Tuileries (Metro
line1); this station is
the furthest from the
museum but you get
to walk across the
beautiful Tuileries
gardens.
■ **FROM ORLY AIRPORT**
Take the suburban
RER (line C) train in
the direction of
Champs de Mars-
Tour Eiffel, alight at
St-Michel/ Notre-
Dame, walk to the
Boulevard St-Michel,
take the 27 bus
(direction St-Lazare),
alight at Musée-du-
Louvre, opposite
the Pyramide.
■ **FROM CHARLES-DE-GAULLE (ROISSY)
AIRPORT**
Take the RER (line B)
in the direction of
Massy-Palaiseau,
change at Châtelet-
les-Halles, take the
Metro (line 1,
direction La Défense)
and alight at Palais
Royal/ Musée du
Louvre.

→ **BY BUS**
Nos 21, 27, 39, 48,
68, 69, 72, 81, 95
pass by the Louvre.
The *Paris l'Open Tour*
bus stops outside the
Pyramide.

→ **BY BATOBUS**
(Jardin des Plantes to
the Eiffel Tower). One
of the eight stops is
by the Louvre, on the
François-Mitterrand
quay. Every 15 mins
in summer, every
30 mins in winter.
Forfait 1, 2 or 5 days.
Tel. 0825 05 01 01
www.batobus.com

→ **BY CAR**
■ **PARKING LOTS**
Entry is sometimes
limited to certain
times of the day but
drivers can collect
their cars 24/7.
**Carrousel-Louvre
underground parking
lot** (7am–11pm);
access by the
underpass on Ave du
Général-Lemonier
from the Quai des
Tuileries or Pont
Royal.
St-Germain-
l'Auxerrois (8am–
8pm); entrance at
1, place du Louvre.
Parking Vendôme
(open 24 hrs); access
on Place Vendôme.
■ **TAXIS**
Place du Palais-
Royal.

ENTRANCES TO THE MUSEUM

→ **PYRAMIDE**
The main entrance
■ for visitors without
a ticket.
■ priority entrance
for disabled visitors
(who can also enter
Porte des Lions, via
passage Richelieu,
or via the Carrousel).

→ **PASSAGE RICHELIEU**
■ for visitors who
already have a
ticket, a museum
pass, or are entitled to
special concession
(read further down).
■ groups.

→ **GALERIE DU CARROUSEL**
(99, rue de Rivoli
or through the
Carrousel gardens)
■ priority access (no
queuing) for visitors
who already have a
ticket, a museum
pass, or are entitled
to special
concessions (read
further down) and for
groups.
■ for visitors without
a ticket.

→ **PORTE DES LIONS**
The entrance is
closed most of the
time but can be used
as a possible exit
from the collection
of African and Asian
arts and arts of the
Americas (Pavillon
des Sessions,
entrance via the
Denon wing).

OPENING TIMES

→ **PERMANENT COLLECTIONS**
Daily (except Tue
and some bank hols)
9am–6pm
Late nights Wed and
Fri until 9.45pm
Last entrance
The ticket desks
close at 5.15pm
(9.15pm Wed and
Fri); the rooms close
at 5.30pm (9.30pm
Wed and Fri).

→ **PYRAMIDE ENTRANCE**
Daily (except Tue)
9am–10pm.

→ **GALERIE DU CARROUSEL**
Daily (except Tue).
9am–10pm.

**CALENDAR OF ROOM
OPENING**
Beware: all the
rooms aren't always
opened; consult the
calendar
■ at the entrance
of the Pyramide
■ in the Hall
Napoléon
■ on the Louvre
website:
www.louvre.fr

→ PASSAGE RICHELIEU
Daily (except Tue)
9am–6pm.

→ PORTE DES LIONS
Daily (except Tue and Fri) 9.20am–8.45pm;
entrance usually closed but can be used as exit.

→ HALL NAPOLÉON
Daily (except Tue)
9am–10pm;
temporary exhibitions 9am–6pm (10pm Wed and Fri).

TICKETS

■ PERMANENT COLLECTIONS
Tickets are valid for the whole day (you can leave the museum and resume your visit later), for the permanent collection and the temporary exhibitions (except those in the Hall Napoléon) and the Delacroix Museum.
Full price:
€8.50.
Late nights:
Wed and Fri until 9.45pm: €6.
■ TEMPORARY EXHIBITIONS
In the Hall Napoléon: approx. €9.50.
■ COMBINED TICKET
Permanent collections, temporary exhibitions and the Delacroix Museum.
Full price: €13;
Late nights: €11.

→ GROUPS
Advance booking compulsory for groups of seven people or more.
Independent groups with their own guide are asked to make advance booking on:
Tel. 01 40 20 57 60
to book a guide from the museum:
Tel. 01 40 20 51 77
Call ahead to find out the cost of a visit:
entrance ticket + advance booking + guide from the museum.

FREE ADMISSION

To the Louvre (except for the temporary exhibitions in the Hall Napoléon) and the Delacroix Museum.

→ FOR ALL
On the first Sunday of each month and on July 14.

→ FOR THE FOLLOWING
(upon presentation of identification;)
■ those under 18
■ those under 26 on Fridays from 6pm (except for the temporary exhibitions in the Hall Napoléon);
■ the unemployed, those on low income or receiving social security benefits;
■ people with major disabilities and the accompanying adult;
■ staff from other museums; teachers in art history, applied arts, decorative arts, graphic arts, etc.;
art school students;
■ artists, journalists, those with museum passes, etc.
Tel. 01 40 20 53 17

PASSES

Information and sale:
Espace adhésion, allée du Grand Louvre, below the Pyramide, 9am–5.15pm (9.15pm if late night opening).
Tel. 01 40 20 51 04

→ MUSEUM AND MONUMENTS CARD
It gives free and priority access to the permanent collections of 60 French monuments and museums, including the Louvre.
■ PRICE
One day: €18;
Three days: €36;
Five days: €54.
■ ON SALE
In the Espace Adhésion of the Louvre Museum, at ticket offices of other

participating museums and monuments, main Metro stations and the Paris Tourist Office in the Carrousel du Louvre.

→ YEARLY PASSES
They give free and immediate access to the permanent collections.
■ "LAISSEZ-PASSER"
Free; valid for one year; for teachers and their students on class visits, for art students etc.
■ "LOUVRE JEUNES" PASS
For those under the age of 26; € 15.
■ "LOUVRE PROFESSIONNELS" PASS
For teachers, artists, art critics, etc. €30.
■ "AMIS DU LOUVRE" PASS
The "Friends of the Louvre" pass costs from €50 to €650 for individuals, from €40 for groups.
Information
Société des Amis du Louvre
Tel. 01 40 20 53 34

ADVANCE BOOKING

→ ADVANTAGES
It gives free and priority access (entrances via Passage Richelieu and the Galerie du Carrousel) to the permanent collections and temporary exhibitions.

→ CONDITIONS
For the purchase of less than 20 tickets at one time. They cannot be collected from the Louvre. Non refundable, non exchangeable.

→ WHERE TO BUY
Department stores
Le Bon Marché, Printemps, Galeries Lafayette, BHV;
Music stores and bookstores
Fnac,

Virgin Megastore;
Hypermarket
Carrefour, Continent, Leclerc, Auchan.

→ INTERNET SALES
Commission and postage charges apply.
■ MUSÉE DU LOUVRE
www.louvre.fr
■ FNAC
Tel. 0 892 684 694
(€0.34 /min),
from abroad:
33 (0)1 41 57 32 28
http://louvre.
fnacspectacles.com
■ TICKETNET
Tel. 0 892 697 073
(€0.34 /min),
from abroad:
33 (0)1 46 91 57 57
www.ticketnet.fr
■ TICKETWEB
Payment in US dollars US; tickets are mailed to North American only.
www.ticketweb.com

→ COMBINED TICKET
■ RATP-LOUVRE COMBINED TICKET
It gives you two RATP transportation tickets (Metro, bus, tramway or RER) + one ticket (with priority entrance) to the permanent collections (and, on the same day, to the Delacroix Museum).
Sales points
Paris Tourist Office
- 25, rue des Pyramides, 75001
- 11 rue Scribe, 75009
- at the Gare-de-Lyon railway station
- at the Gare-du-Nord railway station
- at the Eiffel Tower (from May to Sep).
Tel. 0 892 683 000
(€0.34/min)
www.parisinfo.com

→ GROUP TICKET
If you need more than 20 tickets at one time.
■ MUSÉE & COMPAGNIE
49 rue Etienne Marcel, 75001 Paris
Tel. 01 40 13 49 13
Fax 01 40 13 49 11

◆ Finding your way around the museum

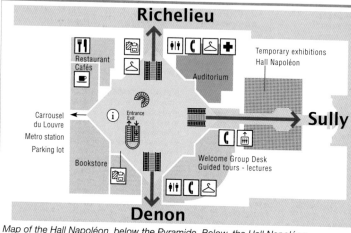

Richelieu

Restaurant
Cafés

Auditorium

Temporary exhibitions
Hall Napoléon

Carrousel
du Louvre
Metro station
Parking lot

Entrance
Exit

Sully

Bookstore

Welcome Group Desk
Guided tours - lectures

Denon

Map of the Hall Napoléon, below the Pyramide. Below, the Hall Napoléon.

INFORMATION DESK

This desk, in the main reception area, in the Hall Napoléon, below the Pyramide should be your first port of call, if you need to talk to a museum employee or pick up the free quarterly program of activities, a map of the museum etc.

FINDING YOUR WAY

→ **MAP-GUIDE**
Free booklet, available in ten languages at the Information Desk; it contains a plan of the museum and color-coded signs for finding your way around the various rooms.

→ **AUDIO-GUIDE**
■ **EARPHONES GUIDE**
Available in six languages, the tapes offer commentaries on a thousand works displayed in the three wings, and the works' location within the museum is indicated on the accompanying leaflet. You can search the tape for any particular commentary you

require by using a numbered code; in this way your visit can be organized in any order you wish. (You will also find these commentaries as mp3 files on the DVD *The Louvre, Virtual Visit*, 2006, sold in the museum's bookstore).

■ **WHERE TO GET THEM**
At the entrance to the collections, in the Richelieu, Sully and Denon wings.

→ **BOOKS, CDROMS, GUIDEBOOKS**
To prepare or remember your visit:
■ *Louvre, 300 Masterpieces*, published by Hazan and the Louvre Museum, 2006, in four languages
■ *The Louvre*, published by the RMN and the Louvre Museum, 2005, in nine languages: 600

masterpieces with commentaries by the curators of the various departments.
■ **MUSEUM BOOKSTORE**
Hall Napoléon ◆ 321.

VISITORS WITH DISABILITIES

Wheelchairs and a special guidebook (in English and French) are available free of charge at the Information Desk.

FACILITIES

■ **ATM MACHINES**
Hall Napoléon
Next to the Information desk.
Galerie du Carrousel
At the end of the Allée Rivoli, at the foot of the escalator.
■ **BUREAU DE CHANGE**
By the inverted Pyramid, at the end of the Allée du Grand Louvre.

Mon, Wed-Sat 10am–7.30pm, Sun 10am–6pm
■ **TELEPHONES**
Hall Napoléon
At the foot of the three escalators.
Galerie du Carrousel
At the end of the Allée Rivoli, at the foot of the escalator and at the end of the Allée de France.
■ **POST OFFICE**
Allée du Grand Louvre.
Daily (except Tue) 9.30am–7pm (9.45pm Wed and Fri)

A FEW RULES

Smoking, drinking, eating and using a mobile phone are strictly forbidden in the exhibition rooms.
■ **FILMS AND PHOTOS**
The use of flash is strongly discouraged. It is also prohibited to videotape or take photographs in some rooms – check the signs at the entrance to each room.

FREE FACILITIES
Cloakrooms, left-luggage (for small items), pushchairs and wheelchairs (identification required), first aid, baby changing room, lost property

LEGEND

- ☐ Arts from Africa, Asia, South Sea Islands and the Americas
- ▒ Oriental antiquities
- ▒ Islamic art
- ▒ Egytian antiquities
- ▒ Greek, Etruscan and Roman antiquities
- ■ Decorative art
- ■ Sculpture
- ▒ Graphic arts
- ■ Painting
- ■ Medieval Louvre

→ THREE WINGS
DENON
To the south, along the quays bordering the Seine.
RICHELIEU
To the north, running parallel to the Rue de Rivoli.
SULLY
To the east, around the Cour Carrée.

→ FOUR FLOORS
The **entresol** (mezzanine level), the **ground floor**, the **first floor** and the **second floor**.

■ **EIGHT DEPARTMENTS**
Spread over the four floors.
HISTORY OF THE LOUVRE AND MEDIEVAL LOUVRE
An archeological tour covering two rooms (entresol).
ARTS FROM AFRICA, ASIA, SOUTH SEA ISLANDS AND THE AMERICAS
Pavillon des Sessions, ground floor, rooms 1 to 8. Entrance through the Denon wing and exit through Porte des Lions.

→ ROOMS
The rooms corresponding to each department are color coded.
■ The rooms themselves are numbered in the direction of the visit; rooms are identified either by a letter of the alphabet or their own name.
■ On each level, detailed plans show the layout of the collection. The small panels with a pyramid on them indicate the exit.
■ In the most important rooms, an information sheet available in several languages comments some of the most significant works exhibited, or summarizes major art movements and techniques.

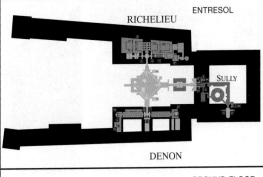

ENTRESOL

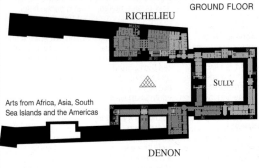

GROUND FLOOR

Arts from Africa, Asia, South Sea Islands and the Americas

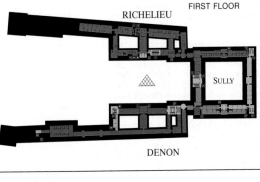

FIRST FLOOR

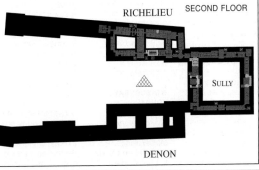

SECOND FLOOR

◆ Guided tours, lectures and workshops

Guided tour

Activities in the studio

TOUR-OPERATORS

→ GUIDED TOURS
There are several organizations to contact if you wish to visit the Louvre with an English-speaking guide.

■ **CITYRAMA PARIS**
149 rue St-Honoré, 75001 Paris
Tel. 01 44 55 61 00

■ **PARIS VISION**
214, rue de Rivoli, 75001 Paris
Tel. 01 42 60 30 01

→PARIS L'OPEN TOUR
This bus stops at twenty or so main touristic sites, including the Louvre (commentaries in English or French, with headphones or, on the bus, out loud). Four different routes.

■ **ONE- OR TWO-DAY PASS**
It allows you to hop on and hop off at any of the planned stops. Tickets can be bought onboard.

■ **INFORMATION**
13, rue Auber, 75009 Paris
Tel. 01 42 66 56 56
www.paris-opentour.com

GUIDED TOURS

To re-discover masterpieces or to obtain a better understanding of a particular theme, work of art, or artist, a visit led by a professional guide can be invaluable,

whether you are an experienced museum goer or a complete novice.

■ **PROGRAMS**
The dates and times of some tours vary throughout the year – see the quarterly program of activities, available from the Information Desk in the Hall Napoléon, below the Pyramid).
Information
Tel. 01 40 20 52 63
www.louvre.fr

■ **TICKETS**
They can be bought at the Group Welcome Desk (Hall Napoléon). Advance reservations are recommended and opened fourteen days prior to the date of the tour. Call for more information.
Tel. 01 40 20 51 77

■ **TICKETS FOR IN-DEPTH STUDIES AND WORKSHOPS**
The advance reservation option for these tours opens two weeks before the beginning of term.
Sales points:
Fnac, Le Printemps and Bon Marché department stores.
Telephone sale:
0 892 684 694;
Internet sale:
www.louvre.fr
www.fnac.com

→ DISCOVERY TOURS
These tours give an overview of the museum's masterpieces.
■ **WHEN / HOW LONG**
In English: daily

(except Tue, first Sun of the month and public hols)
11am, 2pm, 3.45pm (11.30am and 2pm on Sun, except the first Sun of the month).
Length of tour: 1½ hr.

→ ONE WORK
These lectures focus on the presentation and study of a single work from the museum's collection.
■ **WHEN / HOW LONG**
Mon, Wed-Sat 2.30pm;
7.45pm some Wed.
Length of tour: 1 hr.

→ ONE COLLECTION
These tours aim to give visitors an overview of a department, group of works or collection (French sculpture, Mesopotamian art etc.).
■ **WHEN / HOW LONG**
Mon, Wed-Sat 11.30am;
2.30pm some Sat;
7.30pm some Wed.
Length of tour: 1½ hr.

→ "MONOGRAPH" TOUR
A study of the life and work of one artist (Rembrandt, Titian, Veronese, Raphael, Delacroix etc).
■ **WHEN / HOW LONG**
Mon, Wed-Sat 2.30pm;
Length of tour: 1½ hr.

→ THEMATIC TOURS
Historical study of a particular theme through works from the museum's various collections (Egyptian

temples, landscapes etc.).
■ **WHEN / HOW LONG**
Mon, Wed-Sat 2.30pm;
7.45pm some Wed.
Length of tour: 1½ hr.

→ TOUR OF THE TEMPORARY EXHIBITIONS
Quarterly program.

→ ARCHITECTURAL TOUR
These visits, led by an architect, give an insight into the Louvre's architecture and its relationship with its urban surroundings.
■ **WHEN / HOW LONG**
Days and times are variable.
Length of tour: 2 hrs.

→ TUILERIES GARDENS
To understand the gardens' history, learn about their sculptures and landscape. Guided tours and various activities from spring to fall.

→ INTER-MUSEUM TOUR
The program varies; example "The Tuileries Gardens and the garden of the Rodin Museum", "The Louvre Museum and the Musée de l'Homme"...
■ **WHEN / HOW LONG**
Variable.

→ GALLERY TALKS
In-depth discussions around a theme, an art movement, over

Guided tours, lectures and workshops ◆

Visitors and copyists in the Grande Galerie during the 19th century.

several visits, presented by official lecturers of the Réunion des Musées Nationaux.

■ **WHEN / HOW LONG**
Three, five or ten guided visits, once a week, at a fixed time on the same day of the week; see the quarterly program of activities.

→ **WORKSHOPS**
These workshops consist of an active exploration of the Louvre's collections through artistic experimentation and analysis of ancient techniques. For children, adolescents and adults.
The types of subject covered include "The sculpted body", "Mosaic techniques", "The art of the fresco" and more.
■ **WHEN / HOW LONG**
Variable.

LATE-NIGHT FRIDAYS

Late-night opening of the museum (until 10pm) and of the main facilities (cloakroom, bookstores, cafés and restaurants, shops in the Galerie du Carrousel). Activities geared toward a younger audience are organized (reduced ticket entry to the permanent collections and free entry to the under 26s from 6pm) ◆ *315*.
■ **INFORMATION**
Quarterly program. Tickets for the activities can be bought on the same day, from 5.15pm, at the Group Welcome Desk.
■ **INFORMATION**
Tel. 01 40 20 53 17

→ **ONE-OFF LECTURES**
Curators, scholars, scenographers explain their work during temporary exhibitions (free).

→ **WORKSHOPS**
Discover and experiment with a technique in the course of one evening: mosaic, pastels, fresco etc.

→ **IN FRONT OF THE WORKS**
The class is taught in one of the exhibition rooms. Time is devoted to sketching or photographing a particular work.

→ **VISITS**
Introduction to the collections with lectures dedicated to an artist, a collection, a theme or an exhibition.
Architectural tours explore spaces within the museum or outside the building's walls.

→ **CONTEMPORARY MUSIC, MOVIES AND ART**
Invités sur la scène de l'auditorium, des artistes présentent sous des formes variées des créations originales (rencontres «Face à face», projections cinéma et vidéo, concerts). Billets aux caisses de l'auditorium.

THEMATIC JOURNEYS

Itineraries within the Louvre, without guides but with a brochure, are available from the Information Desk or can be printed from the museum's website:
"Living in the Louvre, discovery of the kings' palace", "The Art of Eating at Table: the Rituals and Symbolism of the Meal", "Eugène Delacroix: Passion and inspiration", Masterpieces of the Louvre: In search of ideal beauty".

◆ Research and documentation

THE AUDITORIUM

→ THE SPACE
Conceived by the same architect as the Pyramide, I. M. Pei, the Louvre auditorium is one of the most beautiful spaces in the museum. The multipurpose room seats up to 450 people and offers perfect acoustics and visibility to everyone in the audience.

→ EVENTS
Some 300 events relating to the Louvre are held here.
■ **DEBATES, LECTURES** given by scholars from France and abroad. Topics include movements in the history of art, certain artists, and themes covering the permanent collections and temporary exhibitions in the museum. Specialists are invited to discuss their most recent research as well as current trends in archeological studies.
■ **READINGS** of texts related to themes or works in the collections.
■ **CONCERTS** The auditorium also puts on a varied program of chamber music concerts.
■ **YOUNG AUDIENCE SPECIAL PROGRAM** Shows, pantomines, tales for children.

■ **MOVIES** The auditorium presents a number of special film series and programs of films about art, mostly produced by the Louvre itself – thematic movie cycles mixing art history with the history of cinematography, recent productions, silent films shown with live scores, documentaries etc. Screenings every hour, from 10am–6pm (every hour and a half at weekends); free entry.

→ THE AUDITORIUM AT LUNCHTIME
An informative way to spend a lunch hour (taking 55–60 mins). Meetings take place between September and June at 12.30pm.
■ **CONCERTS**
■ **DEBATES**
■ **FILMS ON ART**
■ **A WORK IN CLOSE UP** The study of a major work from the museum, commented on by a curator. The work is filmed in close-up, and a large-screen video projection reveals its most minute details.

→ INFORMATION
■ **WHERE** At the entrance to the auditorium, in the Hall Napoléon, to the right of the ticket desks.
■ **PROGRAM** Available at the entrance of the auditorium and published in the Louvre quarterly program of activities. It can also be read on the museum's website: www.louvre.fr
Tel. 01 40 20 55 55 (Mon-Fri 9am–7pm).
■ **RESERVATIONS** By phone:
Tel. 01 40 20 55 00 (Mon, Wed-Fri 11am–5pm).
On site, from the auditorium ticket desk (Mon, Wed-Sat 11am–5.30pm).

CYBERLOUVRE

→ MULTIMEDIA SERVICES
The CyberLouvre offers visitors an opportunity to learn about the museum and its collections using new technology. The ten computers in this room offer a free browsing service of the various multimedia resources of the museum. The staff will help you if you're not at ease with computers.
■ **WHAT'S ON OFFER**
The Atlas database allows the direct online consultation of 35,000 works of art exhibited in the Louvre, with authoritative commentary and analysis by the curators and staff; the RMN picture library, and a selection of cultural Internet links.
CD-Roms on the Louvre collections: *The Louvre, Virtual Visit; The Louvre as told to children; Louvre; The Mona Lisa; Egypt in the Antiquity*, etc.
A selection of cultural websites, including various sites of museums in France and around the world.
■ **WHERE AND WHEN** Free entry, daily (except Tue) 9am–5.45pm. Allée du Grand Louvre.
Tel. 40 20 67 30

MULTIMEDIA LIBRARY

You will find in the Médiathèque books on art history, films, videos, recordings, the museum's publications, etc...
■ **ACCESS** Restricted to holders of the Louvre pass, teachers, guides etc. but open to all who want to borrow audiotapes.
Open Mon 1.30–6pm, Wed-Thu 9am–6pm, Fri 9am–1.30pm.
■ **INFORMATION** Group Welcome Desk Tel. 01 40 20 52 80

RESEARCH CENTERS

There is a research center for each of the eight departments of the Louvre. Apart from the ones below

access is usually restricted to art historians, curators, students, teachers etc.

→ DECORATIVE ARTS

The Department of Decorative Arts library contains books and photographs relating to furniture, jewelry, tapestries, ivories, glass, ceramics, small bronze and enamel pieces, gold and silver works, dating from the end of antiquity to the middle of the 19th century.

■ **ACCESS**
Open to all, daily (except Tue) 2–5.30pm, Richelieu wing, first floor, room 94. Tel. 01 40 20 67 31

→ PRINTS AND DRAWINGS

The Department of Graphic Arts (Prints and Drawings) research center consists of the Drawing Cabinet (130,000 works), the Edmond de Rothschild Collection (30,000 engravings and drawings) and the Orsay Museum drawing collection. It also has a digital database, the Mostra database, with an illustrated inventory of all 130,000 items, which records every exhibition of the department's

drawings since they entered the collections.

■ **ACCESS**
Open to all, Mon–Fri 1–6pm, Flore wing, third floor, Porte des lions. Tel. 01 40 20 51 94

→ NEAR EASTERN ANTIQUITIES

The computer research room of this department has three computers dedicated to browsing of the Encyclopedia of the Oriental and Islamic arts and civilizations.

■ **ACCESS**
The computer room (Richelieu wing, room 1bis, Hall Colbert) is open to the general public during museum opening hours, but the research center itself is only open to graduate and students.

BOOKSTORES

→ THE MUSEUM BOOKSTORE

From the basic museum guide to the more elaborate magazine the RMN bookstore offers a huge selection of books – some 18,000 titles – covering all areas of the visual arts. It also has the most exhaustive stock of books on ancient art in France, and sells many foreign language editions, ranging from English to Japanese, German, Italian and

Spanish, slides, DVDs and CD-Roms.

■ **ACCESS**
Hall Napoléon, at the entrance of the Allée du Grand Louvre. Daily (except Tue) 9.30am–7pm (9.45pm Wed and Fri). Tel. 01 40 20 53 53

→ THE CHILDREN'S BOOKSTORE

This new boookstore is dedicated to children and offers more than 4,000 books, educational games, models, toys, jigsaws and other products geared toward the discovery of art, history etc.

■ **ENTRANCE**
Allée du Grand Louvre. Daily (except Tue) 9.30am–7pm (9.45pm Wed and Fri) Tel. 01 40 20 54 28

THE LOUVRE AS PUBLISHER

If exhibition catalogs and academic works make up the greater part of the museum's publishing activities, the Louvre also uses the expertise of its specialists to produce a wide variety of items for the general public including books, games and CD-Roms for the younger market, products aimed at enriching family visits, beautiful art books and DVDs, and educational material for teachers

on the Internet to make the museum as user-friendly as possible. From basic guidebooks describing lesser-known works on show in the museum, via cutting-edge academic research on art history, to the story of the Louvre in strip-cartoon form, the publishing arm of the museum is simply enormous.

L'ÉCOLE DU LOUVRE

The Louvre School of Art, Archeology and Epigraphy is the most famous in France. Its students are the future researchers, curators and scientific staff in museums. It is possible to join the general history course and the specialized courses as an unregistered student.

■ **EVENING CLASS**
Art, from prehistoric times up to the present day.

■ **OPEN CLASS**
Free courses open to the public on the artistic heritage of the French capital.

■ **INFORMATION**
École du Louvre, Palais du Louvre Porte Jaujard, Place du Carrousel 75001 Paris. Tel. 01 55 35 18 00 Mon–Fri 9am–noon, 2–5pm.

◆ Shopping

THE MUSEUM STORE

→ THE RMN
The museum bookstore, like the museum store on the first floor, is affiliated to the RMN (Réunion des Musées Nationaux), an association formed in 1895 to fulfil three aims: the purchase of works of art, facilitating access to works of art for the public, and the spread of culture. With this in mind, the RMN has many different products available that are related to national museums and their contents, such as books, CD-Roms, copies of exhibits, jewelry and ornaments. Each piece is accompanied by a leaflet explaining the work and its origins, and the craftsmanship is of exceptionally high quality. The RMN aims to sell cultural products related to the national museums and their collections (such as books, CD-ROMs, videos, jewelry and reproductions) that are of the highest quality, and are available in a wide choice.

→ OBJETS D'ART AND MOLDINGS
Copies of works in national and foreign collections made by the Atelier de Moulage du Louvre, which has long had a high reputation for its craftsmanship.

→ CHALCOGRAPHY
Chalcography refers the art of engraving on copper or brass. There are many engraved plates on show: the RMN has no fewer than 16,000 hand-engraved examples by artists

from the 17th century to the present day, from which prints can be made on a flat-bed press.

→ JEWELRY AND ACCESSORIES
Silk squares, neckties, watches and over 250 replicas of pieces of jewelry at all prices: royal gemstones, antique pins and brooches, and the famous range of "Bijoux dérobés", or Hidden Jewelry, inspired by details from works shown in the Musée d'Orsay.

→ TABLEWARE
Items in china, faience, silver and crystal to decorate the table and home.

→ INFORMATION
■ BOUTIQUE DU LOUVRE
Entrance via the bookstore or the mezzanine.
Daily (except Tue) 9.30am–7pm)9.45pm Wed and Fri).
Tel. 01 40 20 52 43
■ THE RMN
The stores
Souvenirs of the Louvre and other national museums are on sale in all the RMN outlets and on the Internet at:
www.museesdefrance.com
Other services
Museum pass, guided tours, ticket offices, etc.
RMN main office
Tel. 01 40 13 48 00
www.rmn.fr

ALLÉE DU GRAND LOUVRE

This passageway links the Hall Napoléon, below the Pyramide, to the Galerie du Carrousel.

→ AMENITIES
Cyberlouvre ◆ 320, Membership desk ◆ 315, post office, bureau de change ◆ 316.

→ STORES
The children's boookstore run by the RMN, a store selling stationary and posters, store of the Paris Mint.
Daily (except Tue) 9.30am–7pm)9.45pm Wed and Fri).

THE GALERIE DU CARROUSEL

At the end of the Allée du Grand Louvre, is the place de la Pyramide Inversée (inverted Pyramide) which also intersects with the shopping mall of the Carrousel du Louvre. Here there are other facilities designed to help visitors discover Paris.

→ THE ÎLE-DE-FRANCE TOURIST OFFICE
It can help in organizing your travel plans – guided tours, transportation, accommodation, excursions in nature parks around the capital, gourmet weekends etc.
Daily 10am–6pm.
Tel. 0 826 166 666 (€ 0,15/min.)
From abroad:
Tel. 33 1 44 50 19 98
www.pidf.com
■ SNCF DESK
(French national railways); information and tickets.
Mon, Wed-Fri 10am–5pm.
■ MUSEUM AND MONUMENTS PASS DESK
Daily 10am–6pm.
■ PARISIANS CABARETS
Information and tickets for: the Lido, the Moulin Rouge, the Paradis Latin and the Crazy Horse.
■ EXCURSIONS AND CRUISES
With the Paris Open Tour, Cityrama, Paris Vision and France Tourisme coach companies; cruises on the Seine with Batobus, Bateaux

Parisiens, or the Paris Marina.

→ THE COMÉDIE FRANÇAISE THEATER STUDIO
Dedicated to short (1 hr) classical and contemporary productions.
Tickets:
Wed-Sun 2–5pm.
Tel. 01 44 58 98 58

→ BOUTIQUES
The Carrousel gallery houses a Virgin Megastore together with about 15 other stores – Bernardaud, Résonances, Bodum, L'Occitane, Séphora – selling decorative items of all kinds for the home, as well as fashion accessories. Several stores also sell a wide range of jewelry: Lalique, Swarowski, Salviati (Murano glass), Agatha, Swatch or Les Minéraux (craftware) ◆ 343.

→ OPENING TIMES
■ GALERIE
Daily 8am–11pm (5pm on Tue).
■ STORES
Most are open 11am–8pm; some are closed on Tue.
■ INFORMATION
Tel. 01 43 16 47 47

→ ENTRANCES
■ through the main entrance hall of the museum.
■ by the staircases on either side of the arch of the Carrousel.
■ at no. 99, rue de Rivoli.
■ from the Palais-Royal/Musée-du-

View from the terrace of the Café Marly.

One of the Universal Resto fast-food counters

Louvre Metro station, by the exit doors of the Carrousel parking lot.

■ from the Carrousel parking lot, below the garden, accessible via the underground passsage from the Ave du Général-Lemonnier.

IN THE HALL NAPOLÉON

→ CAFÉ DU LOUVRE
Snacks to take out.
■ **OPENING TIMES**
Wed-Mon 9am–7pm (9.15pm Wed and Fri).

→ LE GRAND LOUVRE
A gastronomic restaurant serving traditional meat and fish dishes, but also featuring more unusual food in season (such as grouper broiled in coconut milk, and scallops with duck liver), and original dishes inspired by pictures in the museum e.g. a ragout of oysters after Recco's Still Life of Oysters with Quinces, and a paté of boned duck inspired by Desportes's Self-Portrait as a Huntsman.
Set menus lunch and dinner: €29 and €37.
À la carte, allow €45 per person, without wine.
■ **OPENING TIMES**
Wed-Mon noon–3pm; Wed and Fri

7–10pm (last orders 9.30pm).
■ **RESERVATIONS**
Tel. 01 40 20 53 41

ON THE MEZZANINE

→ THE PYRAMIDE CAFÉS
They sell food to take out (sandwiches, muffins, soft drinks).
■ **OPENING TIMES**
Daily (except Tue) 10am–5pm.

→ CAFETERIA
Self-service. Assorted dishes, salad bar (€3.30–8) and a varied range of desserts. Warm and friendly atmosphere, thanks to the parquet floor and subdued lighting. Staff available to assist you.
■ **OPENING TIMES**
Daily (except Tue) 11.45am–3pm.

IN THE DENON BUILDING

→ CAFÉ DENON
Entresol level. Restaurant, tearoom.
■ **OPENING TIMES**
Daily 9.30am–5pm (7pm Wed and Fri).

→ CAFÉ MOLLIEN
First floor. Large terrace in summer, overlooking the Cour Napoléon and the Pyramide.
■ **OPENING TIMES**
Daily 9.30am–5pm (7pm Wed and Fri; 8pm during school hols).

IN THE RICHELIEU BUILDING

→ CAFÉ RICHELIEU
First floor. Restaurant and tearoom whose terrace overlooks the Pyramide in summer. The architecture and décor are the works of three contemporary artists: Buren, Raynaud and Giacobetti, who converted these former offices of the Ministry of Finance.
■ **OPENING TIMES**
Daily 10.30am–5pm (7pm Wed and Fri; 8pm during school hols).

→ CAFÉ MARLY
Cour Napoléon.
◆ *336*.
Restaurant, tearoom, heated terrace under the arcade. Décor in the style of Napoléon III by Olivier Gagnère, where discerning customers come to enjoy breakfast early in the morning. Great views of the Cour Marly and the Pyramide, especially in the evening when it is all illuminated. The menu features a seasonal, international cuisine, from French provincial dishes to Thai specialties, though some staples are always there, such as foie gras, stewed forest mushrooms (cèpes) and roast tuna.

A la carte, around €50 per person, without wine.
■ **OPENING TIMES**
Daily 8am–2am (last orders 1am).
■ **RESERVATIONS**
Tel. 01 49 26 06 60

IN THE GALERIE DU CARROUSEL

→ UNIVERSAL RESTO
The name embraces 14 different fast-food counters, both French and foreign, including Asian, Spanish, Italian, Lebanese, Moroccan, vegetarian, a rotisserie, sushi, Tex-Mex, crêpes, pizza, pies, etc. Average price: €13.
■ **OPENING TIMES**
Daily 8am–9.30pm (11pm Wed and Fri).

→ RAGUENEAU
At the entrance to the Universal Resto. Brasserie, tearoom, take out available. Set menus between 11am and 3pm: €16 and €20.
■ **OPENING TIMES**
Daily 11am–7pm.

OUTSIDE THE MUSEUM

The museum's layout allows you to move freely from galleries to restaurants without leaving the Louvre. But you are free to come and go as you wish, as long as you retain your admission ticket which is valid for the entire day.

◆ The Louvre for the visitor in a hurry

There is of course no such thing as a hurried tour of the Louvre, but the route below has been especially designed for the visitor who only wants to spend a limited amount of time in the museum while seeing as many works as possible. Over the next four pages we lead you from one room to another, guiding you around the museum's labyrinthine wings and levels. The tour covers the majority of the museum's departments – including the Medieval Louvre – and selects the best-known works on display.

A TO Z OF THE LOUVRE

The letters (from A to Z) shown alongside each work or group of works chosen refer to the plans and show where they are to be found in the museum. For greater details on the works, refer to the *Guide to the Louvre*, published by the Louvre Museum and the RMN in 2005 ◆ 316.

DENON WING

A set of two escalators leads to the ground level and the Salle du Manège. Leave the room and turn left.

Ⓐ The Slaves (1513–15) by Michelangelo are two statues carved for the first design of Pope Julius II's tomb.Michel-Ange. (Denon, ground floor)

Take the Mollien staircase up to the first floor to reach room 77.

Ⓑ The Raft of the Medusa (1819) painted by Théodore Géricault depicts the shipwreck of the frigate *Medusa* with only fifteen survivors on board a raft. (Denon, first floor, room 77)

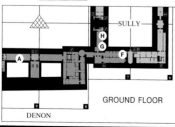

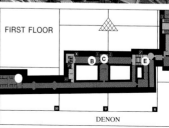

SULLY

GROUND FLOOR

DENON

FIRST FLOOR

DENON

DENON WING

Continue to room 76. On your right is room 6 where the Mona Lisa *and* Wedding Feast at Cana *are hung opposite each other.*

❻ Wedding Feast at Cana (1562–3), painted by Veronese, was commissioned for the refectory of the Monastery of San Giorgio Maggiore in Venice. (Denon, room 76)

❼ Mona Lisa (1503–6) by Leonardo da Vinci, is the portrait of the wife of the eminent Florentine Francesco del Giocondo, which explains its other name of *La Gioconda*. (Denon, room 13)

At the eastern end of the Grande Galerie, cross the Salon

Carré and turn left.

❺ The Victory of Samothrace (c. 190 BC) was discovered on the island of Samothrace in the Aegean Sea. (Denon, first floor, Daru staircase landing)

Continue toward the Sully wing to reach room 74.

❻ Aphrodite, known as the Venus de Milo (end 2nd century BC) was unearthed in 1820 on the island of Milos. It is considered one of the greatest masterpieces of art from antiquity. (Sully, first floor, room 74)

Retrace your steps to the ground floor to room 17.

❼ The Salle des Caryatides with its collection of works from the Greek Hellenic period copied by the Romans.

❽ The Hermaphrodite is on the right. The Caryatids support the musicians' gallery used during balls given at the time of Henri II. (Sully, ground floor, room 17)

Walk in between the Caryatids and go down the staircase to the Medieval Louvre.

❾ Medieval Louvre
Continue into the moats.

SULLY WING

❿ The moats, ditches filled with water, separate the fortress built by Philippe Auguste (on the right) from the Paris city walls (on the left).
Go past several towers. In front of you will be the Sphinx Crypt, through which you can go to the Egyptian Antiquities section. Look at the mastaba (room 4), then come back into the moats to go on to the donjon.

⓫ The donjon of the Louvre was demolished in 1528 on the orders of François I.
Continue into the room containing exhibits found during the excavations. A passage between the display cases leads to the main staircase. Go down as far as the entresol level of the Hall Napoléon in the Richelieu wing. Turn right, toward the sculptures.

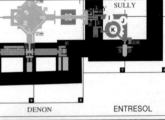

DENON   ENTRESOL

◆ The Louvre for the visitor in a hurry

RICHELIEU WING

Go into the crypt which leads onto two large courtyards. Go into the left-hand courtyard, the Cour Marly.

Ⓛ The Marly Horses is the collective name given to four groups of sculptures: the two groups by Coysevox (1706),

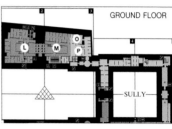

GROUND FLOOR

SULLY

Fame and Mercury, commissioned by Louix XIV to decorate the drinking-trough at the Château de Marly, and the two groups by Coustou (1745) which replaced the first group originally used at the pond. (Richelieu, ground floor, Cour Marly)

Go back into the crypt and walk to the right-hand courtyard, the Cour Puget.

Ⓜ Milo of Croton (1670) was sculpted by Pierre Puget for the park at Versailles. (Richelieu, between the basement and Entresol levels on the right of

room 20, Cour Puget) *Near Milo of Crotona a passage and corridor lead to the Islamic collection.*

Ⓝ The Baptistery of Saint Louis (late 13th–early 14th century) shows just how rich the illustration in Mameluke art was. (Richelieu, entresol level, room 8)

Visit the rooms on this level devoted to Islamic art. Go back to ground level and turn right to reach room 3.

Ⓞ The Law-Codex of Hammurabi (c. 1790–70 bc), engraved on a stele erected by the King of Babylon, is one of the first works ever devoted to the rights of man. (Richelieu, ground floor, room 3)

In the following room, on the right, lies the Cour Khorsabad, room 4.

Ⓟ Cour Khorsabad houses reliefs of the palace of Sargon II. Included are five winged bulls with human heads, the good spirits protecting the palace. (Richelieu, ground floor, room 4)

Go between the two bulls on the right. Continue through rooms 2 and 1 to reach the escalator. Go to the second floor and walk past the staircase.

Ⓞ The Lacemaker by Vermeer. This small painting is a romantic depiction of domestic life. (Richelieu, second floor, room 38)

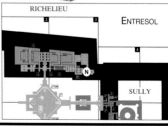

Portrait of the Ⓡ Artist at his Easel (1660) by Rembrandt is a self-portrait of the artist while painting. (Richelieu, second floor, room 31)

RICHELIEU

ENTRESOL

SULLY

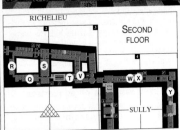

RICHELIEU WING

Continue along, and after a high staircase, turn right.

S In the **Galerie Medici** the cycle in the life of Marie de' Medici (1622–5) is

shown. The work was commissioned by her from Rubens for the Luxembourg Palace.

(Richelieu, second floor, room 18)

Return to the escalator and walk past it. Enter room 1.

T Portrait of King John the Good (c. 1350), anon., is the first known French portrait to have been painted on an easel.
(Richelieu, second floor, room 1)

After room 3, turn left.

The Northern schools
Go into room 4.

V The Virgin of Chancellor Rolin (c. 1435) is the work of Jan van Eyck, who painted at the court of the Duke of Burgundy.
(Richelieu, second floor, room 4).

Keep going to reach room 7, turn right and cross rooms 12 to 16 devoted to paintings of the Northern Schools of the 16th and 17th centuries. Turn left. This is the Sully wing. Continue straight ahead.

W The Cheat (c. 1635) by Georges de La Tour is similar in style to the works of Caravaggio, who was extremely influential during this period.
(Sully, second floor, room 28)

X The Peasant Family (c. 1643) by the Le Nain brothers gives a certain nobility to peasant life.
(Sully, second floor, room 29)

Y The Skate (1728) by Jean-Baptiste-

SULLY WING

Siméon Chardin (above) is one of the two paintings by the artist for which he was elected to the

Académie Royale de Peinture.
(Sully, second floor, room 38)

Pass through the paintings of the French School. Go down the small staircase to room 50, in the Egyptian Antiquities section.

K The Seated Scribe
A masterpiece from the Old Kingdom (2700–2200 BC).
(Sully, first floor, room 21).

To leave the building follow signs showing a pyramid.

◆ The Louvre for children

Within the maze of the Louvre there are plenty of treasures for young art lovers, but in the proliferation of works, periods, schools and styles how can a young visitor find them? The following itinerary has been put together to enable children to pick their way through this world treasury of culture. It takes shortcuts, jumps across the ages and does not observe strict chronology. Instead it wanders through the various rooms to pick out various milestones, and provides something of an overview of world art to the young visitor.

To follow this children's route through the Louvre, it is best to enter the museum through the entrance under the Pyramid and walk toward the Richelieu wing. Richelieu was minister to King Louis XIII. His name is written above one of the three escalators.

Take the large escalator (pass between the two Khorsabad bulls on the right, turn right into room 2, then left into a room with information indicators and cross this room to the right).

GROUND FLOOR
THE KINGDOM OF SCULPTURE

At the top of this escalator go straight ahead into a vaulted room lying between two glass-covered courtyards.

Go into the left-hand courtyard, the Cour Marly.

Ⓐ The Marly Horses
There are four of these. The two furthest away were made by Coysevox by order of Louis XIV to decorate the drinking-trough at his Marly Palace; the two nearest groups were designed by Coustou for Louis XV and replaced earlier ones. All these horses have long since left Marly and are now housed in the pollution-free safety of the Louvre.

Go back through the vaulted room to reach the right-hand courtyard, the Cour Puget.

Ⓑ Milo of Croton has his hand deep in a tree trunk and is being attacked. Milo was an athlete who thought he was invincible and one day decided to split with his own hands a tree which was already partly split. The two sides of the trunk closed up again, trapping one of his hands inside. Milo was devoured by a wolf which the sculptor Puget here depicted as a lion. The animal's claws are dug deep into the man's flesh and his whole body cries out in pain.

Ⓒ The Khorsabad Bulls are a little further on.

To reach them, take the left-hand staircase which leads to the upper level of the Cour Puget. Go into room 33 which adjoins the first room of oriental antiquities. Enter this room and then turn right into the following room.

These enormous bulls with human heads guarded the palace doors of Sargon II, King of Assyria.

FIRST FLOOR
VERY PRECIOUS OBJETS D'ART

On the first floor, go straight ahead and then right.

Ⓓ The little statue known as Charlemagne welcomes the visitor who then goes on into a series of rooms where a number of finely crafted pieces demonstrate the skill of craftsmen in the Middle Ages.

Retrace your steps and take the escalator up to the second floor.

SECOND FLOOR
STILL LIFE AND GENRE SCENES: REALIST PAINTERS

Go past the escalator and go through five rooms dedicated to the Northern School.

Ⓔ Genre scenes by Gerrit Dou and Pieter de Hooch are in room 35. These 17th-century Dutch painters favored scenes taken from everyday life, as is evident from the names of the pictures: *Dutch Housewife, Woman Drinker, Village Grocer.*

Retrace your steps, cross over the landing and go straight ahead.

Ⓕ The collection of French painting begins here with *John the Good.*

Go through three rooms, cross over to the right and then go through eight rooms.

Ⓖ Still life is the name given to paintings depicting inanimate objects. The beautiful baskets of fruit in room 27 are of particular interest.

A little way on, turn left.

Ⓗ Georges de La Tour (room 28) and **Ⓘ the Le Nain brothers** (room 29), are called realist painters because they depicted intimate family scenes. *The Cheat* by Georges de La Tour portrays a scene where everything is said through the play of hands and eyes. In the work *Christ with Saint Joseph in the Carpenter's Shop,* the child Jesus holds

G | J | K

a candle while Joseph works. The Le Nain brothers painted peasants in their homes (see the *Peasant Family*). The clothes and setting are rustic but contrast with an elegant stemmed glass.

Go straight through to room 39.

J Chardin, his still lifes and genre scenes
The painter showed everyday scenes of children and also specialized in still-life subjects.

Go down to room 50 via the small staircase. You are now on the first floor.

FIRST FLOOR
EGYPTIAN ANTIQUITIES

Cross the landing of the Grand Escalier and enter room 21, where the 4,700-year-old famous *Seated Scribe* **K** is on display. Here, you can learn about writing.

Take the Grand Escalier down to the ground floor to see scenes from the daily life of the ancient Egyptians depicted on the walls of the mastaba **L**, room 4.

Go down to room 50 via the small staircase. You are now on the first floor.

ENTRESOL, MEDIEVAL LOUVRE

The Château du Louvre dates back eight hundred years. Philippe Auguste had it built to defend Paris.
M Visit the **moats** – ditches which were formerly filled with water, between the château on the right and the city walls on the left. A passage on the right at the end of the moats, on the left as you leave the Sphinx Crypt,

leads to the **donjon** **N**, or keep, the best-preserved part of the fortress where food and arms were stored.

O Do not forget to visit the room called **Saint Louis.**

Go through the door between the showcases, down the staircase then straight ahead to reach the exit by the Pyramide.

CHILDREN IN THE LOUVRE
TOURS, WORKSHOPS, MOVIES, READINGS

Workshops
Painting, modeling and dancing: activities of all kinds are organized for children aged from 4 to 13 to introduce them to the creative process.
1½-hour, 2-hour and 2½-hour sessions. Booking from 13 days in advance to the day itself.
Family Sunday: while the children are in their

workshop, grown-ups can enjoy a visit on a similar theme.
Themed visits
Guided visits with commentary suitable for children (leaflets at the entrance or printed out via the internet); "Christmas is Coming!", "What a Whopper!" etc.

Auditorium
Movies, story-time, children's concerts etc.

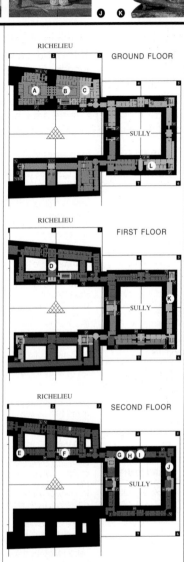

RICHELIEU — GROUND FLOOR
A B C — SULLY — L

RICHELIEU — FIRST FLOOR
D — SULLY — K

RICHELIEU — SECOND FLOOR
E F — G H I — J — SULLY

RICHELIEU — ENTRESOL
SULLY — O N M

◆ Other art museums

The Louvre offers a comprehensive survey of world art down the ages in all its forms, but cannot claim to be completely comprehensive since it only covers the period from the 3rd century BC up to the middle of the 19th century. Some schools and civilizations are represented less exhaustively than others. To make up for these gaps, there are a number of other museums in Paris and the Ile-de-France which are complementary to the Louvre.

PREHISTORY

The Louvre has no collections dedicated to prehistory, but this deficiency can be corrected by visiting the **MUSÉE D'ARCHÉOLOGIE NATIONALE**. It was founded in 1862 by Napoleon III and contains the national archeological collections dating from early man up to the time of Charlemagne. There are stone tools up to one million years old, and the earliest likeness of a human face in the world, *The Lady of Brassempouy*, carved in ivory from a mammoth tusk around 22,000 BC.
◆ Place du Château
78103 St-Germain-en-Laye
Tel. 01 39 10 13 00

ANTIQUITY

In addition to all the treasures on display in the Louvre, many visitors will want to see the **MUSÉE DES MONNAIES, MÉDAILLES ET ANTIQUES** at the Richelieu site of the Bibliothèque Nationale, with its impressive collection of Greek, Roman and ancient oriental coins.
◆ 58, rue de Richelieu
75002 Paris
Tel. 01 53 79 59 59
www.bnf.fr

19TH AND 20TH CENTURY

The Louvre collections come to an end in 1848. Visitors wanting to continue their survey beyond this time should next go to the **MUSÉE D'ORSAY** to see a magnificent collection of naturalist, Impressionist, symbolist, Nabis and also academic paintings from the second half of the 19th century to the beginning of the 20th (1848–1914). On show too are photographic works, sculpture, architectural items and examples of the decorative arts.
◆ 62, rue de Lille
75007 Paris
Tel. 01 40 49 48 14
www.musee-orsay.fr

More art from the end of the 19th century is to be found in the **MUSÉE DE L'ORANGERIE**, which contains the Walter-Guillaume collection of works by Cézanne, Renoir, Matisse, Picasso, Douanier Rousseau, Derain and others, as well as the famous *Waterlilies* in the setting created for them during the painter Monet's own lifetime.
◆ Jardin des Tuileries
75001 Paris
www.musee-orangerie.fr

An entry ticket to the Louvre is also valid for free admission on day of issue to the **MUSÉE NATIONAL EUGÈNE DELACROIX**, the artist's former home and studio containing paintings (including *Magdalene in the Desert*), engravings, drawings, furniture and other objects belonging to the painter, as well as works by his students and friends.
◆ 6, rue de Furstenberg
75006 Paris
Tel. 01 44 41 86 50
www.musee-delacroix.fr

The entire spectrum of French and foreign 20th-century art up to the present day is represented at the **MUSÉE NATIONAL D'ART MODERNE DU CENTRE GEORGES-POMPIDOU**
◆ place Georges-Pompidou
75004 Paris
Tel. 01 44 78 12 33
www.centrepompidou.fr/musee/

Twentieth-century art is also well represented at the **MUSÉE D'ART MODERNE DE LA VILLE-DE-PARIS**, which specializes in contemporary painting.
◆ Palais de Tokyo 11, av. du Pdt-Wilson
75116 Paris
Tel. 01 53 67 40 00
www.mam.paris.fr/

ASIAN ART

Since 1945 the **MUSÉE NATIONAL DES ARTS ASIATIQUES-GUIMET** has been the home of works of art treasures from central Asia and the Far East. Here you can see the famous smile on the faces of the Buddhas of Angkor Wat in southeast Asia, travel the ancient Silk Road, and marvel at gods and demons from Nepal and Tibet.
◆ 6, place d'Iéna
75016 Paris
Tel. 01 56 52 53 00
www.museeguimet.fr

The **MUSÉE CERNUSCHI** consists of a stunning collection of thousands of pieces of Chinese art from Neolithic times to the 13th century, as well as an important collection of Japanese art, housed in a magnificent *hotel particulier* in the Parc Monceau.
◆ 7 av. Vélasquez
75008 Paris
Tel. 01 53 96 21 50
www.cernuschi.paris.fr

DECORATIVE ARTS

The **MUSÉE DES ARTS DÉCORATIFS** contains collections of French decorative arts from the Middle Ages to the present day.
◆ 107, rue de Rivoli
75001 Paris
Tel. 01 44 55 57 50
www.ucad.fr

PRIMITIVE ARTS

In addition to the Pavillon des Sessions in the Louvre, which has retained around 100 works of art from Africa, Asia, the South Seas and the Americas, there is the new **MUSÉE DU QUAI BRANLY**, designed by Jean Nouvel, and entirely dedicated to these civilizations. It contains collections from the Musée de l'Homme, from the former Museum of Arts from Africa and the South Seas, gifts from overseas as well

as new contemporary installations.
♦ 55 quai Branly
75007 Paris
Tel. 01 56 61 70 00
www.quaibranly.fr

ISLAMIC ART

Once you've seen the Islamic collections in the Louvre, remember to visit the **INSTITUT DU MONDE ARABE (IMA)**, which has a museum containing important examples of Arabic-Islamic art, culture and civilization from its origins up to the present.
♦ 1, rue des Fossés-St-Bernard, 75005
Tel. 01 40 51 38 38
www.imarabe.org

FRENCH MONUMENTS

The **MUSÉE DES MONUMENTS FRANÇAIS** contains an exact copy of every single important piece of French monumental art produced between the 12th and19th centuries, and is housed in the new Cité de l'Architecture et du Patrimoine (Heritage) in the Palais de Chaillot. There are 6,000 casts of sculpted works: the masterpieces of French craftsmen. The collection also includes copies of important murals.
♦ Palais de Chaillot
Paris wing
1, place du Trocadéro
75016 Paris
Tel. 01 44 05 39 10
(reopening in 2007).

HISTORY OF PARIS

The history of the Louvre is inextricably bound up with that of the French capital, and no tourist should miss a visit to the **MUSÉE CARNAVALET**, a fascinating museum dedicated to the history of Paris from its origins up to

modern times.
♦ 23, rue de Sévigné
75003 Paris
Tel. 01 44 59 58 58
www.carnavalet.paris.fr

Historic Paris is also on view at the **MUSÉE NATIONAL DU MOYEN ÂGE ET DES THERMES DE CLUNY**, which contains the ruins of the thermal baths of Lutèce (Lutetia), dating from the 2nd and 3rd centuries AD. The museum is inside the 15th-century hôtel of the Abbés (abbots) de Cluny, home to one of the most important collections of medieval art in the world, and is well worth a visit after seeing the Louvre's own collection. Its most famous masterpiece is the series of tapestries known as *The Lady with the Unicorn*.
♦ 6, place Paul-Painlevé, 75005 Paris
Tel. 01 53 73 78 00
www.musee-moyenage.fr

MUSÉE JACQUEMART-ANDRÉ

This museum is housed in a superb Second Empire *hôtel particulier* and contains a splendid collection of French and Dutch paintings from the 17th and 18th centuries as well as from the Italian Renaissance. There are also some fine examples of furniture and other works of art from the time of Louis XV and XVI.
♦ 158, bd Haussmann
75008 Paris
Tel. 01 45 62 11 59

PETIT PALAIS

The splendidly restored **FINE ARTS MUSEUM** (Musée des Beaux-Arts de la Ville de Paris) has a wonderful collection of paintings from

earliest times up to the 20th century, with pride of place being given to the Impressionists and the Barbizon school.
♦ 80 av. Winston-Churchill, 75008 Paris
Tel. 01 53 43 40 00
www.petitpalais.paris.fr

AROUND PARIS

Michelangelo's *Slaves*, which are today in the Louvre, lived for a time in the Château d'Ecouen, having been a gift from Henri II to Anne de Montmorency on whose estate it was. The chateau, an important French Renaissance building, houses the **MUSÉE NATIONAL DE LA RENAISSANCE**, which contains an impressive selection of 16th-century French and European masterpieces.
♦ 95440 Écouen
Tel. 01 34 38 38 50
www.musee-renaissance.fr

The **MUSÉE DU CHÂTEAU DE FONTAINEBLEAU**, is another jewel of French Renaissance architecture. Don't miss the Francois I gallery, decorated by the Tuscan artists Rosso Fiorentino and Primaticcio, who were summoned to France to help create a "New Rome". The Louvre also has some of their surviving work.
♦ 77300 Fontainebleau
Tel. 01 60 71 50 70
www.musee-chateau-fontainebleau.fr

At the **MUSÉE DES CHÂTEAUX DE VERSAILLES ET DE TRIANON** the apartments of the king and the queen are open to visitors, as well as the Grand Trianon and Petit Trianon, which encapsulate the Golden Age of French

decoration. Here is the famous Galerie des Glaces (Hall of Mirrors) with its ceiling decorated in the new French style by Charles Le Brun, whose paintings and drawings are also on view in the Louvre.
♦ 78000 Versailles
Tel. 01 30 83 78 00
www.chateau versailles.fr

The **CHÂTEAU DE CHANTILLY** contains the apartments of the princes of Condé (16th and 17th centuries) as well as the **MUSÉE CONDÉ**, which has an important collection of French art from Clouet to Delacroix, Italian painting and pictures of the Northern schools, and the fabulous 15th-century book, the *Très Riches Heures du Duc de Berry*.
♦ 60631 Chantilly
Tel. 03 44 62 62 62
www.chateaude chantilly.com

The **MUSÉE NATIONAL DE CÉRAMIQUE** at Sèvres contains more than 50,000 ceramics from all over the world, including a priceless collection of 5,000 pieces of Sèvres porcelain, some of which are on view in the Decorative Arts department in the Louvre.
♦ 92310 Sèvres
Tel. 01 41 14 04 20

In the Louvre is the famous picture of *The Coronation of Napoleon I* by David, official painter to the Empire. The Napoleonic era is well covered in the **MUSÉE DES CHÂTEAUX DE MALMAISON ET BOIS-PRÉAU**, which is dedicated to the lives of Napoleon and Josephine.
♦ 92500 Rueil-Malmaison
Tel. 01 41 29 05 55

◆ Chronology of antiquity at the Louvre

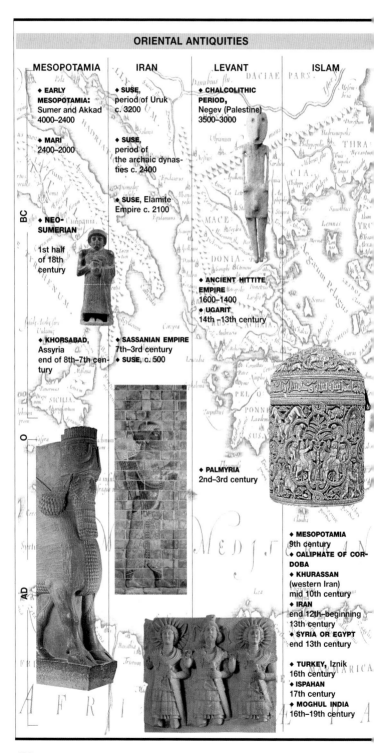

ORIENTAL ANTIQUITIES

MESOPOTAMIA

◆ **EARLY MESOPOTAMIA:** Sumer and Akkad 4000–2400

◆ **MARI** 2400–2000

◆ **NEO-SUMERIAN** 1st half of 18th century

◆ **KHORSABAD,** Assyria end of 8th–7th century

IRAN

◆ **SUSE,** period of Uruk c. 3200

◆ **SUSE,** period of the archaic dynasties c. 2400

◆ **SUSE,** Elamite Empire c. 2100

◆ **SASSANIAN EMPIRE** 7th–3rd century
◆ **SUSE,** c. 500

LEVANT

◆ **CHALCOLITHIC PERIOD,** Negev (Palestine) 3500–3000

◆ **ANCIENT HITTITE EMPIRE** 1600–1400
◆ **UGARIT** 14th –13th century

◆ **PALMYRIA** 2nd–3rd century

ISLAM

◆ **MESOPOTAMIA** 9th century
◆ **CALIPHATE OF CORDOBA**
◆ **KHURASSAN** (western Iran) mid 10th century
◆ **IRAN** end 12th–beginning 13th century
◆ **SYRIA OR EGYPT** end 13th century

◆ **TURKEY,** Iznik 16th century
◆ **ISPAHAN** 17th century
◆ **MOGHUL INDIA** 16th–19th century

BC

0

AD

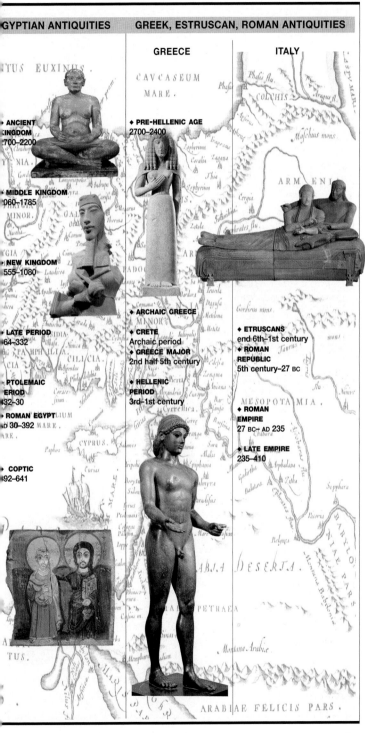

GREECE

ITALY

♦ **ANCIENT KINGDOM**
2700–2200

♦ **MIDDLE KINGDOM**
2060–1785

♦ **NEW KINGDOM**
1555–1080

♦ **LATE PERIOD**
664–332

♦ **PTOLEMAIC PERIOD**
332–30

♦ **ROMAN EGYPT**
AD 30–392

♦ **COPTIC**
392–641

♦ **PRE-HELLENIC AGE**
2700–2400

♦ **ARCHAIC GREECE**

♦ **CRETE**
Archaic period

♦ **GREECE MAJOR**
2nd half 5th century

♦ **HELLENIC PERIOD**
3rd–1st century

♦ **ETRUSCANS**
end 6th–1st century

♦ **ROMAN REPUBLIC**
5th century–27 BC

♦ **ROMAN EMPIRE**
27 BC– AD 235

♦ **LATE EMPIRE**
235–410

◆ Chronology of paintings at the Louvre

				NORTHERN SCHOOLS		
EUROPEAN PAINTING						
PERIODS	FRANCE	ITALY	SPAIN	GERMANY	FLANDERS HOLLAND	GREAT BRITAIN
c.13th		◆ Cimabue (1240–1302) ◆ Giotto (1267–1337)				
c.14th International Gothic	◆ Portrait of Jean II le Bon, King of France (c. 1350, anon.)					
c.15th	◆ Jean Fouquet (1420–77/81) ◆ Enguerrand Quarton (known in Provence from 1444–66)	◆ Fra Angelico (1417–55) ◆ Piero della Francesca (1422–92) ◆ Paolo Uccello (1397–1475) ◆ Leonardo da Vinci (1452–1519) ◆ Raphael (1483–1520)	◆ Bernardo Martorell (1427–52)	◆ Maître de la Sainte Parenté (1470/80–1515) ◆ Albrecht Dürer (1471–1528)	◆ Jan van Eyck (?–1441) ◆ Roger van der Weyden (1390/1400–64) ◆ Quentin Metsys (1465/6–1530)	
c.16th	◆ Fontaine-bleau School	◆ Titian (1488/9–1576) ◆ Veronese (1528–88) ◆ Tintoretto (1518–94)	◆ El Greco (1541–1614)	◆ Lucas Cranach the Elder (1472–1553) ◆ Hans Holbein the Younger (1497/98–1543)	◆ Pieter I Bruegel the Elder (1525–69) ◆ Peter Paul Rubens (1577–1640)	
c.17th	◆ Georges de La Tour (1593–1652) ◆ Le Nain brothers (1600/10–48) ◆ Nicolas Poussin (1594–1665) ◆ Charles Lebrun (1619–90) ◆ J.-Antoine Watteau (1684–1721)	◆ Caravaggio (1571–1610)	◆ Francisco de Zurbarán (1598–1664) ◆ Jusepe de Ribera (1591–1652) ◆ Bartholomé Esteban Murillo (1618–82)		◆ Frans Hals (1581/85–1666) ◆ Rembrandt (1606–69) ◆ Johannes Vermeer (1632–75)	
c.18th	◆ F. Boucher (1703–70) ◆ J.-Honoré Fragonard (1732–1806) ◆ Jacques-Louis David (1748–1825) ◆ Théodore Géricault (1791–1824)	◆ Francesco Guardi (1712–93)	◆ Francisco José de Goya y Lucientes (1746–1828)			◆Thomas Gainsborough (1727–88) ◆ Sir Joshua Reynolds (1723–92)
c.19th	◆ Eugène Delacroix (1798–1863) ◆ J.-A.-D. Ingres (1780–1867) ◆ J.-B.-C. Corot (1796–1875)			◆ Caspar David Friedrich 1784–1840)		◆ Joseph Mallord William Turner (1775–1851)

Useful addresses near the Louvre

GaultMillau classification

Restaurants

Quality of the cuisine:

Marks from ⑩ to ⑫

Marks from ⑬ to ⑳

- Disabled facilities
- Pets not welcome
- Peace and quiet
- Air conditioning
- Grounds, gardens
- Car park
- Swimming pool
- Tennis
- Terrace
- Parking attendant

◆ Restaurants

Restaurants are listed in alphabetical order.
The map coordinates after the name of the establishment refer to the front endpaper map.
A list of logos can be found on page 335.

RESTAURANTS

⑫ BAAN BORAN G4
43, rue Montpensier, 75001
Tel. 01 40 15 90 45
www.baan-boran.com
Closed Sat lunch, Sun.
Last service 11pm.
À la carte: €28;
Menu: €14.50.
It's a good sign that the chef, who has been here since the opening of this Thai restaurant seven years ago and who studied the very best Thai cuisine in Bangkok, has never moved away. The subtle flavors here are created with fantastic sensibility: a straightforward prawn soup with lemon grass is a delight to the palate, while the sweet and sour sea bream as well as the tempting range of meat dishes demonstrate the chef's complete mastery of his art. The ambience is contemporary and most attractive, and the service all you could wish for.
▥

BIOBOA F3
3, rue Danielle-Casanova, 75001
Tel. 01 42 61 17 67
Closed evenings, Sat-Sun and Aug.
À la carte: €25.
This might be the best organic restaurant in Paris. It is certainly the most fun and the most successful – as well as the prettiest, proving that organic food needn't be dull. The design is modern, and the food simple, offering sandwiches, salads, a great gazpacho, and terrific milk shakes.
▥

⑫ BRASSERIE MUNICHOISE F3
5, rue Danielle-Casanova, 75001
Tel. 01 42 61 47 16
Closed Sat lunch, Sun (out of season), Sat (in summer) and three weeks in Aug.
Last service 10.45pm.
À la carte: €24.
A little bit of old Munich in Paris. Just like the Oktoberfest, with draft beer in huge steins and and old-fashioned Bavarian décor. There's a great range of sausages to go with your beer (draft Spaten, the pale and cloudy wheat beer, and an unusual Schwarzbier, which is lightly smoked). Nothing here is really expensive, everything is one hundred percent authentic, and the delightful kitsch atmosphere has a charm of its own. The Sauerkraut with black pudding, Wiener Schnitzel and the Apfelstrudel are perfect pick-me-ups after a hard day in the museum.

CAFÉ MARLY G6
93, rue de Rivoli, 75001
Tel. 01 49 26 06 60
Last service 1am.
Elegant Second Empire décor, a terrace overlooking Pei's famous Pyramide, fresh nouvelle cuisine such as tomatoes with mozzarella, avocado with prawns, smoked Norwegian salmon, and even caviar, who could ask for more? The café is owned by Costes (see below), which is high recommendation enough.
☛

⑰ ☐ CARRÉ DES FEUILLANTS D4
14, rue de Castiglione, 75001
Tel. 01 42 86 82 82
www.carredesfeuillants.fr
Closed Sat-Sun and Aug. Last service 10pm.
À la carte: €110;
Menus: €65–150.
An exceptionally comfortable dining-room in a beautiful part of the city. Dutournier carries himself like a prince as he receives his guests, secure in the knowledge that, like him, they love good food, good wine and good company. His great achievement has been to bring the cooking of south-west France to Paris, transforming hearty peasant food into dishes fit for a king. His cuisine is utterly distinctive and of great character, gradually becoming lighter and more sophisticated over the years, though never losing sight of its origins. Lampreys drizzled with sweet and sour dressing, risotto with morels, or a piquant escabèche of scallops with almonds and forest mushrooms all make memorable first courses. Veal sweetbreads with a jus of oysters, macaroni and mushrooms is one of the master's most popular creations, as is his gigot of lamb cooked in clay and served with a gratin of eggplant. The Carré des Feuillants can also boast a wine list to match the magnificence of the menu, detailing the pedigree and provenance of every bottle in its peerless cellar, and featuring some fine Burgundies that are more than a match for their counterparts from Bordeaux. The service is discreet, friendly though never familiar, and helpful to a degree. Everything a bon vivant could wish for, in fact.
▥ ▨

⑬ ☐ CHEZ LA VIEILLE I7
37, rue de l'Arbre-Sec
1, rue Bailleul, 75001
Tel. 01 42 60 15 78
Closed Sat-Sun and Aug.
Last service 9pm.
À la carte: €50;
Menus: €27.
One of the most famous of all Paris bistros. The Corsican Marie-José Cervoni, who created the establishment, is as well known as the restaurant itself. In a traditional setting, which has been meticulously preserved, the chef offers traditional bistro food such as pot-au-feu, calves' liver or braised oxtail, cooked to perfection. The wine list may not be extensive, but all the vintages in it have been selected with great care.
▨

COSTES D4
239, rue St-Honoré, 75001
Tel. 01 42 44 50 25
Open daily.
Last service 12.30am.
À la carte: €100.
As they used to say: "After champagne and dinner at Costes, who could say no?". What sets this luxurious, modern establishment apart from the rest is its unique ability to serve simple food prepared better than anyone else can do it. And with the best Petrossian at only €175 for 50g, it's no more expensive than anywhere else. Plus you're not anywhere else, you're at Costes!
▣ ▤ ▲

DAVÉ G5
12, rue Richelieu, 75001
Tel. 01 42 61 49 48
Closed Sat and Sun lunch, and one week around Aug 15.
Last service 11pm.

PRICES ARE GIVEN AS A GUIDELINE
À la carte: average prices

xcellent value.
pecialties here
nclude steamed
avioli (dim sum),
piced prawns, and
he juiciest spare ribs
ou've ever tasted.

**⑩ ♀ DELIZIE
'UGGIANO**   C3

8 rue Duphot, 75001
el. 01 40 15 06 69
losed Sat lunch, Sun.
 la carte: €80;
Menus: €36–42.
Directly above the
hop where it sells
pecialist wines, the
estaurant is
ecorated like a
aditional Tuscan
armhouse, with
erracotta tiles on the
oor and wrought-
on chairs. The menu
as a carefully
hosen selection of
alian gastronomic
pecialties, including
ucculent smoked
am and sausage,
 platter of assorted
ortellini filled with
pinach, ricotta and
white truffles, as well
s the traditional
annacotta and fine
asta dishes. The
ervice is friendly and
fficient. The Italian
ines are outstanding
nd can be ordered
y the glass, though
t quite a price.

**⑭ ♀ GÉRARD
BESSON**   I5

, rue du Coq-
Héron, 75001
el. 01 42 33 14 74
www.gerardbesson.com
Closed Sat lunch,
Sun, and Mon lunch.
Last service 9.30pm.
À la carte: €95;
Menus: €60–105.
Forget about bright
ights and noisy fun.
This is a traditional,
lightly old-fashioned
deluxe restaurant with
hick, soft carpeting,
which serves high-
class classic cuisine
ather than the
ashionable food of
he boulevards. Not
exactly what mother
used to make, but
ather what the chef

would have spent all
day preparing in the
kitchens of the family
chateau in the good
old days: fricassée of
lobster in the style of
Georges Garin, roast
breast of duckling
with blackcurrant
sauce and
caramelized onions,
or ragout of sole and
shrimp in a
champagne sauce.
An outdated way of
cooking, almost an
endangered species,
but none the worse
for that, and the
standards are
impeccably high
throughout.
 ♿ ▥ ▨

**⑮ ♀
GOUMARD**   C3

9, rue Duphot, 75001
Tel. 01 42 60 36 07
www.goumard.fr
Open daily. Last
service 10.30pm.
À la carte: €85;
Menu: €46.
If ever a restaurant
in Paris could be
called a temple of
gastronomy, it has to
be Goumard. This is
one of the great fish
restaurants of France,
housed in
surroundings of
sybaritic comfort and
elegance and with
rest rooms designed
by that master of
Art Nouveau, Louis
Majorelle. But all
this style and luxury
comes at a price,
and if you're not keen
on the great vintages
of Bordeaux and
Burgundy, then the
wine list here will be
of little interest. The
service will be all you
could desire, and the
bill at the end
astronomical, so be
prepared. It must be
said that the food at
Goumard is fantastic:
one outstanding
specialty here is
turbot from Guilvinec
served with roast
Breton langoustines,
white asparagus,
parmesan croquants,
country smoked

bacon, chilled goat's
cheese and coriander.
This is the ultimate in
haute cuisine, which
will either shock or
completely seduce
you. But from the
seaweed breadsticks
right through to the
coffee (€10), you'd
have to be smart
indeed to find any
fault with the way
they do it at
Goumard.
 ♿ ▥

IL CORTILE   D3

37, rue Cambon,
75001
Tel. 01 44 58 45 67
www.alain-
ducasse.com
Closed Sat-Sun,
bank hols and Aug.
Last service 10.30pm.
À la carte: €85;
Menu: €55.
Just off a leafy
courtyard belonging
to the beautiful
Hotel Castille is
a restaurant that
many people say
serves the best Italian
food in town. Its
menu is imaginative,
the produce never
less than fresh, and
always seasonal.
Pasta with squid ink,
spit-roasted guinea-
fowl, carpaccio of
scallops, and risotto
with zucchini are all
great dishes, while
the beef braised in
Marsala with truffles
is to die for. Add to
this an excellent list of
Italian wines, as well
as the opportunity to
eat outdoors in
summer, and you
have all the
ingredients of a truly
great evening out.
 ♿ ▥ ▲

⑪ JUVENILES   G4

47, rue de Richelieu,
75001
Tel. 01 42 97 46 49
Last service 11pm.
Tim, the patron
of this attractive,
unpretentious and
friendly wine and
tapas bar, is a man
who understands his
vintages and has

some great value
wines on offer to go
with slices of smoked
ham and sausage, a
really terrific house
chicken salad, or a
range of hot dishes
that change according
to the produce in the
day's market.

**⑭ ♀
KINUGAWA I**   D4

9, rue du Mont-
Thabor, 75001
Tel. 01 42 60 65 07
Closed Sun, Dec 24–
31, first week in Jan.
Last service 10pm.
À la carte: €70;
Menu: €30–108.
The owner of this
celebrated
establishment,
Kiyushi Kinugawa, is
something of a
perfectionist, never
letting the quality of
his food fall below the
level of excellence in
his restaurant and
attached sushi bar.
This has won him
enormous popularity
in the city, with many
international stars
coming regularly to
dine here and also at
the sister restaurant
in the rue St-Philippe-
du-Roule. Teriyaki
salmon, beef with
ginger are just two of
the most tempting
specialties on the
menu, along with
perhaps the best
sashimi it may ever
be your good fortune
to taste.
 ▧ ▥

KONG   I8

1, rue Pont-Neuf,
75001
Tel. 01 40 39 09 00
www.kong.fr
Open daily. Last
service 11.30pm.
À la carte: €42.
Designer Philippe
Starck created this
trendy Asian diner
and cocktail bar on
the top floors over the
Kenzo store, where a
huge glass dome
offers wonderful
views of the Pont
Neuf and the Seine
beneath. The

◆ Restaurants

Restaurants are listed in alphabetical order.
The map coordinates "A1" after the name of the establishment refer to the front endpaper map.
A list of logos can be found on page 335.

cocktails are good but pricey, and the food good too if not exactly imaginative: steaks, crab with avocado, that sort of thing. But this has to be the coolest joint in town, the place to see and be seen, and for some people that makes it all worthwhile. Reservations essential.

🔲 🔳 🔳

LA CLOCHE DES HALLES   H5
28, rue Coquillière, 75001
Tel. 01 42 36 93 89
Closed Sat eve, Sun, and three weeks in Aug.
Last service 9pm.
À la carte: €14.
A friendly neighborhood bistro at the heart of the 1st arrondissement is something of a rarity, but this a delightful and relaxing place to eat tarte à l'oignon, excellent charcuterie and other light meals with a good glass of inexpensive wine. Be warned: the place gets pretty frantic at lunchtime.
🔳

⑫ LA ROBE ET LE PALAIS   J8
13, rue des Lavandières-Ste-Opportune, 75001
Tel. 01 45 08 07 41
www.robe-et-palais.com
Closed Sun.
Last service 11pm.
À la carte: €35.
Menus: €14.50–18.
A small and friendly café-restaurant only a couple of steps from the Théâtre du Châtelet with first-class classic cuisine and fine wines to match (the house wine is also more than adequate). Specialties include roast saddle of lamb with sweet garlic, lambs' sweetbreads in pastry, and a hot

chocolate tart that is out of this world.
🔲 🔳

⑫ L'ABSINTHE   E4
24, place du Marché-St-Honoré, 75001
Tel. 01 49 26 90 04
www.michelrostang.com
Closed Sat lunch, Sun, and two weeks in Aug.
Last service 11pm.
À la carte: €35;
Menus: €29–35.
Owned by the famous restaurateur Michel Rostang and run by his daughter Caroline, L'Absinthe is a fine traditional bistro with two dining-rooms one above the other, in an attractive setting. The cooking is of a uniformly high standard, and dishes include ravioli with langoustines, duck breast with purée of sweet potatoes, cod with aioli, and scallops with bacon poached with sherry.
🔲 🅿 🔳

⑭ L'ARGENTEUIL   F5
9, rue d'Argenteuil, 75001
Tel. 01 42 60 56 22
Closed lunchtimes, Mon, three weeks in Sep, Dec 25–Jan 1.
Last service 10.30pm.
À la carte: €38;
Menu: € 38.
This is the spot where well-briefed visitors to Paris come to feast on classic traditional cooking. The chef, who hails from Lorraine, has many inventive touches to add to the well-known favorites on the menu: there is a delicious tabouleh of lobster, for example, a chaud-froid of lamb with rosemary and a mini-ratatouille, or roast breast of duck with polenta. The wine list is short and to the point, and the service never less than friendly.
🔳

⑭ L'ATELIER BERGER   I6
49, rue Berger, 75001
Tel. 01 40 28 00 00
Closed Sat lunch, Sun and Dec 24–25.
À la carte: €35.
Menus: €35–55.
Conveniently located between the Hotel de Ville and Les Halles, L'Atelier Berger is the perfect place for a slow, comfortable dinner in relaxing surroundings complete with soft lighting and attentive service. There is even a fumoir, a sectioned-off area where diners who smoke may enjoy their aperitif while they indulge their habit. The menu offers a broad selection of well-chosen dishes such as tartare of tuna, a rich and unctuous cream of artichoke soup, mullet with thyme sauce, and many other mouthwatering delights. The wines have been selected with exceptional intelligence to balance the dishes prepared by chef Jean Christiansen.
🔳 🔳

L'AUTOBUS IMPÉRIAL   J6
14, rue Mondétour, 75001
Tel. 01 42 36 00 18
www.autobus-imperial.fr
Closed Sun, Dec 24-25 and Dec 31–Jan 1.
Last service 11pm.
À la carte: €35;
Menus: €16.50–45.
This is exactly the sort of décor one dreams about when thinking of a cozy dinner in Paris: smart, old fashioned and comfortable, with plenty of mirrors, lots of color and traditional food perfectly cooked at amazingly affordable prices. Reservations advised.
🔲

LAVINIA   D
3, bd de la Madeleine, 75001
Tel. 01 42 97 20 20
Closed Sun.
À la carte: €40.
The wines here are amazingly good value (Lavinia is also a wine store, with more than 6,000 bottles). The cuisine is simple, but faultlessly well prepared: try the fillet of Salers beef braised with foie gras and mushrooms, or saddle of Occitan lamb served with a polenta galette. Superb!
🔳 🔲

⑫ LE DAUPHIN   F5
167, rue St-Honoré, 75001
Tel. 01 42 60 40 11
Closed Dec 24-25.
Last service 10.30pm.
À la carte: €37;
Menu: €26.
While not precisely inexpensive, this attractive little restaurant in one of the smartest areas of the city offers almost unbeatable value. The cooking is predominantly traditional bistro fare, including a hearty tournedos of pig's hock, cassoulet, braised rabbit and roast guinea-fowl, all in exceptionally generous portions too. Excellent wine list.
🔳

⑬ LE GRAND VÉFOUR   G4
17, rue de Beaujolais, 75001
Tel. 01 42 96 56 27
Closed Fri eve, Sat-Sun, first week after Easter, end of July-end of Aug, and Christmas-New Year.
Last service 10pm.
À la carte: €175;
Menus: €78–255.
One of the world's great restaurants has long been a household word in France, and held in the highest esteem

since the days when Napoleon himself dined here with Josephine (it first opened its doors in 1784). Other celebrated guests have included Victor Hugo, and nearer our own time the novelist Colette, one of the restaurant's closest neighbors as she lived on the other side of the gardens. Inside, the décor is magnificently over the top and palatial, making much use of velvet, gilding and crystal mirrors. Guy Martin is the chef here, a job with heavy responsibility but one which he carries out with brilliance, uniting great classic dishes with the haute cuisine bourgeoise so dear to French hearts. He is also extremely inventive, the creator of such delights as a fabulous parmentier (a kind of shepherd's pie) of oxtail with truffles, turbot meunière with a purée of peas and radishes, and pigeon Rainier III, devised in honor of the late ruler of Monaco. Other masterpieces at Le Grand Véfour include saint-pierre (John Dory) spiced with verbena and served with asparagus, and chicken Miéral, cooked with salted lemons and accompanied by foie gras and tofu, which is much in demand. One exotic specialty that should be mentioned is an amazing tart of artichokes and preserved vegetables with a sorbet of bitter almonds: you've never tasted anything so wonderful! It goes without saying that the cellar probably has no equal in Paris, and if you can't find the vintage you want then it's probably not

to be had anywhere in France. Incidentally, the restaurant is so supremely self-confident that it happily offers diners a tour of the kitchens, wine cellars, and also of its abundant cigar stocks. For sheer luxury, comfort, personal attention as well as seductive delights for the palate, dinner at Le Grand Véfour stands alone, and probably unmatched anywhere in the French-speaking world.

⑦ ♿ LE MEURICE D4
228, rue de Rivoli, 75001
Tel. 01 44 58 10 55
www.lemeurice.com
Closed Sat lunch, Sun-Mon, two weeks in Feb, and Aug.
Last service 10pm.
A la carte: €160;
Menus: €75–170.
The Meurice, located at the fashionable end of the rue de Rivoli, is one of the smartest restaurant addresses in town, a step back in time to the great days of the fin-de-siècle with ornamental mirrors, chandeliers, richly patterned marble, and an army of floor staff who seemed to have stepped straight out of an operetta! But make no mistake, this is not mere window dressing, but rather a perfect setting for dishes conceived for the noblest and most sophisticated palates of serious, devoted diners. The chef, Yannick Alleno, is also the proprietor, who learned his craft under the great Louis Grondard at Drouant, before starting out as sauce chef here at the Meurice and working his way up through sheer brilliance. In 2004 the

restaurant received its second Michelin star. One delectable way to begin lunch or dinner is with a mousse of avocado, turtle meat and creamed celery. Another is the saddle of Balik salmon served en croûte with potatoes and cream of leeks, or blue lobster accompanied by a sauce made from yellow Jura wine. To follow, there could be red mullet with cream or sardines, Bresse chicken stuffed with foie gras and cooked to retain all the freshness and flavor of these succulent birds, or for hearty appetites, what about fricassee of sucking pig served with artichokes and sage butter? The wine list is, as you would expect, superlative, and though the price beside some of the vintages is simply breathtaking, there are numerous bottles of excellent provenance which are altogether more affordable for the visitor. The service is impeccable, well-informed and friendly without ever descending to the familiar, and one hundred per cent professional. Out of this world, but definitely not for tourists on a budget!

LE PETIT THÉÂTRE E4
15, place du Marché St-Honoré, 75001
Tel. 01 42 61 00 93
Closed Sun-Mon, first three weeks in Aug.
Last service 10.15pm.
À la carte: €35;
Menus: € 18-25.
An attractive bistro in the atmospheric St-Honoré market-place, specializing in traditional dishes prepared from pork

and ham, and served in generous portions too.

LE PLUVINEL E5
2, place des Pyramides, 75001
Tel. 01 42 60 90 34
www.regina-hotel.com
Closed Sat-Sun, Aug.
Last service 10pm.
À la carte: €50;
Menus: €33–40.
Located opposite the Louvre, the restaurant is part of the elegant Hôtel Régina, and very popular with journalists from the satirical weekly Le Canard Enchaîné nearby. In summer there is an attractive courtyard in which to enjoy such delicacies as tempura of grilled prawns with sesame, pan-fried scallops, or roast wild duck with quince jelly.

LE SOUFFLÉ C4
36, rue Mont-Thabor, 75001
Tel. 01 42 60 27 19
Closed Sun, two weeks in Feb, and three weeks beg Aug.
Last service 10pm.
À la carte: €40;
Menus: €29–35.
This has to be the only restaurant in France dedicated to soufflés, sweet and savory. There's even a "tout soufflé" menu, with asparagus, morel mushrooms, foie gras, seafood, pike, chocolate, and apple with calvados, as well as a few more conventional dishes.

⑭ ♿ LES CARTES POSTALES E-F3
7, rue Gomboust, 75001
Tel. 01 42 61 02 93
Closed mid July–mid Aug, and end Dec–mid Jan.
Last service 10.15pm.
À la carte: €45;
Menus: €25–60.
This elegant and attractive restaurant

◆ Restaurants

Restaurants are listed in alphabetical order.

The map coordinates "A1" after the name of the establishment refer to the front endpaper map.

A list of logos can be found on page 335.

---

derives its name from the hundreds of postcards from all over the world adorning its walls. Actually the dining-room is delightful, with light-colored walls and vases of fresh flowers everywhere. The owner and chef, Yoshimisa Watanabe, has devised several dishes that combine the cuisines of east and west, such as carpaccio of tuna, mackerel marinaded in Japanese herbs or fillet of bass with oyster sauce. A specialty here which has its roots firmly planted in French soil is the escalope of warm foie gras in cognac, and wonderfully good it is too. This costly little establishment (though the fixed menu is relatively good value) is just beside the St-Honoré marketplace. Excellent wine list.
▥

⑪ LES DESSOUS DE LA ROBE   I-J8
4, rue Bertin-Poirée, 75001
Tel. 01 40 26 68 18
Closed Sun, Aug, and at Christmas.
Last service 12.30am.
A friendly, old-fashioned bistro, wine bar and wine shop is a real find. Here you can enjoy light, inexpensive meals such as good, homemade soup, plates of appetizing charcuterie and wines by the glass as well as the bottle. The ones from southwest France are particularly good value.
▴

⑪ LESCURE   C4
7, rue de Mondovi, 75001
Tel. 01 42 60 18 91
Closed Sat-Sun, three weeks in Aug, one

week at Christmas.
Last service 10.15pm.
À la carte: €28;
Menus: €22.
A traditional restaurant specializing in beautifully prepared dishes from the Corrèze and Limousin regions: confit of goose or duck, black pudding flavored with chestnuts, pot-roast chicken Henri IV, and prize Limousin beef in a hearty stew with carrots and mushrooms. Perfect for a chilly evening, washed down with a few glasses of St-Emilion or the rich dark wine of Cahors.
▥ ▴

⑯ 🍴 L'ESPADON   D3
15, place Vendôme, 75001
Tel. 01 43 16 30 80
www.ritzparis.com
Last service 10pm.
À la carte: €150;
Menus: €75–180.
L'Espadon (The Swordfish) is the unlikely name of one of Paris's classiest restaurants, the one in the Ritz Hotel. It has one of the most beautiful dining-rooms too, with much use made of gilt, stucco-work, draperies, a gorgeous flower-patterned carpet and even a painted ceiling. Fresh flowers are everywhere. Chef-owner Michel Roth is a traditionalist at heart, though he likes to include his own individual interpretations of many of the great classic dishes that feature on the menu of this magnificent establishment. When cooking comes so close to perfection, it can be difficult to single items out for recommendation, but the pan-roasted langoustines are out of this world, and make an ideal starter. Or you could opt for

sautéed duck foie gras with spices, which is so creamy it literally does melt in your mouth! To follow, you could try red mullet lightly cooked in olive oil and served with a mouthwatering risotto, or the Challans duck roasted with honey and ginger, and the Breton lobster salad is also to die for. Such fine cooking deserves wine to match: this could be the time to splash out and enjoy a rare Romanée Conti or Château Pétrus, but even the less classy vintages are still quite expensively priced: you'll have guessed that L'Espadon, is not a restaurant for visitors on a tight budget! For dessert, try a frisson of chocolate and mandarin oranges, a peach poached in an infusion of hibiscus and raspberry juice, or fresh coconut and lychee sorbet. Actually, making a choice is next to impossible! The service is impeccable, naturally. Every guest is made to feel like royalty, and at these prices, why not?
▤ ▥ ▧ ▴ ▨

⑬ 🍴 L'OSTRÉA   I6
4, rue Sauval, 75001
Tel. 01 40 26 08 07
Closed Sat lunch, Sun, one week at Christmas, one week at easter and three weeks in Aug.
Last service 11pm.
À la carte: €40.
Chef and proprietor of this terrific fish restaurant, Jean-Pierre Devaux, has been here for the last twenty years after giving up his former career as a florist. Specialties concentrate on fish, naturally enough, and vary strictly according to season, but can

include oysters, tuna prepared in any number of different ways, and the juiciest scallops you've ever tasted. The mussels in white wine and cream sauce are simply fantastic, and the wine list includes a crisp, refreshing Chablis that provides the ideal accompaniment.
▧

⑫ MACÉO   G·
15, rue des Petits-Champs, 75001
Tel. 01 42 97 53 85
www.maceorestaurant.com
Closed Sat lunch, Sun, and two weeks in Aug.
Last service 11pm.
À la carte: €50;
Menus: €30–35.
An elegant, stylish but informal wine bar restaurant belonging to Mark Williamson, who is also the proprietor of nearby Willi's Wine Bar, surely one of the most famous addresses in Paris. No more than a couple of steps away from the Palais Royal, with attractive if slightly eccentric décor that can't decide whether to be Second Empire or smart and trendy. The chef here is Thierry Bourbonnais, who cooks the food with a rare savoir-faire: stuffed eggplant with spiced half-smoked salmon, and the delicious Sisteron lamb with artichokes and a pungent poivrade sauce. Though the restaurant can be a bit pricey at times, the €35 menu is usually very good value.
▧ ▥

NODAÏWA   F5
272, rue St-Honoré, 75001
Tel. 01 42 86 03 42
www.nodaiwa.com
Closed Sun, two

weeks end Aug, and nd Dec–mid Jan. ast service 10pm. la carte: €25; Menus: €16–58. Beautifully prepared Japanese cuisine in n attractive and ntimate setting with ubdued lighting. The specialty here s grilled eel (unagi) erved in a variety of vays, a recipe that ates back several enturies.
Ⅲ🔳

② OLIO PANE INO　H5
4, rue Coquillière, 5001
el. 01 42 33 21 15
Closed Sat–Sun, Aug.
ast service 10pm.
la carte: €25.
Following the uccess of tavola alda establishments part deli, part simple estaurants selling harcuterie, cheese nd pasta dishes) in Paris, Olio Pane Vino vas recently set up to ell fresh produce rom Italy made by raftsmen, together vith cheese, sausage nd hams from traight from the arms in Tuscany vhere they were nade. The pasta lishes couldn't be astier, and the tmosphere bustling nd friendly. There re also dishes uitable for egetarians as well as range of tempting lesserts. The imoncello babas ere are extremely opular! Wide election of Italian vines available.
🔳

❸ ♀ PIERRE U PALAIS ROYAL　G5
0, rue Richelieu, 5001
el. 01 42 96 09 17
Closed Sat lunch, Sun, wo weeks in Aug.
ast service 11pm.
la carte: €38;
Menus: €31–38.
n ideal spot for a

business lunch or after-theater supper (they serve up to 11pm) that seems like a nostalgic whiff of old Provence right in the city center. The décor, right down to the menu itself, is unashamedly rustic. Specialties include delicious homemade gazpacho, baked monkfish with rosemary drizzled with a thick red wine sauce, and braised beef with foie gras and apple chutney. Impeccable service and excellent value, particularly the set menus.
Ⅲ🔳

⓭ ♀ PINXO　E4
9, rue d'Alger, 75001
Tel. 01 40 20 72 00
www.pinxo.fr
Closed Aug.
Last service 11.30pm.
À la carte: €50.
There is a new trend in Paris for restaurants that stay open all day, serving light snacks as well as a full-blown dinner, and Alain Dutournier has opened one just near the Palais Royal. The search for a really good steak can be a lengthy one, but here at Pinxo they really know how to get it just right, accompanied by fried diced potato and tapenade. Also good (and hard to find) are the chipirons, crisp fried baby squid with garlic and ginger. Reliable wine list to suit most pockets, as well.
♿Ⅲ🅿🔳

POINT BAR　E3
40, place du Marché St-Honoré, 75001
Tel. 01 42 61 76 28
Closed Sun–Mon.
Last service 11pm.
À la carte: €36;
Menus: €25–36.
A small, friendly restaurant owned and run by Alice Bardet, whose father has two

Michelin stars back at the family establishment in Tours. Alice insists that only the freshest produce will do, and gets as much as she can from the family potager! Try the saddle of cod with honey in a champagne sauce, which is quite superb. Desserts include a delicious French version of apple crumble, and the wine list features some really unusual vintages.
Ⅲ🔳

⓫ RAGUENEAU　G6
202, rue St-Honoré, 75001
Tel. 01 42 60 29 20
Closed Jan 1.
Last service 10pm.
À la carte: €25;
Menus: €19.50–23.
Named after the philanthropic pastrycook in Cyrano de Bergerac, this classic French restaurant and tearoom has an enticing menu, featuring ravioli of snails, a pot-roast of lamb that is really outstanding, and a pungent brandade de morue (salt cod blended with garlic and potato purée). It also has a terrace overlooking the Palais Royal, and the fixed-price menus offer some of the best value in this district.
Ⅲ🔳

⓮ ♀ RESTAURANT DU PALAIS-ROYAL　G5
110, galerie de Valois opposite the 4, rue du Beaujolais, 75001
Tel. 01 40 20 00 27
www.resto-palais-royal
Closed Sun, and two weeks beg Jan.
Last service 10.30pm.
À la carte: €50.
A deluxe restaurant in the gorgeous setting of the Palais Royal gardens has to be one of the city's most romantic places. A

table under the historic arcades, a bottle of good wine (and the wine here is top of the range) are the perfect accompaniment to a dinner that must be classed among the very best in town. In winter, the chef Bruno Hees prepares a coq au vin as good as any you've eaten, while other specialties include a juicy lobster risotto with squid ink, sole so fresh that you'd swear you were at the seaside, and great steaks just as you like them, with thick, English-style fries. The desserts are excellent too, featuring millefeuilles whose filling changes with the seasons.
♿Ⅲ🔳

⓬ RISTORANTE FELLINI　I6
47, rue de l'Arbre-Sec, 75001
Tel. 01 42 60 90 66
Open daily.
Last service 11pm.
Authentic Italian cuisine, with mouthwatering antipasti and a truly magnificent minestrone make this little piece of old Italy between Châtelet and the rue de Rivoli a very popular place to be. Try the rigatoni with four cheeses, or a risotto which simply bursts with flavor. The wine list includes vintages from Piedmont, Tuscany, Sicily and Sardinia, but watch out: the prices can be quite hefty. Reservations advisable.
Ⅲ

⓬ SAUDADE　J7
34, rue des Bourdonnais, 75001
Tel. 01 42 36 03 65
Closed Sun, and Aug.
Last service 10.30pm.
À la carte: €30;
Menus: €20.
Twice winner of the award for the best

◆ Cafés, tearooms, bars

Cafés, tearooms and bars are listed in alphabetical order.
The map coordinates "A1" after the name of the establishment refer to the front endpaper map.
A list of logos can be found on page 335.

foreign restaurant in Paris, Saudade will come as a revelation to those who know little about Portuguese cuisine. Grilled sucking pig, bacalhau *(dried salt cod)* cooked in a number of appetizing ways, and pork à l'alentajana *(with clams)* are some of the great classics on offer here, washed down with a crisp *vinho verde* or a hearty Dao from the Douro valley.
🥢 ▥

⑬ 🍵
VIN ET MARÉE F5
165, rue St-Honoré, 75001
Tel. 01 42 86 06 96
Open daily.
Last service 10.30pm.
À la carte: €40.
A fish restaurant right across the road from the Comédie Francaise, serving only the freshest produce and with a wide selection to choose from. Naturally enough, the menu is liable to change according to the day's catch, but the sole with lemon butter is simply divine, likewise the baby turbot with Hollandaise sauce. For dessert, don't leave without sampling one of their inimitable rum babas, which are so drenched in alcohol, that it would surely be illegal to drive home afterward. Good wine list, mainly featuring bottles from the Rhone valley.
▥ 🦞

WILLI'S WINE BAR G4
13, rue des Petits-Champs, 75001
Tel. 01 42 61 05 09
www.williswinebar.com
Closed Sun, and two weeks in Aug.
Last service 11pm.
À la carte: €32;
Menus: €25–32.

Condrieu de Niero, Manzanilla sherry or 5 Puttonyos Tokay, owner Mark Williamson's eclectic wine list is enough to make anyone thirsty. The menu is inventive, though based on traditional models, including tartare of tuna, tian of lamb with rosemary, and the exotically named strawberry Mikado. Packed at lunchtimes with journalists and financiers, the atmosphere can be much more relaxed in the evenings.

⑫ **YASUBE** F4
9, rue St-Anne, 75001
Tel. 01 47 03 96 37
Closed Sun and public hols.
Last service 10.30pm.
À la carte: €25.
Menus: €13–19.
Sashimi at €15–20, according to the number of pieces, has to be good value. And you can see how fresh it all is, since the food is prepared in full view. The atmosphere is quite formal, but extremely polite and friendly.
🥢 ▥

CAFÉS, TEAROOMS

ANGÉLINA D4
226, rue de Rivoli, 75001
Tel. 01 42 60 82 00
Mon-Fri 8am–7pm;
Sat-Sun 9am–7pm
Since 1947, the famous house of Rumpelmayer has been lending the name of the owner's wife to this adorable tearoom with its Versailles-style décor. This has to be the place to try a montblanc, a rich confection meringue with whipped cream and vanilla-flavored chestnut purée, accompanied by a cup of Angélina's inimitable hot chocolate.

A PRIORI THÉ H4
35-37, galerie Vivienne, 75002
Tel. 01 42 97 48 75
Daily 8.30am– 6pm.
A friendly tearoom set in the elegant calm of the Galerie Vivienne, serving a selection of teas with cakes and other light refreshments. The fascinating mosaic on the floor, which is reproduced on the menu, is the work of the Italian artist Faccina.

BAR HEMINGWAY D3
Hôtel Ritz
15, place Vendôme, 75001
Tel. 01 43 16 30 30
Mon-Sat 6.30pm–2am; Sun 11am–3pm.
When Ernest Hemingway considered life after death, he always thought it would be like living at the Ritz, and was among the first to liberate the hotel in 1944. Pricey, but lots of fun, and more interesting than the hotel's Bar Vendôme.

COLETTE WATER BAR E4
213, rue St-Honoré, 75001
Tel. 01 55 35 33 90
Mon-Sat 11am–7pm.
Located in the basement of the so-called "concept" store, this minimalist bar stocks over 90 varieties of bottled mineral water, but there is also a restaurant serving international cuisine.

LADURÉE ROYALE B3
16, rue Royale, 75008
Tel. 01 42 60 21 79
Mon-Sat 8.30am–7pm; Sun 10am–7pm.
This tearoom first opened in 1862, and still has the original paneling and murals. It also still serves the original macarons

(soft almond cookies with the most extraordinary flavors) that first made its name, and many visitors have said it serves the best Sunday brunch in Paris. Good salads, as well as hot dishes for lunch and dinner.

LE FUMOIR H
6, rue de l'Amiral-de-Coligny, 75001
Tel. 01 42 92 00 24
Daily 11am–2am;
Brunch on Sun noon–3pm.
A comfortable and luxurious establishment, with sash picture window overlooking the Louvre colonnade, rather like the stage set of a Viennese operetta. A great place to enjoy a cocktail and browse the wide selection of newspapers available and they do a hearty Sunday brunch as well.

NIGHTLIFE
BARS

LE COMPTOIR I6
14, rue Vauvilliers, 75001
Tel. 01 40 26 26 66
Bar and restaurant open daily noon–2am
A bar-restaurant designed by Jonathan Amar with a quasi-Oriental theme opposite St Eustache. During the day it serves drinks and light refreshments, but transforms itself into a classy nightclub in the evenings, and is the best one of its kind in the area.

LE RUBIS E4
10, rue du Marché-St-Honoré, 75001
Tel. 01 42 61 03 34
Mon-Fri 7am–10pm;
Sat 9am–3.30pm.
Despite its unprepossessing rustic décor, this is perhaps the best-known wine bar in Paris, attracting a

smart, professional
clientèle. It serves
typical bistro meals
such as boeuf
bourgignon and black
pudding (boudin), and
more than thirty
different wines.

E SOUS-BOCK I6
9, rue St-Honoré,
75001
Tel. 01 40 26 46 61
Daily 9am–5am.
One of the most
popular beer bars in
the city, complete
with shop next door
and serving more
than 250 different
beers, including
Fischer from Alsace
and the Parisian
Lutèce.

**COMÉDIE
FRANÇAISE** G5
, place Colette,
75001
Tel. 0825 16 10 80
www.comedie-
francaise.fr
Known to Parisians
simply as "Le
Francais", this is the
home of classical
French theater,
especially Molière.
Since Antonio Vitez
took over the
management, the
theater has been
opened up to foreign
directors of stage and
screen, and designers
too. It has also
branched out into
producing Feydeau
farces and
contemporary works
by foreign playwrights.

OPÉRA-GARNIER E1
Place de l'Opéra,
75009
www.operadeparis.fr
Reservations tel.
0 892 89 90 90
Mon-Fri 9am–6pm;
Sat 9am–1pm.
Ticket office: Mon-Sat
10.30am–6.30pm.
(closed public hols).
In accordance with
tradition, the
productions of the
Opéra Garnier are
mainly oriented
toward dance, with
productions mounted

by the Ballet de
l'Opéra de Paris.
Each year, a foreign
ballet company is
also invited to
perform here.

PRIVATE THEATERS
Except for the
Daunou, which
stages contemporary
productions, all
theaters listed here
stage conventional
Broadway-style
shows.

THÉÂTRE DAUNOU E2
7, rue Daunou, 75001
Tel. 01 42 61 69 14
**THÉÂTRE DE LA
MICHODIÈRE** F2
4 bis, rue de la
Michodière, 75001
Tel. 01 47 42 95 22
**THÉÂTRE DES
BOUFFES-
PARISIENS** G4
4, rue Monsigny,
75002
Tel. 01 42 96 92 42
**THÉÂTRE
DU PALAIS-ROYAL** G4
38, rue de
Montpensier, 75001
Tel. 01 42 97 59 81

**LE LOUVRE DES
ANTIQUAIRES** F5
2, place du Palais-
Royal, 75001
Tel. 01 42 97 27 27
Tue-Sun 11am–7pm.
Closed Sun in July-
Aug.
In a magnificent
building constructed
in 1854 to house the
Grand Hôtel du
Louvre with 700
rooms, there are now
250 antique dealers
of all types in an area
covering 100,000
square feet. Bar,
restaurant, bureau de
change, shipping
service if required,
and expert advice by
appointment are all
available here.
Exhibitions of the
collections of private
connoisseurs, French
and foreign museums
and the Louvre
dealers are also held
here.

BOUCHERON D-E3
26, place Vendôme,
75001
Tel. 01 42 61 58 16
Mon-Sat 11am–7pm.
The famous jewel
merchant has been in
the Place Vendôme
since 1893, and
features rock crystal
in many of its
exquisite designs.

CARTIER D-E3
23, place Vendôme,
75001
Tel. 01 44 55 32 20
Mon-Sat 11am–7pm.
The bestiary, which
is Cartier's famous
trademark, first
appeared in 1914
in the shape of
a panther.

CHAUMET D-E3
12, place Vendôme,
75001
Tel. 01 44 77 24 00
Mon-Sat 10.30am–
6.30pm.
In 1804, the
celebrated house
of Chaumet was
commissioned to
make the Napoleon
I's crown jewels.

LES MINÉRAUX F6
Le Carrousel du
Louvre, 99, rue de
Rivoli, 75001
Tel. 01 42 60 05 40
Open daily from
10am.
If a souvenir from the
Place Vendôme is
beyond your reach,
the next best thing
might be a semi-
precious stone.
These are specially
imported here, to be
mounted and
transformed into
ornaments on
commission
according to the
customer's
requirements.

MAUBOUSSIN D-E3
20, place Vendôme,
75001
Tel. 01 44 55 10 00
Mon-Sat 11am–7pm.
Founded more
than a century ago,
Mauboussin is one
of the oldest jewel

merchants in Paris.
Its work is
characterized by
the blending and
contrasting of
colors in its pieces.

MELLERIO E3
9, rue de la Paix,
75002
Tel. 01 42 61 57 53
Mon-Sat 11am–7pm.
The oldest jeweler
in Paris, and the
only remaining
independent dealer
in the square.

SALVIATI F6
Carrousel du Louvre,
99 rue de Rivoli,
75001
Tel. 01 40 20 12 66
Daily 10am– 8pm.
Founded in Murano
in 1859, the famous
house of Salviati was
a major contributor
to the revival of the
Venetian glass
industry. It still has its
workshop in Murano,
and uses traditional
techniques such as
blowing, stretching
and mosaic to create
decorative objects
and jewelry in
contemporary style
that are as amazing
as ever.

AU PANETIER H4
10, place des
Petits-Pères, 75002
Tel. 01 42 60 90 23
Mon-Fri 8am–7pm.
A beautiful baker's
shop from the late
19th century selling
traditional bread
baked in wood-fired
ovens. Specialties
here are saint-fiacre
loaves and the pavé
des Petits-Pères,
both made from
stone-ground flour.

FAUCHON C2
24-30, place de la
Madeleine, 75008
Tel. 01 70 39 38 00
Mon-Sat 8am–7pm.
Perhaps the finest,
and certainly the
most famous grocery
store in Paris. The
place is practically
a museum of food,

◆ Shopping

Stores are listed in alphabetical order.
The map coordinates "A1" after the name of the establishment refer to the front endpaper map.

filled with rare delicacies such as redcurrant jelly from Bar-le Duc, honey collected from the roof of the Opéra here in Paris, and thousands of other exotic foods to marvel at.

HÉDIARD   C2
21, place de la Madeleine, 75008
Tel. 01 43 12 88 88
Mon–Sat 9am–10pm.
Another fine foodstore in the square, Hédiard specializes in fresh fruit and vegetables from all over the world, rare herbs and spices, and jars of exotic jelly such as banana, green tomato or ginger, and gorgeous crystallized fruit as well. It has a number of other retail outlets in Paris.

LA FONTAINE AU CHOCOLAT   E4
201, rue St-Honoré, 75001
Tel. 01 42 44 11 66
Mon–Sat 10am–7pm.
A shop specializing in high-quality chocolate, from 60% to 90% pure cacao, traditional pralines made from almonds and hazelnuts, crystallized oranges, and chocolate bars stuffed with nuts and tricked out to look like wood bark, called Chocoblock.

LEGRAND FILLES ET FILS   H4
1, rue de la Banque, 75001
Tel. 01 42 60 07 12
Mon 11am–7pm; Tue–Sat 10am–7.30pm (7pm Sat).
First opened almost 100 years ago, this must be one of the prettiest stores in Paris, and is now run by the third generation of Legrands. The range of wines on sale here is greater than ever, and there are also

many other items to do with the storage and consumption of wine, including elegant glassware. Their warehouse for bulk purchases is in the 13th arrondissement.

FASHION

CHRISTIAN LOUBOUTIN   H6
19, rue Jean-Jacques-Rousseau, 75001
Tel. 01 42 36 05 31
Mon–Sat 10.30am–1pm, 2–7pm.
Known in the trade as "The man with the red-soled shoes", Roger Vivier's former assistant designs highly original clothes that have made his name famous all over the world.

COLETTE   E4
213, rue St-Honoré, 75001
Tel. 01 55 35 33 90
Mon–Sat 11am–7pm.
Arranged over three floors are designer products from all over the world that fit the store's discerning requirements: the "Colette" image of style, originality and minimalism. The goods on display are constantly changing, though there is a certain consistency in the type of goods sold, where everything related to art, accessories, electronic gadgetry and design is given pride of place on the shelves.

CHANEL   D3
29-31, rue Cambon, 75001
Tel. 01 42 86 28 00
Mon–Sat 10am–7pm.
The historic boutique of the celebrated "Coco", featuring accessories such as spectacle frames, perfumes and jewelry side by side with ready-to-wear designs by Karl Lagerfeld.

ON AURA TOUT VU   G4-5
Palais-Royal, 23, rue de Montpensier, 75001
Tel. 01 42 60 75 66
By appointment only.
Original designs for jewelry and buttons, clothes, accessories. A boutique-cum-exhibition space opened by three designers, where artists are regularly invited to design jewelry and exhibit it in one of the fashion shows.

PHILIPPE MODEL   E3-4
33, place du Marché-St-Honoré, 75001
Tel. 01 42 96 89 02
Mon–Sat 10am–1pm, 2–7pm. Closed Aug.
One of the most famous hat designers in France, whose creations are always to be seen at the Prix de Diane in Chantilly – the French "Oaks" horserace. He also designs shoes and accessories which are very popular.

INTERIOR DESIGN, FURNISHING

BOUTIQUE DE LA COMÉDIE FRANÇAISE   G5
1, place Colette, 75001
Tel. 01 44 58 14 30
Mon–Sat 11am–8.30pm; Sun and public hols 1–8.30pm.
A fantastic store where theater lovers can furnish their living-room with the sofa from Cyrano de Bergerac or the bench from Chekhov's The Cherry Tree. The company produces limited editions of eight items of furniture copied from sets in the classical repertory.

107 RIVOLI   F5
107, rue de Rivoli, 75001
Tel. 01 42 60 64 94
Mon–Sat 10am–7pm.
This establishment sets out to prove that

museum shops need not be dull and old-fashioned. Among the items on sale are products from the Artcodif workshops, an exclusive brand and part of the State Art Decoratif institution. Also here are designer jewelry and accessories, specialist books, high-quality stationery, toys, tableware, copies of old and contemporary designs. A great place to find original gifts at all prices in over 10,000 square feet of showrooms.

MAISON DE VACANCES   G4
63-64, Galerie Montpensier, 75001
Tel. 01 47 03 99 74
Mon–Sat 11am–2pm, 2.30–7pm.
Imaginative blends of raw materials with synthetic textiles come as something of a revelation. Fine tableware and accessories on sale, and household linens can be ordered in the colors of your choice.

BOOKSTORE

LA LIBRAIRIE DES JARDINS   B4
Grille d'honneur du jardin des Tuileries, place de la Concorde, 75001
Tel. 01 42 60 61 61
Daily 10am–7pm.
The gardener's bookshop par excellence! Over 4,000 books on every aspect of the art, from garden design and layout, through botanical works to gardens in literature. On the subject of wildlife, there is also a good little department of children's books and wooden toys as well, which make ideal gifts.

List of illustrations ◆

Cover
View of the Salon Carré at the Louvre, Alexandre Brun.

1 Cleaning the display case of the *Mona Lisa*, during filming for N. Philibert's *La Ville Louvre* de © M. Chassat. **2–3** Moving some of the works in the Louvre for the "David" exhibition: an installer from the I.A.T. with the Léonidas aux Thermopyles by David, © M. Chassat. **4–5** Moving the frame of the *Sabines* of David, during the setting up of the "David" exhibition, © M. Chassat. **6–7** Mounting the "David" exhibition at the Louvre © M. Chassat. **9** Pei's Pyramide seen from Richelieu passage. **17** Archeological excavations, © P. Charniot. **18** Hubert Robert, *Pieces of Classical sculpture in front of the Petite Galerie*, canvas, 0.46 x 0.47; Details of different materials of the Louvre, © Patrick Horvais/Gallimard. **19** Sébastien Leclerc, *The construction of Colonnade* (detail), engraving, 1672; Details of different materials of the Louvre, © Patrick Horvais/Gallimard. **21** Pierre Antoine De Machy, *View of Paris, from Pont-Neuf* (detail), 1783, canvas, Musée de Versailles. **25** Victor Chavet , *Napoleon III's Louvre*, canvas, 2.12 x 2.22, 1857. **26** Maître de St-Germain-des-Prés, *Piéta de St-Germain-des-Prés* (detail), c. 1500, wood, 0.97 x 1.98; Excavations of the Cour Carrée: donjon, 1985, © F. Huguier/EPGL.; Pol. of Limburg, *The Book of Hours of the Duc de Berry*, "October, Sowing and the Louvre", Musée Condé, Chantilly, © Giraudon. **26–7** Anon., *View of the Tuileries Palace*, watercolor, © Bibl. Nat. **27** Titian (1488/89– 1576), *François I*, canvas, 1.09 x 0.89; Dupré, *Henri IV and Marie de' Medicis* bronze medal, 1603, © Bibl. Nat.; Anon. c. 1660 and repainted in the 19th century, *Henri IV's Grand Plan for the Louvre*, Musée de Fontainebleau. **28** Charles Lebrun (1619–90), *Profile of Louis XIV*, pastel; Sébastien Leclerc, *The construction of the Colonnade*, engraving; Gabriel de Saint-Aubin (1724–80), *The Salon du Louvre*, drawing, 1765. **29** Joseph Siffred Duplessis (1725–1802), *Comte d'Angiville, Royal Director of Buildings*, 1774, canvas, 1.44 x 1.06, Musée de Versailles; Anon. late 18th century, *Riot of August 10, 1792, storming the Tuileries*, gouache, Musée Carnavalet, © J.-L. Charmet; Gioacchino Sérangeli (1768–1852), *Napoleon receives the army deputies at the Louvre following his coronation, December 8, 1804* (detail), Musée de Versailles; *Arc de triomphe of the Carrousel and the entrance to the Cour des Tuileries*, engraving, all rights reserved **30** Pierre-François Fontaine, *State opening of Parliament*, quill, watercolor and pencil; Anon. c. 1820, *Fateful night of February 14, 1820; assassination of the Duc de Berry*, colored engraving, Bibl. Nat., © J. Vigne; François-Joseph Heim (1787–1865), *Charles X awarding prizes to artists at the 1824 Salon*, canvas, 1.73 x 2.56. **31** Ange Tissier (1814–76), *Visconti presenting Napoléon III with the plan of the Nouveau Louvre*, 1866, Musée de Versailles; *Conversion project for the Carrousel (SARI)*, © EPGL **32–3** Relief plans of the Louvre and surroundings, work carried out by R. Munier and S. Polonovski, 1/1000. 1.60 x 0.60: the Louvre in 1200, in 1380, in 1572, in 1610, in 1643, in 1715, in 1848, in 1870, in 1980 and in 1989.© Caroline.Rose/ RMN. **34** Fragment of painted plaster from Pierre des Essarts manor, 14th century, Direction des Antiquités d'Île-de-France, © EPGL; Carrousel courtyard excavations, 1990, © P. Astier/EPGL; Excavations of the Carrousel courtyard excavations and Charles V's city wall, 1990, © G. Meguersan; France, 14th

century, *Charles V*, stone. **35** Detail from map by François Quesnel, *The Louvre, Tuileries and surrounding area*, 1609, all rights reserved; Flemish painter working in Paris, mid-15th century, *Retable du Parlement de Paris* (detail), wood, 2.26 x 2.70; *Charles V in his library*, manuscript, 1372, © Bibl. Nat.; Israël Silvestre, *Church of the Quinze-Vingt*, engraving, all rights reserved **36** Joseph-Nicolas Robert-Fleury (1797–1890), *Scene from St Bartholomew's Day Massacre*, canvas, 1.64 x 1.30; François Dubois (1529–84), *St Bartholomew's Day Massacre*, Musée cantonal des Beaux-Arts, Lausanne. **37** Anon., France 16th century, *Ball of the Duc de Joyeuse*, copper, 0.41 x 0.65; *Catherine de' Medici receiving the ambassadors of Poland at the Tuileries*, tapestry, Uffizzi, Florence, © Scala; Excavations in the Carrousel: ventilation room, 1986, © B. Descamps; *Figure of the Paris League*, engraving, 1594, all rights reserved **38** Duplessis-Bertaux (1747–c. 1819), *Storming of the Tuileries Paris, Carrousel courtyard, August 10, 1792*, canvas, 1.24 x 1.92, Musée de Versailles; Pierre-Antoine Demachy, *Fête de l'Unité; burning the emblems of royal power*, canvas, Musée Carnavalet, © Spadem 1994. **39** Anon., France 18th century, *Louis XVI passing in front of the Louvre in 1789*, watercolor, Musée Carnavalet © Spadem 1994; baron Gérard, *August 10 1792*, quill with brown wash ; Duplessis-Bertaux, *Assassination of deputy Ferraud during the national convention*, engraving, Year II, © Bibl. Nat.; idem, *Festival of the Supreme Being*, June 3, 1794, engraving, © idem **40–1** and bottom p. 40, Sèvres porcelain, *Etruscan vase* , Musée de la Céramique, Sèvres; Benjamin Zix (1772–1811), *Salle du Laocoön*, drawing. **41** Zix, *Salle des Antiques*, the Louvre, drawing, 1807; Bartolini, *Bust of Napoleon*, bronze; Zix, *Cortège nuptial de Napoleon and Marie-Louise in the Grande Galerie*, pen and brown wash. **42** The naval museum at the Louvre in 1858, all rights reserved; *Salle La Pérouse at the naval museum*, engraving, © Bibl. Nat.; *La salle Pelliot*, 1910, © idem **43** The museum of ethnography in 1856, engraving, © idem; the Egyptian museum in the 19th century, © idem; The Assyrian museum in the 19th century. **44** Barricades of the Communards, rue de Castiglione, photo, May 1871, Musée Carnavalet, J.-L. Charmet; the destroyed Vendôme column , photo, 1871, Musée Carnavalet, © idem; The burning of the Tuileries, the Metz, © idem, 1871, all rights reserved **45** Barricades, place de la Concorde, 1871, photographs, archives Préfecture de Police, © J. Vigne; Ernest Meissonier (1815–91), *The Tuileries in ruins*, canvas, Musée de Compiègne; Giuseppe de Nittis (1846–84), *The place du Carrousel, Tuileries in ruins, 1882*, wood, 0.45 x 0.60, Musée d'Orsay **46** Antoine Durandeau (1854–1941), *Interior of the nave of the Jacobin Church of Toulouse in 1918*, canvas, 0.50 x 0.65, Musée d'Orsay; Paul Jamot (1863–1939), *Interior view of the Jacobin Church of Toulouse in 1916*, canvas, 0.41 x 0.32, Musée d'Orsay; idem *Interior view of the Jacobin Church of Toulouse in 1918*, canvas, 0.41 x 0.27, Musée d'Orsay. **47** Relocating the masterpieces of the Louvre for safekeeping, photo,1939, © Archive Photos; packing the Venus de Milo, photo, 1939, all rights reserved; Jaujard in 1940, © Lapi-Viollet; Works of the Louvre in cases;1939, © Archive Photos. **48** *Médor, or the faithful dog of the Louvre*, popular print by Belfort, 1830, Musée Carnavalet, © J.-L. Charmet; G. de Saint-Aubin, the *Salon, 1779*, wood; idem, *The crowning of Voltaire*, drawing, 1778; Hubert Robert, *View of the "guichet" at the Louvre*, canvas, 0.46 x 0.38. **49** Guérard, *Children's games at the Tuileries, Allée des Feuillants*, c. 1856, Musée Carnavalet, © J.-L. Charmet. **50** Anon. 18th century, *Selling paintings and prints, Cour Carrée*, engraving, Musée Carnavalet, © musées de la Ville de Paris/SPADEM 1994; C.N. Cochin fils, *Royal Press at the Louvre Louvre*, print, © Bibl. Nat.; The Imperial Library at the Louvre, in Paris Nouveau Illustré, c. 1870, all rights reserved **51** Pierre-Antoine Demachy (1723–1807), *Print-dealers*, canvas; New

List of illustrations ◆

Nicolle, *View of the Hôtel des Monnaies*, watercolor, Musée de la Malmaison; *Elevation of the Palais-Royal*, drawing, Arch. nat. de France, © J.-L. Charmet. **80–1** Charles De Wailly (1729–98), *Design for the main door of the Louvre*, Year II (1794), drawing. **81** General design for planned decorations for the Tuileries Palace by Percier and Fontaine, Year IX (1802), drawing, Archives nationales de France, © J.-L. Charmet; Eleation of the Arc du Carrousel, by G. Nicot; *Grand escalier of the Colonnade*, engraving by Hibon, Bibliothèque du Louvre; Armand de Kersaint, *Plan for the Museum*, in "Discours sur les Monuments publics", 1792, © Bibl. Nat.; Percier and Fontaine, *Maison rue de Rivoli*, elevation, engraving, Musée Carnavalet © SPADEM 1994; Section plan for a building of the Palais-Royal, drawing, Archives nationales de France, © J.-L. Charmet, colorist Laure Massin; Elevation of a building in the rue d'Aboukir de Jules de Joly, engraving, all rights reserved. **82** *Plan for the completed Louvre and Tuileries*, after Visconti, 1853, bibliothèque du Louvre; The Cour Napoléon before building work, coll. of photographs 1852–7, Bibliothèque municipale de Versailles. **82–3** Elevation of the pavillon Denon, cour Napoléon, by G. Nicot. **83** Detail of the front pavillon Denon; Charles Garnier, *Façade of the new Opéra de Paris*, engraving, bibliothèque de l'Opéra, © Bibl. Nat.; Pavillon de Rohan, the "guichets", collection of photographs 1852–7, Bibliothèque municipale de Versailles, © Jean Vigne. **84** View of the Louvre, all rights reserved and © P. Ballif/EPGL;. M. Pei, *Design for the Pyramide*, drawing, © EPGL; I. M. Pei, © P. Astier/EPGL **84–5** The Pyramide, © Alfred Wolf/Explorer; The inverted Pyramide, © Robinson/EPGL. **85** La Samaritaine, P.L./G.; The inverted Pyramide, S. de Luigi/EPGL. **86** I.M. Peï, *Technical drawing*, © EPGL; staircase of the Hall Napoléon, © EPGL; The Pyramide, P.L./G.; Section through the Pyramide, © EPGL. **87** Georges Leroux (1877–1957), *In the Grande Galerie of the Louvre Museum*, canvas, 0.89 x 1.51, © A.D.A.G.P., 1994. **88–9** Hubert Robert (1733–1808), *The Grande Galerie of the Louvre*, between 1794 and 1796, canvas, 0.37 x 0.41; *The Grande Galerie of the Louvre undergoing restoration*, c. 1798–9, canvas, 0.42 x 0.55; *Plan to develop the Grande Galerie of the Louvre, in 1796*, canvas, 1,12 x 1.43; *A gallery of the museum*, canvas, 0.65 x 0.81.**90–1** Hubert Robert, *Artist's impression of the Grande Galerie of the Louvre in ruins*, canvas, 1.15 x 1.46. **92** Madeleine Goblot, *View of the Salle des Saisons*, late 19th century, canvas, 0.38 x 0.55; Alphonse Hirsch (1843–84), *View of the rotonde de Mars and the Salle de Mécène at the Louvre c. 1880*, canvas, 1,00 x 0.73.**93** Paul Hugues (1891–1972), *Scenes of of the Salle B of Egyptian Antiquities section of the Louvre during reinstallation of collections, 1946*, canvas, 0.46 x 0.38; Guillaume Larrue (1851–1935), *Egyptian room, the Louvre. In front of the large sphinx*, canvas, 0.69 x 0.88. **94–5** Marco Terenzio Müller de Schongor (1865–1938), *View of the Salon Carré at the Louvre with the "Wedding Feast of Cana"*, wood., 0.34 x 0.24; Alexandre Brun (1853-1941), *View of the Salon Carré at the Louvre*, canvas, 0.24 x 0.32; Anon., France, early 20th century, *View of the Salle Duchâtel and the Salon Carré au Louvre*, before 1914, canvas, 0.46 x 0.61. **96** Louis Béroud (1852–1930), *The Salle Rubens at the Louvre*, canvas; idem. *Homage to Rubens*, canvas, 0.65 x 0.92; idem. *In the Salon Carré*, canvas, 0.65 x 0.92. **97** Charles Renouard, *Wreck of the Medusa*, drawing, Musée communal d'Ixelles (Bruxelles). **98** *The large sphinx of Tanis*, engraving, 1851, © Bibl. Nat. **99** *Talma on the stairway of the Colonnade*, engraving, © Bibl. Nat.; *Soldiers at a cultural visit to the Louvre*, in Supplément Illustré of Le Petit Journal, 1902, © Jean Vigne. **100–1** The Salon in 1843, engraving, © Bibl. Nat. **102** Dromart, *View of the Salle des Antiques, taken from the Salle de Pan*, canvas, 0.59 x 0.69; Charles Renouard, *The Sleeper*, drawing, Musée communal d'Ixelles (Bruxelles). **103** Visitor wearing paper slippers, 1964, © Archive Photo. **104–5**

Charles Renouard, *Painting and cuisine*, drawing, Musée communal d'Ixelles (Bruxelles); idem, *Up a ladder*; idem, *The critic*; idem, *Religious painting*. **106** Night tour of the Apollon gallery in 1880, engraving, © Bibl. Nat. **107** *The Musée Assyrien in 1860*, engraving, © Bibl. Nat. **108–9** *The Louvre Salon in 1787*, engraving , © Bibl. Nat **110** *The Musée des Antiques in 1875*, engraving, © Bibl. Nat. **111** Charles Renouard, *Do not touch*, drawing, Musée communal d'Ixelles (Bruxelles); Moving a sculpture, © M. Chassat. **112** Poster for the film *On a volé la Joconde*, by Michel Deville © Christophe L. **113** Victor Navlet (1819–1886), *View of Paris, taken from the Observatoire*; (detail); canvas, 3.90 x 7.08, 1855, Musée d'Orsay. **114–15** Plan of the different levels of Louvre giving details .**116–19** Perspective view and details, original drawings by Philippe Biard and Jean-Michel. Kassedan **120** Aerial photograph of the Louvre and the surrounding area, © Yann Arthus-Bertrand Altitude. **121** François Biard (1798–1882), *Four hours at the Salon*, canvas, 0.57 x 0.67. **123** Jean Goujon's workshop, *The Justice of Cambyse* (detail).Archeological crypt: keep and moats of Philippe Auguste. **124** *The new underground rooms of the Old Louvre*, engraving, coll. Debuisson; Salle Saint-Louis: column detail ; © C. Rose/RMN; Golden helmet Charles VI, (reconstruction) © EPGL. **124–5** View of the tribune of the Salle des Caryatides, © C. Rose/RMN. **126** Vaulting of the Henri II staircase, © C. Rose/RMN. **126** Apartment of Anne of Austria: Ceiling of the Salle des Saisons, stuccos by Anguier and paintings by Romanelli, © C. Rose/RMN; idem: view of the building; idem, Cour du Sphinx : detail of Le Vau wall **127** Eugène Delacroix, *The Triumph of Apollon*, Ceiling of the Galerie d'Apollon; Ceiling of the Apollon rotonda; Stairway of the Victoire de Samothrace. **128** Ceiling of the Salle Henri II : Georges Braque (1882–1963), *Les Oiseaux*, © SPADEM 1994; Joseph Auguste , 19th century, *The Salle des Bijoux and the Musée Charles X*, canvas, 1.00 x 0.81; Auguste Couder (1789–1873), *Napoleon viewing the staircase of the Louvre with Percier and Fontaine*, canvas, 1.77 x 1.35. **129** Salle Duchâtel by Charles Meynier, detail (1768–1832); Giuseppe Castiglione (1829–1906), *The Salon Carré at the Louvre*, canvas, 0.69 x 1.03. **130** Frederick Nash (1782–1856), *View of th Grande Galerie*, watercolor, c. 1820. **130–1** Benjamin Zix, *Wedding procession of Napoleon I and Marie-Louise in the Grande Galerie, April 2, 1810* (detail), ink and watercolor, 1.72 x 0.24. **131** The Cour Caulaincourt, in *Paris Nouveau Illustré*, c. 1870; Opening of a parliamentary session at the Louvre in 1859, watercolor, Musée Carnavalet, © J.-L. Charmet. **132** Salle Daru, postcard, 1906, © Bibl. Nat., The stables of the Emperor, at the Louvre, in Paris Nouveau Illustré, c. 1870, all rights reserved; Royal stables of the Louvre; Calaincourt riding ring, in L'Illustration, 1867, all rights reserved **133** Woman's head, Mari, c. 2400 BC; Victory Samothrace, 3rd–2nd century BC, marble; Statue of a woman, New Kingdom, red quartzite. **134** Figurine of a woman (Halaf), c. 4500 BC, terracotta; Sumerian tablet; Sumerian priest-king, Uruk period, c. 3200 BC, limestone; The Urnanshe Relief , Tello, c. 2500 BC, limestone; Statue of Ebih II, Superintendent of Mari , Mari, c. 2500 BC, alabaster. **136** Royal seal of Sharikalisharri, Agadé c. 2100 BC, chlorite; Libation vase to Gudea, Tello, c. 2150 BC, chlorite; Victory stele of Naram Sin, Suse, limestone. **137** Little Gudea seated, Tello, diorite; Foundation figurine of Ur Ba'u, Tello, copper; Lady from Tello, Tello, diorite; Gudea bearing a vase that spouts water, Tello, calcite. **138** Adoration of Larsa, c. 1700 BC, bronze and gold. **138–9** Sacrificial priest, Mari, Zimrilim Palace, fresco; Law-Codex of Hammurabi (detail), c. 1760 BC, basalt; Statuette of Astarte, Babylonia, alabaster , garnet and gold. **139** Pendant in the Shape of a God, Yogzat, gold; Rhython in the shape of a lion, Kültepe, c. 1950–1750 BC, terracotta; Ashurbanipal in his chariot (detail), Nineveh, gypseous alabaster **140–1** Palace of Sargon at Khorsabad,

◆ List of illustrations

◆ List of illustrations

List of illustrations ◆

◆ List of illustrations

List of illustrations ◆

Aubin, *Completion of a façade of the Cour du Louvre*, drawing, 1755, Musée Carnavalet, © J.L. Charmet; Nicolle, *An oeil-de-bœuf of the Colonnade*, watercolor, Musée Carnavalet, © J.L. Charmet; Demachy, *View of the Colonnade of the Louvre*, canvas, 1772.

Practical information
314 Perspective © Philippe Biard. **316-317** Maps of the Louvre © Musée du Louvre. graphic design B. Pell. Artistic input Ph. Apeloig; Beneath the Pyramide © Patrick Horvais /G; **318** A guided tour, © M. Chassat / Service culturel du Louvre; The workshops, © idem **319** *Copyists at the Louvre*, engraving, 1874. © Bibl. Nat. **320** Entrance to the auditorium © Patricia Canino. **321** The bookshop © RMN. Daniel Arnaudet **322** The inverted Pyramide © RMN. Caroline Rose **323** Terrace of the Café Marly. © P. L. / G; Universal Resto © Serge Cohen **324** Leonardo da Vinci, *Mona Lisa*; Géricault, *Raft of the Medusa*; Michelangelo, *The Slaves*; Veronese, *Wedding Feast at Cana* (detail). **325** *Venus de Milo*; *Victory of Samothrace*; Salle des Caryatides; © C. Rose / RMN; *Mastaba of Akhethetep*. **326** Guillaume Coustou, *Marly Horse*; Vermeer, *The Lacemaker*; *The Law-Codex of Hammurabi*; *Winged bull in the Cour Khorsabad*; Rembrandt, *Portrait of the Artist at His Easel*; Puget, *Milo of Croton*. **327** Van Eyck, *The Virgin and Chancelor Rolin*; *Portrait of Jean II Le Bon*; Rubens, *Marie de' Medici Landing at Marseille*; *Seated Scribe*; Chardin, *The Skate*. **328** *Portrait of Jean II Le Bon*; Delatour, *The Cheat ;* equestrian statue of Charlemagne; Puget, *Milo of Croton*; Guillaume Coustou, *Marly Horses*. **329** Lubin Bauguin, *Dessert with Wafers*; Chardin, *Copper pot with pepper mill, leek, three eggs and earthenware pot on a table*; *Seated Scribe*. **332** *Statuette of a man*; Goudéa; *Pyx of Al-Mughira*; *Archers of Darius*; *Khorsabad bull*; *Trio of Gods, Palmyra*. **333** *Seated scribe*; *Effigy of Amenhotep IV*; *Dame d'Auxerre*; *Sarcophagus of husband and wife*; *Christ and Abbot Mena*; *Apollo of Piombino*. **334** Leonardo da Vinci, *Mona Lisa* **335** Café Marly © Café Marly.

Illustrators :
Cover and fold out: Philippe Biard, Jean-Michel Kacédan.
Maps: Dominique Duplantier.
Nature : Anne Bodin, Frédéric Bony, Jean Chevallier, François Desbordes, Claire Felloni, Gilbert Houbre, Jean-Michel Kacédan, Catherine Lachaud, Pascal Robin, John Wilkinson.
Practical information: Maurice Pommier.

Computer graphics:
Maps of the Louvre © Louvre. Graphic design B. Pell; artistic input Philippe Apeloig.

Acknowledgements:
We would like to give special thanks to: Dominique Camus (practical information), Clio Karageorghis, Guy Nicot, Marie-Claude Parisis, Béatrice Tambafandouno, and the team of Nino and Salvo Pecora.

◆ Bibliography

GENERAL READING

◆ Sir Lawrence Gowing, Michel Laclotte, *Paintings in the Louvre* Stewart, Tabori & Chang, 1994
◆ *Grand Louvre, le musée, les collections, les nouveaux espaces*, Réunion des Musées Nationaux / Connaissance des Arts, special edition, 1993.
◆ Michel Laclotte, Jean-Pierre Cuzin, *The Louvre: Paintings*, Scala Publishers, London, 2004.
◆ Michel Laclotte, Mark Polizzotti (Translator), *A Museum Stories: Memoirs of a Curator*, Abbeville Press Inc
◆ Michel Laclotte, Françoise Broyelle, *The Louvre*, Réunion des Musées Nationaux/ Scala Books, London 1993.
◆ Jean-Baptiste Lebrun, *Réflexions sur le Muséum* Réunion des Musées Nationaux, Paris 1992.
◆ Andrew McClellan, *Inventing the Louvre: Art, Politics and the Origins of the Modern Museum in Eighteenth-century Paris*, University of California Press, 1999
◆ Vincent Pomarede (Editor), *1001 Paintings from the Louvre: From Antiquity to the Nineteenth Century*, 5 Continents Editions, 2006
◆ Annette Robinson, *Le Louvre*, Scala, Paris, 1994.
◆ Frédéric Vitoux, *Paris vu du Louvre* A. Biro, Paris, 1993.
◆ Jacqueline de Romilly, Jacques Lacarrière, *Au Louvre avec Jacqueline de Romilly et Jacques Lacarrière*, Somogy and Musée du Louvre, Paris, 2001.

GUIDES

◆ *A Guide to the Louvre*, Réunion des Musées Nationaux, Paris, 2005.
◆ *Les Arts de l'islam, guide du visiteur*, Réunion des Musées Nationaux, Paris, 1993.
◆ Pascal Bonafoux, David Rosenberg, *Louvre Game Book: Play With The Largest Museum In The World*, Assouline, 2005
◆ Marie-Thérèse Genin, *Le Louvre, guide du visiteur pressé*, Réunions des Musées Nationaux, Paris, 1993.
◆ Marianne Hamiaux, *Les sculpture grecques*, Réunion des Musées Nationaux, Paris, 2001.
◆ *Knopf Guide to Paris*, Alfred A. Knopf, New York, 2004
◆ *The Lady and the Unicorn Tapestry*, Réunion des Musées Nationaux, Paris, 1989.
◆ Claude Mignot, *The Pocket Louvre: A Visitor's Guide to 500 Works*, Abbeville Press Inc.
◆ Pierre Quoniam, *Louvre, A Visit*, Réunion des Musées Nationaux, Paris, 1993.
◆ *Le Peinture française, guide du visiteur*, Réunion des Musées Nationaux, Paris, 1993.
◆ *Les Peintures flamande, hollandaise et allemande, guide du visiteur*, Réunion des Musées Nationaux, Paris, 1994.
◆ Tony Ross (Illustrator), *Let's Visit the Louvre* (First Discovery / Art S.) Moonlight Publishing Ltd, 2005
◆ Anne Sefroui, *The Louvre: 500 Masterpieces*, Réunion des Musées Nationaux / Scala Publishers, London, 1999

COLLECTIONS

◆ Alexandra Bonfante-Warren, *The Louvre*, Hugh Lauter Levin Associates, 2000.
◆ Arnauld Brejon de Lavergnée, *Ecoles flamande et hollandaise*, Réunion des Musées Nationaux, Paris, 1980.
◆ Annie Caubet,
Marthe Bernus-Taylor, *The Louvre: Near Eastern Antiquities*, Réunion des Musées Nationaux/ Scala Publishers, London, 1991.
◆ Jean René Gaborit, *The Louvre: European Sculpture*, coed. Réunion des Musées Nationaux / Scala Books, London, Paris, 1994.
◆ Sir Lawrence Gowing, Michel Laclotte, *Paintings in the Louvre* Stewart, Tabori & Chang, 1994
◆ Stéphane Loire, *La Peinture au Louvre*, F. Hazan, Paris, 1992.
◆ Alain Madeleine-Perdrillat, *Un dimanche au Louvre* Skira, Paris, 1994.
◆ Alain Pasquier, *The Louvre: Greek, Etruscan and Roman Antiquities*, Réunion des Musées Nationaux / Scala Publishers, London, 1991.
◆ Renaud Temperini, *Leonardo da Vinci at the Louvre Album*, Réunion des Musées Nationaux, Paris, 2003.
◆ Christiane Ziegler, *The Louvre: Egyptian Antiquities*, Réunion des Musées Nationaux / Scala Publishers, London, 1990.

HISTORY

◆ Christiane Aulanier, *Histoire du palais et du musée du Louvre*, 10 vol., Réunion des Musées Nationaux, Paris, 1948–1971.
◆ Germain Bazin, *Souvenirs de l'exode du Louvre, 1940–1945*, Somogy, Paris, 1992.
◆ Claude Daufresne, *Louvre et Tuileries, Architecture de papier*, Pierre Mardaga editor, Liège, 1987.
◆ Jean-Marc Leri, Alfred Fierro, *Le Louvre, 1180–1989*, Guide Historia-Tallendier, Paris, 1989.
◆ Jean-Jacques Leveque *La Louvre: From the Palace to the Museum*, ACR Edition, 1999
◆ Andrew McClellan,
Inventing the Louvre: Art, Politics and the Origins of the Modern Museum in Eighteenth-century Paris, University of California Press 1999

ARCHITECTURE

◆ Emile Biasini, Dominique Bezombes, Jean Lebrat, Jean-Michel Vincent, *Le Grand Louvre*, Electa Moniteur, Paris, 1989.
◆ Ieoh Ming Pei, *L'Invention du Grand Louvre*, Odile Jacob, Paris, 2001.
◆ Ieoh Ming Pei, Emile Biasini, *Les Grands Dessins du Louvre*, Hermann, Paris, 1989.

VIDEO/MULTIMEDIA

◆ Richard Copans, *Au Louvre avec les maîtres*, Réunion des Musées Nationaux / Editions Montparnasse, 1993.
◆ Alain Fleischer, *Louvre, le grand musée*, Réunion des Musées Nationaux / Editions Montparnasse, 1993.
◆ Alain Jaubert, *Palettes*, various titles, Editions Montparnasse, 1989–1994.
◆ *The Louvre, CDRom*, Monterey Video, Jarvis Collection
◆ Stan Neumann, *Louvre, le temps d'un musée*, Réunion des Musées Nationaux / Editions Montparnasse, 1993.
◆ Nicolas Philibert, *La Ville Louvre*, Editions Montparnasse, 1990.

LITTERATURE

◆ Dan Brown, *The Da Vinci Code*, Anchor, 2006.
◆ Henry James, *The American*, in *Novels 1871–1880*, Library of America, 1983.
◆ Emile Zola, *L'Assommoir*, Oxford University Press, USA, 1999

Index of artists and famous people

◆ Index of artists and famous people

Index of artists and famous people ◆

Index of styles and works of art ◆

◆ Index of sites and rooms